W9-DAS-703

Trade and Poverty

Trade and Poverty

When the Third World Fell Behind

Jeffrey G. Williamson

The MIT Press
Cambridge, Massachusetts
London, England

For information about special quantity discounts, please email special_sales @mitpress.mit.edu

This book was set in Stone Sans and Stone Serif by Toppan Best-set Premedia Limited. Printed and bound in the United States of America.

Library of Congress Cataloging-in-Publication Data

Williamson, Jeffrey G., 1935–
Trade and poverty : when the Third World fell behind / Jeffrey G. Williamson.
 p. cm.
Includes bibliographical references and index.
ISBN 978-0-262-01515-8 (hardcover : alk. paper)
1. Industries—Developing countries—History. 2. Deindustrialization—Developing countries—History. 3. Developing countries—Commerce—History. 4. Poverty—Developing countries—History. 5. Developing countries—Economic conditions—Regional disparities. I. Title.
HC59.7.W536 2011
338.9009172′4—dc22

                                                          2010028163

10 9 8 7 6 5 4 3 2 1

To our amazing, talented, and wonderful grand children
Maya, Nell, Erin, AJ, and Sarah

Contents

Acknowledgments   ix

1   When the Third World Fell Behind   1

2   The First Global Century up to 1913   11

3   Biggest Third World Terms of Trade Boom Ever?   25

4   The Economics of Third World Growth Engines and Dutch Diseases   45

5   Measuring Third World De-industrialization and Dutch Disease   59

6   An Asian De-industrialization Illustration: An Indian Paradox?   75

7   A Middle East De-industrialization Illustration: Ottoman Problems   101

8   A Latin American De-industrialization Illustration: Mexican Exceptionalism   119

9   Rising Third World Inequality during the Trade Boom: Did It Matter?   145

10   Export Price Volatility: Another Drag on Third World Growth?   167

11   Tying the Knot: The Globalization and Great Divergence Connection   181

12   Better Late Than Never: Industrialization Spreads to the Poor Periphery   199

13   Policy Response: What Did They Do? What Should They Have Done?   215

14   Morals of the Story   231

Notes   235
References   251
Index   281

Acknowledgments

When I was a graduate student at Stanford in the late 1950s, I wanted to write a book like *Trade and Poverty: When the Third World Fell Behind*. But my mentors at that time—Irma Adelman, Ken Arrow, Hollis Chenery, Bob Mundell, and especially Moe Abramovitz—wisely advised against it. After all, the third world had yet to establish a long enough postindependence track record to assess the questions raised in this book, questions about the connection between globalization and what is now called the great divergence. "Why not use economic history to start exploring the connection," they asked? Why not indeed!

And so this book has been brewing for about half a century. An early (and very incomplete) assessment was given in Stockholm as the Ohlin Lectures in October 2004, subsequently published as *Globalization and the Poor Periphery before 1950* (MIT Press, 2006). *Trade and Poverty* deepens the argument, extends the evidence for the century before W. Arthur Lewis's starting point of 1870 (an important extension since, as we will see, that's where the action was), combines time series with case studies, and is written in a way that I hope speaks to a much wider audience. Were my still very active mentors at Stanford to read this, and had Moe Abramovitz lived long enough to read it as well, they might best decide whether the half century was worth the wait.

Trade and Poverty relies heavily on past collaborations that resulted in: "The Impact of the Terms of Trade on Economic Development in the Periphery, 1870–1939: Volatility and Secular Change," *Journal of Development Economics* 82 (January 2007), with Christopher Blattman and Jason Hwang; "Measuring Ancient Inequality," NBER Working Paper 13550, National Bureau of Economic Research, Cambridge, Massachusetts (October 2007), with Peter H. Lindert and Branko Milanovic; "Mughal Decline, Climate Shocks and British Industrial Ascent," *Explorations in Economic History* 45 (July 2008), with David Clingingsmith; "Mexican

Exceptionalism: Globalization and De-industrialization 1750–1877,"
Journal of Economic History 68 (September 2008), with Aurora Gómez Gal-
varriato and Rafael Dobado González; "Commodity Price Shocks and the
Australian Economy since Federation," *NBER Working Paper 14694*, National
Bureau of Economic Research, Cambridge, Massachusetts (January 2009),
with Sambit Bhattacharyya; "Commodity Price Volatility and World
Market Integration since 1720," *NBER Working Paper 14748*, National
Bureau of Economic Research, Cambridge, Massachusetts (February 2009),
with David Jacks and Kevin H. O'Rourke; "Ottoman De-industrialization
1800–1913: Assessing the Shock, Its Impact and the Response," *NBER
Working Paper 14763*, National Bureau of Economic Research, Cambridge,
Massachusetts (March 2009), with Şevket Pamuk; and "Was It Prices, Productivity or Policy? The Timing and Pace of Industrialization in Latin
America 1870–1910," *Journal of Latin American Studies* 41 (December 2009),
with Aurora Gómez Galvarriato. My warmest thanks to Aurora, Branko,
Chris, the two Davids, Jason, Kevin, Peter, Rafa, Sambit, and Şevket, won-
derful collaborators and good friends all.

In addition other friends and colleagues have over the years listened to
the arguments in *Trade and Poverty*, corrected some, sharpened others,
offered better tools to make the points, and even supplied what they
thought was better evidence. They are: Daron Acemoglu, Bob Allen,
Lee Alston, Leticia Arroyo Abad, Carlos Bazdresch, Ted Beatty, William
Bernstein, Luis Bértola, Leah Platt Boustan, Huw Bowen, Luis Catão,
Amilcar Challu, William Clarence-Smith, Greg Clark, Michael Clemens,
John Coatsworth, Bill Collins, Metin Cosgel, Javier Cuenca Esteban, Brad
Delong, Steve Dowrick, Barry Eichengreen, Charles Engel, Rui Pedro
Esteves, Ron Findlay, Zephyr Frank, Hector Garcia, Regina Grafe, David
Greasley, Bob Gregory, Bishnupriya Gupta, Steve Haber, Yael Hadass, Peter
Harnetty, Tim Hatton, Phil Hoffman, Hilary Williamson Hoynes, Greg
Huff, Alejandra Irigoin, Doug Irwin, Paul Krugman, Sandra Kuntz, Andrew
Leigh, Norman Loayza, Enrique Llopis, Debin Ma, Noel Maurer, Graciela
Márquez, Gustavo Marrero, Ian McLean, Adolfo Meisel, Javier Moreno,
Aldo Musacchio, Patrick O'Brien, José Antonio Ocampo, Kevin O'Rourke,
Roger Owen, Michael Palairet, Steve Poelhekke, Carlos Ponzio, Leandro
Prados de la Escosura, Om Prakash, Saif Shah Mohammed, Jaime Salgado,
Dick Salvucci, Blanca Sánchez-Alonso, Ananth Seshadri, Mike Smith,
T. N. Srinivasan, Tirthanker Roy, Alan Taylor, Peter Timmer, Insan Tunali,
Rod Tyers, Miguel Urrutia, Tony Venables, Javier Rodríquez Weber,
Amy Williamson-Shaffer, and Tarik Yousef. The title owes a lot to Ken
Snowden.

Trade and Poverty has been greatly improved by student responses in classrooms at Harvard and audience reactions to public lectures at the University of Adelaide, the Australian National University, the Canadian Development Economics Group, Carlos the Third University, University of Göttingen, Harvard University, Kiel Institute, Luca d'Agliano Turin, University of Melbourne, Middlebury College, Oxford University, Universitat Pompeu Fabra, Queens's University, Washington and Lee University, Universidad de la Republica, Stanford University, Vanderbilt University, and York University.

A team of able, amazing, and intense Harvard undergraduates has, over the years, helped with the data heavy lifting. Wherever they are now, they have my thanks: Pedro Glaser, Ignacio de la Huerta, Martin Kanz, Kyle Nasser, Taylor (Owings) Downer, Rodrigo Parral, Abdallah Salam, Carolyn Sheehan, Miray Topay, and Pablo Tsutsumi. To help pay these talented young people, I acknowledge with pleasure financial support from the National Science Foundation and the Harvard Faculty of Arts and Sciences.

1   When the Third World Fell Behind

1.1   The World Economic Order in 1960

Before the Gang of Four (Hong Kong, Singapore, South Korea, Taiwan) had completed their postwar growth miracle, before China, India and the rest of Asia began to play with double-digit growth rates, and just as Africa gained independence from their European colonial masters, there was a *world economic order* in place that had been two hundred years in the making. Income per capita in Asia and Africa was less than 14 percent of western Europe in 1960, Latin America was a little more than 41 percent, and the three combined were about 16 percent (table 1.1). Thus one characteristic of the *world economic order* in 1960 was the wide gap in per capita income and living standards between what this book will call the rich industrial core and the poor pre-industrial periphery. The second characteristic of the *world economic order* was that the poor periphery exported primary products or what we call today commodities, while the rich core exported manufactures: indeed 85 percent of the poor periphery's exports were either agricultural or mineral products (for sub-Saharan Africa it was 94 percent), while the figure for western Europe was only 30 percent. Trade, specialization in commodities, and poverty were closely correlated.

Thus today's wide economic gap between the post-industrial OECD and the third world is hardly new. It was there more than a half century ago before the aid and cheap loan largess of the World Bank, before the International Monetary Fund bailouts, before the health and education delivery systems of the United Nations, before activist nongovernmental organizations, before the global trade boom, and before the exploration of pro-development policies in much of the recently autonomous third world. If the *world economic order* was with us in 1960, then we need to look at least at the two centuries between 1760 and 1960 to understand its origin,

Table 1.1
World economic order in 1960

Region	GDP per capita 1990 GK$	GDP per capita relative to western Europe	Share of exports in manufactures (%)
Western Europe	7,582	100	70
Latin America	3,136	41.4	11
Africa	1,055	13.9	6
Asia	1,025	13.5	na
Africa and Asia	1,030	13.6	na
Africa, Asia, and Latin America	1,239	16.3	15

Sources: GDP per capita calculated from Maddison (March 2009), http://www .ggdc.net/maddison. Manufactures export shares for 1960 Africa and 1960 Africa + Asia + Latin American are taken from Martin (2003: fig. 3, 194), while Latin America and western Europe are 1965 from World Development Indicators online.

perhaps even before. Indeed the new institutional growth economics led by Douglas North (1990, 2005), and Daron Acemoglu, Simon Johnson, and James Robinson (2001, 2002, 2005) suggests that we must go back at least five centuries to find the sources of today's wide divergence between the OECD and the third world. Others have argued that we need to go back more than a millennium and even into pre-history to get the right answers (Diamond 1997; Olsson and Hibbins 2005; Comin et al. 2008).

1.2   When Did the Great Divergence Take Place?

Let's start by identifying exactly when the great divergence between the west European leaders—a economic group often augmented by the United States—and the poor periphery emerged. Table 1.2 shows that there was already a big income per capita gap in 1820 when the industrial revolution was just warming up in Europe: the poor periphery had only half the GDP per capita that the west European leaders had. So whatever explanation one hopes to find for the appearance of the gap, the search for it must be before the industrial revolution. And we see it over the long century 1700 to 1820, where although pre-modern per capita income growth was almost glacial the world around, it was still four times as fast in western Europe than in the periphery (0.16 versus 0.04 percent per annum). Still the gap was already large in 1700, with the periphery only 56 percent of the core.

Table 1.2

World per capita GDP growth performance, 1700 to 1820

Regional group	GDP per capita in 1990 GK$		Per annum growth (%)	GDP per capita relative to western Europe	
	1700	1820	1700–1820	1700	1820
Western Europe	1,032	1,243	0.16	100.0	100.0
European periphery	653	737	0.10	63.3	59.3
Latin America	540	712	0.23	52.3	57.3
Middle East	564	571	0.01	54.7	45.9
South Asia	550	530	−0.05	53.3	42.6
Southeast Asia	580	601	0.03	56.2	48.4
East Asia	595	605	0.01	57.7	48.7
Periphery unweighted average	580	626	0.04	56.2	50.4

Source: Maddison (March 2009), http://www.ggdc.net/maddison

Regional definitions: Western Europe: Austria, Belgium, Denmark, Finland, France, Germany, Italy, Netherlands, Norway, Sweden, Switzerland, United Kingdom. European periphery: Albania, Bulgaria, Czechoslovakia, Hungary, Poland, Romania, Yugoslavia, Russia; Ireland, Greece, Portugal, Spain. Latin America: Brazil, Mexico. South Asia: India. Southeast Asia: Indonesia. East Asia: China, Japan.

True, some parts of the periphery had done better than others: the European periphery to the south and east of the leaders was at the top of the list, about 63 percent, while South Asia and Latin America were at the bottom, about 52 or 53 percent. But what distinguished living standards the world around in 1700 was that western Europe was already ahead while the rest of the world was tightly clustered together behind: that is, the divergence between regions in 1700 was almost entirely the divergence between western Europe and the rest.

Thus we have to search even earlier in pre-industrial times to find the explanation for the great divergence, and the recent historical literature on the pre-1800 economic divergence is lively and contentious. Robert Allen (2001) led the way in documenting a great divergence within Europe starting with the early modern era, when living standards in the northwest pulled ahead of countries to the east and south. Kenneth Pomeranz's book *The Great Divergence: China, Europe, and the Making of the Modern World* gave us the phrase and focused the debate on when the China–Europe gap first appeared. Since then, pre-industrial evidence on the great divergence has deepened and widened (Parthasarathi 1998; Bengston et al. 2004; Allen 2005; Allen et al. 2009). Thus it is clear that divergence has been with us for 500 years or more, but while it took western Europe many centuries to achieve incomes per capita double those of the periphery in 1820, it took only one century to drive that figure up to 3.5 times in 1913 (the gap was 29 percent: table 1.3). Note, however, that the gap was no higher in 1940, and perhaps even a little lower (34.7 percent: table 1.4). Thus the 19th century looks like a period of exceptionally rapid divergence between core and periphery, and that divergence was most dramatic over the half century 1820 to 1870.

1.3   A Trade and Divergence Connection?

The correlation between the world trade boom and accelerating divergence during the first global century up to 1913 is a seductive fact.

As the next chapter will make clear, the world became global at a spectacular rate from the early 19th century to World War I. While the world trade boom was accompanied by mass migrations and the development of an international capital market, that boom had never happened before and it would not happen again until after World War II, closer to our time. The European economies went open, removing long-standing mercantilist policies and lowering tariffs. Their colonies did the same, and European and American gunboats forced many others to follow suit. Much of the world integrated their currencies by going on the gold standard and other currency unions, lowering exchange risk. Led by new steam engine technologies, the world also underwent a pro-trade transport revolution. As the cost of trade fell dramatically, the ancient barriers of distance began to evaporate. The telegraph, another pro-trade technology, lowered uncertainty about prices in distant markets, stimulating trade still more. Most important, the industrial revolution in Europe raised GDP growth rates many times faster than what had been common over the previous two millennia, and the demand for everything soared, especially traded goods. To give the world trade boom yet another nudge, *pax Britannica* brought peace.

There is that seductive correlation, the first world trade boom occurring at the same time as the acceleration in the great divergence. Correlations like this invite causal interpretations: Did globalization contribute to the great divergence? This question was debated during the first global century, and it is debated now in the midst of the second global century.

Table 1.3
World per capita GDP growth performance, 1820 to 1913

Regional group	GDP per capita in 1990 GK$			GDP per capita relative to western Europe			Growth rates per annum		
	1820	1870	1913	1820	1870	1913	1820–1870	1870–1913	1820–1913
Western Europe	1,243	2,087	3,688	100.0	100.0	100.0	1.04	1.15	1.18
English-speaking offshoots	1,202	2,419	5,233	96.7	115.9	141.9	1.41	1.81	1.59
European periphery	737	992	1,607	59.3	47.5	43.6	0.60	1.13	0.84
Latin America	712	742	1,618	57.3	35.6	43.9	0.08	1.83	0.89
Middle East	571	707	978	45.9	33.9	26.5	0.43	0.76	0.58
South Asia	530	533	679	42.6	25.5	18.4	0.01	0.56	0.27
Less India	462	544	765	37.2	26.1	20.7	0.33	0.80	0.54
Southeast Asia	601	604	890	48.4	28.9	24.1	0.00	0.91	0.42
East Asia	605	555	646	48.7	26.6	17.5	-0.17	0.35	0.08
Less China	648	748	1,270	52.1	35.8	34.4	0.29	1.23	0.73
Periphery unweighted average	626	689	1,070	50.4	33.0	29.0	0.19	0.92	0.51
Periphery unweighted average, no China, India	622	723	1,188	50.0	34.6	32.2	0.29	0.96	0.67

Source: Maddison (March 2009), http://www.ggdc.net/maddison.

Regional definitions: Western Europe: Austria, Belgium, Denmark, Finland, France, Germany, Italy, Netherlands, Norway, Sweden, Switzerland, United Kingdom. English-Speaking Offshoots: Australia, Canada, New Zealand, United States. European Periphery: Albania, Bulgaria, Czechoslovakia, Hungary, Poland, Romania, Yugoslavia; Russia; Ireland, Greece, Portugal, Spain. Latin America: Argentina, Brazil, Chile, Colombia, Mexico, Peru, Uruguay, Venezuela. Middle East: Western Asia plus Egypt, Morocco, Tunisia. South Asia: Burma, Ceylon, India, Nepal. Southeast Asia: Hong Kong Indonesia, Malaysia, Philippines, Siam, Singapore. East Asia: China, Japan, Korea, Taiwan.

Table 1.4
World per capita GDP growth performance, 1913 to 1940

Regional group	GDP per capita in 1990 GK$		Per annum growth (%)	GDP per capita relative to western Europe	
	1913	1940	1913–1940	1913	1940
Western Europe	3,688	4,984	1.12	100.0	100.0
European periphery	1,607	2,087	0.97	43.6	41.9
Latin America	1,618	2,122	1.01	43.9	42.6
Middle East	1,213	1,675	1.20	32.9	33.6
South Asia	681	695	0.08	18.5	13.9
Southeast Asia	892	1,231	1.20	24.2	24.7
East Asia	1,270	2,567	2.64	34.4	51.5
Periphery unweighted average	1,214	1,730	1.32	32.9	34.7

Source: Maddison (March 2009), http://www.ggdc.net/maddison.
Regional definitions: Western Europe: Austria, Belgium, Denmark, Finland, France, Germany, Italy, Netherlands, Norway, Sweden, Switzerland, United Kingdom. European Periphery: Albania, Bulgaria, Czechoslovakia, Hungary, Poland, Romania, Yugoslavia; Russia; Ireland, Greece, Portugal, Spain. Latin America: Argentina, Brazil, Chile, Colombia, Mexico, Peru, Uruguay, Venezuela. Middle East: Turkey. South Asia: Ceylon, India. Southeast Asia: Indonesia, Malaysia, Philippines. East Asia: Japan, Korea, Taiwan.

Before we move much farther along in this book, some issues must be laid to rest. Most important, look again at the evidence in table 1.3, and note two big facts reported there. First, the periphery did *not* suffer a fall in GDP per capita during the first global century. Indeed GDP per capita growth there was just short of 1 percent per annum between 1870 and 1913. More to the point, percent per annum GDP per capita growth rose from 0.04 between1700 and 1820 up to 0.19 between 1820 and 1870, then up to 0.92 between 1870 and 1913. The periphery growth rate was, of course, less than the core, which rose from 0.16, to 1.04, to 1.15 percent, per annum. Second, no economist since Adam Smith has ever found the evidence or the argument to reject the gains from trade theorem: all participants gain from trade. By exploiting specialization and comparative advantage, trade raises GDP. Some residents, classes, and regions may gain more than others, but average incomes will rise in all trading countries as a consequence of trade. Then again, in the long run will some countries gain more from trade than others? Indeed, did the rich core gain more than poor periphery?

The last question motivates this book: Did the global trade boom between 1820 (or even 1750) and 1913 serve to augment the great divergence? Trade certainly creates gains from specialization, but it can also be growth-enhancing. It can, after all, be a conduit for knowledge, technological transfer, and political liberalism. Trade can also be growth-enhancing if it fosters agglomeration and scale economies, and if it fosters capital flows and accumulation in capital deficient countries. In modern terminology, this would be called trade-driven endogenous growth (Krugman 1981, 1991a, 1991b; Romer 1986, 1990; Helpman 2004; Lucas 2009). Fair enough, but couldn't these growth-enhancing forces be weaker, absent, or even negative in some circumstances? For example, could trade have growth-diminishing effects in poor countries exporting primary products? What about de-industrialization there? What about the price volatility associated with their primary products? What about the contribution of global-induced inequality to anti-growth rent-seeking by the increasingly powerful rich in the periphery? Did trade augment growth rates in the rich core by much more than the poor periphery, contributing to the great divergence?

1.4   What Do We Mean by "Open" Economies?

Some otherwise very clever economists get a little confused when talking about countries being "open" to trade. Typically, in exploring the correlation between "openness" and growth, the former is measured by trade ratios, that is, exports plus imports all divided by GDP. But trade shares may be high simply because income is high, and trade shares may rise simply because income rises. Instead, a country's openness should be measured by the height of trade barriers around it—including tariffs, nontariff barriers, distance from foreign markets, cost of transportation to and from foreign markets, and anything else that adds to the barriers. But even if we agree on how to measure the trade barriers, it is the *change* in the trading environment that will induce *changes* in the domestic economy, and the *changes* in the trading environment that matter are *changes* in relative prices in the home market. How might relative prices change? Two ways: by a decline in trade barriers from any source, and/or by a change in world market conditions. Both of these will induce a change in the (net barter) terms of trade (the price of exports over the price of imports) facing the country in question, as well as the prices of these tradables relative to all the nontradables that poor countries produce, like local services and ordinary foodstuffs. So, if we are looking for ways that trade might foster (or inhibit) growth, we need to look at the magnitude and duration of exogenous changes in the country's terms of trade, not trade shares.

The next source of confusion is this. If the share of exports in GDP is only, say, 10 percent, and if the terms of trade improves by only 10 percent (by a rise in the export price facing local producers), would this simply translate in to a once and for all 1 percent increase in GDP (10 percent times 10 percent equals one percent)? No! The external terms of trade shock will permanently change all relative prices in the economy, thus causing labor, skills, and capital to move to sectors where prices are improving and flee sectors where they are deteriorating, thus causing growth effects to the extent that the structure of the economy has an impact on growth.

1.5   *Trade and Poverty*: Looking over the Terrain

Trade and Poverty begins in the next chapter by describing the first global century between 1820 and 1913. It then moves on in chapter 3 to report the behavior of the terms of trade facing the poor periphery over that century. The price of their primary product exports relative to their imports (mainly manufactures) boomed everywhere in the poor periphery. In some places the terms of trade increased by a factor of three, probably the biggest sustained terms of trade boom the world has ever seen. Since trade fosters specialization, resources flowed in to the export sector and out of the import-competing sector in the poor periphery, the import-competing sector being industry. So chapter 4 explores the economics of de-industrialization and what is called Dutch disease in the poor periphery. Because de-industrialization is thought to have had a negative impact on growth, the book spends three chapters exploring how India, Ottoman Turkey, and Mexico dealt with it. Chapter 9 raises another issue: Did the trade boom create greater inequality in the poor periphery, and did this fact serve to reinforce anti-growth institutions as many have argued (Engerman and Sokoloff 1997)? Chapter 10 brings another potential anti-growth factor to the table: Did greater price volatility for primary products add another drag to growth in the poor periphery? With this background, chapter 11 is then able to offer an historical assessment of the central question of the book: Was the globalization and great divergence correlation causal? Furthermore, if the terms of trade boom (a fall in the relative price of manufactures) across most of the 19th century caused de-industrialization in the poor periphery, would not symmetry predict that a secular collapse in the terms of trade (a rise in the relative price of manufactures) foster industrialization there? Thus chapter 12 turns Raúl Prebisch (1950) and Hans Singer (1950) on their heads by exploring the extent to which a secular slump in the terms of trade—rather than protectionist policy or technological transfers—might help explain much of the early industrialization that was observed in the late 19th and early 20th centuries in Brazil, Mexico, Russia, Bombay, Shanghai, and Japan? Chapter 13 documents a steep rise in tariffs in what we now call the third world before 1913, long before the inward-looking ISI polices of the 1930s through the 1970s. What was the motivation underlying this anti-trade backlash? Infant industry arguments? Government revenue needs? Compensation for the losers?

We have a long way to go before we reach the concluding chapter 14. Let's start to negotiate this terrain with a description of the first global century.

2 The First Global Century up to 1913

2.1 What Made It the First Global Century?

Four things happened to the world economy from the early 19th century to World War I, four things that had never happened before and that would not happen again until after World War II. First, the richest and fastest growing European economies went open, removing long-standing mercantilist policies, lowering tariffs, and removing nontariff barriers. Their colonies in Africa and Asia did the same, and many of the others were forced to follow suit with gunboat diplomacy. In addition much of the world integrated their currencies by going on the gold standard and other currency unions, lowering exchange risk. Thus liberal commercial and exchange rate policy gave trade one good reason to boom. Second, led by new steam engine technologies, the world underwent a pro-trade transport revolution. As the cost of trade fell dramatically, the ancient barrier of distance was broken down, and all forms of global communication boomed, especially trade. The revolution was given added impetus by the appearance of the telegraph, another pro-trade technology that lowered uncertainty about prices in distant markets. Third, and carried by an industrial revolution in Europe and its offshoots, economic growth rose steeply to rates many times faster than what had been common over the previous two millennia. As a consequence the demand for everything soared, especially imports of intermediate inputs in to manufacturing (cotton, wool, tin, rubber), fuel (coal), and luxury foodstuffs (sugar, tea, coffee, meat). Fourth, the world was at peace. Frequent wars between the European economic leaders and between their trading partners in the periphery (and civil unrest within them) had shut down trade much of the time over the three centuries after Christopher Columbus discovered the Americas and Vasco de Gama emerged on the Indian Ocean. Wars shut down trade by: embargo, privateering, the draft of merchant marine bottoms for naval use, and the creation of market uncertainty. By the early 19th century, *pax Britannica* reigned, and a trade-stimulating peace would prevail for a century.

Thus trade had four reasons to boom during the first global century.

2.2   Western Europe Goes Open: Liberal Moves to Pro-trade Policies

Despite all the attention that the age of discovery and the age of commerce get in our history books, the descriptive phrase "global economy" only applied to a tiny share of world economic activity before the 19th century. Nor was there much evidence of world market integration over the three centuries following 1492 and 1502 even for that tiny share of the world economy. Commodity prices in Asian, American, and European markets did not converge even for spices and quality textiles, and not at all for grains, fuels and building materials. And why should they have done so? After all, state trading monopolies did what monopolies do so well: they choked off supply by internalizing any fall in transport costs, and by keeping the price markup between producer and consumer high or even rising (O'Rourke and Williamson 2002a, 2009). Mercantilism was a weapon of economic power, aggression and diplomacy (Findlay and O'Rourke 2007): it certainly did not foster global trade.

The battle of Waterloo (1816)—where Wellington finally thumped Napoleon—was a turning point. After the wars with the French were over, Britain emerged self-confident and the dominant hegemony, confident enough to start dismantling its trade barriers.[1]

European trade policies were almost universally protectionist just after the Napoleonic Wars. The exceptions to the rule were smaller countries such as the Netherlands, which adopted a relatively liberal trade policy in 1819, and Denmark, which had already abolished import prohibitions and adopted low tariffs as early as 1797. But the first major economy to liberalize was Britain, where power was shifting to export-oriented urban interests. A series of liberal reforms in the 1820s and 1830s were followed by Robert Peel's momentous decision to abolish the Corn Laws in 1846, which moved the United Kingdom unilaterally to free trade, against the objections of landlords whose agricultural interests had been protected for so long (Schonhardt-Bailey 2006; O'Rourke and Williamson 1999: ch. 5). It is important to stress that this movement to free trade by the world's hegemony did not happen as a one-shot political event in 1846. Instead, going open proceeded in four major steps over the previous thirty years (Williamson 1990: 125–26): between 1815 and 1827, the ad valorem tariff equivalent was about 70 percent; between 1828 and 1841, it dropped to 50 percent; between 1842 and 1845, it fell farther to 19 percent; and, finally, in 1846 Britain went to free trade. Thus, Europe's biggest economy opened its markets to all comers.[2] The rest of western Europe—Austria–Hungary, the Netherlands, Belgium, Sweden, Norway, and Denmark (Bairoch 1989: 20–36)—followed Britain's liberal lead, and average tariffs on the continent fell throughout the 1850s. A further breakthrough came in 1860, with the Anglo-French Cobden–Chevalier Treaty. This treaty abolished all French import prohibitions as well as the British export duty on coal, and lowered British tariffs on wine. The treaty also established most-favored-nation (MFN) relations between the two countries, and laid the basis for a series of further bilateral trade deals between the countries of western Europe, all of which incorporated an MFN clause. Even though tariffs were already falling in Europe by the time of the treaty, the non-discriminatory nature of the MFN principle greatly strengthened the multilateral nature of the 19th-century trade regime. MFN clauses also implied that bilateral concessions were automatically generalized to all participants in this network of treaties, which speeded up tariff reductions. According to Bairoch (1989), average tariffs on the European mainland had fallen to some 9 to 12 percent by the mid-1870s, by which time "Germany had virtually become a free trade country" (Bairoch 1989: 41).

Then things changed. The turning point came in the late 1870s and 1880s, when the impact of cheap New World and Russian grain began to make itself felt in European markets (O'Rourke and Williamson 1999: ch. 6). But this late 19th-century European tariff backlash had little impact on exporters in the poor periphery whose primary products did not compete with grain (or wine) producers in European markets.

Much of East Asia and Latin America were not interested in free trade. As chapter 13 will show, the English-speaking New World offshoots and the young Latin American republics had the highest tariffs in the world. East Asia was also less enthusiastic about free trade, but the naval muscle of the industrial leaders made them comply. Under the persuasion of Commodore Perry's American gun ships, Japan signed the Shimoda and Harris ("unequal") treaties and, in so doing, switched from autarky to free trade in 1858. It is hard to imagine a more dramatic switch in trade policy since Japan's foreign trade quickly rose from nil to 7 percent of national income (Huber 1971). Other Asian nations followed the same liberal path, most forced to do so by colonial dominance or gunboat diplomacy. Thus, following the Opium Wars, China signed a treaty with Britain in 1842 that opened her ports to trade and set a very low 5 percent ad valorem tariff limit. Siam avoided China's humiliation by going open and adopting an even lower 3 percent tariff limit in 1855. Korea emerged from its autarkic "hermit kingdom" stance about the same time, undergoing market integration with Japan long before colonial status became formalized in 1910 (Brandt 1993; Kang and Cha 1996). In South Asia, India, Ceylon, and Burma all went the way of British free trade in 1846, and Indonesia followed Dutch commercial liberalism in the same way.

But what mattered most for the poor periphery was that European markets be open to their exports, and they certainly were throughout the century. Furthermore the European leaders, their offshoots, and their colonies bound themselves more closely together by integrating currencies with the gold standard and other currency unions, adding more pro-trade policies to the mix.

2.3   The World Transport Revolution[3]

Until well into the 19th century, the cost of overseas trade was too great to allow much long-distance trade in the bulky primary products that were the poor periphery's comparative advantage. Thus most foodstuffs, most industrial intermediates, and most fuels were not traded long distance. These goods are called nontradables, and until the transport revolution their prices were determined by supply and demand in local markets, not in world markets. Long-distance trade between core and periphery involved only precious metals, spices, silk, porcelain, and other consumption goods of the rich, and, of course, slaves. These tradable goods were typically noncompeting: that is, they were not produced in local European markets and thus their import did not directly compete with or crowd out any local industry (O'Rourke and Williamson 2002a, 2005).

Things changed quickly around the start of the 19th century, and it involved a transport revolution over both water and land. Furthermore the periphery played a very important part in it, indeed, perhaps the most important part.

Investment in river and harbor improvements increased briskly in the European core following the French wars. British navigable waterways quadrupled between 1750 and 1820 and canals offered a transport option 50 to 75 percent cheaper than roads. On the European continent, French canal construction boomed, while the Congress of Vienna recognized freedom of navigation on the Rhine. In the United States, construction of the Erie Canal between 1817 and 1825 reduced the cost of transport between Buffalo and New York by 85 percent, and cut the transit time from

21 to 8 days. The rates between Baltimore and Cincinnati fell by 58 percent from 1821 to 1860 and by 92 percent between Louisville and New Orleans from 1816 and 1860. While it took 52 days to ship a load of freight from Cincinnati to New York by wagon and riverboat in 1817, it took only 6 days in 1852. The US internal transport sector recorded productivity growth rates something like 4.7 percent per annum in the four decades or so before the Civil War (Williamson and Lindert 1980: 171). As a result regional price differentials underwent a spectacular fall (Slaughter 1995: 13). In the first half of the 19th century, transportation improvements began to destroy regional barriers to internal trade and integrated national goods markets began to emerge within the United States, within Britain, within the German *Zollverein*, and within other countries on the continent.

Steamships made the most important contribution to 19th-century shipping technology. The *Claremont* made its debut on the Hudson in 1807; a steamer had made the journey up the Mississippi as far as Louisville by 1815, and steamers had traveled up the Seine to Paris by 1816. In the first half of the century, steamships were mainly used on important rivers, the Great Lakes, and inland seas such as the Baltic and the Mediterranean. A regular trans-Atlantic steam service was inaugurated in 1838, but until 1860 steamers mainly carried high-value goods similar to those carried by airplanes today, like passengers, specie, mail, and gourmet food.

The other major 19th-century transportation development was, of course, the railroad. The Liverpool–Manchester line opened in 1830, and early continental emulators included Belgium, France, and Germany. Table 2.1 documents the phenomenal growth in railway mileage during the second half of the 19th century, particularly in the United States where it played a major role in creating a truly national market. Indeed the railroad was in many ways to the United States what the 1992 single market program was to the European Union. By 1850, there were more than 9,000 railroad miles in the United States. At the same date there were more than 1,700 railroad miles to report for France, more than 3,600 for Germany, and more than 6,600 for the United Kingdom. Note, however, the tiny railroad mileage entries in table 2.1 for Austria-Hungary, Italy, and Russia— and their complete absence before 1870 for Bulgaria and Romania, or for Portugal and Spain, or for Greece (Mitchell 1978: 315–18)—facts that helped postpone the involvement of the European periphery in the world trade boom until the second half of the century. But, by the 1850s, every major port in the northwest of Europe was within relatively inexpensive reach of every small town in its rural hinterland.

Table 2.1
World railway mileage, 1850 to 1910

Country	1850	1870	1890	1910
Austria-Hungary	954	5,949	16,489	26,834
Australia	—	953	9,524	17,429
Argentina	—	637	5,434	17,381
Canada	66	2,617	13,368	26,462
China	—	—	80	5,092
France	1,714	11,142	22,911	30,643
Germany	3,637	11,729	25,411	36,152
India	—	4,771	16,401	32,099
Italy	265	3,825	8,163	10,573
Japan	—	—	1,139	5,130
Mexico	—	215	6,037	15,350
Russia (in Europe)	310	7,098	18,059	34,990
United Kingdom	6,621	15,537	20,073	23,387
United States	9,021	52,922	116,703	249,902

Source: Hurd (1975: app. 2, 278)

To get a sense of the timing and magnitude of the transport revolution in the Atlantic economy, consider figure 2.1. What is labeled the North index (North 1958) drifted down over many decades before accelerating its fall after the 1830s—its most dramatic decline by far being 1840 to 1860, and what is labeled the British index (Harley 1988) underwent the same big fall. The North index measures freight rates along Atlantic routes connecting American to European ports, and it dropped by almost 55 percent in real terms between the 1830s and 1850s, while other evidence documents a fall in nominal rates of 75 percent between Antwerp and New York (Prados 2004: 10–11). The British index measures major trade routes involving Liverpool and London, and it fell by about 70 percent, again in real terms, in the half century after 1840. These two indexes imply a steady decline in Atlantic economy transport costs of about 1.5 percent per annum, for a total of 45 percentage points up to 1913, a big number indeed. Figure 2.2 expands the index to cover all trade costs, and it documents a similar big fall in 1870 to 1913.

One way to get a comparative feel for the magnitude of this decline is to note that tariffs on manufactures entering OECD markets fell from 40 percent in the late 1940s to 7 percent in the late 1970s, a 33 percentage

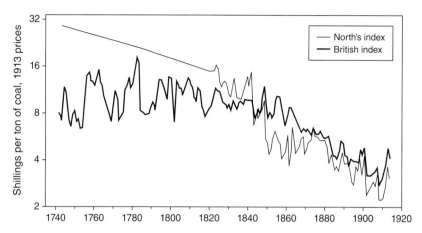

Figure 2.1
Real freight rate indexes, 1741 to 1913: Nominal rates divided by a UK GDP deflator.
Source: Harley (1988: fig. 1)

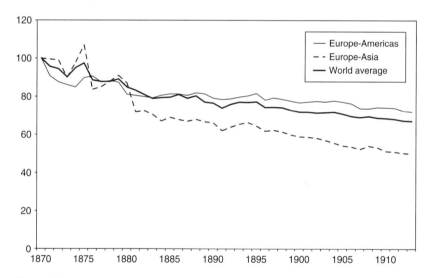

Figure 2.2
Trade costs, 1870 to 1913 (1870 = 100).
Source: Jacks, Meissner and Novy (2009: fig. 2)

point decline over this thirty-year resurrection of free trade in the industrial economies. This spectacular postwar reclamation of free trade from
interwar autarky is still smaller than the 45 percentage point fall in trade
barriers induced by transport improvements over sea lanes between 1870
and 1913. Furthermore, since the impact of railroads was probably even
more important than transport improvements on ocean shipping, that big
45 percentage point fall is almost certainly an understatement. In addition
it was probably even bigger in the three or four decades before 1870 than
afterward.

Steamships made the most important contribution to improved shipping technology. As was noted above, steamers mainly carried high-
value goods until around 1860. A series of innovations changed all that
in subsequent decades: the screw propeller, the compound engine, steel
hulls, bigger ships, more efficient crews, increased fuel efficiency, more
ships, more predictable schedules, and shorter turnaround time in port all
served to produce a spectacular fall in intercontinental transport costs.
Furthermore the opening of the Suez Canal in 1869 halved the distance
from London to Bombay, and the Panama Canal in 1914 cut the distance
from New York to Shanghai. Refrigeration was another innovation with
major trade implications. In 1876, the first refrigerated ship sailed from
Argentina to France carrying frozen beef, and by the 1880s, Australian
meat and New Zealand butter were being exported in large quantities to
Europe.

The transport revolution was not limited to the Atlantic economy. The
decline in freight rates was just as dramatic on routes involving Black Sea
and Egyptian ports, and perhaps even more so (Harlaftis and Kardasis 2000;
Shah Mohammed and Williamson 2004). Over the fifty years after 1820,
freight rates fell by 51 percent along routes connecting Odessa with
England (Harley 1988: table 9). And after 1870, the railroads had a big
impact in Eurasia and Asia too: they tied the Ukraine interior wheat lands
with Odessa, the Black Sea, and thus with world markets. The same was
true of Latin America: freight rates between Antwerp and Rio de Janeiro
fell by 40 percent from 1820 to 1850, and those between Antwerp and
Valparaiso in the Pacific fell by 40 percent from 1850 to 1870 (Prados
2004: 11).

Asia was affected most dramatically by the transport revolution (Shah
Mohammed and Williamson 2004; see also figure 2.2). Except for "exotic"
products like silk, fine cottons, spices, porcelain, and precious metals, distance seemed almost to have isolated Asian producers and consumers from
Europe until well into the 19th century.[4] By 1914, transport innovations

had erased much of that isolation, and for the first time in recorded history, railroads served to moderate local famines on the Indian subcontinent by connecting regional grain markets (Hurd 1975; MacAlpin 1979). True, the Suez Canal, cost-reducing innovations on seagoing transport, and railroads penetrating the interior did not completely liberate Asia from the tyranny of distance.[5] But it was the *change* in the economic distance to the European core that mattered to the Asian periphery, and those changes were spectacular. An Indonesian freight rate index divided by an export price index fell by 83 percent between 1825 and 1875, and by another 45 percent between 1875 and 1912 (Korthals Altes 1994: 159–60). To take another example, the tramp charter rate for shipping rice from Rangoon (Burma) to Europe fell from 74 to 18 percent of the Rangoon price between 1882 and 1914, and the freight rate on sugar between Java (Dutch East Indies) and Amsterdam fell by 50 or 60 percent. There were equally dramatic changes taking place *within* Asia. For example, the freight rate on shipping coal from Nagasaki (Japan) to Shanghai (China) fell by 76 percent between 1880 and 1910, and total factor productivity on Japan's tramp freighter routes serving Asia advanced at an amazing 2.5 percent per annum between 1879 and 1909 (Yasuba 1978: tables 1 and 3).

Railroads were an important part of the transport technologies that contributed so much to world market integration in the first global century. Furthermore in many parts of the periphery they were even more important than they were in the core. Some time ago Nobel *laureate* Robert Fogel (1964) showed that railroads in the United States were hardly indispensable since second-best transport alternatives—canals, inland rivers, extensive coastlines, and the like—were abundant. Similar findings emerged for Belgium, Britain, France, and Germany (Caron 1983; Fremdling 1983; Hawke 1970; Laffut 1983; Vamplew 1971). However, where regions were fragmented by rough topography, poorly endowed with inland rivers, and isolated from coastlines, railroads had a spectacular market integrating impact. Indeed the social savings of the railroads were very big in Argentina (Summerhill 2001), the Brazilian southeast (Summerhill 2005), Mexico (Coatsworth 1979, 1981), and Spain (Gómez Mendoza 1982; Herranz-Loncán 2003). Thus the railroad had a profound impact on integrating domestic commodity markets in much of the periphery and connecting them to the world economy, as illustrated by Mexico in the decades up to World War I (Dobado and Marrero 2005).

Before the completion of the Panama Canal in 1914, the Andean economies—Chile, Peru, and Ecuador—were seriously disadvantaged in European and East Coast US trade. And prior to the introduction of an effective railroad network, landlocked Bolivia and Paraguay were at an even more serious disadvantage. This was also true of the Mexican interior (Coatsworth 1981), the Argentine interior (Newland 1998), the Colombian interior (Ocampo 1994: 185–88), and elsewhere. Thus the economic distance to the European core varied considerably depending on Latin American location. In 1842, the cost of moving a ton of goods from England to Latin American capital cities was (in pounds sterling): Buenos Aires and Montevideo 2; Lima 5.1; Santiago 6.6; Caracas 7.8; Mexico City 17.9; Quito 21.3; Sucre or Chuquisca 25.6; and Bogotá 52.9. The range was huge, with the costs to Bogotá, Chuquisca, Mexico City, Quito, and Sucre nine to twenty-seven times that of Buenos Aires and Montevideo, both well placed on either side of the Rio de la Plata (Brading 1969: 243–44). Furthermore most of the difference in transport costs from London to Latin American capital city was the overland freight from Latin American port to interior capital (Prados 2003). The most populated areas under colonial rule were the highlands. Mexico City, Lima, and the other Andean capital cities were far from accessible harbors, thus increasing transport costs to big foreign markets. In contrast, the Latin American regions bordering on the Atlantic, with long coastlines and good navigable river systems, have always been favored. These include Argentina, Uruguay, Brazil, Cuba, and the other Caribbean islands. These regional economies may have failed for other reasons, but geographic isolation certainly wasn't one of them.

It has been estimated that distance, geography and access to foreign markets explained a third of the world's variation in per capita income as late as 1996 (Overman, Redding and Venables 2003; Redding and Venables 2004). Not surprisingly, geographic isolation therefore helped explain much of the economic ranking of the young Latin American republics in 1870 too, with poor countries being the most isolated: Peru, Ecuador, Bolivia, and Paraguay were at the bottom of the income per capita list; Colombia and Brazil were next; Cuba and Mexico were a little higher; and Argentina and Uruguay were at the top.[6] Railroads helped unlock the Latin American interior that had been so isolated: for example, between 1870 and 1913, freight rates on overseas routes connecting Uruguay with Europe fell by 0.7 percent per annum, but they fell by 3.1 percent per annum along the railroads penetrating the interior pampas, more than *four times* as big (Bértola 2000: table 4.1, 102). Railroads were vital in integrating the periphery with core markets.

It is also important to note that the impact of the transport revolution on overseas freight rates was unequal along different sea routes. Overseas freight rates fell much less along the southward leg to Latin America than along the northward leg back to Europe, and the fall along the latter does not seem to have been as great as that for Asian and North Atlantic routes (Stemmer 1989: 24). The northward leg was for the bulky Latin American staple exports—like beef, wheat, and guano, the high-volume low-value primary products whose trade gained so much by the transport revolution. The southward leg was for Latin American imports—like textiles and machines, the high-value low-volume manufactures whose trade gained much less from the transport revolution. The transport revolution served to erase price differentials between periphery and core *much* more dramatically for primary products than for manufactures simply because primary products had much bigger price differentials to erase when the transport revolution began in 1820.

2.4   Growth Miracles in the Core and the World Trade Boom

Late 20th-century growth rates in the East Asian gang of four and then China, set a modern standard of "growth miracles" hard to beat, making impressive and then unique growth spurts in the distant past look pretty modest. But the first growth miracle was carried by the industrial revolutions in western Europe and its English-speaking offshoots two centuries ago. As panel A in table 2.2 shows, the size of markets (GDP) in the rich core were very slow to grow over the long century from 1700 to 1820, 0.6 percent per annum in western Europe or 0.7 percent per annum when the English-speaking offshoots are included. Over the first global century between 1820 and 1913, the rates increased by almost four times, to 2.4 percent per annum. Furthermore this increase is understated to the extent that, in 1700, even these rich economies were populated by farms and families that were close to subsistence, self-sufficient and hardly even connected to markets. Thus the upward jump in the growth rate in the "surplus" above subsistence must have been much bigger than four times. And it was the surplus that drove trade. Indeed the world share of trade in GDP rose eight times between 1820 and 1913, from 1 to 7.9 percent, and the trade share for western Europe reached 16.3 percent by the end of the period (Maddison 1995: 38).

Finally, much of the exports from the poor periphery were essential inputs into manufacturing. The canonic example is raw cotton to produce cotton textiles, but there were many more like copper, hemp, hides, iron, jute, lead, nitrates, rubber, silk, silver, tin, wool, and woods of all types, as well as foods to be processed. As I will argue in chapter 3, these intermediates were driven by industrial output expansion in the rich core

Table 2.2
GDP and industrial output performance in the rich core, 1700 to 1913

Panel A			
GDP levels	1700	1820	1913
Western Europe	70,988	142,399	840,612
Western Europe offshoots	833	13,499	582,941
Total rich core	71,821	155,898	1,423,553
GDP growth (% per annum)		1700–1820	1820–1913
Western Europe		0.58	1.93
Western Europe offshoots		2.35	4.13
Total rich core		0.65	2.41
Panel B			
Industrial output levels	1750	1830	1913
Developed countries	34	73	863
Third world	93	112	70
Industrial output growth (% per annum)		1750–1830	1830–1913
Developed countries		0.96	3.02
Third world		0.23	−1.56

Panel A sources and notes: Maddison (2009). Western Europe = France, Germany, Italy, Netherlands, Norway, Sweden, Switzerland, United Kingdom. Offshoots = Australia, Canada, New Zealand, United States. In millions of PPP Geary-Khamis US$. Panel B sources and notes: Bairoch (1982: table 3). Developed = as in panel A less Netherlands and Norway plus Austria-Hungary, Belgium, Russia, Spain plus Canada, Japan and United States. In absolute volumes, UK 1900 = 100.

where the rates of growth were much faster than for GDP. The time periods in panel B of table 2.2 documenting the industrial output growth accelera- tion are not quite comparable to those for GDP,[7] but they serve to make the point: industrial output grew even faster than did GDP in the rich core. Note also, by the way, that industrial output growth in the third world or the poor periphery was much slower in 1750 to 1830, and that it was *nega- tive* in 1830 to 1913. This fact will attract a lot of our attention in chapters 5 through 8.

2.5   Which Mattered Most?

Liberal Policy, Transport Revolutions, or Growth Miracles?
The world trade boom across the first global century was impressive. In the six decades before 1913, world trade grew about 3.8 percent per annum,

well above the growth rate in core GDP, 2.4 percent per annum, and even above core industrial output growth, about 3 percent per annum. So the world trade share in GDP rose: according to one estimate it rose from 1 to 2 percent between 1700 and 1820, and then increased almost nine times to 17.5 percent in 1913![8]

The fact that after 1820 world trade shares were rising so steeply suggests that income growth, industrialization, transport revolutions, communication improvements, and more liberal policy were all playing a role. Which mattered most? The answers depend on whether the focus is on market integration, trade/GDP shares, or trade alone.

If the focus is on trade, then income and growth miracles matter most. Over the three centuries between 1500 and 1800, European income growth explained between 50 and 65 percent of the intercontinental trade boom between Europe and Asia (O'Rourke and Williamson 2002a: 439), say 57.5 percent. During the 18th century alone, when European growth rates began their slow rise, between 59 and 75 percent of the Euro-Asian trade boom can be explained by European income growth, say 68.5 percent. Between 1870 and 1913, 57 percent of the world trade boom can be explained by income growth (Estevadeordal, et al. 2003: table III). And from the late 1950s to the late 1980s 67 percent of the OECD trade boom can be explained by the European postwar "growth miracle" (Baier and Bergstrand 2001). So income growth obviously matters greatly: world growth miracles foster trade booms, and world depressions (like the 1930s) do the opposite. Still there is 100 − 57 = 42 percent of the trade boom between 1870 and 1913 left to explain.

If instead the focus is on trade shares in GDP, then income growth drops in importance and changing barriers to trade become the leading forces. Between 1870 and 1913, the main sources of the rising world trade share were the gold standard (and other currency unions) and falling transportation costs (Estevadeordal et al. 2003; López-Córdova and Meissner 2003). Since the gold standard and other currency unions were late 19th-century institutions, and given that the move to liberal trade policy took place before 1870 not after, it seems likely that the fall in tariffs and transportation costs played a much bigger role in the first three-quarters of the 19th century. Other scholars have focused on world market integration—the convergence of prices between markets—rather than trade or trade shares. For world grain markets over the two centuries since 1800, trade costs were influenced more by commercial policy and monetary regimes than by transport costs (Jacks 2006; Federico and Persson 2007), but for European trade over the 19th century, falling transport costs played the biggest role (Keller and Shiue 2008). Finally, many studies have found that peace paid big trade dividends in the first global century (Olson 1963; O'Rourke 2006; Jacks 2006; Glick and Taylor 2009).

The next chapter will show how the appearance of these pro-trade forces during the first global century changed the world economic environment facing the poor periphery.

3 Biggest Third World Terms of Trade Boom Ever?

3.1 Globalization and the Great Divergence

The economic impact of the industrializing core on the poor periphery during the long century before World War I was carried by four dramatic global events: a world transport revolution, a liberal policy move in industrial Europe toward greater openness, an acceleration in GDP growth rates associated with the industrial revolution, and colonialism. As chapter 2 pointed out, the transport revolution was driven by technological events along sea lanes and by railroads connecting ports to interiors. All of this helped integrate world commodity markets, lowered price gaps between exporters and importers, and fostered trade. Since falling trade costs from all sources accounted for more than half of the trade boom between 1870 and 1914 (Jacks et al. 2008: 529), it must have accounted for even more than that before 1870 when the fall in transport costs was more rapid and the move to free trade was in full swing. In any case, it is clear that falling trade costs played a major role in fueling the trade boom between core and periphery, and that it created commodity price convergence for tradable goods between all world markets: that is, commodity price differentials between locations diminished, raising export prices for producers and lowering import prices for consumers. By raising every country's export prices and reducing every country's import prices, it also contributed to a rise in every country's external terms of trade, especially, as it turned out, in the periphery. The move by the European industrial core toward more liberal commercial policy (Estevadeordal et al. 2003), a commitment to the gold standard (Meissner 2005), and perhaps even imperialism itself (Ferguson 2004; Mitchener and Weidenmier 2007), made additional contributions to the world trade boom.

The accelerating growth in world GDP, led by industrializing Europe and its offshoots, was the second force driving the trade boom before 1913, and especially before 1870. The derived demand for industrial intermediates—like fuels, fibers, and metals—soared as manufacturing production led the way. Thus manufacturing output growth raced ahead of GDP growth as the European core and their offshoots raised industrial output shares. Rapid manufacturing productivity growth in the core lowered their supply costs and output prices, added to the demand for inexpensive factory-made manufactures, and by so doing generated a soaring derived demand for raw material intermediate inputs. This event was reinforced in the core by accelerating GDP *per capita* growth and a high income elasticity of demand for luxury consumption goods, like meat, dairy products, fruit, tea, and coffee. Since industrialization was driven by an unbalanced productivity advance favoring manufacturing relative to agriculture, other natural resource based activities, and services (Clark et al. 2008), the relative price of manufactures fell everywhere, including the poor periphery from where they were imported.

All three forces—liberal trade policy, transport revolutions, and fast manufacturing-led growth in Europe—produced a positive, powerful, and sustained terms of trade[1] boom in the primary-product exporting periphery, an event that stretched over almost a century. As we will see, some parts of the periphery had much greater terms of trade booms than others, and some reached a secular peak later than others, but all (except China and Cuba) underwent a secular terms of trade boom. Factor supply responses facilitated the periphery's reaction to these external demand shocks, carried by South–South migrations from labor abundant (especially China and India) to labor scarce regions within the periphery, and by financial capital flows from the industrial core (especially Britain) to those same regions. Thus countries in the periphery increasingly specialized in one or two primary products, reduced their production of manufactures, and imported them in exchange.

Let me rephrase these events in a different way. Whether due to advantages of culture (Polanyi 1944; Landes 1998; Clark 2007), geography (Diamond 1997; Gallup et al. 1999; Easterly and Levine 2003), or institutions (North and Weingast 1989; Acemoglu et al. 2001, 2002, 2005), western Europe launched modern economic growth first, carried by rising productivity growth rates, especially in manufacturing. The economic leaders had to share these productivity gains with the rest of the world by absorbing a decline in the price of their manufactured exports. Had the industrial leaders been closed to trade, their export sectors would have faced an even bigger price decline as supply shifted outward. A less elastic domestic demand would have generated a bigger fall in the price of manufactures, smaller profits, lower investment, and slower growth. Thus openness was an important ingredient for rapid industrialization in the rich core, even if it meant a diminished terms of trade. But since the industrial leaders retained for themselves most of the export sector productivity advance, and since they did not have to share any of the productivity advance that took place in their big nontradable sectors, the terms of trade slump did not entail a big enough transfer to their trading partners to make it possible for the poor periphery to keep up with economic growth in the industrial core.

Thus, even though trade made it possible for the periphery to share some of the fruits of the industrial revolution taking place in the core, an industrialization-driven great divergence still emerged. To add to the forces of divergence, globalization fostered de-industrialization (e.g., specialization) in the periphery so that, as we will see in chapters 5 and 11, growth rates in the periphery fell behind those in the core still further. In addition globalization-induced specialization in primary products must have meant greater price volatility in the periphery, and thus, as we will see in chapters 10 and 11, even greater divergence in growth rates. The positive effects of globalization and European industrialization on the third world were dubbed an "engine of growth" by W. Arthur Lewis (1980), in helping account, one supposes, for the nearly 1 percent annual GDP per capita growth rate achieved in the poor periphery between 1870 and 1913 (table 1.3). But critics have always argued that globalization had its downside for the poor periphery, namely de-industrialization, Dutch disease, commodity price volatility, and rising inequality. Which dominated, Lewis's positive engine or the critics' negative drag? This debate is as old as the great divergence, and this book will take a position before too long. But an elaboration of the de-industrialization and Dutch disease forces will have to wait until chapters 4 and 5. Here we will simply measure the size of terms of trade boom which triggered those events.

All these pro-global forces eventually abated. A protectionist backlash swept over continental Europe and Latin America (Williamson 2006a). The rate of decline in real transport costs along sea lanes slowed down before World War I, and then stabilized for the rest of the 20th century. Most of the railroad networks were completed before 1913. The rate of growth of manufacturing slowed down in the core as the transition to industrial maturity was completed and manufacturing began to grow at rates closer to those of GDP. As these forces abated, the resulting slowdown in primary-product demand growth was reinforced by resource-saving innovations in the industrial core, induced, in large part, by those high and rising primary-product prices during the century-long terms of trade boom. Thus the secular boom faded, eventually turning into a 20th-century secular bust during the interwar slowdown and the great depression of the 1930s. Exactly when and where the boom turned to bust depended, as we will see, on export commodity specialization, but throughout the poor periphery each region's terms of trade peaked somewhere between 1860 and 1913. Typically that peak occurred very early in that half century, rather than late, most often between the 1870s and 1890s, and it was *long* before the crash of the 1930s, in some cases seven decades earlier.

This chapter reports this terms of trade experience for twenty-one countries located everywhere around the poor periphery except sub-Saharan Africa (where the data are missing): Italy, Portugal, Russia, and Spain in the European periphery (1782–1913); Argentina, Brazil, Chile, Cuba, Mexico, and Venezuela in Latin America (1782–1913); Egypt, Ottoman Turkey, and the Levant in the Middle East (1796–1913); Ceylon and India in South Asia (1782–1913); Indonesia, Malaya, the Philippines, and Siam in Southeast Asia (1782–1913); and China and Japan in East Asia (1782–1913). We focus on the 19th-century secular boom since so much has already been written about the subsequent 20th-century bust, the latter triggered by the writings of Rául Prebisch (1950) and Hans Singer (1950) more than a half century ago. As we will see, the most dramatic boom took place between the 1780s and the 1870s, after which it had pretty much run its course. This focus is in sharp contrast with that of W. Arthur Lewis whose famous writings in the 1970s dealt almost exclusively with the 1870 to 1913 period (Lewis 1978a, 1978b). This chapter suggests that his new international economic order—the poor periphery exporting primary products and the rich core exporting manufactures—had been established long before the late 19th century. Indeed there were strong signs of a *retreat* from Lewis's new international economic order between the 1870s and WWI (see chapter 12).

3.2 The Biggest Terms of Trade Shock Ever? The Poor Periphery 1782 to 1913

A Word about the Terms of Trade Data

Before we get to the secular trends, it might be helpful to take a brief look at the heterogeneous character and limitations of the net barter terms of trade data that underlie the analysis. Twenty-one important regions in the periphery offer terms of trade estimates from points well before 1865, some deep into the 18th century, thus covering the era prior to the late 19th century when typically the relative price of primary products had already reached its peak. In every case but Argentina and Mexico, these new series are taken up to 1913 and replace the 1865 to 1939 series used in my previous work with two collaborators (Blattman, Hwang, and Williamson 2007: hereafter BHW). For Argentina and Mexico, the new series are linked to the BHW series at 1870.

For the purposes of this chapter and the rest of the book, the best measure of the terms of trade is the ratio of a weighted average of export and import prices quoted in local markets, *including* home import duties, that captures the impact of relative prices on the local market. The weights, of course, should be constructed from the export and import commodity mix for the country in question. Unfortunately, the data are sometimes unavailable for such estimates—what might be called the worst-case scenario. It is easy enough even in those cases to get the export prices (and the weights) for every region in our sample. However, these prices are rarely quoted in the local market, but rather in destination ports, like Amsterdam, London, or New York. To the extent that transport revolutions caused price convergence between exporter and importer, primary product prices quoted in core import markets will understate the rise in the periphery country's terms of trade. On this score alone, any reported boom in a periphery country terms of trade, where it is based on the worst-case scenario estimation, was actually somewhat bigger than that measured. However, since the terms of trade booms are, as we will see, so big, these worst-case scenario flaws on the export side are unlikely to matter much for the analysis. Things are a bit less accommodating on the import side in the worst-case scenario. As with export prices in the worst-case scenario, import prices are taken from export markets in the industrial core. Since transport revolutions reduced freight costs on the outward leg from the industrial core much less (they were high-value, low-bulk products: see Shah Mohammed and Williamson 2004), the periphery import price estimates are less flawed in the worst-case scenario than are the export price estimates. The more serious problem on the import side is the difficulty of documenting the import mix for many of the periphery countries, especially as we move earlier in the 19th century. Elsewhere I have described the proxies used to solve this worse-case scenario problem (Williamson 2008: app.).

Having pointed out the flaws in the worst-case scenario, it should be stressed that there are only 6 of these (out of 21). The other 15 are taken from country-specific sources and do an excellent job in constructing estimates that come close to the ideal measure: Argentina 1810–1870

(Newland 1998), Brazil 1826–1913 (Prados de la Escosura 2006), Chile 1810–1913 (Braun et al. 2000), Cuba 1826–1913 (Prados de la Escosura 2006), Egypt 1796–1913 (Williamson and Yousef 2008), India 1800–1913 (Clingingsmith and Williamson 2008), Indonesia 1825–1913 (Korthals 1994), Japan 1857–1913 (Miyamoto et al. 1965; Yamazawa and Yamamoto 1979), the Levant 1839–1913 (Issawi 1988), Malaya 1882–1913 (Caggiano and Huff 2007a, 2007b), Mexico 1751–1870 (Dobado et al. 2008), Ottoman Turkey 1800–1913 (Pamuk and Williamson 2008), Portugal 1842–1913 (Lains 1995), Spain 1750–1913 (Williamson 2008: app.), and Venezuela 1830–1913 (Baptista 1997). The worst-case scenarios apply to Italy 1817–1913 (Glazier et al. 1975) and the remaining five (see Williamson 2008: app.): Ceylon 1782–1913, China 1782–1913, the Philippines 1782–1913, Russia 1782–1913, and Siam 1782–1913.

Finally, there is one more reason why we might expect that the terms of trade boom in the third world is understated. Then and now, manufactures undergo much more dramatic improvements in quality over time than do primary products: for example, while copper ore is copper ore, a textile machine improves in capacity, speed, and durability over time. To the extent that prices fail to reflect fully improvements in quality, a rise in the price of imported manufactured goods will be overstated, and so the rise in the terms of trade facing the third world country importing manufactures and exporting primary products will be understated. However, based on experiments with Latin American terms of trade data, the quality adjustments would probably be minor (Williamson 2006c: fig. 1).

Still, if we think we see a big third world secular terms of trade boom out there, it was probably even bigger.

The Big Picture: Stability, Boom, and Bust

Although the number of countries underlying the poor periphery average is limited for most of the 18th century,[2] what we do have reveals no trend in the net barter terms of trade, that is, in the ratio of the poor periphery's average export price to its average import price. The averages are calculated so that the price of each commodity exported or imported is weighted by the importance of that traded commodity in the country's total exports or imports. Furthermore the poor periphery average is calculated using fixed country 1870 population weights. The resulting series plotted in figure 3.1 is certainly volatile, but there is no long-run trend whatsoever. Secular stability in the poor periphery's 18th-century terms of trade is consistent with a world still waiting for the industrial revolution, the transport revolution, peace in Europe, liberal trade policy, and a world trade boom.

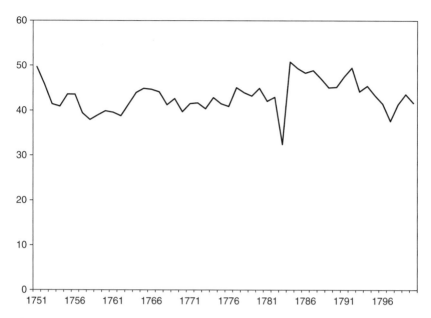

Figure 3.1
Terms of trade in the 18th century: Calm before the storm in the poor periphery.
Source: Williamson (2008: fig. 1)

Figure 3.2 describes a very different world, the first global century. Excluding China and the rest of East Asia (more on that below), the terms of trade in the poor periphery soared from the late 18th century to the late 1880s and early 1890s, after which it underwent a decline up to 1913, before starting the interwar collapse about which so much has been written. The timing and the magnitude of the boom up to the late 1860s and early 1870s pretty much replicates—but in the opposite direction—the decline in the British terms of trade over the same period. The secular price boom was huge in the poor periphery: between the half-decades 1796 to 1800 and 1856 to 1860, the terms of trade increased by almost two and a half times, or at an annual rate of 1.5 percent. This rate was vastly greater than per capita income growth in the poor periphery—0.1 percent per annum, Asia 1820 to 1870—and even greater than per capita income growth in western Europe—1.2 percent per annum, 1820 to 1870 (see table 1.3).

Had Britain and Europe been closed to trade, the industrial revolution would have generated an even sharper fall in the price of manufactures, since productivity growth would have driven supply curves outward and downward along downward-sloping domestic demand curves. By being

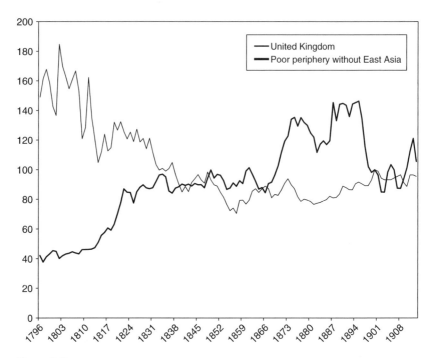

Figure 3.2
Terms of trade, 1796 to 1913: United Kingdom versus the poor periphery.
Source: Williamson (2008: fig. 2)

open to trade, these industrializing economies could vent their surplus output on world markets with a much smaller fall in price. The gain to industrializing Europe was higher prices of manufactures than otherwise, higher profits, and higher rates of accumulation. But Britain and Europe had to share some of the productivity gains with their trading partners by the gift of lower prices for their manufactured exports. Although it may have been a magnificent gift for the poor periphery, that 1.5 percent annual rate of terms of trade growth still applied only to that portion of GDP which was traded. Thus a poor country trading with Britain whose exports were 10 percent of GDP would have had its annual GDP growth augmented only by (1.5 times 0.10 =) 0.15 percentage points. Still it was an impressive transfer from rich industrial Europe to the poor periphery.

Not everybody gained in the poor periphery, of course. As we have seen, a rise in the primary-product specializing country's terms of trade implied a fall in the relative price of imported manufactures. And the decline in that price implied a penalty to domestic manufacturing, eroding their profits and inducing the sector to shrink. Thus those economies de-industrialized. When Lewis published his now-famous *The Evolution of the International Economic Order* in 1978 dealing with de-industrialization in what we now call the third world, he placed his emphasis on "the second half of the nineteenth century" (1978a: 14). But if we are looking for Dutch disease forces that caused de-industrialization in the poor periphery—the same forces that helped create Lewis's new international economic order, the century *before* 1870 is the place to look, not after.

Chinese and East Asian *Exceptionalism*

Not every part of the poor periphery underwent a big terms of trade boom since what a region traded mattered.[3] The best example of this is the biggest country in our sample, China. Figures 3.3 and 3.10 plot the terms of trade for China, for the poor periphery with East Asia (and thus China[4]) included, and for the poor periphery without it. The difference is astounding. First, China did not undergo a terms of trade boom over the century before 1913,

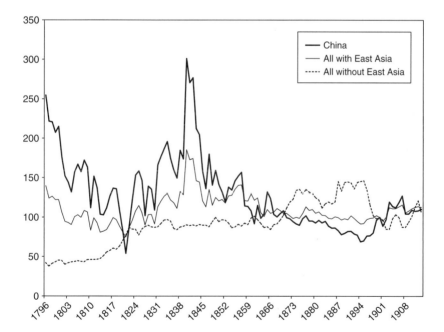

Figure 3.3
Chinese exceptionalism: Terms of trade in the poor periphery, 1796 to 1913 with and without East Asia.
Source: Williamson (2008: fig. 3)

but rather underwent a secular slump! Second, as the rest of the periphery began the boom between 1796 and 1821, China underwent its first big *collapse*, with its terms of trade falling to one-fifth (sic!) of the 1796 level. Third, when China finally joined the boom taking place in the rest of the periphery, it was very brief since its terms of trade peaked much earlier than the rest, in 1840 after only a two decade boom. Following the early 1860s, China underwent the same slow secular decline in its terms of trade that was common across much of the poor periphery.[5] China's terms of trade *exceptionalism* was, of course, driven by its unusual country-specific mix of imports and exports. On the import side, what distinguished China from the rest of the periphery was opium. The price of imported opium rose sharply from the 1780s to the 1820s, partly because of a successful monopoly by the East India Company (Chaudhuri 1978; Farrington 2002; Bowen et al. 2003), and it maintained those high (but volatile) levels until the 1880s (Clingingsmith and Williamson 2008).[6] Since opium imports rose from about 30 to 50 percent of total Chinese imports over the period, the rise in the opium price helped push China's terms of trade downward, and in a direction opposite to that of the rest of the poor periphery. Reinforcing that secular fall in China's terms of trade, was the fact that it also exported the "wrong" products since the price of silk and cotton fell dramatically over the century between the 1780s and 1880s, by 60 and 71 percent, respectively (Mulhall 1892; 471–78).[7] Chinese *exceptionalism* indeed!

While China was certainly big enough to dominate East Asian trends, it should be pointed out that Japan was exceptional as well. First, it remained closed to world trade until the mid-1850s, so that there is no terms of trade trend worth reporting up to that point since its trade sector was so tiny, even with smuggling included. Second, when Japan was forced to go open in 1854 by the threat of American gunships commanded by Matthew Perry, it underwent the biggest 19th-century terms of trade boom by far: the price of its exportables boomed and the price if its importables slumped, just when the rest of the poor periphery had pretty much completed its secular boom. But its exports were manufactures, not commodities!

East Asian *exceptionalism* indeed.

Poor Periphery Variance around the Average
While each region in the poor periphery had much the same import mix (except for China and its opium), each specialized in quite different primary products on the export side. Endowments and comparative advantage

dictated the export mix, and different commodity price behavior implied different terms of trade magnitudes during the secular boom, as well as different terms of trade peak years. Figures 3.4 through 3.10 document terms of trade performance in each of the six poor periphery regions, some starting as early as 1782. The regional time series are constructed as a fixed 1870 population weighted average of the region's countries (listed above: the European Periphery four, the Latin American eight, the Middle East three, the South Asian two, the Southeast Asian four, and the East Asian two). Table 3.1 and figure 3.4 summarize the magnitude of the boom and its length by region and by major country members, making a comparative assessment possible. Table 3.1 reports the starting year in each region's terms of trade time series, the peak year of the secular boom in the series, the annual growth rate between half-decade averages from start to peak, and the annual growth rate from start to the half-decade 1886 to 1890. While there was a terms of trade boom everywhere outside of China, some had bigger and longer booms than others.

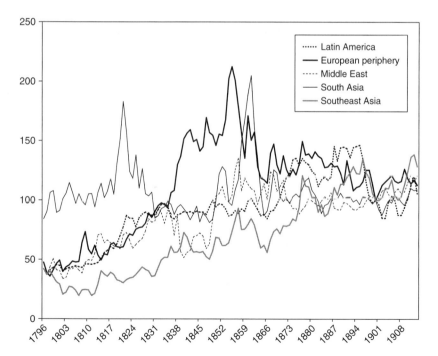

Figure 3.4
Terms of trade in the poor periphery, 1796 to 1913.
Source: Williamson (2008: fig. 4)

European Poor Periphery, 1782 to 1913   Figure 3.4, figure 3.5, and table 3.1 suggest that the shape of the secular boom and bust in the European periphery was pretty much like that of the overall poor periphery average, with peaks very close together (1855 vs. 1860). However, the *magnitude* of the booms certainly differed. The terms of trade boom in the European periphery was *much* greater than the average (2.4 vs. 1.4 percent per annum), especially for Italy and Russia. This was also true of the century-long boom up to 1885 through 1890 (1.2 vs. 0.7 percent per annum). As I suggest below, these powerful Dutch disease effects may help explain why the industrial revolution was slow to spread from the European northwest to the European east and south. Although the historical literature documenting lagging industrial revolutions in eastern and southern Europe is extensive (Gerschenkron 1962; Pollard 1982), rarely does it stress the contribution of Dutch disease forces. Perhaps it is time to add globalization forces to an agenda that explores the roles of culture, institutions, bad government, and geography in the European periphery.

Latin America, 1782 to 1913   Figure 3.4, figure 3.6, and table 3.1 report that Latin America also deviated significantly from the poor periphery

Table 3.1
Terms of trade boom across the poor periphery: Timing and magnitude

Region	Starting year in the series	Peak year	Annual growth rate between half-decades start to peak (%)	Annual growth rate between half-decades start to 1886–90 (%)
All periphery excluding East Asia	1796	1860	1.431	0.726
European periphery	1782	1855	2.434	1.234
Latin America	1782	1895	0.873	0.851
Middle East	1796	1857	1.683	0.872
South Asia	1782	1861	0.904	0.037
Southeast Asia	1782	1896	1.423	1.423
East Asia	1782	None	na	−2.119
European periphery	1782	1855	2.434	1.234
Italy	1817	1855	3.619	0.697
Russia	1782	1855	2.475	1.335
Spain	1782	1879	1.505	1.264

Table 3.1
(continued)

Region	Starting year in the series	Peak year	Annual growth rate between half-decades start to peak (%)	Annual growth rate between half-decades start to 1886–90 (%)
Latin America	1782	1895	0.873	0.851
Argentina	1811	1909	1.165	1.284
Brazil	1826	1894	1.115	1.067
Chile	1810	1906	0.966	0.140
Cuba	1826	None	na	−1.803
Mexico	1782	1878	1.096	0.989
Venezuela	1830	1895	0.692	0.677
Middle East	1796	1857	1.683	0.872
Egypt	1796	1865	2.721	1.571
Ottoman Turkey	1800	1857	2.548	1.233
South Asia	1800	1861	0.904	0.037
Ceylon	1782	1874	0.670	0.366
India	1800	1861	0.932	0.024
Southeast Asia	1782	1896	1.423	1.423
Indonesia	1825	1896	3.294	3.335
Philippines	1782	1857	1.480	0.720
Siam	1800	1857	1.534	0.397
East Asia	1782	None	na	−2.119
China	1782	None	na	−2.342

Source: Williamson (2008: table 2).
Notes: The following countries are excluded from the table's detail since their series begin too late (starting date in parentheses): Portugal (1842); Columbia (1865), Peru (1865), Venezuela (1830); the Levant (1839); Malaysia (1882); and Japan (1857). These country observations were used, however, when constructing the regional aggregates and the all periphery aggregate. Where it says "start," the calculation is the average of the first five years. Where it says "peak," the calculation is for the five years centered on the peak year. The regional and all the periphery averages are weighted by 1870 population.

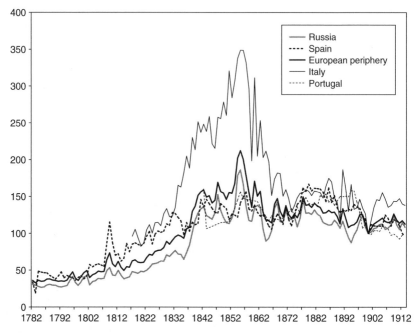

Figure 3.5
Terms of trade in the European poor periphery, 1782 to 1913.
Source: Williamson (2008: fig. 5)

average, but on the down side. First of all, most of the secular boom there took place up to about 1830, that is during the late colonial and revolutionary years. Afterward, the terms of trade boom up to 1860 was much more modest. Indeed there was very little change at all in the Latin American terms of trade between about 1830 and 1870. At least the new Latin American republics emerging after the 1820s did not have to deal with global de-industrialization forces during their "lost decades" of poor growth when violence and political instability was already doing enough economic damage (Bates, Coatsworth and Williamson 2007; Williamson 2007). Still the Latin American terms of trade boom lasted far longer (1895) than was true for the average periphery region (1860), more than three decades longer. The more modest early boom in republican Latin America and its great length about balanced out, such that the century-long boom was much the same as in the average poor periphery region (0.9 vs. 0.7 percent per annum up to 1886–1890). To summarize, de-industrialization forces were very weak in republican Latin America during its *lost decades,* when they were stronger everywhere else in the poor periphery; they were

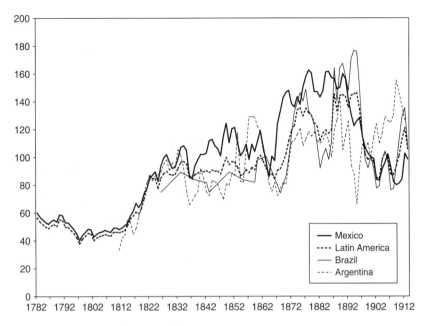

Figure 3.6
Terms of trade in Latin America, 1782 to 1913.
Source: Williamson (2008: fig. 6)

very strong during its *belle époque*,[8] when they were weaker everywhere else in the poor periphery. Presumably these differences left their mark on the economic performance of the new Latin American republics compared to the rest of the poor periphery. Chapter 8 will explore the terms of trade impact on Mexico up to 1879 at great length. Since Mexico and the rest of Latin America had terms of trade experience less dramatic up to the 1870s than elsewhere, our expectation is that Dutch disease forces were weaker; that helped make local industry stronger and gave Mexico a much better industrial base from which to launch its precocious industrialization after 1870.

Middle East, 1796–1913   Figure 3.4, figure 3.7, and table 3.1 document that the terms of trade boom facing the Middle East was even more dramatic than it was for the poor periphery average. While the peak was about the same (1857 vs. 1860), the magnitude of the boom was greater (1.7 vs. 1.4 percent per annum), and it was *much* greater for Egypt and Ottoman Turkey (2.7 and 2.5 percent per annum).[9] The magnitude of the century-long boom up to 1885 through 1890 was also greater for the Middle East

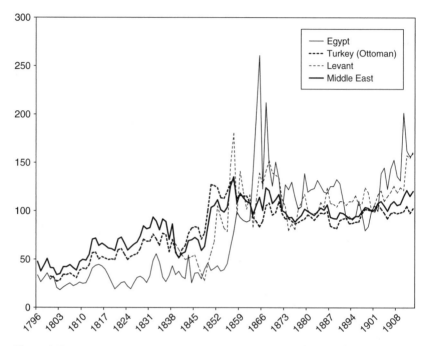

Figure 3.7
Terms of trade in the Middle East, 1796 to 1913.
Source: Williamson (2008: fig. 7)

than the periphery average (0.9 vs. 0.7 percent per annum), and it was, once again, *much* greater for Egypt and Ottoman Turkey (1.6 and 1.2 percent per annum). Since the Middle East seems to have undergone an unusually big terms of trade shock even by poor periphery standards, chapter 7 will explore its impact on Egypt and the Ottoman empire in much greater depth.

South Asia, 1782 to 1913 Our South Asia sample has only two observations, Ceylon and India, but the latter is so large that the South Asian weighted average lies on top of the India series in figure 3.8. Like Latin America, India (and thus South Asia) had a very weak terms of trade boom up to mid-century.[10] The South Asian and the average periphery terms of trade (still excluding East Asia) peaked only one year apart (1861 vs. 1860), but beyond that similarity there are only differences. The boom in South Asia up to 1861 was far weaker than the average (0.9 vs. 1.4 percent per annum), and this was even more true over the century up to

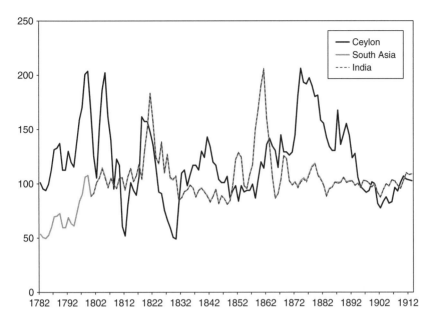

Figure 3.8
Terms of trade in South Asia, 1782 to 1913.
Source: Williamson (2008: fig. 8)

1885 through 1890 (no growth at all vs. 0.7 percent per annum). Indeed all of that early growth in India's terms of trade took place up to the 1820s; after that decade India exhibited great volatility (like the spike up to 1861) but no secular growth whatsoever. And, to repeat, there was no growth at all in India's terms of trade between 1800 and 1890. Like China, India was exceptional, an especially ironic finding given that the literature on 19th-century de-industrialization in British India has been the most copious and contentious by far, starting with the words of Karl Marx about the bones of the weavers bleaching on the plains of India (Roy 2000, 2002; Clingingsmith and Williamson 2008). Chapter 6 will explore this Indian paradox—big de-industrialization but small terms of trade shocks, and special domestic supply side factors will be found to explain it.

Southeast Asia, 1782 to 1913   Like Latin America, the terms of trade boom in Southeast Asia persisted much longer, in this case to 1896, and the size of the century-long boom up to 1885 through 1890 was much greater (1.4 vs. 0.7 percent per annum). Yet there was immense variance within the

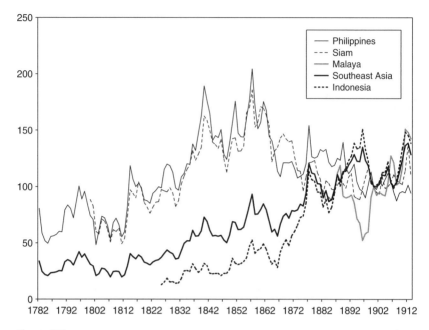

Figure 3.9
Terms of trade in Southeast Asia, 1782 to 1913.
Source: Williamson (2008: fig. 9)

region (figure 3.9), much more than elsewhere in the poor periphery. For example, the terms of trade for Siam (a rice exporter) grew at "only" 0.4 percent per annum over the century up to 1885 through 1890, but it grew almost twice as fast in the Philippines (an exporter of hemp, sugar, copra, and tobacco) at 0.7 percent per annum, and more than eight times as fast in Indonesia (a coffee exporter) at 3.3 percent per annum. Because of its size, the latter dominates the Southeast Asian weighted average, and the terms of trade experience suggests that globalization must have done bigger damage to industry in Indonesia than almost anywhere else in the non-European periphery.

East Asia, 1782 to 1913   We have already discussed Chinese *exceptionalism*, but figure 3.10 also highlights Japan's unusual experience. That is, after being forced by American gunboat diplomacy to go open in 1857—after centuries of autarchy, Japan underwent a textbook response (Bernhofen and Brown 2005)—the price of importables collapsed, and the price of exportables soared. Thus Japan's terms of trade improved, and by a factor

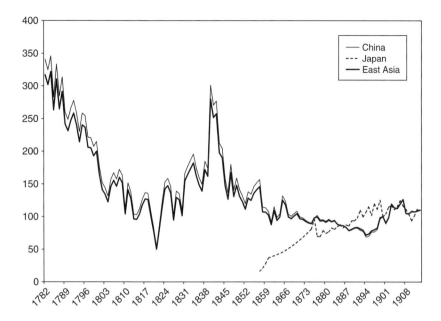

Figure 3.10
Terms of trade in East Asia, 1782 to 1913.
Source: Williamson (2008: fig. 10)

of six or more (sic!) between 1857 and 1913 (Huber 1971; Yasuba 1996). Japan's experience was different from much of the poor periphery for two reasons: first, it missed the terms of trade boom across the first half of the 19th century by opting to remain closed to world trade; second, when it was forced to go open after 1857, this resource-scarce and labor-abundant country should have found its manufacturing favored since that's where its comparative advantage lay. How much of the early and spectacular industrialization during the Meiji years (the 1870s to World War I: Ohkawa and Rosovsky 1973; Smith 1955) was due these globalization forces, and why is the conventional literature so quiet about it?

3.3   An Agenda

The first chapter of this book established that a great divergence took place between the European industrial core (plus its offshoots), and the poor agrarian periphery, a divergence that was especially dramatic over the long century 1800 to 1913. This divergence created a great gap in income per capita, living standards, and levels of development that persisted into the late 20th and the early 21st century. Chapter 2 established that this long century also recorded a boom in world trade, an integrated world financial capital market, and mass migration. In addition a new international economic order emerged, where what we now call the third world came to specialize in the production and export of primary products, while what we now call the OECD came to specialize in the production and export of manufactures. This chapter has now shown that the Third World underwent a spectacular terms of trade boom, forces that might be able to help account for both the great divergence and the emergence of the new international economic order. The remainder of the book will make these connections much clearer.

4 The Economics of Third World Growth Engines and Dutch Diseases

4.1 Laying out the Steps

This chapter will try to make the underlying economics of this book as clear as possible. We know there were gains from 19th-century trade, and we know opening up to trade should have augmented the growth rate in the third world *unless the underlying growth fundamentals were altered*. The next section repeats the standard arguments for the gains from trade and shows how the terms of trade boom might have augmented third world growth rates. Section 4.3 demonstrates, at least theoretically, how de-industrialization, rent-seeking, and price volatility, also induced by global forces, could have offset the gains from trade. No empirical resolution is offered to these two contending forces until chapter 11. Finally, since the de-industrialization we observe in the 19th-century third world was not just the result of external global forces but also the result of local supply-side forces, section 4.4 develops a simple neo-Ricardian model that helps us discriminate between the two forces. The chapter concludes with an agenda for the rest of the book.

4.2 Gains from Trade and Engines of Growth

When David Ricardo (1817) proposed the theory of comparative advantage two centuries ago, he used an example very relevant to this book, namely the exchange of Portuguese wine for English cloth. Since Ricardo stated his comparative advantage theorem, no anti-global critic has ever been able to destroy the logic of his argument. It follows that if all trading partners gain from trade, then trade must have increased third world GDP everywhere across the 19th century, at least in the short run and holding everything else constant. Those countries that were landlocked, and had no railroads or extensive river system, had less trade and smaller gains.

Those that were distant from European markets, and faced high transport costs between ports, also had less trade and smaller gains. Those that had huge interiors had less external trade and smaller gains. Currency arrangements and colonial connections also played a role in determining how much was gained from trade. But *all* countries in the poor periphery gained.

Clearly, the higher the price a third world country got for its exports, and the lower the price it paid for its imports, the greater were the gains from trade. Just as clearly, if that third world country's terms of trade improved every year, it should have raised the growth performance of the country, at least in the short run. Furthermore those countries with a big trade share (e.g., exports divided by GDP) would have had their growth rates augmented by more than those with small shares. This is one component of what W. Arthur Lewis (1978a, 1980) was talking about when he referred to *trade as an engine of growth*. What is surprising, however, is how modest the gains turn out to be when you do the math on a poor preindustrial slow-growing economy during that era. Consider some primary-product exporter whose export share in GDP was about 10 percent (the third world average between 1870 and 1913: table 4.1; see also Hanson 1986), and enjoyed an impressive 1 percent rise in its terms of trade every year, year in and year out (about the third world average between 1796 and 1890, excluding China: table 3.1). What should this have done to the country's growth rate? If GDP was growing at a very modest 0.7 percent per annum (third world average 1820–1913, Maddison 2007)—enough to keep up with slow pre-modern population growth rates with a little to spare (0.4 percent per annum 1820–1913: Maddison 2007), then the terms of trade improvement would have increased the growth rate to $(0.7 + 0.10 \times 1 =)$ 0.8 percent per annum. That increase from 0.7 to 0.8 percent per annum may seem pretty tiny, but it was significant by 19th-century third world growth rate standards (after all, 0.1/0.7 implies a 15 percent increase). But that's not all since it seems likely that trade would also induce a transfer of technology, an event that would raise the underlying growth fundamentals and thus the growth rate to something higher than 0.8. In addition the growth rate increase would have been a lot larger if the country's trade share was larger. If we double the trade share from 10 to 20 percent (that of Latin America and the Mideast in 1913: table 4.1), then we raise the growth rate to 0.9 percent per annum $(0.7 + 0.20 \times 1 = 0.9)$. True, these augmented figures hardly inspire confidence that the third world would have caught up with Europe, but at least they would have helped lower the growth gap between the two.

Table 4.1
Export shares in GDP: Poor periphery, 1870 and 1913

Country	1870	1913	1913/1870
Argentina	12.6	21.3	1.7
Brazil	14.1	20.9	1.5
Chile	16.1	20.5	1.3
Colombia	2.0	6.8	3.4
Cuba	38.8	45.3	1.2
Mexico	3.6	8.8	2.4
Peru	29.4	13.0	0.4
Uruguay	20.4	20.6	1.0
Latin America	*17.1*	*19.7*	*1.2*
Burma	10.6	17.3	1.6
Ceylon	11.1	16.4	1.5
China	0.5	1.3	2.6
India	2.3	5.5	2.4
Indonesia	1.6	8.1	5.1
Japan	0.7	5.8	8.3
Philippines	6.3	4.7	0.8
Thailand	1.3	5.4	4.2
Asia	*4.3*	*8.1*	*1.9*
Egypt	25.5	33.1	1.3
Greece	4.4	6.7	1.5
Turkey	5.0	11.5	2.3
Mideast	*11.6*	*17.1*	*1.5*
Italy	0.7	2.8	4.0
Portugal	4.1	6.1	1.5
Russia	2.8	4.6	1.6
Serbia	5.2	5.9	1.1
Spain	3.6	5.6	1.6
European periphery	*3.3*	*5.0*	*3.0*
All periphery	*9.5*	*12.4*	*1.3*

Source: Data underlying Blattman et al. (2007). Averages are unweighted.

The second component of Lewis's engine of growth was getting the third world country's export share from a lower to a higher level, that is, to better exploit trade opportunities as time went on. Countries with growth-friendly institutions, good government, effective factor markets, access to cheap foreign capital to help build the infrastructure, and access to cheap unskilled foreign workers to labor in the mines and plantations were able get more resources to the export sector faster, increase the export share in GDP quicker, and get the bigger gains in growth rates.

Table 4.1 summarizes what we know about export shares in GDP for the poor periphery in 1870 and 1913.[1] With rare exceptions (Peru and the Philippines), all 24 countries listed there increased their export shares over the four decades. Large countries with large interiors tended to have low export shares—like China, India, and Russia, and small economies with extensive coastlines had large ones—like Argentina, Brazil, Cuba, Chile, and Uruguay. But there is a lot of variance across these 24 economies in the poor periphery left to be explained by institutions, the quality of government, the effectiveness of factor markets, access to foreign capital and labor, supportive currency arrangements and perhaps even colonial connections. In any case, the average for the periphery was a little more than 12 percent by 1913.

4.3   The De-industrialization, Rent-Seeking, and Price Volatility Downsides

If the gains from trade are so obvious, and if the impact of the terms of trade boom so significant, why the big fuss about globalizations' potential negative impact on growth performance? Note we are talking about *growth rates*, not *levels* of GDP. To repeat, no economist denies the gains from trade. What's being debated is the possible asymmetric impact of globalization on growth rates, raising them in industrial Europe and not raising them in the pre-industrial third world, thus contributing to the great divergence. Note also that there is no mention of *diminished* third world growth rates in this paragraph, but rather of an asymmetric *no increase* in growth rates. How is this possible when the previous section just showed how the terms of trade boom should have raised growth rates in the poor periphery? The answer is that there were three potential long-run offsets to the short run increase in GDP growth: de-industrialization, rent-seeking, and price volatility.

De-industrialization and Dutch Disease

First consider de-industrialization. Most theories of economic growth—especially the more recent endogenous growth theories (e.g., Krugman 1981, 1991a, b; Krugman and Venables 1995; Romer 1986, 1990; Galor and Mountford 2006; Lucas 2009)—imply that industrial-urban activities contain far more cost-reducing and productivity-enhancing forces than do traditional agriculture and traditional services. This notion is so embedded in mainstream economic thinking that it gets important exposure in modern surveys of growth theory (e.g., Helpman 2004: ch. 5). Indeed, how else can industrialization—that is, an increase in the share of economic activity based in industry—take place without more rapid rates of total factor productivity growth there? After all, it is relatively rapid productivity advance in industry that lowers its relative costs and prices, raises demand for its output, pulls resources from other less dynamic sectors to augment its capacity to meet that increased demand, and makes it expand in relative size. Thus, given that industry achieves much higher growth rates during the industrial revolution than do other sectors, GDP growth rates quicken as the dynamic sector pulls up the average. And as industry grows in relative importance, its impact on overall GDP growth rates rises as well. The explanations offered for this asymmetric effect favoring rapid productivity growth in urban industry are many. To name just four, urban clusters foster agglomeration economies, denser urban product and factor markets imply more efficient markets, a more skill-intensive industry and its modern support services fosters the demand for and accumulation of skills, and a denser urban-industrial complex tends to generate a more extensive productivity-enhancing knowledge transfer between firms.

The historical evidence certainly confirms the theory. Figure 4.1 plots the correlation, both in logs, between current GDP per capita (observed between 1820 and 1950: Maddison 2001), and past levels of industrialization per capita (50 or 70 years earlier: Bairoch 1982). The correlation is steep and strongly significant. Today's more industrial countries are able to achieve much higher levels of per capita income in the distant future than those less industrial: in other words, faster growth comes with industrialization. The corollary, of course, is that de-industrialization today lowers your growth capacity for the future. Any external price event in the third world that favors the primary-product export sector and penalizes import-competing industry should breed de-industrialization, or what has come to be called Dutch disease.[2] The term "Dutch disease" is used to describe the response of an economy not only to external price shocks but

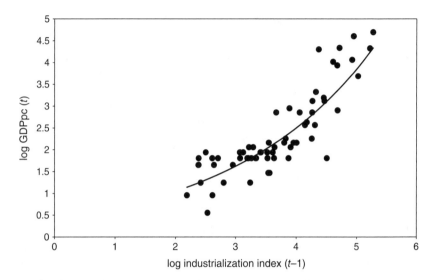

Figure 4.1
Do industrial countries get richer?
Source: Data from Bairoch (1982: table 4, p. 281) and Maddison (2001: tables A1–A3, pp. 185, 195, 215)

also to technological change or resource discovery, typically for commodity exports. The "disease" takes the form of a shift in resources to the favored commodity sector from other sectors. While an external terms of trade boom favoring commodities certainly gives resources an incentive to move, the commodity boom also augments the supply of foreign exchange, lowers (raises) the real cost of the foreign (domestic) currency, and cheapens imports, thus fostering de-industrialization. We shall return to real exchange rate effects in chapter 12.

In short, de-industrialization should contribute to a growth slowdown if industry is the carrier of growth that theory says it is, and that figure 4.1 supports. Thus de-industrialization, induced by global forces, offers a potential offset to the gains from trade and the growth engine. Chapter 5 will explore the de-industrialization magnitudes across the third world between 1750 and 1913, and they were very big.

Rent-Seeking and Resource Curse
Consider now rent-seeking, or what has come to be called *resource curse*.[3] Chapter 9 will document what happened to the distribution of income as the primary-product exporting third world responded to the terms of trade

boom. While there were gains from trade everywhere, those elite who held most of the productive land, the mines, and the other natural resources gained the most, that is, the rent-to-wage ratio soared, and income distribution became more unequal. To the extent that these elite at the top found their political power strenghtened, institutions must have been bent to favor their rent-seeking and disfavor the growth-oriented entrepreneur (Tulloch 1967; Krueger 1974; Bates 1997, 2008). In short, rising inequality and rent-seeking, induced by global forces, offer a second potential offset to the gains from trade and the growth engine.[4] This offset may also be strengthened by institutional forces as elaborated by Douglas North and Robert Thomas (1973), Daron Acemoglu (2009), and Acemoglu, Simon Johnson and James Robinson (2001, 2002, 2005).

Commodity Price Volatility

Finally, consider price volatility and export concentration. Chapter 10 will elaborate on the evidence and argument, but it has long been appreciated that primary products have much higher price volatility than do manufactures (Deaton and Miller 1996; Mendoza 1997; Bleaney and Greenway 2001; Poelhekke and van der Ploeg 2007). Furthermore those primary-product exporters that exploit comparative advantage by specializing in one or two products, expose themselves to higher price risk, than those that have a wider range of export products. Table 4.2 shows just how high measures of export concentration had become in the third world by the end of the 19th century and the beginning of the 20th century. Of the 24 poor periphery countries listed there, 6 had all their export earnings coming from two products, and some, like Siam (rice) and Egypt (cotton) had all their export earnings coming from just one. The average share of total export earnings coming from just two commodities was 72 percent in 1900. While it was highest in Latin America (83 percent) and lowest in the European periphery (71 percent), export concentration was obviously a common attribute of the poor periphery under the *new international economic order*. Furthermore table 4.3 documents that in 1900 export concentration was about three times higher in the poor periphery than in the industrial European core.

Did export concentration in the poor periphery rise in response to 19th-century globalization? Some time ago, John Hanson (1977) showed that export concentration did not rise in the poor periphery *after* 1860. Indeed W. Arthur Lewis thought export diversification took place there between 1880 and 1913 (Lewis 1970). Evidence such as this would, of course, be quite consistent with the facts of chapter 3 where we noted that, on

Table 4.2
Export concentration in the poor periphery around 1900

Country	Two major export commodities	Percentage of total exports
Latin America		83
Argentina	Wool, wheat	65
Brazil	Coffee, rubber	90
Chile	Nitrates, copper	100
Colombia	Coffee, tobacco	100
Cuba	Sugar, tobacco	100
Mexico	Silver, copper	90
Peru	Sugar, silver	54
Uruguay	Wool, hides	72
Venezuela	Coffee, cacao	73
South and Southeast Asia		79
Burma	Rice, oil products	92
Ceylon	Tea, coffee	100
India	Rice, jute	35
Indonesia	Sugar, coffee	60
Philippines	Hemp, sugar	89
Siam	Rice	100
East Asia		78
China	Silk, tea	78
Japan	Silk, cotton goods	79
Middle East		78
Egypt	Cotton	100
Turkey	Fruits and nuts, silk	55
European periphery		71
Greece	Fruits and nuts, lead	91
Portugal	Wine, cork	74
Serbia	Livestock, fruits and nuts	73
Spain	Iron, fruits and nuts	46
Russia	Wheat, wool	70
Total		72

Source: Venezuela 1913 from Bulmer-Thomas (1995: table 3.2). All others based on data underlying Blattman et al. (2007).
Note: All regional averages are unweighted.

Table 4.3

Changes in export concentration in the poor periphery: Share of most important export in total exports, 1860 to 1900 (in percent)

	1860		1900	
	Core	Periphery	Core	Periphery
Mean	37	58	22	52
Median	39	62	18	54

Source: Hanson (1977: table 2).

average, the third world terms of trade reached its peak in the 1860s or 1870s, and underwent a secular fall thereafter. On the upswing, export concentration must have been encouraged while on the downswing, diversification must have been encouraged. Table 4.3 reports a reworking of Hanson's evidence for 1860 and 1900: the share of export earnings accounted for by the major export.[5] First, and consistent with table 4.2, export concentration was much higher in the poor periphery than in the European industrial core in both years. Second, a trend toward export diversification was quite dramatic in the core over the four decades. Third, while there is also some evidence of a trend toward greater export diversification in the periphery, it was nowhere near as dramatic as in the core.

What's missing from table 4.3, however, is the pre-1860 experience. This was when soaring terms of trade should have increased export concentration in the periphery.

We know that price volatility is bad for growth (chapter 10: Blattman et al. 2007; Poelhekke and van der Ploeg 2007). To the extent that specialization in primary products, induced by global forces, implied higher export price volatility, we have a third potential offset to the gains from trade and the growth engine.

4.4   A Neo-Ricardian Model of De-industrialization[6]

As we have seen, if, by the generous endowment of natural resources, climate, good harbors, and other environmental factors, a country has a comparative advantage in some primary product, trade with the rest of the world will make it possible to exploit that comparative advantage. Improvements in the terms of trade will serve to reinforce that comparative advantage, exports of the primary product will rise, and trade will boom. In a world without mass migration and global capital markets, the export boom can only be achieved by the movement of labor and capital into the export sector from elsewhere in the domestic economy. Foreign immigration and capital inflows may ease the transition, but the strong pull of resources out of other domestic sectors will still be powerful. But which domestic sectors? It can pull those mobile resources away from sectors not engaged in international trade—like basic agriculture, or it can pull them away from import-competing industry and urban support services. If it's the latter, then de-industrialization will take place as those sectors contract. After all, that's what specialization is all about. However, the 19th-century de-industrialization we will document in the next chapter need not have been caused solely by globalization since domestic supply side forces may also have played a role.

In order to formalize our intuition about domestic supply-side and foreign demand-side causes of de-industrialization, this section develops a simple neo-Ricardian model that relies on the formal contribution of Ronald Jones (1971), and the economic insights of Adam Smith,[7] Alexander Gerschenkron (1962), and W. Arthur Lewis (1954, 1978a). Consider a perfectly competitive economy in which there are three sectors: textiles (T), grain (G), and commodity or primary-product exports (C). Commodity exports include nongrain items such as sugar, coffee, cacao, tea, indigo, jute, hemp, raw cotton, silk, or rubber, but they also include products of the mines, like silver, gold, copper, and tin. Textiles and export commodities are traded in the world market and sell for the world prices p_T and p_C, respectively. Labor (L) is mobile between all three sectors, is the only factor of production, and costs nominal wage w per unit. Of course, labor is never perfectively mobile in any economy, especially a pre-modern economy, but we only require that labor tends in the long run to seek out the highest rewards. Note that, for simplicity, the model also abstracts from capital and land, but these factors are not needed to make the points of this section.

We also assume that grain is not traded on the world market, so that p_G is determined only by local supply and demand. Grain was the key foodstuff in poor, pre-modern economies, and it was an activity employing something like three-quarters of the labor force. Treating agricultural output as a nontradable good turns out to be a reasonable assumption until well in to the late 19th century. Grain prices—rice, wheat, millet, oats, and barley—in the third world exhibited independent movement prior to the 1870s (Dobado Gonzáles and Marreno 2008; Studer 2008), suggesting the absence of a world grain market and one fragmented into local markets. The transport revolution changed all of that. For example,

prior to the nineteenth century the grain trade in India was essentially local, while more distant markets remained fragmented. It was only in the second half of the nineteenth century that . . . a national grain market emerged. (Studer 2008: 393)

A series of papers have shown that a world grain market began to include the third world in the 1870s, so that by 1913 grain prices there were tied closely to world markets. This included South and East Asia (Latham and Neal 1983; Latham 1986; Brandt 1985, 1993). The same seems to have been true of Latin America (Dobado Gonzáles and Marreno 2005b; Gómez Galvarriato and Williamson 2009). Thus third world grains can be treated as nontradables during most of the great terms of trade boom across the 19th century.

To create a link between agricultural productivity and wages in the textile sector, which chapters 6 through 8 will argue helps explain whether a poor periphery country lost or gained competitiveness in the home or even world textile market, we follow Lewis (1954, 1978a) in assuming that the real wage in grain units is constant. This reflects the Malthusian assumption that in a pre-industrial economy the supply of labor will be unlimited as long as the wage assures subsistence. Any lower wage leaves laborers unable to sustain the physical capacity for work. The Lewis assumption of perfectly elastic labor supply requires that there be unemployment (or underemployment), so L represents employment rather than the population, which we denote by P.

Suppose that output in each sector is produced according to a Cobb–Douglas production function of the following sort:

$$Y_G = GL_G{}^\alpha, \tag{4.1}$$

$$Y_C = CL_C{}^\beta, \tag{4.2}$$

$$Y_T = TL_T{}^\gamma. \tag{4.3}$$

Here G, C, and T are technology parameters; changes in them imply productivity changes. In good Malthusian style, the elasticities α, β, and γ are all less than 1, assuring diminishing returns. The labor market is such that each individual will supply one unit of labor as long as the grain wage w/p_G is at or above the reservation price (equal to the subsistence consumption basket) of 1. We assume that there is no rationing of labor, so that $L = L_G + L_C + L_T < P$. Perfect competition in each sector ensures through zero-profit conditions that labor demand will be given by

$$L_G = (p_G G/w)^{(1/1-\alpha)} = G^{(1/1-\alpha)}, \tag{4.4}$$

$$L_C = (p_C C/w)^{(1/1-\beta)}, \tag{4.5}$$

$$L_T = (p_T T/w)^{(1/1-\gamma)}. \tag{4.6}$$

If we assume that there is no technical change in any of the three sectors, the growth rates of labor demand are simply

$$L_G^* = 0, \tag{4.7}$$

$$L_C^* = -(1/1 - \beta)(w^* - p_C^*), \tag{4.8}$$

$$L_T^* = -(1/1 - \gamma)(w^* - p_T^*). \tag{4.9}$$

Since the nominal wage is equal to the price of grain, employment in the grain-producing sector is fixed. Growth in the own wage[8] in either commodity exports or import-competing textiles leads to a decline in the absolute number of workers employed there. Thus *absolute de-industrialization results from an increase in the own wage in textiles.* The own wage in either sector would increase due to a decline in the world price for its output. It would also increase if the price of grain rose, for example, from a negative productivity shock in agriculture generated by war, pestilence or the absence of the monsoon. As we will see in chapters 6 through 8, this connection is very important in understanding why some 19th-century third world countries de-industrialized faster than others, and why some strongly resisted these global forces.

The growth rate of the share of textile workers in total employment, our measure of *relative de-industrialization*, is:

$$L_T^* - L^* = \frac{-1}{(1-\beta)(1-\gamma)}\left([(1-\beta)(1-\theta_{TL})(w^* - p_T^*)] - [(1-\gamma)\theta_{CL}(w^* - p_C^*)]\right).$$
$$\tag{4.10}$$

The shares of import-competing textiles and commodity exports in total employment are given by θ_{TL} and θ_{CL}, respectively. Thus *relative de-industrialization will result whenever the own wage in textiles is growing sufficiently fast compared to the own wage in commodity exports.* Moreover, with employment shares held constant, relative de-industrialization will be most severe when the difference in own wage growth rates is largest. More formally, the condition that must be satisfied for relative de-industrialization is

$$w^* - p_T^* > \frac{(1-\gamma)\theta_{CL}}{(1-\beta)(1-\theta_{TL})}(w^* - p_C^*). \tag{4.11}$$

Given that both commodity export- and import-competing textile sectors are small shares of total employment in the 19th-century third world,[9] the ratio on the right-hand side is likely to be less than one. This implies that own wage growth in commodity exports would have to be even higher to counteract the relative de-industrialization effect of own wage growth in textiles. In short, we expect to see relative de-industrialization whenever own wage growth in import-competing textiles is positive, unless own wage growth in commodity exports is much greater. Own wage growth in commodity exports dampens the relative de-industrialization effect because it reduces L_C, which is in the denominator of our relative de-industrialization measure. As the share of the labor force employed in the commodity export sector increases, the greater growth in the own wage in textiles needs to be bigger to overcome growth of the own wage in export commodities and for de-industrialization to ensue. We can also rewrite condition (4.11) to relate nominal wage growth to the terms of trade between textiles and commodity agriculture as

$$\frac{(1-\gamma)\theta_{CL}+(1-\beta)(1-\theta_{TL})}{(1-\beta)(1-\theta_{TL})}w^* > p_T^* - p_C^*. \tag{4.11'}$$

Relative de-industrialization results when nominal wage growth, which deters production in both nongrain sectors, is sufficiently greater than the growth of the terms of trade favoring textiles, which encourages production in textiles over commodity exports. Thus *relative de-industrialization should have been most severe when nominal wage growth was strongest and when the terms of trade were shifting most strongly in favor of commodity exports.*

In summary, the predictions of the model are: *absolute de-industrialization*, defined as a decrease in employment in textiles, will result if the own wage in textiles increases; and *relative de-industrialization*, defined as a decrease in the share of the labor force employed in textiles, will result if own wage growth in textiles increases sufficiently faster than the own wage growth in commodity exports. Everything hinges on the own wage in import-competing textiles. A terms of trade boom will lower the relative price of textiles in the home market, raising the own wage there, lowering profits, and thus causing de-industrialization. A rise in food prices, caused by some negative productivity shock in agriculture, will raise nominal wages, raise the own wage, lower profits, and thus cause de-industrialization. Of course, a collapse in productivity in import-competing textiles will do the same.

4.5 The Agenda

It now should be absolutely clear where this book is going, and why. The next chapter will document the ubiquitous de-industrialization that was felt everywhere in the third world over the century or more before World

War I. Not every third world country underwent the same de-industrialization magnitudes and timing, however, and chapters 6 through 8 will show why that was so. Chapter 9 will deal with distributional impact of globalization—which must have augmented rent-seeking possibilities. Chapter 10 will deal with export price volatility. Chapter 11 will make an empirical assessment of all of these forces, before we turn to the issues of policy and the more recent third world experience with what will be called re-industrialization.

5 Measuring Third World De-industrialization and Dutch Disease

5.1 Introduction

The idea that the third world suffered de-industrialization during the 19th century has a long pedigree. The image of skilled weavers thrown back on farm employment was a powerful metaphor for the economic stagnation Indian nationalists believed was brought on by British rule. However, quantitative evidence on the overall level of economic activity in the 18th- and 19th-century third world is scant, let alone evidence on its breakdown between agriculture, industry, and services. Most de-industrialization assessments rely on very sparse employment and output data. Price data are more plentiful, and, as a consequence, chapters 6 through 8 will use newly compiled evidence on relative input and output prices to offer what is called a price-dual assessment of de-industrialization in 18th- and 19th-century India, Ottoman Turkey, and Mexico. But this chapter will use more conventional quantitative and qualitative employment and output evidence to describe the timing and magnitude of de-industrialization in Latin America, the Middle East, Asia, and the eastern and southern European periphery. The chapter will show that while de-industrialization occurred everywhere in the poor periphery, it was much more dramatic in some parts than others, that it arrived earlier in some parts, that it ceased earlier in some parts, and that it turned around—what will be called re-industrialization in chapter 12—in some parts but not in others. These differences suggest an important role for independent domestic forces as well as the commonly shared global forces.

The shared global forces can be restated briefly. The mainstream historical literature explains each region's de-industrialization by appealing to British and continental European productivity gains in manufacturing and to the world transport revolution. Improved British productivity, first in cottage production and then in factory goods, led to declining world prices of manufactures, making production in Mexico, São Paolo, Catalonia, Russia, Anatolia, Bengal, Madras, Java, Luzon, and elsewhere increasingly unprofitable. These forces were reinforced by declining sea freight rates, which served to foster trade and specialization for both Europe and its trading partners in the poor periphery. As a result Europe first won over world export markets in manufactures and eventually took over much of the third world's domestic markets as well. An additional explanation for third world de-industrialization also has its roots in globalization forces: relative to textiles, metals, and other manufactures the third world's commodity export sector saw its terms of trade improve significantly and thus drew workers away from manufacturing as well as from food grain production.

There is nothing wrong with this argument, except that it does not leave scope for different experiences around the poor periphery in fending off those external global forces. Some regions faced smaller price shocks or remained more competitive than others, and these underwent less dramatic de-industrialization as a consequence. True, the Latin American, east European, and Mediterranean republics had the political autonomy to impose protective tariffs that others could not (chapter 13), but we will see in the three chapters that follow that these anti-global responses cannot explain all or even most of the third world de-industrialization variety we observe.

Before proceeding to the evidence, we need to agree on a precise definition of de-industrialization. Suppose that an economy produces two commodities: agricultural goods, which are exported, and manufactured goods, which are imported. Suppose that it uses labor, which is mobile between the two sectors, land, which is used only in agriculture, and capital, which is used only in manufacturing. Suppose further that this economy is what trade economists call a "small country," in that it takes its terms of trade as exogenous as dictated by world markets. Given these assumptions, de-industrialization can be defined as the movement of labor out of manufacturing and into agriculture, either measured in absolute numbers (what we called *absolute de-industrialization* in the previous chapter) or as a share of total employment (what we called *relative de-industrialization* in the previous chapter). With those definitions in hand, what did third world trends look like in the century or more before World War I?

5.2 Using Textile Manufacturing to Gauge Third World De-industrialization

Textiles are a very big share of manufacturing activity in all economies starting modern economic growth, whether the gauge is employment, output, or value added. After all, labor-intensive light manufacturing is where it all starts. More mature economies move on to capital and skill-intensive industries, like iron and steel, chemicals, and machine making. Post-industrial economies move on still further from heavy industrial to skill-intensive and knowledge-based services. This sequence is a natural evolution, and it is driven partly by increasing economywide endowment of skills and capital relative to raw labor and natural resources (what international trade economists call the Rybzynski effect) and partly by technical progress.

We can in fact easily document the relative dominance of textiles in early development. Although the issue will be explored at greater length in chapter 8, we know that cotton textile production in Nueva España amounted to a little more than 5 million pesos at the end of the 18th century (Miño 1998: 244), or between 60 and 70 percent of total manufacturing production (7 to 8 million pesos; Humboldt 1822: 451). For Meiji Japan at the start of its industrial revolution in 1874, the share of textiles in total manufacturing output less food processing was almost 63 percent (Shinohara 1972: table 1, 140–41). Even as late as 1891, textiles and clothing employed 53 percent of the manufacturing labor force in Britain (Deane and Cole 1967: table 32, 146). In short, if we understand what drives textile output and employment in an economy embarking on modern economic growth, we pretty much will understand early industrialization.

5.3 A Comparative Quantitative Assessment

About twenty-five years ago, Paul Bairoch (1982, 1991) offered comprehensive benchmark estimates of 19th-century third world de-industrialization. While his estimates have been criticized, they have the advantage of offering a comparative sense of magnitudes and timing around the poor periphery. Table 5.1 measures the share of world manufacturing output being produced by four key regions between 1750 and 1913 —the developed European core where the industrial revolution started, India (plus modern Pakistan, Bangladesh, and Ceylon), China and the rest of the poor periphery (Latin America, the Middle East, Southeast Asia, and eastern and southern Europe).

First, note that China and India together produced more than 57 percent of world manufacturing output in 1750. Of course, everywhere, including Europe, the technology was labor intensive, and the pre-factory organization was the putting-out cottage industry system. But still, the business of

Table 5.1

World manufacturing output, 1750 to 1938 (in percent)

Year	India	China	Rest of the periphery	Developed core
1750	24.5	32.8	15.7	27.0
1800	19.7	33.3	14.7	32.3
1830	17.6	29.8	13.3	39.5
1880	2.8	12.5	5.6	79.1
1913	1.4	3.6	2.5	92.5
1938	2.4	3.1	1.7	92.8

Source: Simmons (1985: table 1, 600), based on Bairoch (1982: tables 10 and 13, 296 and 304).

Note: India refers to the entire subcontinent.

making textiles, ceramics, furniture, building materials, metal products, and primitive machines employed large numbers and had high value added. The point is that while China and the Indian subcontinent produced more than 57 percent of world manufacturing output during the mid-18th century, these two regions claimed "only" about 47 percent of world GDP (GDP in 1700 from Maddison 2007). These two figures imply that China and India had a higher manufacturing output share in domestic GDP than did the rest of the world, about 22 percent higher.[1] The developed core produced 27 percent of world manufacturing output, more than its 22 percent share of world GDP, also implying a higher industrial share than the global average, about 23 percent higher.[2] The amazing implication of these numbers is that China and India were just as "industrialized" as was the European core in 1750! The figures for the rest of the world (eastern Europe, Latin America, the western offshoots, the Middle East, and the rest of Asia) were about 16 percent of world manufacturing output and about 31 percent of world GDP, the ratio of which is 0.5, or less than half the "industrialization" of China, India, and the European core.

Next, note what happened between 1750 and 1800, still a pre-factory episode even in western Europe. India's share of world manufacturing output fell dramatically from 24.5 to 19.7 percent, a fall of almost 5 percentage points, implying an early Indian start with de-industrialization. At the same time early industrialization started in the European core, where the share rose by more than 5 percentage points, from 27 to 32.3 percent. China did not repeat India's early de-industrialization experience, since its share *rose* from 32.8 to 33.3 percent. Chapter 6 will offer some explanations for the difference. Note also that while the rest of the poor periphery underwent a decline in its share of world manufacturing output, from 15.7 to 14.7 percent, the fall was far more modest than it was for India. Chapter 8 will offer some explanations for the difference. By 1830, the regional shares in world manufacturing output were moving everywhere toward what Lewis called the *new economic order*: the developed core manufacturing share rose to 39.5 percent, and it fell everywhere else. Indeed evidence offered by Patrick O'Brien suggests that the evolution was pretty much complete by the 1830s, when the share of United Kingdom exports in manufactures was 91 percent, and the share of third world exports in primary products was 92 percent (O'Brien 2004: table 3). By 1880, the de-industrialization process in the poor periphery was complete, and each region's manufacturing share in GDP relative to the world average was the following: European core 2.39, India 0.23, China 0.73, and the rest of the periphery 0.15. The big fact, of course, is that the industrial output share in Europe was more than three times that of China by 1880, more than ten times that of India, and about sixteen times that of the rest of the poor periphery (and the primary product share of third world exports had reached 98 percent: O'Brien 2004: table 3). In chapters 6 through 8 we will try to grapple with these very different levels and rates of de-industrialization across the poor periphery.

So far we have combined Bairoch's manufacturing output data in table 5.1 with Angus Maddison's GDP estimates to infer relative rates of industrialization and de-industrialization around the world by looking at the share of manufacturing output in GDP. Since the estimates of manufacturing output and GDP come from different sources, the reader might fear that some bias could have crept in due to lack of comparable samples, definitions, and the way the two scholars treated the data. Thus table 5.2 reports Bairoch's *per capita* industrialization indexes. Just looking at table 5.1, the reader might have concluded that the rise of manufacturing in the west was due to its success with the industrial revolution, not necessarily to some de-industrialization "failure" in the rest. By expressing the data as a per capita index, however, table 5.2 is quite specific about third world "failure." First, we note that the per capita index falls everywhere in the poor periphery (except Brazil and Mexico) between 1750 and 1913. Second, most of that fall was completed by 1860, and indeed manufacturing turned around in Brazil and Mexico thereafter (see chapter 12 on re-industrialization). Third, the new evidence has China now joining India with early de-industrialization starting with 1750. And fourth, the decline in the index is much more dramatic for Asia in 1750 to 1860 than it is for Latin America. In short, table 5.2 confirms that the poor and rich parts of

Table 5.2
Per capita levels of industrialization, 1750 to 1913

Region	1750	1800	1830	1860	1913
European core	8	9.2	12.1	22.2	64.6
Asian and Latin American periphery	6.75	5.75	5	4	4.75
China	8	6	6	4	3
India	7	6	6	3	2
Brazil	6	5	4	4	7
Mexico	6	6	4	5	7
Ratio core/periphery	1.2	1.6	2.4	5.6	13.6

Source: Bairoch (1991: table 1, 3). The European core is an unweighted average of Hungary, Belgium, France, Germany, Italy, Spain, Sweden, Switzerland, and the United Kingdom. The Asian and Latin American periphery is an unweighted average of China, India, Brazil, and Mexico. A definition of his industrialization per capita index can be found in his papers cited in Bairoch (1991).

the world economy were "going to the corners" (Krugman and Venables 1995), that the rich industrial core was increasing its specialization in industrial production and the poor periphery was increasing its specialization in primary products. According to Bairoch's data in table 5.2, W. Arthur Lewis's *new economic order* had been firmly entrenched by 1860.

Table 5.3 offers another index of de-industrialization for the 19th-century third world, using quite different sources. For four third world regions—Mexico, Ottoman Turkey, India, and Indonesia—the table measures the loss of domestic textile markets to foreign imports. That is, the figures report the share of domestic textile consumption supplied by local and foreign sources. Take India first. Chapter 6 reports that Bengal exported about 27 percent of domestic consumption (21 percent of its domestic production) in 1750. That figure had fallen, at least for India more generally, to 6 or 7 percent by 1800. Thus, even before the onset of the factory-led industrial revolution in Britain, India had lost a big chunk of its export market. By 1833, India had lost *all* of its (net) export market *and* 5 percent of its domestic market. By 1877, the de-industrial damage was done, with domestic producers claiming only 35 to 42 percent of their own home market. Although the Ottoman empire did not have a large foreign market to lose, it underwent a similar dramatic collapse in its home market, domestic producers undergoing a huge fall in their home market share from 97 down to 11 to 38 percent over the half century between the 1820s

Table 5.3

Comparative de-industrialization: Textile import penetration around the third world, 1800s to 1880s (in percent)

	Home textile market supplied by	
	Foreign imports	Domestic industry
India 1800	−6 to −7	106 to 107
India 1833	5	95
India 1877	58 to 65	35 to 42
Ottoman 1820s	3	97
Ottoman 1870s	62 to 89	11 to 38
Indonesia 1822	18.1	81.9
Indonesia 1870	62	38
Indonesia 1913	88.6	11.4
Mexico 1800s	25	75
Mexico 1879	40	60

Source: Dobado, Gómez, and Williamson (2008: table 4).

and the 1870s.[3] The decline in the Indonesian (or Dutch East Indian) textile industry was a little less spectacular than that for the Ottoman empire, since the local producer share of the home market "only" fell from 82 to 38 percent of the home market between 1822 and 1870. But in the Dutch East Indies case de-industrialization persisted much longer, with the local producer share falling still further to 11 percent in 1913.

So far we note differences in the rate and timing of de-industrialization: it started sooner in India, and fell faster; it started later in the Ottomans, but once started, fell just as fast; and it fell a little less dramatically in Indonesia, but de-industrialization went on for another four decades. Now note Mexico: its level of foreign import penetration was quite a bit higher at the start of the century, but the rate of de-industrialization up to the 1870s is much less than in the other three regions. Once again, while de-industrialization was taking place everywhere around the poor periphery between the mid-18th century and World War I, the timing and the magnitudes were often quite different, suggesting that they were hit by different price shocks or that they responded to them differently, or both.

5.4 A Comparative Qualitative Assessment

So far we have relied on comparative quantitative evidence, evidence that will be elaborated in chapter 6 on India, chapter 7 on the Ottoman empire, and chapter 8 on Mexico. The rest of this chapter will now explore the more qualitative evidence we have for the rest of the periphery, where we focus on Egypt for the Middle East, Indonesia for Southeast Asia, and both China and Japan for East Asia.

De-industrialization and Dutch Disease in Egypt

Figures 3.7 and 7.1 document that the net barter terms of trade boom in Egypt (see also Issawi 1966, 1982; Owen 1969) was even bigger than it was in the rest of the periphery. p_X is a raw cotton export price index (Alexandria 1820–1899 and New York thereafter: see Williamson 2008) and p_M is proxied by the price of British exports. The spectacular rise in the Egyptian terms of trade between 1820–1824 and 1856–1860, 2.7 percent per annum, is even bigger than that of the Ottoman empire over the same period (2.3 percent per annum: table 3.1). Since p_M is the same in both cases, it is clear that cotton prices rose even more in world markets than did the price of Ottoman exports—wheat, wool, fruits, tobacco, and opium. In any case, these terms of trade figures imply an even bigger de-industrialization impact on Egypt than on the rest of the Middle East, spelling especially bad luck for Mohamed Ali's early experiments with Egyptian industrialization. Between 1855–1859 and 1875–1879, the Egyptian terms of trade fell by almost 11 percent, less than half the fall experienced by the Ottoman empire, 27 percent, and thus presumably less re-industrialization stimulation. Finally, between 1875–1879 and 1909–1913, the Egyptian terms of trade drifted upward at roughly the same modest rate as elsewhere in the Middle East (0.5 vs. 0.4 percent per annum).

Over the century-long terms of trade upswing between 1796 and 1886–1890 shared by all regions in the poor periphery, Egypt underwent about the biggest increase, 1.6 versus 0.7 percent per annum (table 3.1). Did Egypt therefore also undergo the biggest de-industrialization and the most pronounced Dutch disease? Perhaps, but the missing evidence makes the judgment impossible, and if we had the evidence, the timing would be difficult to assess because of a unique intervention.

Almost exactly when the Egyptian terms of trade boomed most dramatically between 1805 and 1849, Mohamed Ali intervened in Egyptian markets in an attempt to improve the competitive position of domestic industry and to foster industrialization.[4] First, he restricted imports by tariffs and nontariff barriers. Second, the state took over and invested in much of Egypt's manufacturing factories. Mohamed Ali's prototype establishments were protected by state monopolies from the beginning, and these factories "suffered from great inefficiencies, including lack of fuel and metallic raw materials and the total absence of skilled labor" (Issawi 1982: 154). They were also poorly managed with military elite serving as supervisors, rather than young men that had been technically trained in Europe. In addition Ali's factories had dilapidated machinery and inadequate power sources, both of which would have been very expensive to remedy (Owen 1993: 72 and 76). If this was one of the first infant industry experiments, it did not work out very well. In his famous report to the British Secretary of State for Foreign Affairs, Sir John Bowring had this to say about Mohamed Ali's experiment:

Could it be averred that the character of the people had been elevated by the various factories which have been created . . . and that the early rude attempts had been progressively improved upon . . . there would have been . . . justification of those sacrifices which the government made in the beginning . . . But those attempts have been eminently costly and not successful . . . the progress made has been small; they have added nothing to the resources of the country. . . . (Bowring 1840: 84)

Indeed Mohamed Ali's factories "did not survive his death in 1849" (Issawi 1961: 7).

Third, the state created something like a modern marketing board, whereby it purchased food from farmers at low prices and as a consequence kept the urban cost of living and nominal wages in manufacturing lower than they would have been otherwise:

In the Nile valley, high [grain] yields kept labor costs low. Under Muhammad-Ali's rule, grain in Egypt was three times cheaper than in France. While in both countries daily wages were close to the biological minimum, in Egypt [their nominal values] were three times lower than in France. (Batou 1991: 197)

Thus Mohamed Ali kept the Egyptian manufacturing wage competitive with foreign producers.

We know that all of these policies were effective in fending off de-industrialization, even if we cannot measure it. Again, in the words of John Bowring:

Cotton cloth [production] has injured commercial importation; . . . it appears that England sends these articles far less frequently [1837/38 vs. 1823], especially cloths of low quality; and India muslins, formerly so much used, are now scarcely at all sent to Egypt since muslins have been woven in the new factories. (Bowring 1840: 103)

The Egyptian state apparatus also purchased commodity export products (cotton, wheat) at low prices and sold them on world markets at higher prices, a policy equivalent to an export tax (Issawi 1961: 5; Owen 1993).

The low purchase prices for cotton, wheat, and nontradable foods reduced farmer incentive and thus Egyptian farm productivity, but Mohamed Ali also invested some of the "marketing board" revenue in irrigation, which might have partially offset any productivity decline coming from the farmer disincentive caused by low prices.

In short, during the terms of trade boom phase, Egypt went anti-global to the extreme, much like Latin America after the 1930s and post-independence Africa in the late 20th century. Although it is almost impossible to measure its impact, Mohamed Ali's precocious policy clearly muted the de-industrialization effects before mid-century.[5] But the policy was purchased at great cost: that is, Egypt gave up all possible gains from trade to achieve it, recording 'lost decades' of poor growth performance during the world's first great trade boom.[6]

After Mohamed Ali's death in 1849, the export tax, import restriction, the food price squeeze, and state intervention at the firm level all eventually disappeared. By 1870, a pro-global (and pro-British) laissez faire regime emerged, and the average tariff rate was only about 7 percent (Williamson 2006b). Another pro-trade force was carried by productivity improvement on Mediterranean sea-lanes that reduced transport costs on trade involving Egypt (especially on bulky raw cotton exports: Harlaftis and Kardasis 2000). Geography offered some additional protection for Egypt's interior markets in Mohamed Ali's time: since European imports couldn't be brought cheaply into the more remote areas before the 1860s, domestic manufactures could still supply local demand in those parts of the interior. In the second half of the century, increasingly dense rail networks, improved navigability on waterways, and better roads all served to lower transportation costs to the interior, thus creating price convergence between Upper and Lower Egypt and internal trade (Yousef 2000: 356).

Paradoxically, just when the terms of trade boom began to lose its steam after mid-century, Egypt switched from an extremely anti-global to an extremely pro-global policy. The impact on de-industrialization was therefore postponed in the Egyptian case, from the first to the second half of the century. Had we the evidence to measure it, it seems likely we would find much more dramatic de-industrialization in Egypt after the 1850s than most everywhere else in the poor periphery.

De-industrialization and Dutch Disease in Indonesia

Figure 3.9 plots the net barter terms of trade for Indonesia from 1825 to 1913, and it can be compared there with the Philippines (1782–1913) and Siam (1800–1913).[7] While the latter two underwent a spectacular price boom up to mid-century—1.5 percent per annum up to 1857 (table 3.1)—Indonesia's coffee-driven boom was more than twice as steep (3.3 percent per annum: table 3.1) and much longer, peaking in 1896. Not only was that the biggest terms of trade boom in Southeast Asia, chapter 3 reported that it was the biggest in the poor periphery. Since the Indonesian population was so large compared with the other two, its trend dominates the Southeast Asian regional average.

Did the biggest terms of trade boom produce the biggest Dutch disease and thus the biggest de-industrialization?[8] If we make the assessment starting with the 1820s, the answer is definitely yes. Table 5.3 documents that the share of the home textile market supplied by Indonesian producers dropped from about 82 to 11 percent from 1822 to 1913.

Apparently the impact of Indian exports on Indonesia before the European 19th-century invasion of manufactures was more complex. William Clarence-Smith argues that "Indian exports probably did more to stimulate than to undermine local production of cotton textiles [in Indonesia] . . . and it appears to have been fairly general across the Indian Ocean" (Clarence-Smith 2005: 1). Like elsewhere in the pre-industrial periphery, cotton cloth was the leading manufacture in Southeast Asia (Reid 1988: 90–94), and it satisfied the lower end of the market, with little exporting. Raw cotton was abundant from Java east to Sumbawa (Pires 1944: 169–70, 180). Silk dominated the top end of the market. But the idea that Indian exports to Indonesia stimulated local production derives from its cheap intermediate supply:

Some imports from India stimulated Southeast Asia production, with Java's batik sector especially reliant on cambric from Coromandel and Malabar. This plain white South Indian fabric, with its high thread density and even surface, was ideally suited to dyeing with wax. As for coloured Indian cloths, Sumatran artisans stamped them with gold flowers and decorated them with borders. (Clarence-Smith 2005: 5)

Others have argued that it was rising costs of Indian imports that stimulated local production in Java and Sumatra (Andaya 1989), a position that is consistent with the decline in sales of Indian cloth before the early 19th century and with India's loss of competitiveness in world markets (chapter 6). But these need not be competitive hypotheses: increased Indonesian relative competitiveness could have made it possible for domestic producers to displace Indian imports of common muslin, while the development of batik and other local fabrics increased the demand for intermediate white cambric.

Indonesian textile manufacturing was an important economic activity in the early 1800s. Indeed Jan Luiten van Zanden estimates that it was about 15 percent of GDP in the 1820s (van Zanden 2002), figures that suggest manufacturing may have been as much as a fifth of total Indonesian GDP at that time. By the early 1850s, textile manufacture had fallen by half, to 6 to 7 percent of GDP. And, as we have seen in table 5.3, the share of the home textile market supplied by Indonesian producers dropped from almost 82 to 38 percent between 1822 and 1870, before falling still further to about 11 percent in 1913. Dramatic de-industrialization indeed! Pierre van der Eng, from whom these estimates come, interprets them differently. He points out that value added in textile manufacturing increased between 1820 and 1871 (van der Eng 2007: 1). But in a growing economy, it is the sector's performance *relative* to the overall economy that matters, and Anne Booth agrees (Booth 1998: 96–97). Although per capita income hardly grew at all over the half century following 1820, only 0.1 percent per annum (Maddison 2007), population grew at 1.2 percent and GDP at 1.3 percent per annum. Thus it's the relative de-industrialization measure that matters in judging the impact of Dutch disease effects in Indonesia, and they were enormous.

Indonesia was not alone in suffering de-industrialization, since it happened everywhere in Southeast Asia, including Burma, the Philippines, and Siam. By the late 1890s Burma's "textile industry had suffered a serious decline, and it was finally . . . destroyed by the 1920s" and "weaving . . . , spinning, iron and metal making, pottery . . . and paper making" had declined in Siam (Resnick 1970: 57, 60). Like Indonesia, the Philippines started the 19th century with a well-developed textile industry. Indeed by 1818 local cloth accounted for 8 percent of Manila's exports:

The province of Iloilo . . . developed valuable *piña*, dyed in bright and varied colours. This was woven chiefly with pineapple fibre, but might also contain cotton, silk and *abacá*. The industry sucked in migrants from far and wide . . . selling as far afield as Europe and the Americas. (Clarence-Smith 2005: 8)

But the Dutch disease generated by its terms of trade boom spelled trouble for Philippine industry too. By 1847, almost 60 percent of Philippine imports were textiles, and they increased ninefold over the half-century that followed (Legarda 1999: 149–50), while the dominant exports were copra, hemp, sugar, and tobacco products. By the 1880s, "native textiles were in a sad state" especially in southern Panay (around Iloilo) and Ilocos (Legarda 1999: 155). Nor did Spanish authorities use tariffs to fend off the flood of European manufactures since the average tariff rate in the

Philippines never rose above 7 percent between 1844 and 1874, and the tariff system was otherwise thoroughly liberalized in the late 1860s (Legarda 1999: 198, 205), as it was in Indonesia (Booth 1998: 215–16).

In short, it does appear that the biggest terms of trade boom produced the biggest Dutch disease and thus the biggest de-industrialization in Indonesia and Southeast Asia.

Forced to Go Open: Industrialization and Dutch Disease in Japan

Not every region in the poor periphery was resource abundant; some, like Japan and China, were labor abundant and resource scarce. In this case, going open fostered exports of labor-intensive manufactures, not resource-intensive primary products.

While the fall in transport costs, the fall in European tariffs, and the boom in European income advanced Asian trade, they were hardly the greatest globalization events affecting the region. Recall that under the persuasion of Commodore Perry's American gun ships, Japan signed the Shimoda and Harris ("unequal") treaties in 1858 and, by doing so, switched from complete autarky to unfettered free trade. As we noted in chapter 3, Japan's foreign trade rose from nil to 7 percent of national income in just a few years (Huber 1971; Bernhofen and Brown 2004, 2005; Williamson 2006a: 43–44). Other Asian nations followed the same liberal path, most forced to do so by colonial dominance or gunboat diplomacy. Thus China signed a treaty with Britain in 1842 that opened her ports to trade and that set a 5 percent ad valorem tariff limit. Seeing the handwriting on the wall, Siam went open and adopted a 3 percent tariff limit in 1855. Korea emerged from its autarkic "hermit kingdom" stance about the same time, undergoing market integration with Japan long before colonial status became formalized in 1910 (Brandt 1993; Kang and Cha 1996). Thus the mid-century removal of restrictions and embargoes by East Asia on its trade with the core added greatly to the convergence forces—whether East Asia liked it or not.

When Japan was forced to emerge from isolation after 1858, prices of its labor-intensive exportables soared, rising toward world market levels while prices of its land- and capital-intensive importables collapsed, falling toward world market levels. One scholar estimates that as a consequence the terms of trade rose by a factor of 3.5 over the fifteen late Tokugawa and early Meiji years following 1858 (Huber 1971), while another thinks the multiple was even bigger, 4.9 (Yasuba 1996). These were massive and permanent relative price shocks. Just how permanent can be seen in figure 3.10: not only did Japan's terms of trade increase almost five times after the country opened up to trade, but it continued to increased still further up to the 1890s.[9]

What was the impact? Not surprisingly, Japan's industrialization effort, led by labor-intensive silk and cotton textiles, was powerfully reinforced while agriculture and other resource-intensive activities suffered. That is, Japan's latent comparative advantage was reinforced by going open: Dutch disease helped industrialization. The spectacular (by the standards of that time) industrialization experience Japan recorded in the four decades up to World War I is well known (Lockwood 1954; Ohkawa and Rosovsky 1973; Patrick 1976). Between 1874 and 1900, textile industry production grew at 8.6 percent per annum, pig iron by 8 percent, and nonferrous metals by 8.9 percent (Shinohara 1972: 187, 226, 229). How much of this impressive industrial performance can be claimed by being forced to go open by foreign powers, and how much to other internal forces? We do not yet know, but the work of Richard Huber (1971), Shinya Sugiyama (1987, 1988), and Daniel Bernhofen and John Brown (2004, 2005) suggests that the share caused by going open was large indeed.

Weak De-industrialization and Modest Dutch Disease Effects in China

As indicated in the previous section, between 1842 and 1860 China was forced to sign a series of free trade treaties that opened her ports to European imports and set a 5 percent ad valorem tariff limit. Like Japan, this "opening up" should have raised prices of its exportables—like ceramics and silk textiles—toward world market levels while it should have lowered prices of its importables—like factory-made cotton and wool textiles and metal products. No doubt they did, putting upward pressure on China's terms of trade (favoring manufactures), *in the absence of other forces*. But what about the other forces? Unfortunately, we can only guess at magnitudes, since it appears that no scholar has yet made any assessment of China's going open matching what has been done for late Tokugawa and early Meiji Japan. Still we can guess that the impact of going open on China's economy was likely to have been much smaller than on Japan's, and for three reasons. First, trade was a much smaller share of a much bigger economy, where only the coastal regions would have been greatly affected (Ma 2004). Second, for centuries before 1842 Chinese merchants had found ways to overcome imperial restriction on external trade, so that the impact of being forced *officially* to "go open" had a smaller actual impact. Third, it appears that there were offsetting forces that had been muting the rise in China's terms of trade across the whole century. Figure

3.3 serves to remind us of China's exceptionalism in this regard: China's terms of trade never did undergo its otherwise ubiquitous rise in the poor periphery across the first two-thirds of the 19th century. Indeed China's terms of trade *fell* between the 1830s and the 1890s, an event that implies that the relative price of manufactures at home rose. Furthermore "going open" does not seem to have left its mark on a downward trend from the late 1830s to the turn of the century.

As a consequence it should come as no surprise to learn that China resisted the invasion of European manufactures far better than any other region in the poor periphery. Chinese de-industrialization forces were very weak,[10] and the best place to see that is in Albert Feuerwerker's (1992: 123–63) magisterial summary of the ability of domestic handicraft and factory textiles to fend off the foreign competition.[11] Feuerwerker begins his account with the following striking statement:

Until 1831 England purchased more "nankeens" (that is, cloth manufactured in Nanking and other places in the lower Yangtze region) each year than she sold British-manufactured cloth to China. (Feuerwerker 1992: 125)

Subsequently European manufactures did invade China. After the open port treaties and the completion of the Suez Canal, cotton goods and yarn imports boomed, but we must remember that the latter were inputs to the domestic production of the former. Domestic handicraft and factory produced textiles also boomed. The amazing fact is how much of the domestic market for cloth local producers retained. In the 1870s domestic mills (mainly in Shanghai) and domestic handicraft supplied more than 81 percent of the market (Feuerwerker 1992: table 8, 142), a figure bigger than anywhere else that we can document around the poor periphery (table 5.3). Three decades later (1901–1910) the figure (74 percent) was lower as foreign penetration had increased, but not much lower.

Of course, Chinese producers did less well in defending the yarn market: between 1871–1880 and 1901–1910, the share of China's yarn market supplied by imports rose from 2 to 40 percent (Feuerwerker 1992: 154). Yet, after the dust had settled, China could still claim 60 percent of its domestic yarn market.

In contrast to Karl Marx's assertions, Chinese spinners and weavers did not suffer greatly from foreign competition during the first global century up to the 1900s, at least compared to the rest of the poor periphery. De-industrialization forces were weaker than anywhere else—as predicted.

5.5   De-industrialization and Dutch Disease in the Periphery

Thus de-industrialization and Dutch disease pervaded the poor periphery throughout most of the long 19th century up to World War I. For some, the domestic industrial wreckage was spectacular—like the Ottoman empire, Egypt, India, and Dutch Indonesia; for some the damage was more limited—like China and Mexico; and for at least one—Japan—the effect was to foster industrialization, not de-industrialization. This regional variety can be attributed to the size of the terms of trade shock, to domestic factor endowments, and to domestic supply side resistance. The next three chapters will sort these forces out by looking at India, the Ottoman empire, and Mexico in greater detail.

6   An Asian De-industrialization Illustration: An Indian Paradox?

6.1   A De-industrialization Paradox?

That India suffered de-industrialization during the 19th century has long dominated the historiography. The image of skilled weavers thrown back on the soil was a powerful metaphor for the economic stagnation Indian nationalists believed was brought about by British rule, a metaphor used by Karl Marx to great effect. Like the rest of the third world national economic histories, the literature attributes most of India's de-industrialization to Britain's productivity gains in textile and metal manufacture and to the world transport revolution. Improved British and European productivity in manufacturing led to declining world textile and metal product prices, making their production in India less and less profitable (Roy 2002). These forces were reinforced by declining sea freight rates, which served to foster trade and specialization for both Britain and India. As a result Britain first won over India's export market and eventually took over much of its domestic market as well. This conventional thesis is reinforced by an additional globalization force adding to India's de-industrialization: relative to textiles and other manufactures, India's commodity export sector saw its terms of trade improve significantly in the 18th century and it drew workers away from manufacturing.

As chapter 4 argued, if globalization was the root cause of de-industrialization in 19th-century India, we should see a secular boom in India's net barter terms of trade (p_X/p_M) after 1800 or 1810. That is, productivity events in British industry, and the subsequent invasion of British manufactures in both India and third markets everywhere, should have driven down India's prices of its imports (p_M) and of its manufactures. The rising demand for primary goods in British markets—to satisfy the demand for intermediate inputs generated by a booming manufacturing there as well as for food generated by rising incomes—

should have also served to raise the price of India's commodity export prices (p_X).

Why, then, do we *not* see a big terms of trade boom for India across the 19th century, while we *do* see it everywhere else in the poor periphery? Figure 3.4 compared the terms of trade for India in 1800 to 1913 with population-weighted series for other regions of the poor periphery, consisting of Latin America, the Middle East, and Southeast Asia. India underwent a significant improvement in its terms of trade from 1800 to the mid-1820s, followed by a collapse through the early 1830s. India's terms of trade rose and collapsed again between 1850 and 1865. After that, India's terms of trade maintained an average level of about 115 (1800 = 100). Between 1800 and 1870, then, India's terms of trade rose only 15 percent, or about 0.2 percent per annum. The experience of other regions around the poor periphery was much more dramatic. To recap chapter 3, the Middle Eastern terms of trade rose by 270 percent between 1800 and 1870, or 3.9 percent per annum; the Southeast Asian terms of trade increased by 231 percent, or 3.3 percent per annum; and the Latin American terms of trade increased by 247 percent, or 3.5 percent per annum.[1]

In addition India underwent at least as great, and perhaps even greater, de-industrialization than did the rest of the poor periphery. Section 9.3 will offer additional evidence on India's 19th-century de-industrialization experience, but recall that table 5.3 reported some comparative evidence. The table estimates the share of the domestic textile market claimed by net foreign imports (negative figures imply a net export position, as for India 1800) for four regions around the poor periphery and at various points in time after the early 1800s. As in the previous chapter, we use textiles to illustrate import penetration and de-industrialization because textiles are better documented and were such a big share of manufacturing activity. To begin with, Sushil Chaudhury (1999) estimates that in the mid-18th century Bengal exported about 21 percent of domestic output, or, equivalently, exported 27 percent of domestic consumption.[2] By 1800, although still a net exporter, India's exports had dropped dramatically to 6 to 7 percent of the domestic textile market, a fall of 20 percentage points, or 0.4 percentage points a year over the half century. By 1833, it had become a net importer, amounting to 5 percent of the domestic market. Between 1800 and 1833, this amounted to a fall of 11 to 12 percentage points, or about 0.35 percentage points a year. By 1877, the foreign import share of the domestic textile market had risen to between 58 and 65 percent. Over three-quarters of a century the foreign import share of the domestic market rose, and the domestic producers' share fell by the huge factor of between 64 and 72 percentage points, an average of 68 percentage points. The figures for the Ottoman empire between the 1820s and the 1870s were similar, an average of 73 percentage points, experience that will get our attention in chapter 7. Similarly Indonesia's local supply share fell by almost 44 percentage points between 1822 and 1870. In contrast, Mexico, which gets our attention in chapter 8, did far better in fending off foreign competition, since the domestic producer's share fell by "only" 15 percentage points between the 1800s and 1879.

So much for 19th-century comparative de-industrialization rates. What about the 18th century? Here, India's de-industrialization was clearly more dramatic than that of the rest of the periphery. Based on Paul Bairoch's (1982) estimates, table 5.1 reported that between 1750 and 1800 India's world manufacturing output share dropped by 4.8 percentage points, from a 1750 base of 24.5 percent, *much* bigger than the fall elsewhere around the periphery: China actually *gained* 0.5 percentage points, and the rest of the periphery only lost 1 percentage point. Bairoch's data suggest that during the half century before 1800, well before European factories flooded world markets with manufactures, India suffered much more pronounced de-industrialization than did the rest of the periphery.

How do we resolve this Indian paradox of relatively dramatic de-industrialization with relatively modest terms of trade improvements? Obviously the paradox can only be resolved by some domestic supply-side conditions that must have been unique to India and that apparently played a far more important role in accounting for de-industrialization there than elsewhere. While Indian historiography does occasionally note a possible role for supply-side forces, the connection has never been pursued extensively. This chapter argues that the economic woes India suffered following the dissolution of Mughal hegemony in the 18th century ultimately led to aggregate supply-side problems for Indian manufacturing, even if some producers in some regions benefited from the new order. In addition India suffered a profound secular deterioration in climate conditions in the century or so following the early 1700s, events that appear to have added greatly to the slump in agricultural productivity, to the rise in grain prices, to an increase in nominal wages, and thus (as we will see) to de-industrialization. The chapter argues that these explanations are complementary, not competitive.

While chapter 5 showed that de-industrialization is easy enough to define, an assessment of its short- and long-run impact on living standards and GDP growth is more contentious and hinges on the root causes of de-industrialization. One possibility is that a country de-industrializes because its comparative advantage in the agricultural export sector has been strengthened by productivity advance on the land or by increasing openness in the world economy, or both. A second possibility is that a country de-industrializes due to deterioration in home manufacturing productivity and/or competitiveness. The economic impact of de-industrialization from this source is unambiguous, and also a potential explanation for India's role in the great divergence.

The next section explores all three (noncompeting) hypotheses about the causes of India's de-industrialization experience. Section 6.3 elaborates on the efforts in chapter 4 to measure India's de-industrialization. Section 6.4 briefly reviews the simple, neo-Ricardian, general equilibrium model of de-industrialization in order to restate chapter 4 predictions about relative prices and their relationship to employment measures of de-industrialization. Section 6.5 presents three price series, three wage series, the intersectoral terms of trade between agricultural export commodities and textiles, and the external terms of trade. This input and output price evidence is then used to assess the three hypotheses. India's experience is also compared with its primary competitor, England.

6.2 India's De-industrialization: Three Hypotheses and One Offset

Any account of India's de-industrialization must embrace three contending hypotheses. First, there is the impact of globalization and industrial productivity advance in Europe. Second, there are the political changes that might have impacted costs and productivity in Indian industry. The dissolution of the Mughal empire into a constellation of small successor states was followed, after a time, by the initial phase of reintegration of these states under the East India Company. Historians have long thought that India underwent an overall economic decline during the transition between hegemonies. This proposition has recently become controversial, but this chapter stakes out a position in favor of it. It argues that the political fragmentation of the 18th century engendered a rise in grain prices that was reinforced by a second negative supply-side force, a devastating climatic shift that generated a steep upward trend in drought frequency.[3]

The Mughal Collapse Hypothesis

The dissolution of Mughal hegemony could have affected manufacturing through several channels. It could have reduced agricultural productivity through an increased rent burden, shifting of settlement owing to insecurity, and warfare. Reduced agricultural productivity would increase the price of grain, the key nontradable, and therefore reduced the relative price of textiles, a key tradable.[4] We know that grain was the dominant consumption good for Indian workers[5] and that the grain wage was close to subsistence (Allen 2007b; Roy 2009), so this negative productivity shock should have put upward pressure on the nominal wage. Indeed East India Company officials in Surat were already complaining in the 1720s that rising grain and raw cotton prices were putting upward pressure on the prime cost of textiles they were sending to England (Chaudhuri 1978: 299–300). Wages started from a low "cheap labor" nominal but high real base in the mid-18th century (Parthasarathi 1998; Allen 2005, 2007b; Prakash 2004: 268, 383). Declining textile prices and rising nominal wages put downward pressure on "profits" both from below and above. An increase in the own wage in textiles would have hurt the competitive edge India had in export markets, such as the booming Atlantic economy.[6] Any Indian agricultural productivity decline, even before factory-driven technologies appeared after 1780, would have helped Britain break India's powerful "cheap labor" grip on the world export market for textiles.[7] India was even losing its grip on its traditional Southeast Asian market where for the century before 1850 there were "reduced sales of Indian cloth" an event that "appears to have been fairly general across the Indian Ocean" (Clarence-Smith 2005: 1; see also Reid 1988: 96).

This connection between labor productivity in pre-industrial agriculture, nominal wages in industry, and the resulting competitiveness in world markets for manufactures has been stressed before in classic studies. Alexander Gerschenkron (1962), W. Arthur Lewis (1978: ch. 2), and even Adam Smith all used the argument to good effect in explaining why low productivity in agriculture helps explain the absence or delay of industrial revolutions. More recently Prasannan Parthasarathi (1998) has argued that while low nominal wages in pre-colonial and early colonial India gave it the edge in world textile markets, living standards for labor in the south of India were just as high as that in the south of England. Indian productivity in grain production was higher, and thus grain prices were lower.

The evidence for an overall 18th-century economic decline begins with unskilled wages in grain units, which are a good measure of the overall level of economic activity in a largely agricultural economy. Figure 6.1 presents three grain-wage series, two for north India and one for south India (Mukerjee 1939; Broadberry and Gupta 2005). The figure documents a long-run decline in grain wages beginning in the last decades of the 17th century and continuing until early in the century. The wage data in

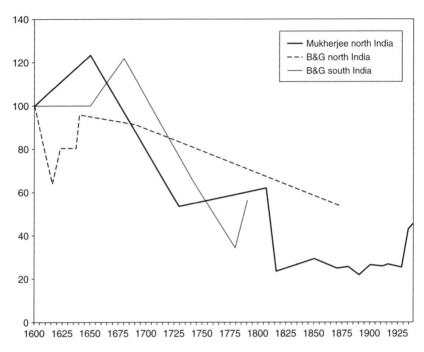

Figure 6.1
Grain wages in India in 1600 to 1938 (1600 = 100).
Source: Cliningsmith and Williamson (2008: fig. 1)

17th- and 18th-century India are particularly thin, but they provide one of the few indicators of the condition of ordinary people across time.

Historians traditionally viewed India's 18th century as a dark era of warfare, political chaos, and economic decline sandwiched between the stable and prosperous Mughal and British hegemonies. This view has been vigorously challenged by the most recent generation of Indian historians, who have emphasized the continuities between the earlier Mughal and later British states and the constellation of small successor states that emerged with the ebbing of Mughal power (e.g., Alam 1986; Bayly 1983; Marshall 1987). Their rulers were former provincial governors, Mughal officials, and other men powerful enough to assert de facto sovereignty. They collected the land revenue, sometimes using a modification of the old Mughal system, but submitted less and less of it to Delhi in favor of building up their own armies and courts.

While it has been widely accepted that the successor states provided a greater degree of political continuity and stability than was previously thought, no consensus has been reached about the implications of this fact for the Indian economy (Marshall 2003).[8] Still, this chapter favors the position that aggregate economic output declined following the dissolution of a strong empire into contending states. The more optimistic narrative tends to place too much emphasis on the prosperity of a few areas and groups, such as the towns of the successor states and their middle classes, and too little emphasis on the evidence for decline in the rural areas and peripheries of these states. Agriculture overwhelmingly dominated the 18th-century Indian economy,[9] so the economic performance of that sector largely dictated the course of the overall economy, and not what happened in the towns.[10] The optimistic narrative also seems to discount the strength of the Mughal empire and the economically favorable stability it brought. A regime powerful enough to extract 40 percent of the economic surplus from distant provinces must have also ensured peace and security, which were in turn favorable for agricultural investment and productivity.

A number of features of the transition of political authority from the Mughal empire to the successor states provide further evidence supporting an overall economic decline, one that resulted from reduced agricultural productivity. As central Mughal authority waned, the state resorted increasingly to revenue farming, and the practice became even more widespread in the successor states. This served to raise the effective rent share to 50 percent or more, far greater than the maximum said to have been extracted by the Mughal state (Raychaudhuri 1983: 17; Bayly 1983: 10; Marshall 1987: 62). "With revenue assessment geared to 50 per cent or more, in contrast to China's 5 to 6 per cent, the Indian peasant had little incentive to invest labour or capital" (Raychaudhuri 1983: 17). The economics is familiar to development analysts, economic historians, and observers of modern agrarian backwardness: the lower the share of output received by the peasant, the less incentive he has to carefully monitor the crop, to invest in the land, and to remain in place rather than fleeing. Scattered evidence suggests that the rent burden was quite extreme in some locations (Bayly 1983: 42). North of Delhi in Rohilla, cultivators were stripped of their land rights entirely and reduced to direct dependence. Under the *savak* system in north Awadh, cultivators received as little as one-sixth of the produce and their wives and children were required for *corvée* for a large part of the year. The Sayyids of Moradabad employed the *batai* system in which they "appropriated all 'save a bare subsistence' from the cultivators and invaded the villages for several months a year with bullock teams, armed retainers, and weighmen to secure the best portion of the crop." Productivity must have suffered as a result of the increased rent burden, and Tapan Raychauduri claims that grain prices "increased by 30 percent or more in the 1740s and 1750s" as a result (Raychaudhuri 1983: 6).

Rulers of the successor states also engaged in territorial disputes, and it is possible that the increased rent burden reflected added military expenses. These wars drew key resources out of agriculture and led to the destruction of capital (Bayly 1983: 70). Areas at the edges of successor states were particularly prone to agricultural decline, perhaps because these were most affected by territorial disputes, both between states and between local strongmen, who in remote areas were relatively free to plunder their neighbors. This led to population shifts as cultivators retreated to more secure areas. Bayly describes large areas of agricultural decline, particularly in the northwest (1983: 76) where "warfare withdrew both men and animals from agriculture" (Bayly 1983: 70–71), yielding a dearth of animal power, less efficient cultivation, and increased grain prices. Cultivators who relied on the bullocks owned by others would have been particularly vulnerable to fluctuations in their availability due to warfare. To cite one example, when Ahmed Shah Durrani invaded India from the northwest in 1759, bullock hire rates between Benares and Patna, a route nearly 600 km from the furthest extent of the fighting, increased by 500 percent (Bayly 1983: 68). Since most long-distance transport was by bullock, the scarcity of bullock power resulting from warfare would have increased transport costs. Political fragmentation and warfare also disrupted India's major internal trade routes, increased transport and insurance costs (Habib 2003), and reduced the gains from regional trade.

Thus a contemporary observer's claim that the dissolution of the Mughal empire led to "a scarcity of grains in all parts, [and] the wages of labour [were] greatly enhanced" seems credible (Holwell 1766–1767, cited in Raychaudhuri 1983: 6). This presumed rise in nominal wages would have slowly eroded the long-standing source of Indian competitiveness in foreign textile markets, long before Britain flooded those markets with factory-made products, and declining agricultural productivity in India must have been at the heart of it.

The Monsoon, El Niño, and Agricultural Crisis Hypothesis

There was another force at work that may also have served to lower agricultural productivity and raise grain prices in 18th- and early 19th-century India—El Niño, the periodic rise in Pacific sea surface temperature that can cause India's monsoon rains to fail. Charles Darwin stressed the influence of climate in *The Origin of the Species*, in particular when he wrote that "drought seems to be the most effective of all checks" (1972: 72). Indeed, for some time now, climate historians have developed evidence documenting frequent and deep droughts in South Asia over the late 18th and 19th century (e.g., Grove 1997; Grove, Damodaran, and Sangwan 1998; Grove and Chappell 2000) and modern Indian data clearly document the powerful role of rainfall on grain yields (Kapuscinski 2000).

Elsewhere, David Clingingsmith and I have plotted the occurrence of drought in India between 1525 and 1900 (Clingingsmith and Williamson 2008: fig. 2). The data we used were archive-based drought data reported in Richard Grove and John Chappell (2000: table 1) and culled from various sources (Habib 1977; Dyson 1989; and 19th-century publications). The pattern is striking. The average likelihood of a drought occurring was 34 percent for the period 1525 to 1649, or about one drought year every three. The average then fell to 18 percent for the long century from 1650 to 1774, or about one drought year every six. Indeed between 1720 and 1765 there were two fifteen-year spans without a single drought. However, drought incidence increased substantially from 1775, reaching a devastating likelihood of 40 percent for the years 1785 to 1825. Moreover the five-year drought of 1788 to 1793 surpassed in severity any drought of the previous century (Grove and Chappel 2000: 18). The monsoon failed to arrive for three years straight in southeast India, and annual rainfall was less than 40 percent of the pre-drought level.

Thus India experienced a historically low rate of drought during the long century 1650 to 1774, years that hailed the Mughal empire's golden age under Shah Jahan, its overextension and collapse under Aurangzeb, and the rise of competing successor states. The Mughals increased the territory under their control by about half during the reigns of Shah Jahan and Aurangzeb, moving deep into southern and western India. The empire reached its territorial maximum at around the end of the 17th century, when only the very southern tip of the subcontinent was excluded (O'Brien 1999). The last decades of Aurangzeb's life were spent trying to subdue the tenacious Marathas in western India, at great cost in both blood and treasure. During the fractious succession following Aurangzeb's death in 1707, the Marathas surged out of their Deccan strongholds, extending their control across almost a third of India by 1757. The low drought occurrence during these years must have augmented agricultural productivity and thus the resources available for territorial conquest. But these unusually good climatic conditions soured at the end of the 1760s, when India was politically fragmented and conflict widespread, thus making a bad agricultural situation worse.

The combined influence of drought and the disintegration of the Mughal empire on diminishing grain yields in the second half of the 18th and early 19th century can be inferred from various fragmentary sources. For example, the evidence documenting deserted villages in rural Tamil Nadu in southern India (Lardinois 1989: 34–43) reveal very high rates between 1795 and 1847, but they were more than twice as high in 1795 to 1814 (21.4 percent) than in 1816 to 1847 (10.1 percent). This evidence certainly suggests low and falling agricultural productivity in the second half of the 18th and the early 19th century, but the best evidence of poor agricultural conditions in India was the soaring relative price of grains, evidence that will be discussed at much greater length below.

A De-industrialization Offset: Short-Run Financial Drain and Textile Boom

Even if we had good data on Indian employment and output in the late 18th and early 19th centuries, long-term de-industrialization forces might still be difficult to identify since there was a huge net financial transfer, or "drain," from India to Britain between 1772 and 1815. The "drain resulting from contact with the West was the excess of exports from India for which there was no equivalent import" (Furber 1948: 304), including "a bewildering variety of cotton goods for re-export or domestic [consumption], and the superior grade of saltpeter that gave British cannon an edge" (Esteban 2001: 65). Indian textiles were at this time an important vehicle by which Britons repatriated wealth accumulated in India to England, increasing demand for them. Javier Cuenca Esteban estimates these net financial transfers from India to Britain reached a peak of £1,014,000 annually in 1784 to 1792 before declining to £477,000 in 1808 to 1815 and –£77,000 in 1816 to 1820 (Esteban 2001: table 1, line 20). However, even at their peak these net Indian transfers still amounted to less than 2 percent of British industrial output (Deane and Cole 1967: table 37, 166, using 1801 "manufacture, mining, building"). As a share of Indian industrial output, these net transfers were probably about the same.[11] Thus, while a secular fall in the "drain" after the 1784 to 1792 peak must have served to speed up the pace of de-industrialization in early 19th-century India by reducing demand for Indian textiles, the effect could not have been very big. In any case, the fall in the "drain" after 1784 to 1792 was equivalent to the rise before, thus implying little effect on de-industrialization over the full half century of 1750 to 1810.[12] There must have been other fundamentals at work that mattered far more.

The Globalization Hypothesis: Britain Did It

Around the beginning of the 19th century, the fundamental economic dynamics underlying de-industrialization in India started to change from agricultural productivity decline at home to globalization shocks induced by factory-based industrialization abroad. The change did not necessarily eliminate the role of agricultural productivity decline at home, but it must have reduced it. Globalization has, of course, long been the most popular explanation for India's de-industrialization, and it is an important component of the historiography of colonial India constructed by the Indian nationalists. For example, Jawaharlal Nehru's classic *Discovery of India* (1947) argued that India became progressively ruralized in the 19th century owing to the destruction of artisanal employment by British factory-made goods. Nehru laid the blame squarely on colonial economic policy, which almost entirely eschewed tariff protection and did nothing to help nurture Indian industry (Nehru 1947: 247–53). Similar arguments can be found in the work of the 19th-century nationalist Dadabhai Naoroji, pioneering Indian economic historian R. C. Dutt, and the Marxist historian D. D. Kosambi.

The economic logic underlying the de-industrialization-through-globalization hypothesis is that rapid productivity advance in European manufacturing—led by Britain—lowered the relative price of textiles, metal products, and other manufactures in world markets. Having first defeated India in its export markets, ever cheaper British factory-made yarn and cloth took away more and more of India's local market from her own producers (Moosvi 2002: 341). While poor agricultural productivity performance, rising grain prices, and increasing nominal wages might still have been eroding competitiveness of Indian manufacturing, the globalization hypothesis has it that Indian de-industrialization over the half century following 1810 was driven increasingly by globalization manifested by a rising terms of trade. India's textile producers would have faced a big negative price shock on that score alone. To make matters worse, newly independent Latin America, United States, Australia, Canada, and New Zealand raised their tariffs on imported manufactures to enormous heights (Williamson 2005: ch. 13). Failing to keep up with European factory-based productivity growth, facing new high tariffs in its old export markets, and unable to defend their own markets with tariffs, the Indian textile industry became less profitable, and de-industrialization ensued. These foreign-productivity-induced price shocks were reinforced by another global event, the transport revolution (Shah Mohammed and Williamson 2004). Thus the relative supply price of manufactures in India was driven down still further. In short, the standard globalization hypothesis has it that world events served to create Dutch disease effects in India: the import-competing sectors slumped, the export sectors boomed, and de-industrialization took place. While this globalization hypothesis certainly sounds plausible, recall that India's terms of trade rose only modestly between 1800 and 1870 (15 percent), suggesting that negative domestic supply-side forces were still playing a very active part.

The decline in world textile prices caused by British productivity advance made production in India less attractive. It also contributed to a shift in the terms of trade between India's own textiles and commodity export sectors, a shift reinforced by booming world demand for Indian commodity exports. This shift alone would have caused a decline in the relative employment in textiles. The most important export commodities for India in the first half of the 19th century were opium, raw cotton, raw silk, and sugar, and they were a growing fraction of India's exports. By 1811 they accounted for 57 percent of India's exports by value, compared to 33 percent for cotton piece goods (Chaudhuri 1983). The role played by the terms of trade in reallocating resources to commodity export sectors is noted in the literature on the commercialization of Bengali agriculture in the late 18th century (Chowdhury 1964), but it has not yet become a part of the de-industrialization debate.

In sum, the long-run sources of India's de-industrialization were both the globalization price shocks induced by European productivity advance in manufacturing —and the derived demand for industrial intermediates such as cotton and indigo—plus the negative productivity shocks to Indian agriculture induced by the earlier Mughal decline and deteriorating climate conditions.[13] These foreign and domestic effects were not competing. They were both at work, although each had its most important influence in different epochs.

6.3 Measuring India's De-industrialization

Inputs, Outputs, and De-industrialization

Owing to the dearth of statistical evidence, there have been only four attempts to directly measure India's de-industrialization using estimated employment shares, and that only for the 19th century. This chapter tries something new, the application of relative price evidence to the Indian de-industrialization question, and, by doing so, offers previously missing evidence, tentative though it may be, about de-industrialization in the 18th century.

Tirthankar Roy (2000) offers a useful survey of the existing direct 19th-century evidence, starting with this big fact: it seems likely that the share of the labor force engaged in industry was quite a bit higher in 1800 (probably 15–18 percent[14]) than it was in 1900 (about 10 percent), implying that labor force share de-industrialization took place over the 19th century.[15] The first evidence supporting labor force share de-industrialization was offered more than a half century ago by Colin Clark (1950). Clark published tabulations of the 1881 and 1911 census records of India showing that the share of the Indian workforce in manufacturing, mining, and construction declined from 28.4 to 12.4 percent from 1881 to 1911, implying dramatic late 19th century de-industrialization. Daniel Thorner (1962) re-examined the census data and convincingly argued that the tabulations used by Clark were misleading. His revised estimates show that the sectoral employment structure was stationary after 1901, with only a very small decline in male nonagricultural employment between 1881 and 1901. Thorner used these revisions to make an important point: if there was a major shift out of industry, it occurred before 1881, not after. Indeed Om Prakash (2005: 28) reports that Indian textile employment fell by 3.6 million between 1850 and 1880.

The third attempt to measure de-industrialization looks to the early 19th century, closer to the years that the qualitative literature has always suggested were those of most dramatic de-industrialization.[16] Amiya Bagchi (1976a, b) examined evidence on handloom spinning and other traditional industry in Gangetic Bihar, data collected between 1809 and 1813 by the East India Company surveyor Francis Buchanan Hamilton.[17] Bagchi compared Hamilton's data with the 1901 census estimates for the same area. First, he removed commercial workers from the 1901 data to make them consistent with the 1809 to 1813 data. Second, the population dependent on industrial employment requires an estimate of family size, and Bagchi offered two estimates using alternative assumptions. In either case, Bagchi's evidence suggests a substantial decline in the industrial employment share during the 19th century, from more than 21 percent to less than 9 percent. The Bagchi and Thorner evidence suggests that most 19th-century de-industrialization took place during its first half, and that it was big.

While the employment share in other industrial occupations also fell over the century, it is important to note that the largest component of de-industrialization was the decline of cotton spinning.[18] Of the population that depended on cotton weaving and spinning in 1809 to 1813, more than 80 percent depended on spinning (Bagchi 1976b). Since cotton spinning was performed part-time by women at home using extremely simple technology, it may seem implausible to argue that the demise of cotton spinning in the early 19th century destroyed India's platform for modern industrialization. Yet European economic historians assign the same importance to home-based cotton spinning: 17th- and 18th-century proto-industrial cottage industries are said to have supplied the platform for the factory-based British industrial revolution that followed (Mendels 1972; Mokyr 1993: chs. 1–3; Weisdorf 2006). Furthermore women and children were key players then too (de Vries 1994).

Finally, in an unpublished study reported by Irfan Habib (1985), Amalendu Guha calculated the amount of cotton yarn available for Indian handloom production by subtracting the quantity used in local machine production from total local yarn production and imports. The result documents a huge decline in yarn used for handloom production, from 419 million pounds in 1850, to 240 in 1870 and to 221 in 1900. This indirect evidence suggests that the decline in hand spinning documented for Gangetic Bihar in the early 19th century was widespread, that it was followed by a decline in hand weaving during the mid-century, and that the decline of both hand spinning and weaving was almost complete by 1870.

Chapter 5 (table 5.1) noted that Paul Bairoch had used evidence similar to that reviewed above to assess de-industrialization not only in India but across the rest of the periphery. According to his estimates, China and India together accounted for 57 percent of world manufacturing output in 1750, while India alone accounted for about a quarter. By 1800 India's world share had already eroded to less than a fifth, and by 1860 to less than a tenth. In short, India's share in world manufacturing output declined precipitously in the half century 1750 to 1800, *before* factory-led industrialization took hold in Britain and consistent with the hypothesis that significant de-industrialization took place in the second half of the 18th century. World output shares can also change due to different rates of output growth across countries. The economic implications of faster growth abroad are much more benign than those of slow growth at home. Anticipating this criticism, Bairoch (1982: tables 6 and 9) also documented that per capita levels of industrialization in India fell from an index of 7 to 3 between 1750 and 1860.

Real Wages and De-industrialization

If de-industrialization is driven by declining productivity and competitiveness in domestic industry, rather than by the specialization response to globalization forces, it should be accompanied by a decline in real wages. The evidence for 18th- and 19th-century India is not yet of high quality, but it does document a secular deterioration (figure 6.1).

Parthasarathi (1998) argues that real wages in mid- to late 18th-century south India were comparable to those in the south of England, and thus that the rising living standard gap between the two was a late 18th- and early 19th-century phenomenon. Robert Allen (2005) uses Mughal manuscript sources to compute the real wage in 1595 Agra, then the capital of the Mughal empire. He compares it to the real wage in 1961, based on a common market basket of consumer goods. Allen's evidence documents a fall in the real wage by about 23 percent over those 366 years, and if Parthasarathi is correct, most of that fall must have taken place after the mid- to late 18th century. While based on sparse data, the most telling evidence on the timing of real wage performance come from Radhakamal Mukerjee (1939) and Stephen Broadberry and Bishnupriya Gupta (2005), reproduced in figure 6.1. Mukerjee reports 1600 to 1938 real wages of unskilled and skilled labor in northern India (nominal wage rates deflated by grain prices), and Broadberry and Gupta offer grain wage trends up to the late 19th century in both north and south India. According to these estimates, real wages had fallen 30 to 44 percent from their 1600 level by 1789, and 50 to 75 percent by 1875.

This evidence suggests that more than half of the real wage and living standards fall (30/50 = 60 percent, and 44/75 = 59 percent) took place *before* about 1800. Was de-industrialization responsible for the fall, or can Mughal decline and bad climate shocks account for both? Were the de-industrialization forces just as powerful before 1800 to 1810, as after? Were the sources of de-industrialization before and after 1800 to 1810 quite different, the first due to local supply side problems and the second due to globalization forces and the European industrial revolution?

6.4 Some Neo-Ricardian De-industrialization Economics Once More

In order to formalize intuitions about the relationship between relative prices and de-industrialization in India between the 1750s and 1850s, it might be useful to summarize the neo-Ricardian economics developed in chapter 4 for this purpose. The economy is characterized by three sectors: textiles (T), grain (G), and agricultural commodity exports (C). Grain was too bulky and low value to be traded internationally, so we assume as much.[19] In contrast, high value agricultural commodities like opium, tea, indigo, jute, and raw cotton were exported. Thus, we take textiles and agricultural commodities to be traded in the world market and sell for the world prices p_T and p_C, respectively. Labor is assumed to be mobile between all three sectors, to be the only factor of production, and to receive a nominal wage w per unit. We also assume that there is no technical change in this pre-industrial economy. To create a link between agricultural productivity and wages in the textile sector—which was likely to have been a key driver in India's loss of competitiveness in the 18th-century world textile market, we follow Lewis (1954, 1978) in assuming that the real wage in grain units is constant at subsistence. Since the nominal wage is equal to the price of grain, employment in the grain-producing sector is fixed. Growth in the own wage in either commodity exports or textiles leads to a decline in the absolute number of workers employed there.

The neo-Ricardian model predicts that *absolute de-industrialization*—or a decline in the labor force in manufacturing—results from an increase in the own wage in textiles (i.e., the nominal textile wage deflated by the price of textile output) either due to a decline in the world price for its output or to an increase in the nominal wage driven up by a rise in the grain price (from a negative productivity shock in grain production) or by other forces. *Relative de-industrialization*—the decline in the share of the labor force in manufacturing—will result whenever the own wage in textiles is growing sufficiently fast compared to the own wage in agricultural commodity exports, and de-industrialization will be most severe when the difference in own wage growth rates is largest. This implies that own wage growth in agricultural commodity exports would have to be even higher to counteract the de-industrialization effect of own wage growth in textiles. In short, a decline in the industrial labor force share is expected whenever own wage growth in textiles is positive, unless own wage growth in agricultural commodity exports is much greater. Own wage growth in agricultural commodity exports dampens the relative de-industrialization effect because it reduces employment in the commodity export sector, which is in the denominator of the de-industrialization measure. As the share of the labor force employed in agricultural commodities increases, the greater growth in the own wage in textiles needs to be to overcome growth of the own wage in agricultural commodities and for de-industrialization to ensue. Relative de-industrialization results when nominal wage growth, which deters production in both nongrain sectors, is sufficiently greater than the growth of the terms of trade favoring textiles, which encourages production in textiles over agricultural commodities. Thus relative de-industrialization should have been most severe when nominal wage growth was strongest and when the terms of trade were shifting most strongly in favor of agricultural commodities.

6.5 Relative Prices and the Own Wage in Manufactures, 1750 to 1913

Indian de-industrialization experience over the two centuries between 1700 and 1913 can be divided into four distinct epochs. Explanations for the sources of de-industrialization within these epochs implies predictions regarding Indian relative price trends.

The first epoch ran from about 1700 to 1760, and it was India's high watermark as a global manufacturing powerhouse. Indian textiles clothed tens of millions of Indians, Southeast Asians, the fashionable men and women of Europe, American slaves and peons, Africans, and others throughout the Middle East. This success rested in part on the high productivity of Indian agriculture, which was supported during this epoch by unusually reliable monsoons and a flourishing empire.

The second epoch, about 1760 to 1810, was one during which India lost its significant share of world textile markets to Britain. What was an important export sector at the beginning of the epoch became an important import-competing sector at the end. While that result can be partly explained by increasing cost competitiveness favoring Britain, superior factory technology was not yet the main force at work. Instead, reduced agricultural productivity in India—driven by the decline of the Mughal empire and bad climate shocks—was likely to have mattered most. Grain prices rose and, in a subsistence economy where grain was the key consumption good, pushed up nominal wages economy-wide. The own wage rose in textiles, damaging cost competitiveness there.[20] Textiles therefore experienced a contraction. To the extent that the price of textiles relative to agricultural export commodities fell, the effect of reduced agricultural productivity would have fallen more heavily on textiles than export commodities, a labor force share de-industrialization effect.

During the third epoch, about 1810 to 1860, India lost much of its domestic textile market to Britain. This result can be explained in large part by the combined influence of relatively rapid factory-based productivity advance in Britain and by increased world market integration, the latter driven by declining transport costs between the two trading partners, and to the free trade policy imposed on India by her colonial ruler. However, manufacturing's contraction was also explained by continued domestic supply-side problems. While the effects of the Mughal decline were over, the effect of unfavorable climate was not and thus low Indian grain productivity persisted, implying continued high nominal wages in manufacturing.

The rate of de-industrialization slowed down early in the fourth epoch, about 1860 to 1913, and then reversed as India slowly re-industrialized (see chapter 12). This slow down and reversal can be explained by the subsidence in productivity advance in European manufacturing and in the world transport revolution. As a result, the terms of trade trend was flat and did not raise the penalty on import competing manufacturing. In addition climate conditions improved for Indian agriculture. In any case, the emergence of an integrated world grain market (see chapter 4) probably served to put downward pressure on grain prices and nominal wages in India, thus increasing the competitiveness of local manufacturing.

These predictions are largely confirmed by the relative price, terms-of-trade, and own-wage evidence reported in figures 6.3 through 6.6 covering the 150 years 1700 to 1850. The price evidence includes three series for grains, textiles, and agricultural commodities (figure 6.2).[21] These are used

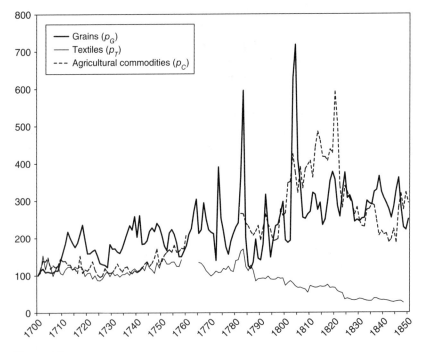

Figure 6.2
Prices of key Indian goods in 1700 to 1850 (1700 = 100).
Source: Cliningsmith and Williamson (2008: fig. 3)

to measure the intersectoral terms of trade between textiles and agricultural export commodities and the own wages in the two sectors.[22] The analysis that follows will focus on the century between the 1750s and the 1850s, when de-industrialization appears to have been most dramatic, and in two parts.

The first epoch corresponds to the dissolution of the Mughal empire. Despite favorable climate, the price of grain nearly doubled between 1700 and 1760, putting upward pressure on nominal wages and hurting India's competitiveness in both textile and commodity exports (figure 6.2). Textile and commodity prices were roughly constant from 1700 to 1740 before climbing steadily between 1740 and 1760. There is no evidence here of falling textile prices due to improvements in European technology or sea-going transport. The intersectoral terms of trade between textiles and agricultural commodities moved slightly in favor of commodities during this period, putting some pressure on the allocation of resources between export sectors (figure 6.3). Grain prices rose while nominal wages fell from 1700 to 1740 (figures 6.3 and 6.5). The fall in textile's own wage from 1700 to 1730 favored local industry, after which it stayed flat (figure 6.5), suggesting India actually became more competitive in its textile export market during 1700 to 1760. Figure 6.5 offers no support for the view that

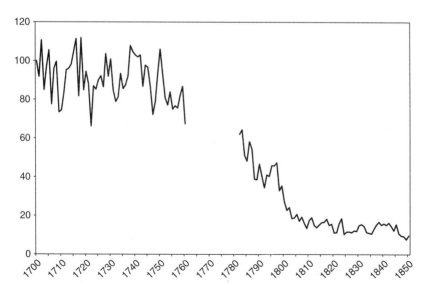

Figure 6.3
Intersectoral terms of trade (p_T/p_C) in 1700 to 1850.
Source: Clingingsmith and Williamson (2008: fig. 4)

de-industrialization was induced by an own wage rise in textiles during 1700 to 1760, but figure 6.3 does offer some support for the view that de-industrialization was induced by a small twist in the intersectoral terms of trade in favor of agricultural commodities.

Now consider the case for absolute de-industrialization over the century after 1760, recalling that absolute de-industrialization is defined as a decline in the industrial workforce, driven in the first half century by a rise in the own wage. Figure 6.5 shows that the own wage in textiles rose spectacularly between 1765 and 1810, more than tripling, with faster growth in the latter part of the period. Why the spectacular rise in w/p_T in the late 18th century? The answer is that grain prices, while volatile in the short run, soared upward in the long run (figure 6.2). This did not serve to reduce real wages (w/p_G): Figures 6.1 and 6.4 show that grain wages appear to have been largely stable following the early to mid-18th century,[23] consistent with a Lewis-like assumption about long-run real wage stability. But the grain price boom did serve to inflate nominal wages. Since textile prices also began to fall after 1785 to about half that level in 1810, w/p_T soared.

There is no qualitative evidence suggesting significant productivity advance in Indian textiles and other manufacturing production before

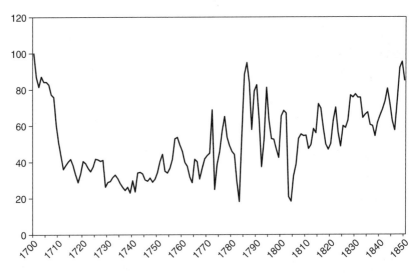

Figure 6.4
Grain wage in India (w/p_G) in 1700 to 1850 (1700 = 100).
Source: Clingingsmith and Williamson (2008: fig. 5)

1810,[24] so the evidence on the own wage is taken to offer powerful support for the thesis that reduced agricultural productivity attendant on the dissolution of Mughal hegemony and more frequent droughts can indeed explain much of India's pre-1810 loss of world markets and resulting de-industrialization. India lost much of its cost competitiveness as the own wage in home manufacturing underwent that spectacular rise, and it was the rise in the price of nontradable grains that pushed up the nominal wage to such high levels. Most of the secular rise in grain prices stopped after around 1810, but they stayed at high levels. Thus, while the upward pressure on nominal wages eased, wage competitiveness was not recovered. Still, the fall in p_T dominated de-industrialization conditions in Indian manufacturing. The own wage continued to rise after 1810 and de-industrialization persisted, but it was now driven mainly by exogenous world market forces (e.g., p_T). Between 1810 and 1850, the own wage roughly tripled.

Consider now relative de-industrialization (i.e., a declining manufacturing labor force share) across the middle two epochs; recall that it should have been more intense when the own wage in textiles was growing faster *and* when the intersectoral terms of trade was shifting most strongly in favor of agricultural commodities. Figure 6.5 shows the own wage almost tripling between 1765 and 1810, and more than tripling between 1810 and 1850. Thus own wage growth was slightly stronger in the third epoch. However, the intersectoral terms of trade shift appears to have been strongest in the second epoch, that is before 1810 not after (figure 6.3). Figure 3.8 documents India's external terms of trade from 1800. It shows two big spikes, the first over the decade of the 1810s and the second over the decade of the 1850s. When the series is smoothed, the measured trend in the terms of trade favoring India (thus penalizing the import competing sector) is very modest, as we saw in this chapter's introduction. In contrast, between 1750 and 1810 the intersectoral terms of trade between textiles and agricultural commodities (figure 6.4: p_T/p_C) underwent a very sharp decline: by 1810 it was only 20 percent of its 1780 level. Thus, while the own wage in export commodities was stable during this period (figure 6.5), it rose in textiles. This pattern suggests that de-industrialization was likely to have been greater during the half century before 1810 than in the half century thereafter. Before 1810, workers left textiles due to their demand for higher nominal wages to buy increasingly expensive grain and to a strong shift in the terms of trade favoring commodity exports and disfavoring textiles, whereas after 1810, workers left mainly due to falling world textile prices and a sagging demand for their output.

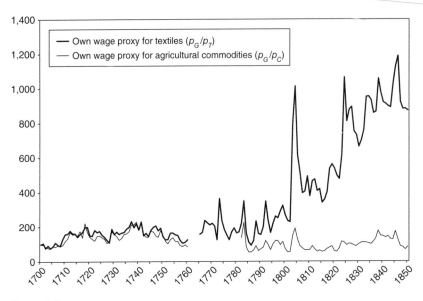

Figure 6.5
Proxy for own wage in textiles and agricultural commodities in 1700 to 1850
(1700 = 100).
Source: Clingingsmith and Williamson (2008: fig. 6)

Since England was India's main competitor in world markets, a comparison of trends in the own wage in textiles between the two should be a useful indicator of relative productivity change. Caution should be exercised here, since a measured increase in the ratio of Indian to English w/p_T will understate the role of own wage inflation to the extent that English labor productivity growth performance was superior to India even before the great factory boom. Figure 6.6 plots indexes for w/p_T in India and England, and their ratio. The India/England own wage ratio was relatively stable between 1705 and 1760. The own wage in England grew by about 80 percent between 1765 and 1845, but the own wage in India grew much faster. The ratio of w/p_T in India relative to England shot up from 79 in 1760 to 181 in 1810 and 492 in 1845. Nearly half of that 85-year increase was completed by 1810, before the great flood of factory-produced textiles hit Indian markets in the third de-industrialization epoch. But even after 1810 it appears that some part of Indian de-industrialization was explained by poor productivity performance in grains: after all, p_T was pretty much equalized between India and Britain, so the faster rise in India's p_G/p_T implies a poorer productivity performance in grains there, and perhaps even compared with the rest of the periphery. And rise it did!

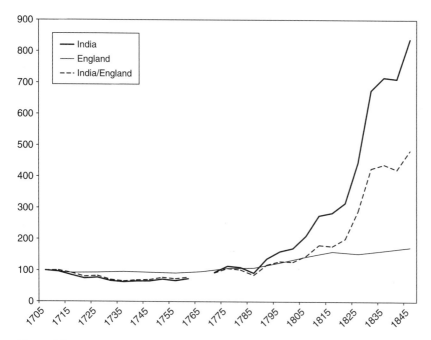

Figure 6.6
Textile own wages in India and England (1705 = 100).
Source: Clingingsmith and Williamson (2008: fig. 9)

Grain prices rose almost four times faster in India than England, an event that must have put far greater upward pressure on wage costs in India than England, thus raising the Indian own wage in textiles relative to England.

Is our evidence inconsistent with the fact that India's textile export volume grew strongly in the last decades of the 18th century (Datta 1999)? No: this fact does not counter our stress on 18th-century de-industrialization, and for two reasons. First, it has already been noted that the period from 1772 to 1812 saw an artificial increase in demand for Indian textile exports from East India Company servants, who used them as a vehicle to transmit their fortunes back to England. This artificial demand shock served to mask the longer run fundamentals driving the Indian textile industry. Second, exports were by 1800 a relatively small component of the Indian textile market, ranging between 4 and 12 percent in 1800 (Clingingsmith and Williamson 2008: table 5, panel C), where 6 to 7 percent seems most plausible. In short, India had lost much of its world market by 1800, and stronger growth in export volume thereafter would have had only a modest effect on India's textile industry as a whole.

6.6   A New View of Indian De-industrialization

Chapters 4 and 5 stressed that de-industrialization appeared everywhere around the 19th-century periphery, although the size of the terms of trade boom and de-industrialization varied considerably from place to place. This variety could have been due to the magnitude of the terms of trade boom, dictated by the commodities in which each region specialized. But the de-industrialization response could have varied for other reasons coming from the domestic supply side. While globalization played a major role everywhere around the poor periphery, Indian historiography has given more space to de-industrialization than do other historiographies from the poor periphery, laying the blame with Britain. Yet the de-industrializing global price shocks facing India were relatively modest. This apparent paradox is resolved once we pay attention to negative domestic supply-side forces, since they played a far more important role in India than elsewhere.

India's de-industrialization between 1760 and 1860 contained two main epochs, with somewhat different de-industrialization causes. The first epoch ran from about 1760 to 1810, when Indian manufacturing lost so much of its export market. This de-industrialization experience was a direct result of poor climate conditions and an indirect result of the dissolution of the Mughal empire. The deterioration in climate conditions lowered agricultural productivity, raised grain prices, and thus increased nominal wages in home manufacturing, lowering India's competitiveness with England and other world producers. Furthermore, as central authority waned, these forces were strengthened: revenue farming expanded, the rent burden increased, warfare raised the price of agricultural inputs, and regional trade within the subcontinent declined, all serving to drive down the productivity of food grain agriculture still further. So grain prices had another reason to rise, and given that ordinary workers lived near subsistence, the nominal wage rose even faster, hurting India's competitiveness in the export market all the more. India thus lost ground to Britain in the world textile market during a period when most British production was still carried out using the cottage system. Additionally the intersectoral terms of trade moved against textiles, encouraging a shift to agricultural commodity production. India's share of world industrial production fell faster than in any other part of the non-European world. During the second epoch, running from about 1810 to 1860, Indian manufacturing lost much of its domestic market. The European productivity advance resulting from the adoption of the factory system drove down the relative price of textiles worldwide, a trend that was magnified as a world transport revolution lowered the price of European textile imports even further everywhere in the periphery. Thus, while the productivity of Indian agriculture stopped its decline during this period, under the relative security of company rule and reinforced by a secular fall in drought frequency, and while the rise in grain prices slowed down and then stabilized, nominal grain prices remained high, and their *relative* price continued to rise.[25] By 1860 India had completed a century-long two-part transition from being a major net exporter to a major net importer of textiles. India's terms of trade were relatively flat over most of the 19th century, especially compared to the booms in the rest of the poor periphery, suggesting that domestic supply-side conditions played a relatively important role in India. India's de-industrialization was over by the late 19th century, and a period of slow reindustrialization began, as it did in Shanghai, Japan, Brazil, Mexico, and other parts of the poor periphery.

7 A Middle East De-industrialization Illustration: Ottoman Problems

7.1 Ottoman Issues

If a country de-industrializes because its comparative advantage in agriculture has been strengthened, either by productivity advances on the land (or more land) or by increasing openness in the world economy, or both, then GDP increases in the short run. In the case of more land or more productive land, and assuming the country to be "small" in the sense that international economists use that term—a condition that clearly applied to the Ottoman empire—then the country faces no change in its terms of trade.[1] In the case of increasing openness, the country enjoys an unambiguous terms of trade improvement as declining world trade barriers raise export prices and lower import prices in the home market. Whether real wages and living standards of landless labor also increase depends on the direction of the terms of trade change, whether foodstuffs are among the export commodities, and whether foodstuffs dominate the worker's budget. That is, it depends on whether the export commodities are wheat and barley (a big share of the Ottoman worker's budget) or silk, tobacco, and opium (a small share). This is a feature of the Ottoman economy that made it different than India (chapter 6) and Mexico (chapter 8). So, since the Ottomans exported foodstuffs, rising terms of trade must have translated in to rising nominal wages and falling wage competitiveness in industry.

This chapter documents Ottoman experience with its terms of trade over the century 1800 to 1913, explores the connection between de-industrialization and those external price shocks, and compares this experience with that of the rest of the eastern Mediterranean, as well as with Asia, Latin America, and the European periphery. The next section sets the stage by outlining Ottoman experience with trade policy, world transport costs, and thus with world market integration. Section 7.3 reviews the de-industrialization debate as it applies to the Ottoman empire and the rest of the eastern Mediterranean, and section 7.4 assesses the Ottoman de-industrialization evidence. The chapter then reports the external terms of trade estimates for the Ottoman Turkish and Balkan core, for Levant in the empire's eastern wing, and for the more autonomous Egypt. Section 7.6 reviews our neo-Ricardian model of de-industrialization, and the section that follows uses it to answer these questions: How much of Ottoman de-industrialization was due to falling world trade barriers—ocean transport revolutions and European liberal trade policy, how much due to factory-based productivity advance in Europe, how much to changing Ottoman competitiveness in manufacturing, how much to Ottoman policy, and how much to Ottoman railroads as they opened the interior?

7.2   Changing Trade Barriers in the Eastern Mediterranean: Setting the Stage

In response to the influx of cheaper manufactured goods from Britain and the rest of western Europe, de-industrialization was, as we have seen, the norm for most of the poor periphery during the 19th century. The great Middle East scholar Charles Issawi placed the Ottoman case in this general context:

The Revolutionary and Napoleonic wars gave the region a respite, but in the 1820s and 30s it was hit by the full blast of European competition. Factories were pouring out cheap goods, and peace and increased security in the Mediterranean and improvement in shipping made it possible to land them at low costs. To this should be added the effects of the various commercial treaties, which froze import duties at low levels and opened up the region's markets. (Issawi 1982: 151)

Thus the 1838 Treaty is one of the most widely discussed events pertaining to the collapse of Ottoman industry in the 19th century. Most European industrial countries were still protectionist before they went liberal in the 1860s (chapter 2), so Britain's agenda was to sign free trade agreements with as many periphery countries as possible in order to gain foreign markets for their manufactures. The 1838 Anglo-Turkish Commercial Convention was one such commercial agreement, and the "convention eventually became the basis of practically all foreign trade in Turkey" as the Ottoman empire signed similar treaties with several other European countries in the following three years (Puryear 1969: 83). The Convention was viewed as the next step in the empire's transition to economic liberalism after the sultan eliminated the Janissary corps in 1826, urban guildsman on the military payroll that were the strongest advocates of protection (Quataert 1994: 764).

The 1838 Treaty eliminated all local monopolies, allowed British merchants to buy goods anywhere in the empire, and exempted foreign (but not domestic) merchants from an 8 percent internal customs duty that had previously been levied on goods transported within the empire.[2] Export duties were raised from 3 to 12 percent and import duties from 3 to 5 percent (Issawi 1966: 38).[3] Şevket Pamuk (1987: 20) has argued that the importance of these treaties has been overstated since they did not represent a drastic revision from the liberal course already set in 1826. It appears that Donald Quataert agrees: "Commerce between [Britain and the Ottoman empire] already was increasing dramatically: British exports to the empire had doubled in value during the late 1820s and doubled again before 1837" (Quataert 1994: 825). However, by locking the government into fixed import duties these treaties did prevent the Ottomans from providing any subsequent protection to domestic industry. Indeed, between 1865 and 1905, their average tariff rates were fairly stable at 7.5 percent. These low revenue-producing tariffs were consistent with free trade policy, and they were equivalent to the tariff rates prevailing in Asia. In contrast, average tariff rates in protectionist Latin America and the United States were about 30 percent in the middle of the period,[4] or *four times* that of the Ottoman empire (chapter 13). It is interesting that the literature never mentions the political pressure exerted by export interest groups who, after all, stood to gain significantly from the treaties, and how they came to overwhelm import-competing interest groups, when the opposite was true of Latin America and the United States. The elimination of monopolies also had a powerful short run impact on de-industrialization, as we will see below.

The move to free trade and the dramatic decline in transportation costs (Harlaftis and Kardasis 2000) contributed to a boom in Ottoman trade during the 19th century, especially with western Europe. Imports increased from £5.2 million in 1840 to £39.4 million in 1913, about 3.3 percent per annum, and since "the prices of the traded commodities were considerably lower on the eve of World War I than in 1840, the increases in trade volumes were actually greater" (Pamuk 1987: 23). Between 1840 and 1873, trade grew even faster with the volume doubling every 11 to 13 years. Placed in a comparative framework with other periphery countries,

for the period 1840–1913 as a whole per capita exports from the Ottoman Empire expanded at rates close to but lower than those of per capita world trade and per capita center-periphery trade. Within [the first] three quarters of [the] century, the Ottoman-center trade grew faster than the periphery-center trade until the early 1870s, but the rate of growth of Ottoman exports lagged behind the rate of growth of total exports from the periphery after the 1870s (Pamuk 1987: 37).

Steamships and railroads constitute the two major transport innovations that contributed to the booming Ottoman trade during the period. Steamships could be built much larger than their sail counterparts and their rise to dominance lowered freight costs and stimulated trade for the region. The decline in freight rates between 1870 and 1914 was just as dramatic on routes involving Black Sea and Egyptian ports as it was in the Atlantic, perhaps even more so (Harlaftis and Kardasis 2000; Shah Mohammed and Williamson 2004). Shipping boomed in the Mediterranean. For example, tonnage entering Beirut went from 40,000 in 1830, to 600,000 in 1890, and to 1,700,000 in 1913. Other cities in the eastern Mediterranean show similar tonnage increases (Issawi 1982: 48).

Over the 19th century as a whole, the Ottoman empire was more active in world trade than either Asia or Africa, but less so than Latin America. Why? Did its shorter distance to European markets matter? Did the Ottoman empire enjoy more favorable terms of trade shocks than Asia and Africa, but less favorable than Latin America? As a consequence, did it undergo greater de-industrialization than Asia and Africa, but less than Latin America?

7.3 The Eastern Mediterranean De-industrialization Debate

In the simple two-sector model set out in chapter 4, de-industrialization can be gauged as the movement of labor out of manufacturing and in to agriculture, measured either as a fall in the total employment share or as a fall in absolute numbers. Either measure could, in theory, also be constructed for value added, but such evidence is almost impossible to find for the 19th-century Ottoman economy. Alternatively, absolute de-industrialization could be supported by information on the capital stock in manufacturing, like the number of spindles and handlooms. In any case, de-industrialization is easy enough to define. Debate over its *magnitude*, its *causes*, and its *impact* on living standards and GDP growth is more complicated and contentious.[5]

The literature dealing with Ottoman and Middle Eastern 19th-century de-industrialization exhibits an impressive solidarity. Charles Issawi, Roger Owen, Şevket Pamuk, Donald Quataert, and other Ottoman scholars all promote similar, or at least reconcilable, views. Yet the de-industrialization narrative is usually supported only by qualitative accounts, anecdotal evidence, or spotty time series, making long period quantitative analysis difficult. Twenty-five years ago Orhan Kurmuş (1983: 411–12) commented that anecdotal evidence was being "accepted as constituting some part of the historical truth" which would serve "to substitute antiquarianism for scientific work." The Kurmus challenge produced a response by Pamuk in his book *The Ottoman Empire and European Capitalism, 1820–1913*, which will be used extensively in this survey. Still Pamuk and Issawi appear to be the only Ottoman economic historians that base their claims on hard evidence. Even in those exceptions, previous debate has rarely been engaged in comparative terms. How did the Ottomans do relative to the rest of the 19th-century periphery? Where the experience was different, why was it different?

As is true with the de-industrialization literature written about other parts of the 19th-century periphery, Ottoman industry has too often been considered solely as capital-intensive, large-scale, urban, factory production since those were the modes of production in Britain and the rest of Europe by mid-century. This is a mistake when analyzing any part of the poor periphery during the 19th century (or even Britain before 1800), where most manufacturing was labor intensive, small scale, household based, and rural. Since cotton spinning and handweaving were performed part-time by family members using extremely simple technology, it may seem implausible to argue that their demise destroyed a 19th-century Ottoman platform for modern industrialization. Yet, as the previous chapter noted, economic historians assign the same importance to home-based cotton spinning and weaving in Britain: proto-industrial cottage industries are said to have supplied the platform for the factory-based British industrial revolution that followed in the late 18th century (Mendels 1972; Petmezas 1990; de Vries 1994; Mokyr 1993: chs. 1–3; Weisdorf 2006). Hence this chapter and chapters 6 and 8 consider both cottage and factory industries.

7.4 Measuring Ottoman De-industrialization

The traditional view of Ottoman manufacturing is that it steadily collapsed in the wake of the influx of European manufactured goods. Consular and traveler's reports are riddled with anecdotal accounts relating the demise of industry (Quataert 1994: 888). Certainly de-industrialization did occur between about 1815 and 1860, and in response to three forces. First, the end of the Napoleonic Wars opened the gates for British exports of manufactures. Britain had already accumulated productivity advantages in manufacturing, and peacetime conditions made it possible for the leading European economy to exploit them in world markets. Second, additional rapid productivity advance in British manufacturing increased its competitive edge in foreign markets still further. Third, the move to liberal policies in Asia and the Ottoman empire between the 1830s and the 1850s deepened the de-industrialization shock still further. After all, the terms of trade soared between 1815 and the late 1850s (figure 3.7), and it more than doubled over the two decades after the late 1830s.

The Ottoman empire was completely self-sufficient in cotton textiles until about 1820, but the deluge of cheap European industrial goods changed all of that. Pamuk reconstructs the decline of Ottoman cotton textile industry by using an identity to estimate the domestic consumption and production of textiles.[6] He identifies the period from the late 1830s to the mid-1870s as the crucial one for the decline of cotton handicrafts, a result consistent with the fact that the biggest terms of trade improvement took place in this period, as we will see below. Weavers suffered, but domestic spinning also declined dramatically in the face of import competition: spinning output "fell from 11,550 tons per year in 1820–2, to 8,250 tons in 1840–2, to 3,000 tons in 1870–2" (Pamuk 1987: 118). Note that the biggest collapse in local spinning output was between 1840–1842 and 1870–1872 at 74 percent, not between 1820–1822 and 1840–1842 at 29 percent, an observation consistent with the fact that the external price shock was *much* bigger in the latter period. De-industrialization hit the Balkans hard, but in Syria, at the eastern edge of the empire, de-industrialization forces hit hard too (Issawi 1988: 374). Aleppo was estimated to have had 40,000 handlooms in the 18th century, while the numbers were down to 25,000 in the 1820s—a 37 or 38 percent fall from the 18th-century highs, and averaged 5,125 between 1838 and 1850—for an 80 percent fall from the 1820s. Damascus was estimated to have had 34,000 handlooms in the 18th century, while the numbers were down to 12,000 in the 1820s—a 65 percent fall from the 18th-century highs, and averaged 2,355 between 1838 and 1850—an 80 percent fall from the 1820s. One wonders how much of the decline between "the 18th century" and the 1820s can be attributed to competition from modern British factories after 1815 and the peace, and how much of it can be attributed to the late 18th century when Britain, before the factories, began to take over the Atlantic and European market from India, the Middle East, and other competitors (chapter 6).

Table 5.3 offered another de-industrialization indicator for the 19th-century Ottoman empire, where comparisons with other parts of the third world were offered. For four third world regions—Mexico, the Ottomans, India, and Indonesia—the table measured the loss of domestic textile manufactures markets to foreign imports. That is, the figures document the decline in the share of domestic consumption supplied by local sources. Take India first. Chapter 6 reported that Bengal exported about 27 percent of domestic consumption (21 percent of domestic production) in 1750. That figure had fallen to 6 or 7 percent by 1800. Thus India had lost a big chunk of its export market even before the onset of the factory-led industrial revolution in Britain. By 1833, India had lost *all* of its (net) export market *and* 5 percent of its domestic market. By 1877, the de-industrial damage was complete, with domestic producers claiming only 35 to 42 percent of their own home market. Although it did not have as large a foreign market to lose, domestic producers in the Ottoman empire also lost a huge share of the home market, their share falling from 97 percent down to 11 to 38 percent over the half century between the 1820s and the 1870s. The decline in the Dutch East Indian textile industry was only a little less spectacular since the local producer share of the home market fell from 82 to 38 percent between 1822 and 1870. But in the Dutch East Indies case de-industrialization persisted much longer, with the local producer share falling still further to 11 percent in 1913. Finally, Mexico seems to have resisted these de-industrialization forces more successfully since domestic producers could still claim 60 percent of its home market in 1879. In short, the Ottoman empire had one of the more dramatic de-industrialization episodes around the poor periphery.

After 1880 the rapid growth in imports from Europe slowed down, and although domestic spinning output continued to decline, weaving actually doubled from 1880 to World War I. This industrialization about-face is consistent, as we will see, with the fact that the terms of trade also underwent an about-face, gradually *falling* for most of the second half of the century. Hence we would expect the de-industrialization forces to be powerful up to the 1850s and weak thereafter. On the eastern edge of the empire, the handloom numbers in both Aleppo and Damascus show no downward trend between 1850 and World War I (Issawi 1988: 374), after more than five decades of decline.

Not all Ottoman industries were severely damaged by foreign competition in the first half of the 19th century. Carpet making, copper work, earthenware, inlaid woodworking, lace making, silk reeling, and embroidery were able to hold their own in the face of foreign competition and trade liberalism (Issawi 1982: 153; Quataert 1994: 890). Indeed some of these industries, and even the textile industry itself, persisted until the First World War and after.

While domestic industry suffered badly, how was some of it able to survive at all in the face of the foreign competition? There are a number of hypotheses suggested by the literature. First, perhaps foreign goods were not able to penetrate into regions distant from major trade routes or ports, especially before the railway boom late in the century. Geography offered considerable protection for those parts of the Ottoman empire distant from the Mediterranean coast, just as it did for the Latin American interior (Coatsworth and Williamson 2004; Bértola and Williamson 2004; Williamson 2006b). Support for this hypothesis can also be inferred from the price convergence in another part of the Middle East, between upper and lower Egypt. These results are especially relevant because they speak to the impact of the transport breakthroughs that occurred in one part of the Middle East very late in the century. Denser rail networks and more navigable waters and roads lowered transportation costs and fostered internal trade in Egypt (Yousef 2000: 354–56). Thus, since European imports couldn't be brought cheaply into the more remote areas of the empire during most of the century, domestic manufactures could still supply local demand in those parts of the interior.

Second, domestic tastes afforded Ottoman handicrafts some staying power. Although British companies attempted to imitate Ottoman styles, often they could not do so satisfactorily, and thus there was still demand for domestic cloth (Pamuk 1987: 124). Their knowledge of local preferences helped domestic manufactures survive in the short run, and the import of foreign techniques and foreign managers increased their efficiency and competitiveness in the longer run. For example, local textile makers eventually became more familiar with synthetic dyestuffs, which allowed them to import European plain cloth and take advantage of cheaper Ottoman labor to dye it (Quataert 1994: 889), as with the Indonesian conversion of imported plain Indian cloth into local *batik*. Third, Issawi argues that "weavers were able to cut their costs greatly by using imported yarn; thus the Industrial Revolution, which had wiped out the spinners, gave the weavers a precarious reprieve" (Issawi 1982: 152). We are skeptical of this argument, since this advantage was given just as freely to weavers abroad who were competing with local weavers. A fourth potential explanation seems more promising. Namely the late 19th-century resistance of Ottoman handicrafts can be explained by what economic historians call the "great depression" from 1873 to 1896 when the terms of trade ceased to boom, and may have even moved *against* the Ottomans. This relative price event may have afforded local manufacturing some relief.

For all these reasons domestic handicrafts and industry, although badly hurt by foreign competition in the first half of the 19th century, resisted and adapted in the second half of the 19th century and in the early 20th century.

While the destruction of Ottoman industry across the 19th century was ubiquitous, observers then and now may exaggerate what was still a big collapse. The demise of small industrial establishments in the cities was closely monitored, both because the operations were centralized and because they were in the cities where foreign observers were most likely to visit. Urban manufacturing centers were also "affected first and most profoundly by the offensive of European industrial products" (Pamuk 1987: 110–11). However, much of the production in the Ottoman empire—like elsewhere in the poor periphery—was a rural household activity, shielded from the watchful eyes of British consuls, official travelers, and other observers. Furthermore, while spinning was a predominantly rural activity, contemporary observers referred mostly to the decline of weaving because the weaving that was destroyed was urban and visible. Spinning could have been even harder hit, but it was hidden in the rural hinterland.

Large capital-intensive factories were not common in the Ottoman empire, or anywhere in the poor periphery for that matter, hardly a surprising fact in a region where relative factor scarcities favored instead small-scale and labor-intensive technologies (Allen 2007a). Nevertheless, there were two waves of factory building in the Middle East during this period. The first wave occurred before the treaties, consisting of state-owned factories like Mohamed Ali's prototype establishments in Egypt. While they were protected by monopolies from the beginning, the factories were inefficient and lacked fuel, raw material inputs and skilled labor to operate equipment (Issawi 1982: 154). They were also poorly managed, and used dilapidated machinery of inadequate power (Owen 1993: 72 and 76). The liberal treaties ensured these factories a short life. The second wave appeared after the 1870s. These new factories were owned by private interests, and they received little or no financial support from the state. Although Quataert thinks that these factories expanded rapidly in number, both Issawi and Pamuk disagree, arguing that this second wave was also modest (Quataert 1994: 901; Issawi 1982: 155–58; Pamuk 1987: 127) and that their production was still very small compared to handicrafts. Modest perhaps, but that second wave certainly looks like a supply response to a much more favorable price environment facing local manufacturing. And while it may be true that Turkish (no longer Ottoman) industrialization really took hold only in the 1930s (Issawi 1982: 159), it might be relevant to point out that the terms of trade took a nose dive during this decade as well.

We have argued that relative factor prices did not make capital-intensive industry profitable in the Ottoman empire. In addition Quataert (1992: 6–10) offers three additional reasons for the lack of capital-intensive industrialization: population density, religion, and wars. He argues that population density fostered local industry by creating local demand, and while the Balkans had the empire's greatest population density and the most pervasive industry, the Arab provinces were very thinly populated and had the least industry. Correlation is not causation, and couldn't this local demand just as easily have been satisfied by foreign imports? As for Quataert's second reason, why was the Muslim religion incompatible with large-scale industry in the Balkans when it was compatible with it in Egypt? Quataert's third reason seems more plausible, namely that the wars waged by the Ottomans may have delayed technology transfer at a time when such assimilation would have been crucial. In any case, no hard evidence is offered in support of these propositions. In its absence we will explore more mundane explanations—factor endowments and the external terms of trade.

7.5   The Ottoman External Terms of Trade

Figure 3.7 plots the net barter terms of trade for the Ottoman empire (the ratio of the price of exports p_X to the price of imports p_M) covering the century 1800 to 1913. As it turns out, the first half of the century was probably the most crucial one. For comparison, figure 3.7 also plots Egypt from 1796 to 1913, the Levant from 1839 to 1913 (present-day Iraq, Israel, Lebanon, Palestine, Jordan, and Syria), and the Middle East region as a whole.

Like most of the periphery, the Ottoman empire specialized in the export of primary products, while importing manufactures, so between 1800 and 1854 p_X refers to an unweighted average of wheat, wool, raisins, figs, tobacco, opium, and raw silk. These seven prices are taken as an unweighted average because the share of each commodity in total exports is not available until 1879, although we know those weights changed dramatically over the decades before the late 1870s. The p_M refers to what were primarily manufactured goods and intermediate inputs, and it is proxied by British export prices.

As we saw in chapter 3, between 1800 and the late 1860s the price of British manufactured exports fell far faster than did the price of British imported primary products, swinging the terms of trade against Britain and in favor of the periphery (figure 3.4). If p_M for the Ottoman empire moved anything like p_X for Britain, then the Ottoman empire certainly received a massive positive price shock over those 45 years before the Crimean War decade. The magnitudes were enormous: over the four decades up to the late 1850s, the Ottoman terms of trade rose almost 2.6 times, for an annual rate of 2.4 percent. Hence domestic resources were pulled in to commodity export sectors, while the glut of cheap, foreign manufactures flowed into the empire, pushing domestic resources out of industry and perhaps even out of some nontradable activities.

Between 1855–1859 and 1875–1879, terms of trade trends reversed, falling by 27 percent. Over the three decades or so between the late 1870s and World War I, the terms of trade was relatively stable, drifting up at a modest annual rate of 0.4 percent. Furthermore all of the pre–World War I rise took place after 1896.

To summarize, if we are looking for evidence of a big de-industrialization shock on the Ottoman empire, we should see plenty of it in the half century before the late 1850s when its terms of trade soared. We should see little or no evidence of de-industrialization between the late 1850s and the mid-1890s, when the boom subsided and the terms of trade were quite stable. And we should see only very modest evidence of de-industrialization in the two decades before World War I when the rise in the terms of trade was also modest. These predictions are confirmed by the de-industrialization evidence.

Were these terms of trade trends common to all parts of the empire? Issawi claims that the terms of trade improved for both Syria and Iraq between 1836 and 1913. He bases his claim concerning Syria on the prices of raw silk and cocoons prevailing in Beirut from 1836 to 1913 and on prices for some other commodities exported from Aleppo between 1891 and 1913. His claims for Iraq are based on an unweighted five-commodity index covering the period from 1864 to 1913. Issawi extrapolates both the Syrian and Iraqi terms of trade backward, concluding that the terms of trade improved there from 1800 to 1913 (Issawi 1988: 147–51). These estimates are consistent with the de-industrialization experience in that part of the empire: "it destroyed a large part of the handicrafts both directly through competition and indirectly by turning consumers' taste to western-type goods," without causing technology spillovers or import substitution (Issawi 1988: 151).

Figure 3.7 offers an index of the terms of trade for Egypt between 1796 and 1913, as well as the Ottoman empire between 1800 and 1913, and the Levant between 1839 and 1913. The spectacular rise in the Egyptian terms of trade between 1820–1824 and 1856–1860, 2.7 percent per annum, is even bigger than that of the Ottoman empire over the same period, 2.3 percent per annum: cotton prices rose even more in world markets than did the Ottoman export mix of wheat, wool, fruits, silk, tobacco, and opium. These terms of trade figures imply an even bigger de-industrialization impact on Egypt than on the rest of the Middle East, spelling especially bad luck for Ali's early experiments with Egyptian industrialization. Over the two decades after the late 1850s, the Egyptian terms of trade fell by almost 11 percent, less than half the fall experienced by the Ottomans, 27 percent, and thus presumably less stimulation to import-competing industry. Finally, in the three decade run up to World War I, the Egyptian terms of trade drifted upward at roughly the same modest rate as elsewhere in the Middle East (0.5 vs. 0.4 percent per annum).

7.6   Neo-Ricardian Economics in the Ottoman Setting

Booming terms of trade must have contributed to Ottoman de-industrialization in the 19th century through Dutch disease effects. As export prices rose, labor, capital, and other resources would have been pulled out of failing industry (and nontradable sectors) and into the thriving export sector so as to augment its capacity. The size of the Dutch disease effects could, of course, have been moderated or intensified by anti-global or pro-global policies, but other domestic supply-side forces might well have augmented or diminished Ottoman competitiveness with foreign manufactures.

During the century before about 1860, most foodstuffs for village peasants and the urban working class (like maize and fava beans) were not traded internationally, and foodstuffs were a very large share of family budgets. Under those conditions, labor productivity in the nontraded part of food production must have influenced manufacturing competitiveness. After all, in a pre-industrial economy with relatively stable subsistence wages, any decline in Ottoman food productivity would have put upward pressure on food prices and thus on the nominal wage in every nonfood sector, eroding competitiveness with foreign producers. Alternatively, any rise in Ottoman food productivity or increase in arable land in the interior would have had the opposite effect. But there was another Ottoman force at work too, a force absent in Mexico (chapter 8) and India (chapter 6). As the Ottoman empire became more integrated into world commodity markets, increased specialization took the form of rising exports not only of wool, silk, and opium but also of foodstuffs like wheat, figs, raisins, and even barley. Thus, any rise in the price of traded grains and fruit would have put more upward pressure on food prices and thus on the nominal wage in every nonfood sector, eroding competitiveness with foreign producers. This would have been manifested by rising food prices relative to other products, by falling profitability in manufacturing, and by a decline in industrial output.

Which of these domestic supply-side forces dominated the Ottoman empire, especially before the 1860s? The global trade boom must have raised the price of exportable food stuffs at home, augmenting nominal wages and reducing competitiveness in import-competing textiles and other manufacturing activities. Increasing commercial crop land-use must have competed with locally consumed foodstuffs, raising their price still further. But these forces would have been offset by the increase in arable land in the interior, thus lowering the price of locally consumed foodstuffs, at least in the pre-railroad era. What was the net effect of all these complex forces on the relative price of food?

Chapter 6 applied an explicit and testable Lewis-like model to British India, and it worked well in helping account for the spectacular demise of Indian manufacturing in the face of British competition after 1750. We will see in the next chapter that it also works well in helping account for exceptional Mexican success in minimizing the damage inflicted by foreign imports on its domestic textile industry. But conditions were quite different in the Ottoman empire to the extent that it was a major exporter of foodstuffs, in contrast with India and Mexico. So how do the Ricardian economics work when applied to the Ottoman empire?

Since the Ricardian model was fully elaborated in chapter 4, we can cover the same territory much more briefly here. Again, we assume a perfectly competitive economy in which there are three sectors: textiles: the manufacturing importable (T); wheat, fruit, opium, silk, and wool—the primary-product commodity exportables (C); and maize and beans, the nontradable foodstuffs (F). Assume that textiles and commodity exports are traded in world markets and sell for the world prices p_T and p_C, respectively,[7] while p_F is determined endogenously by local supply and demand. Labor (L) is assumed to be mobile between all three sectors and paid the nominal wage w. For greatest clarity, the model continues to abstract from capital and land. Finally, since we will show below that the Lewis assumption of real wage stability holds for most of the Ottoman 19th century, the model assumes that it was constant in food units.

Since the nominal wage is equal to the price of a unit of food, village employment in food production is fixed. Growth in the own wage in textile production (w/p_T) leads to a decline in the absolute number of workers employed there. Thus absolute de-industrialization results from an increase in the own wage in textiles. There are three forces pushing the own wage (and thus wage competitiveness with imports), one foreign and two domestic. First, the own wage in textiles would increase if the world price for its output fell (i.e., if the Ottoman external terms of trade rose due to a fall in the price of imports). Second, it would also increase if the nominal wage rose in response to a rise in food prices, induced in turn by some negative shock to local food output productivity, or, third, it would increase by a rise in the price of exported wheat. One source of such negative shocks would have been the shift of food production off high yielding hectares to accommodate the expansion of wheat, fruit, and tobacco cultivation, a shift encouraged by booming world export prices.

Relative de-industrialization will result whenever the own wage in textiles is growing fast compared to that in wheat and other commodity exports. Moreover, holding employment shares constant, de-industrialization will be most severe when the difference in own wage growth rates is largest, and this can only result when the external terms of trade booms ($p_C^* > p_T^*$), since, by assumption, w^* is everywhere the same in the domestic economy. As it turns out, own wage growth in wheat and other commodity exports would have to be even higher to counteract the relative de-industrialization effect of own wage growth in textiles. In short, we expect to see relative de-industrialization whenever own wage growth in textiles is positive, unless own wage growth in commodity exports is much greater. Own wage growth in the commodity export sector seems unlikely to the extent that nominal wages and prices in export sectors, like wheat, should have been moving alike, but any own wage growth in the export sector would have dampened the de-industrialization effect because it would have reduced L_C, which is in the denominator of the relative de-industrialization measure. As the share of the labor force employed in commodity exports increases, the greater the growth in the own wage in textiles needs to be to overcome growth of the own wage in the export sector and thus for de-industrialization to ensue. Thus relative de-industrialization in the Ottoman empire should have been most severe when nominal wage growth was strongest and when the terms of trade were shifting most strongly in favor of wheat and other commodity exports.

7.7 Assessing the Causes of Ottoman De-industrialization

It appears that the evidence in table 7.1 is consistent with our simple neo-Ricardian model. First, we invoked the Lewis assumption of stable real wages, and they were indeed stable, at least over the first eighty years of the 19th century. Second, the model predicted that a rapid rise of the own wage in manufacturing (here proxied by textiles), especially compared with the commodity export sector, would generate powerful de-industrialization forces. And indeed we find that the own wage in textiles rose most rapidly between 1800 and 1860–3.5 percent per annum—precisely the decades of most dramatic de-industrialization. Third, the rise in the own wage in manufacturing between 1800 and 1860 was being pushed partly by a nominal wage boom (1 percent per annum), accounting for 29 percent of the own wage increase—but mostly by the collapse in manufactures prices (–2.4 percent per annum)—accounting for 71 percent of the own wage increase. Fourth, the predicted rise in food prices seems to have taken place as the consumer price index (dominated by foodstuffs) doubled between 1800 and 1860. The rising CPI pushed up the nominal wage by almost the same amount—confirming the predictions of Alexander Gerschenkron, W. Arthur Lewis, and Adam Smith, thereby diminishing Ottoman wage competitiveness in manufacturing.

Fifth, the rise of the own wage in manufacturing slowed down between 1860 and 1880 to 1.5 percent per annum—precisely the decades when de-industrialization rates diminished and when there was even some evidence of re-industrialization. Furthermore, during these two decades the

Table 7.1
Wage and price trends for the Ottoman empire (1860 = 100)

Item	1800	1860	1880	1913
Nominal wages	55	100	103	156
Consumer prices	50	100	86	106
Real wages	110	100	114	148
Imported textile prices: c.i.f	430	100	76	63
Wheat export prices: f.o.b.	126	100	86	90
Other export foodstuff prices: f.o.b.	127	100	92	84
All export foodstuff prices: f.o.b.	127	100	89	87
Raw material export prices: f.o.b.	114	100	63	54
All export prices: f.o.b.	123	100	65	55
Own wage in textiles	13	100	136	248
Own wage in exports	45	100	158	284
Price exports/price imports	46	100	83	89

Sources: Pamuk and Williamson (2009: table 2). Nominal wages in unskilled construction and consumer prices are in grams of silver (Istanbul).

modest rise in the nominal wage (0.1 percent per annum) accounts for only 7 percent increase in the own wage in manufacturing, while the fall in manufacturing prices (−1.4 percent per annum) accounts for 93 percent. Sixth, and finally, the neo-Ricardian model loses its relevance in the late 19th century as the real wage rises quite impressively after 1880 to 0.8 percent per annum—presumably because the rate of productivity advance in both the export and import competing sectors rose.

Next table 7.2 reports an effort to identify the domestic sources of Ottoman de-industrialization that supported the external sources coming from the terms of trade boom. The table focuses on *changes* in Ottoman policy and the appearance of the railroads penetrating the interior in the late 19th century.[8] The importance of these two changing domestic forces should be judged by comparing them with the dramatic 260 percent increase in the external terms of trade between 1800 and 1860 (table 7.1). While domestic policy and the railroads also fostered de-industrialization, these domestic forces were pretty modest compared with the impact of changing world market conditions in the six decades before 1860.

Consider first the impact of the Ottoman free trade treaties of 1838 to 1841 about which so much has been written. Table 7.2 estimates that this oft-cited liberal move raised p_X/p_M in Ottoman ports and coastal cities by only 7 percent, a trivial impact compared with the 260 percent rise in p_X/p_M coming from world market forces. True, the policy impact was twice as big in the Ottoman interior (15 percent), but it was still relatively small even there. Ottoman policies in the 1860s had the opposite effect, reducing the terms of trade by 14 percent in both coast and interior, thus favoring industry. Since world market forces alone caused p_X/p_M to fall by 17 percent between 1860 and 1880 (table 7.1), the combination of Ottoman policy and world markets served to reduce the relative price of manufactures (p_M) by 31 percent, an event that must have greatly eased the de-industrialization pressures on local manufacturing. Neither the external terms of trade nor Ottoman policy changed much thereafter, so coastal industry was neither penalized nor rewarded. Things were different in the interior, however, as the railroads opened up those markets to import penetration by foreign manufactures and to primary product exports to world markets. Table 7.2 estimates that the terms of trade in the interior rose by 28 percent, as declining transport costs served to push exportable (e.g., wheat) prices up to world levels and to push importable (e.g., textiles) prices down to world levels.[9] So, while de-industrialization forces were quiet on the Ottoman coast after 1860, they were still a presence in the Ottoman interior.

Table 7.2

Impact of Ottoman policy and railroads on p_X/p_M in 1800 to 1913: Percentage impact on price

	Coastal		Interior	
	Imports	Exports	Imports	Exports
Policy and transport cost conditions before free trade treaties, 1838–1841				
Import tariff or export tax	3	3	3	3
Tax on interior trade	0	0	8	8
Transport cost	0	0	25	43
Policy and transport cost conditions from free trade treaties to 1860				
Import tariff or export tax	5	12	5	12
Tax on interior trade	0	0	0	8
Transport cost	0	0	25	43
Policy and transport cost conditions, 1861–1869				
Import tariff or export tax	8	1	8	1
Tax on interior trade	0	0	0	8
Transport cost	0	0	25	43
Policy and transport cost conditions, 1870–1906				
Import tariff or export tax	8	1	8	1
Tax on interior trade	0	0	0	0
Transport cost	0	0	18	18
Policy and transport cost conditions, 1907–1913				
Import tariff or export tax	11	1	11	1
Tax on interior trade	0	0	0	0
Transport cost	0	0	18	18
Changes in 1838–1841: assuming no change in transport cost (pre-rails)				
Total p_M or p_X	+2	+9	−6	+9
p_X/p_M	+7		+15	
Changes in 1860: assuming no change in transport cost (pre-rails)				
Total p_M or p_X	+3	−11	+3	−11
p_X/p_M	−14		−14	
Changes in 1870: including change in transport cost (rails)				
Transport cost	0	0	−7	+21
Total p_M or p_X	0	0	−7	+21
p_X/p_M	0		+28	
Changes in 1907: assuming no change in transport cost (post-rails)				
Total p_M or p_X	+3	0	+3	0
p_X/p_M	−3		−3	

7.8   The Eastern Mediterranean versus the Rest of the Periphery

How does the terms of trade boom for the Ottoman empire and the rest of the eastern Mediterranean compare with Latin America, Asia, and the European periphery? Figure 3.4 documented terms of trade performance for the five major regions in the poor periphery between 1796 and 1913, where each region is a population-weighted average of individual countries. Figure 3.4 does not break out the country experience of which the five regions are aggregates, but table 3.1 and the original source does (Williamson 2008).

First and most important, the secular terms of trade boom was even bigger in Egypt and the Ottoman empire than in the rest of the poor periphery. If we ignore the few years around 1820 when the terms of trade spikes, it appears that India and the rest of South Asia underwent relatively modest improvements in its terms of trade from 1800 to the mid-1820s, and in fact it *fell* thereafter up to 1850. Over the half century up to the late 1850s, India's terms of trade rose less than 0.5 percent per annum. No doubt this was a significant secular price shock, but it was *far* smaller than what happened in Egypt, the Ottoman empire, and the Middle East as a whole. The Latin American terms of trade increased by 1.7 percent per annum between 1820–1824 and 1855–1859. The Ottoman terms of trade increased by 2.4 percent per annum over the same period while the Indonesian terms of trade (which dominates the Southeast Asia regional experience) increased by 2.5 percent per annum. The Egyptian terms of trade rose by 2.7 percent per annum up to the late 1850s. In short, Egypt and the Ottoman empire underwent one of the biggest terms of trade booms in the poor periphery. It is therefore no surprise that the region also underwent one of the biggest de-industrialization experiences.

What went up then came down with a crash, as the terms of trade fell everywhere in the periphery from the 1870s or 1890s to World War II. But Egypt and the Ottoman empire reached a relatively early peak in their terms of trade, the series leveling off and even falling after the 1850s and 1860s. This implies that de-industrialization forces lost their power much earlier in the region than in Latin America and other parts of the poor periphery where their terms of trade continued to rise during the late 19th century.

8 A Latin American De-industrialization Illustration: Mexican Exceptionalism

8.1 Mexico in the Latin American Mirror

Latin America underwent a steady increase in its terms of trade from the 1810s to the early 1890s, and the improvement was especially dramatic during the first few decades. Its quality-adjusted terms of trade probably grew at about 2.2 percent per annum over the four decades up to the late 1850s, and about 1.4 percent annum over the eight decades up to the early 1890s (figure 3.4 and table 3.1). This was a very big terms of trade boom, but up to 1870 it was considerably less pronounced than it was in almost everywhere else in the poor periphery. Thus Ceylon, Egypt, the Ottoman empire, Indonesia, the Philippines, Russia, Italy, and Spain all had greater terms of trade booms up to 1870 than did most of the new Latin American republics.

Of course, a terms of trade boom does not guarantee fast GDP growth. Indeed chapter 1 showed that during the 19th century terms of trade boom, rates of technological advance, and human capital accumulation were so modest in the poor periphery that the living standard gap between it and the industrial countries rose to levels that were much wider in 1913 than in 1800. All economic historians agree that the terms of trade boom caused de-industrialization in the poor periphery through Dutch disease effects. Whether these negative Dutch disease effects offset the positive gains from trade has, however, never been resolved until recently, but chapter 11 will confirm that the terms of trade boom never raised long-run growth in the poor periphery, and terms of trade volatility lowered it. But whether the modest rates of technological advance and human capital accumulation in the poor periphery were *caused* by de-industrialization has still not been resolved.

This chapter establishes that Mexico obeyed the same laws of motion as the rest of the poor periphery during the century before the 1870s. However, the magnitudes were quite different, so different that we will speak of Mexican *exceptionalism*. Since the rate of de-industrialization was far less than elsewhere in the periphery, it suggests that either Dutch disease forces were weaker, or that there were offsetting local forces at work, or both. These local forces served to blunt de-industrialization during the first half century of the republican era, sufficiently so to give Mexico a much more effective platform for modern industrialization[2] starting in the 1870s than almost anywhere else in the periphery (see chapter 12). The next section revisits chapter 5 and places Mexican de-industrialization in context. We then use the neo-Ricardian economics of chapter 4 to explore the sources of Mexican *exceptionalism*. It appears that there were three forces at work: first, the terms of trade and Dutch disease effects were weak compared with the rest of the periphery; second, Mexico maintained better wage competitiveness vis-à-vis the industrial countries compared with the rest of the periphery, a result determined by relative productivity performance in food production; and third, the Mexican republic had the autonomy—something that most of the poor periphery did not—to devise more pro-industrial policies. Between the 1820s and the 1870s the first two forces were far more important than the third, mainly because politically unstable and weak young republican governments did not introduce very effective pro-industrial and pro-growth policies.

8.2 Mexican De-industrialization in the Transition before *Porfiriato*

It is very important to distinguish between economywide productivity levels and rates of growth, on the one hand, and industrial output and employment performance, on the other. We start with the former before dealing with the latter.

Mexican Economic Growth: Bourbon Reform, *Insurgencia,* and Lost Decades

Debates about colonial growth in Mexico (or Nueva España, as the Spanish colony was called) have been lively, mostly because the evidence is so scarce. Some take an optimistic view (Klein 1998; Dobado Gonzáles and Marrero 2001, 2005a; Ponzio 2005). Indeed Angus Maddison (2003) estimates that Mexican per capita GDP was about 77 percent of the continental European periphery in 1820,[1] and that it was well ahead of Asia and Africa. Some take a more pessimistic view. John Coatsworth (2003, 2005) has documented stagnation between 1700 and 1800, followed by the economic disruption caused by *Insurgencia* (1810–1821).[2] Maddison's estimates are more optimistic, and reveal the apparent belief that economic disruption during *Insurgencia* had no lasting impact. Note, however, that both authors document a significant increase in Mexican GDP during the 18th century: Maddison estimates a doubling between 1700 and 1820, while Coatsworth estimates an increase by 2.3 times between 1700 and 1800. Thus the difference in their per capita GDP growth estimates lies with very different views about population change.[3]

Debate over GDP per capita levels and growth before 1820 will, no doubt, continue, but there is other evidence supporting significant economic achievement in 18th-century Nueva España. For example, the urban share of the population was at least 9.1 percent around 1800.[4] This figure was higher than that of Scandinavia, Ireland, Germany, France, Switzerland, Portugal, Austria-Hungary, and Poland, and very close to the European 10 percent average (de Vries 1984: table 3.8). This urban performance seems impressive for a pre-industrial economy, especially for one in the new world that was land abundant and labor scarce. Growing towns implied declining agricultural self-sufficiency, rising commercialization, developing internal markets, and an industrial base equivalent to the proto-industrial platform from which Germany, France, Switzerland, and so much of the rest of the European continent was to develop their industrial revolutions between 1800 and 1870 (Mendels 1972; Mokyr 1993: chs. 1–3; Weisdorf 2006).

While the debate about Mexican growth before the *Insurgencia* may be intense, there is far less disagreement about its growth between the *Insurgencia* and the start of the *Porfiriato*. During the five "lost decades" from 1820 to 1870, the per capita GDP growth rate estimates range between –0.2 (Maddison 2003) and +0.3 (Coatsworth 2003) percent per annum, for an average of hardly any growth at all.[5] These lost decades took place when the European and North American economies were undergoing industrial revolutions and vigorous modern economic growth. Most analysts of the poor economic performance during the lost decades point to post-independence institutional weakness and political instability (Ponzio 2005). Others would, no doubt, emphasize the legacy of inefficient colonial institutions and culture (Harrison 1985; Engerman and Sokoloff 1997; Landes 1998; Acemoglu et al. 2002).

Foreign Trade and Openness

Commerce between Spain and Spanish America was strictly regulated until 1765. Only one port in Spain—Cádiz—and four in America—Cartagena, Portobelo, La Habana, and Veracruz—were authorized to trade. The rationale for this system was to make it easier for the Crown to collect taxes on its colonial trade. Some observers argued that the trade regulations actually hurt the Crown, since they limited commerce and thus the tax potential. They reasoned that lower taxes, more ports, fewer smugglers, and a pro-global policy would increase Crown revenue. The Crown listened, and in 1765 restrictions regulating commerce between Spain and Spanish America were substantially reduced. By 1789 Nueva España had gone open. But how open?

As is common in the trade-development literature, openness is defined here as the trade share, that is, exports plus imports as a share of GDP. The trade share averaged 9.6 percent between 1796 and 1820, 12.5 percent between the mid-1820s and the mid-1850s, and 17 percent by 1872 (Dobado Gonzáles et al. 2008: figure 1). The 1796 to 1820 trade share was higher than that of France in 1815 (8.4 percent; Mitchell 2003: 571 and 905), and comparable to the United States. Thus the late colonial and the early post-colonial Mexican economy was open by the standards of that time.

The structure of Nueva España's foreign trade with the Atlantic economy can be summarized without much exaggeration as an exchange of silver, augmented by cochineal,[6] for textiles (table 8.1). Pacific trade with Asia was similar, mainly consisting of textile (and handicraft) imports and silver

Table 8.1
Mexican textile imports/total imports and silver exports/total exports, 1802 to 1872 (in percent)

	Textiles	Silver
1802	72.9	63.7
1803	84.9	42.2
1804	53.0	56.3
1805	23.8	3.5
1806	39.4	36.5
1807	62.8	52.0
1808	50.4	56.4
1809	40.1	57.9
1821	62.5	84.0
1823	59.0	56.5
1824	68.1	62.2
1825	63.9	72.5
1826	63.9	77.6
1827	70.5	79.5
1828	58.6	85.5
1856	59.9	96.3
1872	52.0	80.1

Source: Dobado et al. (2008: table 1).

exports through the *Galeón de Manila*. Independence did not bring about a substantial change in the structure of foreign trade, dictated as it was by fundamental resource endowments and geographical location. Indeed export specialization was reinforced, and textiles kept their dominant position among imported items. The textile import share in total imports was almost 65 percent in the decade before the *Insurgencia*[7] and about 63 percent in the decade thereafter. Thus the new republic's foreign trade mix was much like that of the colonial period—silver in exchange for textiles.

8.3   De-industrialization and Industrialization in Young Republican Mexico

As chapter 5 pointed out, textiles are a very big share of manufacturing activity in all economies embarking on modern economic growth, and Mexico was no exception. Manuel Miño Grijalva estimates that cotton textile production in Nueva España was a little more than 5 million pesos by the end of the 18th century, or between 60 and 70 percent of total manufacturing production (7 to 8 million pesos).[8] Fortunately, textiles are also the best documented manufacturing activity for Nueva España and republican Mexico. Thus this chapter's account of Mexican de-industrialization over the century or so before 1877 will focus on woolens and cottons.

Domestic Textiles and Industry, before 1820

Richard Salvucci (1992: 222–23, 237) estimates that *obraje* production (integrated woolen textile manufactories with as much as one hundred workers employed) rose from about 1.5 million pesos in 1600 to between 1.5 and 2 million pesos in 1700. Woolen textiles underwent a sharp secular decline late in the colonial era, so that by the end of the 18th century production had decreased to between 1 and 1.5 million pesos, and was negligible by 1812. The *obrajes* heyday had passed by the 1810s. While 40 *obrajes* were operating in 1579 Nueva España, there were only 30 in 1770 and 19 in 1810. Increasingly woolen textile production was carried out in domestic workshops (*trapiches*), which "expanded in Querétaro from 30 to 340 between 1693 and 1803" (Salvucci 1992: 211).

The rise of *trapiches* was part of a cost-reducing response to the inflow of cheap foreign cloth, reflected by a steep decline in the price of textiles relative to corn (figure 8.1). After 1750 the Mexican woolen industry had to face increasingly fierce competition from imported British and Catalan

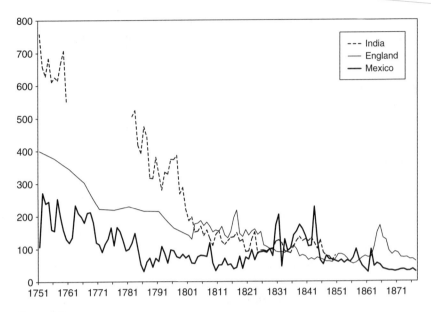

Figure 8.1
Grain price of textiles, Mexico versus England and India, 1751 to 1877 (p_T/p_C 1828 = 100).
Source: Data underlying Clingingsmith and Williamson (2008)

cloth as well as from a growing domestic cotton textile industry. While foreign cotton goods certainly penetrated the Mexican market, domestic cotton textile firms fared much better than did *obrajes* in the competition. Indeed cotton textiles expanded in Nueva España between 1750 to 1800, and by the end of the century cotton textile production was far more important than woolens: there were about 11,000 Castillian treadle looms working in Nueva España by 1800, of which 87 percent were weaving cotton (Miño 1998: 583). This cotton textile production was based on a putting-out system similar to that which flourished in proto-industrial Europe, and it was located mainly around the cities of Puebla, Tlaxcala, Mexico, and Guadalajara (Miño 1998: 79–107; 1993: 170).

The cotton textile industry diversified in the second half of the 18th century, evolving from the production of only basic cotton drill (*manta*) to calico prints (*indianas*, *pintadas* or *zarazas*) (Thomson 1991: 259). Several *indianilla* factories were established in Nueva España, and specialized in printing and finishing cotton yarn and cloth produced by the domestic putting-out system or imported from China and India. These factories were similar to those that were being developed in Catalonia, and they represented the most elaborate manufacturing organization that had yet appeared in Nueva España (Miño 1998: 185–93). There were several of these *indianilla* factories, and one in Mexico City employed close to 500 workers in 1804.[9]

Although *obrajes* underwent a steep secular decline in the late 18th century, cotton textiles underwent an even steeper rise, and total textile production expanded. The number of looms increased from 1,323 in 1781, to 9,981 in 1793, and to 11,692 in 1801, providing work for approximately 90,000 spinners and weavers in 1800 (Miño 1998: 285–87; Thomson 1991: 258). Cotton textile manufacturing flourished partly because European imports were cut off by wartime conflict. The good times ended after 1802 when a change in Spanish policy allowed neutral powers to trade directly with Nueva España, triggering an invasion of foreign cloth.[10] Between 1802 and the 1830s Mexican textiles faced the most intense foreign competition they had ever experienced.

The War of Independence (1810–1821) raised de-industrialization forces to "apocalyptic" proportions (Miño 1998: 270), and it hit hardest those regions where the textile industry was concentrated, Bajío and Puebla-Tlaxcala. Raw materials became scarce, and the commercial routes to the north, traditionally an important market for domestic textile production, were cut off. Many textile workers abandoned their looms to join the contending armies, and many died as a consequence of epidemics (Salvucci 1992: 238; Miño 1998: 269–72; Thomson 2002: 245). The *Insurgencia* delivered the death blow to the woolen *obrajes*: Querétaro could report only four still working in 1812.

Cotton textile production was also greatly affected by the intense post-1802 foreign competition. The Consulate of Mexico reported that in 1818 foreign trade had left 12,000 textile workers unemployed. The city of Puebla, where an important part of the cotton cloth industry was located, experienced a population decrease of 19 percent from 1791 to 1821. Guadalajara's cotton textile production "was virtually eliminated by competition from imports through the newly opened Pacific ports" (Miño 1998: 269). Although the cotton textiles sector was heavily damaged, it survived these three decades of foreign competition and *insurgencia*, and it had fully recovered by the 1830s (Thomson 1991: 244–45; 2002: 260 and 275).

The literature offers several competing explanations for the demise of Mexico's woolen textile sector. In an influential book Salvucci (1987) favored domestic demand. His argument was that woolen textiles were an inferior good: as household incomes and living standards rose, consumption and thus production of *obrajes* fell. But, as we saw above, it is not clear that income per capita actually rose in the 18th century, and given new estimates of a real wage decline (figure 8.5), Salvucci's domestic demand led hypothesis loses its plausibility. In any case, since the logic of Salvucci's domestic demand–led hypothesis requires that Nueva España be viewed as a closed economy, it must be rejected. In a small open economy like colonial Nueva España, domestic demand could not have influenced the relative price of goods actively traded in world markets. If instead the reader thinks that the economy *was* closed, and that income or taste changes were causing domestic demand to shift away from woolens to cottons, then we ought to see a rise in the price of cotton relative to woolen cloth across the 18th century. We do not. Nueva España mimics world relative cloth price trends, and they certainly do not confirm Salvucci's hypothesis. Instead, relatively rapid productivity events in cotton spinning and weaving abroad served to drive down the relative price of cotton goods.

Enrique Florescano thought that the agrarian crisis at the end of the 18th century must have had depressing effects on manufacturing.[11] He reasoned that the sharp increase in corn prices in 1771 to 1772, in 1785 to 1786, and 1809 to 1811 affected the *obrajes* and the cotton textile workshops in several ways. First, the agricultural crises also raised the cost of raw materials (cotton and wool), energy and transport (livestock costs). Second, it reduced available textile workers, since many left for the countryside given that they could no longer support themselves on prevailing urban wages, or were victims of famine and epidemics. Finally, and most important, Florescano thought the agrarian crisis resulted in a general collapse in purchasing power: the upward pressure on food costs reduced the household surplus available for other goods like textiles, causing a fall in textile demand and a decrease in *obraje* output. We agree with the first step in Florescano's argument since real wages fell steeply from the 1750s to the 1800s (figure 8.5). However, we do not agree with his last step since domestic demand could not have played anything but a modest role in this open economy.

The rise in food costs that Florescano stressed (and that figure 8.4 will confirm) put upward pressure on the nominal wage and thus served to reduce competitiveness in domestic textiles: labor costs must have risen while textile prices fell. While woolen textile production declined during the last decades of the 18th century, cotton textile production grew until 1802. Thus the effects of the agrarian crisis were different for cotton and woolen manufacturing, which indicates that cotton textiles were in a better position to adapt to rising input costs than were woolens. We shall

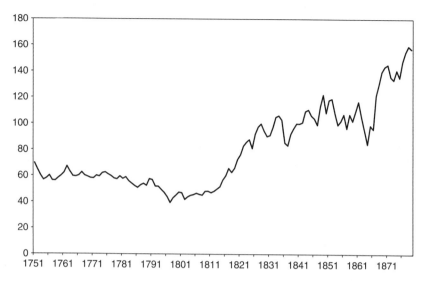

Figure 8.2
Mexican external terms of trade, 1751 to 1879 (1828 = 100).
Source: Dobado et al. (2008: fig. 2)

return to these supply-side forces since they may be central to understanding Mexican de-industrialization.

While falling domestic demand did not cause the demise of woolen textiles after the 1790s, the invasion of foreign textiles clearly did. That invasion was carried in large part by rapid, factory-based productivity advances in Britain, cheap new supplies that crowded out cottage industry in Mexico and everywhere else in the world's periphery. Driven by the productivity gains, the cost of British cottons fell by as much as 70 percent between 1790 and 1812 (chapter 3). Compared with Nueva España's key export product, silver, textile prices collapsed after around 1805 or so (figure 8.2). This dramatic increase in the terms of trade provoked de-industrialization,[12] although, as we will see, its effects were cushioned by a persistent wage competitiveness and, probably to a lesser extent, by protectionist policies introduced by the first republican governments.

Domestic Textiles and Industry, 1820 to 1877
While Mexican (and other Latin American[13]) textile manufactures struggled against foreign imports during the first third of the 19th century, contemporary observers thought it was a losing battle. In 1827 the English diplomat Henry George Ward saw a dismal future for local textiles, writing:

. . . until the end of the last century the value of cotton manufactures was estimated in five million dollars. Currently, they are gradually disappearing, as a result of the more abundant supply of European manufactures, and probably they will cease to exist in the course of a few years. (Ward 1991: 73)

There was clear evidence of de-industrialization when Ward was writing. Indeed he must have been well aware of the fact that "in the capital of Oaxaca, where once 500 looms had clattered in the production of cotton cloth, a mere 50 were working in 1827" (Potash 1983: 27). But Ward's gloomy prediction did not materialize: just a decade later, the industry was experiencing substantial growth and was supplying a large domestic market. Mexico had 5.9 million inhabitants in 1820, the second largest population in the Western Hemisphere after the United States. Thus Mexico had a large domestic market in which to foster industrialization through protectionist policies.

Textile producers were united for protection during the 1820s, and in the early 1830s the government began to foster the establishment of mechanized factories through credit provided by the Banco de Avío, a development bank that supported industrialization, of which more will be said below. From 1835 onward, mechanized textile mills began to be established, and the industry grew at impressive rates during the following decade:

These mills were established around the same time that the Lowell mills were built, and only twenty years after the first mechanized mill was established in the United States. Brazil, the other precocious industrializer in Latin America, established its first mills in the 1840s. Yet, by 1853, it only had 8 mills with 4500 spindles while ten years earlier Mexico's textile manufacture included 59 mills with more than 100,000 spindles. (Gómez Galvarriato 1999: 192)

As in other places, mechanization of spinning preceded that of weaving, but as time went by, weaving began gradually to be carried out in factories as well. Cotton textile factory production grew rapidly in the late 1830s and early 1840s rising from 29 thousand kilos of yarn produced in 1838 to more than 3.7 million kilos in 1843 (table 8.2), while cloth production grew at an annual rate of 11 percent from 1838 to 1843. Growth in cotton textile production slowed down after that date, but the industry still continued to expand up to 1877. Looms and spindles increased by 138 and 241 percent, respectively, and the average firm increased in size as measured by spindles (up 58 percent) and looms (up 126 percent).[14] The cotton textile industry also modernized: while 37 percent of the mills in 1843 used men or mules as their power source and only 3 percent ran on

Table 8.2
Growth in the Mexican cotton textile industry, 1837 to 1879

Year	Number of factories	Number active spindles	Yarn (1,000 kilos)	Cloth (1,000 pieces)
1837				45
1838			29	109
1839			15	125
1840			257	88
1841			467	196
1842			358	218
1843	59	106,708	3,738	327
1844		112,188		508
1845	55	113,813	1,317	657
1853			3,348	875
1850–1857	48	119,278	3,351	727
1862	57	133,122	3,615	1,259
1879	89	253,594	2,925	3,255

Source: Dobado et al. (2008: table 2).
Note: 1850–1857 is a midpoint average.

steam, by 1879, 64 percent employed steam (Gómez Galvarriato 1999: 204–207).

The growth of the Mexican textile industry between the mid-1830s and late-1870s contrasts sharply with the devastating de-industrialization that took place in most parts the poor periphery. Thus Mexico underwent less dramatic de-industrialization up to the 1870s than did Asia and the rest of Latin America. Table 5.2 documented "only" a 17 percent fall in Mexico's per capita industrialization index between 1800 and 1860 (compared with 30 percent for the whole periphery), and the index actually rose between 1830 and 1860. Despite the de-industrialization damage up to the 1830s, Mexico still ranked ninth in machine cotton spinning world-wide in 1842, its spindles per capita just below Germany and Austria-Hungary, and far above Russia (Batou 1991: 185). Most important, recall that by the 1870s local textile producers claimed 60 percent of the domestic market (table 5.3), a fairly big number for a country that had been attacked by cheap European textiles for almost a century. The figures for India and the Ottoman empire were only 35 to 42 percent and 11 to 38 percent, respectively, both much lower than the Mexican 60 percent. Thus, despite the importance of foreign imports, Mexican textiles were doing better than the rest of the poor periphery.

8.4 Applying Neo-Ricardian Economics to Mexican De-industrialization

What were the domestic supply-side conditions that influenced Mexican competitiveness with foreign manufactures? During the century before the Porfiriato, when foodstuffs for peasants and urban workers (like corn and beans) were not traded internationally and when foodstuff expenditures represented a very large share of family budgets, agricultural productivity must have influenced manufacturing competitiveness. To repeat the argument, any decline in agricultural productivity in a pre-industrial economy with relatively stable subsistence wages must put upward pressure on food prices and thus also on nominal wages, eroding competitiveness in import-competing manufacturing. This would have been manifested by rising food prices relative to other products, by falling profitability in manufacturing, and by a decline in its output. As we saw in the previous two chapters, this story seems to work well in helping account for the spectacular demise of Indian and Ottoman manufacturing in the face of European competition after 1750. Now we will learn whether it also works for Mexico.

Since this simple neo-Ricardian model was presented previously, only a brief recap is needed to place it in Mexican context. Here, the three sectors are textiles, the importable (T); silver, the exportable (S); and corn,[15] the nontradable (C). The price of textiles (p_T) is taken to be the price of imports and the price of silver (p_S) to be the price of exports. Textiles and silver are assumed to be traded in world markets at the world prices p_T and p_S, while p_C is determined by local supply and demand. Labor costs a nominal wage (w) per unit economywide. Once again, we follow Lewis in assuming that the real wage in corn units was constant, and the evidence (as we will see below) seems to confirm the assumption.[16]

Since the nominal wage is equal to the price of corn, employment in the corn sector is fixed. The own wage in silver mining (w/p_S) or textile production (w/p_T) could increase due to a decline in the world price for its output or due to an increase in the nominal wage. The latter would increase if the price of corn rises, induced by some negative productivity shock to agricultural output. As we have seen previously, there are three predictions of this neo-Ricardian model: industrial employment will decrease if the own wage in textiles increases; the industrial employment share will decrease if own wage growth in textiles increases faster than the own wage growth in silver and other commodity exports; and productivity in corn production will be an important determinant of the nominal wage and thus competitiveness in domestic manufacturing. These predictions are, of course, made ceteris paribus. If other important forces were not constant— like productivity growth in manufacturing and mining, then these predictions might be technically correct but historically unimportant. However, the remainder of this chapter will show that they *were* historically important. Note also that the small country assumption is important: we assume that the price of textiles and silver were both determined outside the Mexican economy in world markets. This assumption can be readily justified as it applies to textiles, since Mexico was such a small market compared with Europe and Asia. The silver price assumption is another matter: was the price of silver really exogenous to the Mexican economy? Apparently so. Recall that silver is held as a *stock*: it is not consumed as an annual flow like wheat, coffee, or rubber. Thus, while Mexico certainly was a major silver producer (50 percent of the world production in 1801–1820, but only 14 percent in 1861–1875: Schmitz 1979), its annual production and export was a tiny share of the *stock* of world silver. Between 1750 and 1800, the share of Mexican production in the world stock was less than 2 percent, and from 1810 to 1870, it was less than 1 percent. Thus the mainstream literature (e.g., Flynn and Giraldez 1997; Schell 2001) argues that the price of silver was determined by *demand to hold the stock*, and that meant Chinese and Indian households plus governments on silver or bimetallic standards.

8.5 Trends in Mexican Terms of Trade, 1750 to 1877

To repeat, a rise in the terms of trade for a primary product exporter implies a fall in the relative price of import-competing manufactures, the bigger the rise, the bigger the penalty to home manufacturers. The timing and magnitude of such secular terms of trade shocks should have a powerful influence on de-industrialization experience. Mexico's increasing reliance on imported manufactures meant that as the world price of textiles, specifically, and manufactures, more generally, fell, Mexico's terms of trade improved. As chapter 3 showed, relative textile prices certainly fell dramatically the world around up to the 1850s "as the Industrial Revolution drove down the unit cost of production in the exporting countries" and "as technological innovations shifted supply curves downward" (Bulmer-Thomas 1994: p. 43). Mexico was no exception, but was that relative price decline *less dramatic* since it was exporting silver?

Terms of Trade Trends before 1828

For the half century before 1800, Mexican terms of trade trends are estimated by simply plotting the ratio of silver to textile prices, p_S/p_T. This estimate may seem crude, but we doubt that terms of trade reality deviated much from what is plotted in figure 8.2. After all, silver exports accounted for more than three-quarters of total exports and textiles accounted for almost two-thirds of total imports (table 8.1). For the period 1800 to 1828, the terms of trade is estimated by using the British export price index to proxy p_M[17] and, as before, by using silver prices to proxy p_X.

The terms of trade trends in figure 8.2 suggest a surprising moral. Deindustrialization or Dutch disease forces could not have been very strong during the half century before 1802, since the relative price of import-competing textiles did not fall. Rather, it rose. True, the terms of trade jumped up by 81 percent between 1802 and 1830, but, as we will discuss in a moment, it was stable afterward, and especially so when compared to the rest of Latin America (figure 8.3). Mexico failed to undergo the same kind of external terms of trade boom between 1750 and 1830 that the rest of the periphery did, and also the boom was limited to the two or three decades after 1802.[18] Mexican *exceptionalism* indeed!

Terms of Trade Trends after 1828

While primary product export prices were on a steep rise almost everywhere across the periphery in the 19th century, it appears that Mexico missed much of the boom (figure 8.3). Between 1828 and 1881 Mexico's terms of trade did indeed rise, and at 1.4 percent per annum (figure 3.6; Prados 2004: 34–35). However, all of that increase appears to have taken place *after* mid-century, since there was no upward trend in the terms of trade between 1828 and the early 1840s (figure 8.2).[19]

Figure 8.3 documents the secular boom in the terms of trade across the poor periphery between 1828 and 1860: it rose more slowly in Latin America, and more slowly still in Mexico, implying that Dutch disease forces were much weaker in Mexico than elsewhere over these three decades, perhaps even absent. In addition Mexico appears to have been exceptional relative to the poor European periphery, including Spain, Italy, and Russia (table 3.1).

What accounts for the relatively weak terms of trade boom in Mexico? It cannot be explained by a less dramatic fall in import prices, since every member of the poor periphery imported pretty much the same products, dominated by factory-made manufactures from Europe. Rather, the

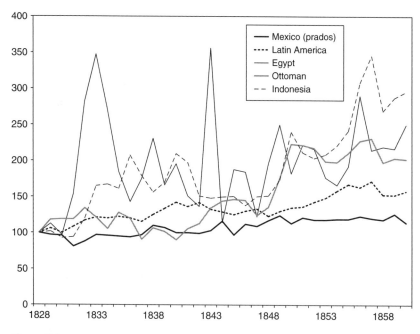

Figure 8.3
Terms of trade trends, 1828 to 1860: Mexico (based on Prados) versus other periphery.
Source: Dobado et al. (2008: fig. 4b)

explanation lies with export prices, namely that silver prices were stable when other primary product prices soared.

In summary, globalization-induced de-industrialization forces were relatively weak in Mexico between independence and the *Porfiriato*. Thus Mexican manufactures should have been in a stronger competitive position than the rest of a poor periphery where de-industrialization was more dramatic. Whether their competitive position was strong enough to repel or only retard the advance of invading foreign manufactures is, of course, another matter entirely.

8.6   Mexican Wage Competitiveness

Food Productivity and Wage Competitiveness
Dutch disease forces were weaker in Mexico than in the rest of the poor periphery but were there other causes of Mexican *exceptionalism*? One possibility might have been relatively stable agricultural productivity, an event that would have kept the price of nontradable foodstuffs from rising too

fast. We are not denying that agricultural productivity and living standards were low in Mexico: indeed as early as 1822 Alexander von Humboldt noted that Mexican agricultural productivity was low compared to western Europe. But he was talking about levels, not trends. Nor do we assert that there were no agrarian crises over the century before the 1870s, only that they were less deep and frequent than elsewhere. Our hypothesis is that the absence of any secular deterioration in agricultural labor productivity would have implied no upward pressure on food prices and the nominal wage, and that import-competing manufacturing would have had a better chance of maintaining its wage competitiveness with foreign producers. What are the facts?

Let us start with the trend in relative commodity prices. Figure 8.4 plots p_M/p_C and p_X/p_C, that is, the price of exports and imports relative to the key nontradable, corn. These relative price trends trace out two distinct epochs. First, there was the dramatic decline in the relative price of tradables in the 60 or 70 years up to the *Insurgencia* and independence. This decline penalized both the mining export industry and the textile import-competing industry, which contributed to de-industrialization by pulling resources out of manufacturing (and mining) and into agriculture. Note

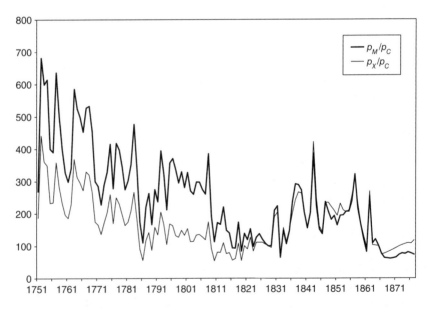

Figure 8.4
Price of tradables relative to nontradable corn in Mexico, 1751 to 1877 (1828 = 100).
Source: Dobado et al. (2008: fig. 5)

that the external terms of trade did not rise over this period (figure 8.2), so it was *not* a source of de-industrialization. But the rise in the price of corn relative to silver and textiles *was* a de-industrialization source, and it looks like it was powerful. The second epoch begins when that secular decline flattened out in the 1810s and turned around in the 1820s. Over the half century before the *Porfiriato*, there was one big cycle but no trend: p_M/p_C and p_X/p_C rose up to around 1850, an event that favored both mining and industry, and fell thereafter. One possible explanation for the absence of a rising trend in p_C is that after independence more people had access to land, and that there was an increase in the cultivated area. Furthermore, between 1821 and 1870 there were no famine episodes like those that took place earlier, between 1785 and 1786 and between 1809 and 1810 (Sánchez Santiró 2006; Chowning 1997). Figure 8.2 shows that the post-1810s were years of rising external terms of trade (albeit, much more modest than elsewhere in the poor periphery), events that penalized Mexican manufacturing and contributed to de-industrialization (albeit, much more modestly than elsewhere in the poor periphery). But trends in the internal terms of trade with agriculture had the opposite influence, and it looks like it might have dominated.

Next, what happened to the Mexican corn price of textiles (p_T/p_C) relative to its main competitors, England and India? Figure 8.1 plots p_T/p_C for England, India, and Mexico. The result is surprising: after about 1810 the relative price of textiles fell faster (the price of grains rose faster) in England and India than it did in Mexico! Thus, while the rise in grain prices tended to lower the relative price of textiles in all three countries, the grain price rise was bigger in England and much bigger in India. The explanation for this cannot be faster productivity growth in English factories (although it certainly was faster), since textiles were internationally traded and textile prices moved the same way the world around. Thus the explanation must lie with local productivity events in agriculture. The relative price of textiles fell much faster in India where a collapse in agricultural productivity after the mid- to late-18th century produced a spectacular rise in the relative price of grains, generating an immense upward pressure on the nominal wage and contributing to diminished wage competitiveness (chapter 6). While a lagging agriculture pushed up the relative price of foodstuffs in England, India, *and* Mexico, it was far less dramatic in Mexico.[20] Since all three countries were competing with the rest of the world for textile market shares at home and abroad, Mexico appears to have been relatively favored by a more modest rise in p_C. Of course, the fact that Britain took the technological lead in textiles gave it a big edge in world markets. But the point

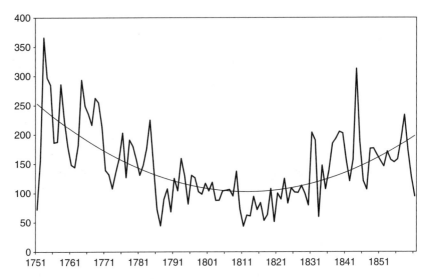

Figure 8.5
Estimated annual and smoothed Mexican grain wages (w/p_C), 1750 to 1860.
Source: Dobado et al. (2008: fig. 7)

of figure 8.6 is that domestic forces partially offset the British de-industrialization impact on Mexico.

Figure 8.5 shows quite clearly that there were other forces at work eroding Mexican grain wages, since they fell quite steeply from the mid-18th century until the 1810s. The downward trend in real wages just before Independence speaks badly for the impact of late colonial conditions on the working poor, and the upward trend after about 1820 speaks well for the impact of independence.[21] That pre-1820 fall should have strengthened wage competitiveness in textiles, while the post-1820 rise should have eroded it. Indeed figure 8.6 shows that while the own wage in textiles (w/p_T) was very stable in Mexico up to the late 1830s, it doubled from then to the 1850s. If we are looking for domestic de-industrialization sources, we have found it here in the three decades or so between the 1820s and 1850s.

To summarize, from 1751 to about 1810, w/p_T showed no trend in any of the three countries: thus Mexico maintained wage competitiveness with both England and India. While Mexican textiles may have increasingly lost its competitive edge in domestic markets by lagging behind in adapting modern technology, at least it did not make matters worse by undergoing a rise in wage costs. Between about 1810 and 1840, Mexican wage

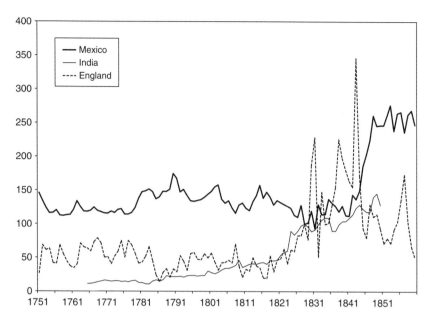

Figure 8.6
Own wage in Mexican, English, and Indian textiles, 1751 to 1860 (w/p_T 1828 = 100).
Source: Data underlying Clingingsmith and Williamson (2008)

competitiveness *improved* relative to England and India, helping domestic industry deal with de-industrialization forces coming from world markets. After about 1840, Mexico lost all the relative wage competitiveness it had gained.

During the century 1750 to 1877 as a whole, the combination of strong wage competitiveness and weak terms of trade effects minimized de-industrialization relative to the rest of the periphery.

8.7   Why Didn't Mexican Manufacturing Compete Even More Effectively?

Was Mexico's inability to compete more effectively with foreign producers before the 1820s, and perhaps even before the 1850s, due to the fact that Mexican wages were too high (even though their growth rates were not)? Of course! After all, Mexico and the rest of the Americas had a comparative advantage in primary products because they were relatively abundant in land and natural resources compared to Europe, and they had a comparative disadvantage in manufactures because they were relative scarce in labor compared to Europe. Thus import-competing textiles and other manufactures *should* have faced heavy competition from European imports, just as Europe *should* have faced heavy competition from American grains, fish, metals, dyes, and other resource-intensive products. But what this chapter confronts is the significant *decline* in the relative importance of industry in the Mexican economy (e.g., de-industrialization), not its low levels of industrial activity dictated by initial comparative advantage.

Another common explanation offered for Mexican industry's inability to compete more effectively is its low labor quality and the culture of its labor market: "In the largest republics (Brazil and Mexico) the primary-education system remained woefully inadequate, forcing employers to rely on a workforce with virtually none of the attributes required for technical progress and innovation" (Bulmer-Thomas 1994: 102). This claim assumes that textile production required a lot of skilled labor, something other authors, like Gregory Clark (1987), have questioned at length. Indeed before the 1840s and the great mass migrations to the New World, New England firms hired unskilled (but literate) country girls, while afterward, they hired unskilled (and illiterate) European immigrants. Since the New England example can be easily multiplied by reference to early factory-based textile development in Catalonia, Japan, India, and even Britain, one wonders how the low labor quality hypothesis could help explain any lack of industrial competitiveness in Mexico. It bears repeating that while skilled labor was certainly scarce in Mexico, things were no better anywhere else in the periphery. And if Mexican labor was of such low quality, why did the textile industry survive foreign competition better than elsewhere in the poor periphery?

It has also been suggested that "Mexican cotton manufacture suffered from technological [backwardness], which limited its capacity to supply the market and vitiated its ability to compete" (Hamnett 1980: 13). This sounds very much like a culture-of-the-labor-market thesis whereby Mexico was unable to compete more effectively because its labor resisted the introduction of the new technologies. While domestic producers certainly faced some severe competitive disadvantages due to technological backwardness, the main reason for its difficulties was increasing productivity abroad, which induced a relative decline in manufacture's prices worldwide, and those forces were no different for Mexico than elsewhere around the poor periphery.

Historians have always added politics to the explanations for Mexican textile troubles. Thus Aurora Gómez-Galvarriato argues that domestic textiles were not necessarily inherently uncompetitive, they just needed support from the government and a stable political environment in which to develop. According to this view, the Mexican government failed to take the steps needed to protect domestic industry, so textile producers were not able to compete successfully with imports. If, however, the government had moved to subsidize and protect the textile sector, it would have had a chance to develop the skills and efficiency necessary to compete successfully with foreign imports after the subsequent removal of the tariff wall. This infant industry argument certainly had become very popular with Alexander Hamilton's followers in the United States and with Frederick List's followers in Germany. After all, government support of industrial development in the form of financial assistance and protective tariffs has always been considered crucial for the American textile industry takeoff (Rose 2000: 44). Support for it in Mexico comes from the fact that when the government finally did take an interest in protecting and developing textiles, the industry did show strong signs of resisting import competition. Only "when political instability was briefly surmounted during the 1830s and 1840s, [did] the mechanization of the industry finally take place," and it occurred with the "support of government policies that gave [the sector] both the necessary protection and the financial support required, through the creation of a development bank: the Banco de Avío" (Gómez Galvarriato 2002: 52–55).

Many scholars share this infant industry view. After all, without active state intervention private interests would have had little incentive to invest in local industry given that foreign competition had already deeply penetrated the market. Thus Guy Thomson (1991: 267–68) argues that once foreign competition grew too intense, Mexican merchants were reluctant to invest in restructuring the cotton textile industry. Only a deliberate government program could have induced Mexican textiles to modernize; economic agents were not going to do it alone given the costs, uncertainty, and risks. According to this view, protective tariffs starting in the 1820s, and subsidies to mechanization starting in the 1830s, were central to improving manufacturing competitiveness and offsetting the de-industrialization forces.

8.8   Tariffs and Other Pro-industrial Policies

Mexican *exceptionalism* can be explained in part by modest terms of trade gains and weak Dutch disease effects. It can also be explained in part by the maintenance of wage competitiveness. Does policy offer a third explanation? After all, independence gave Mexico the autonomy to choose tariff and industrial policies that most of the periphery did not have.

Early Anti-industrial Policy

As chapter 13 will argue, coherent pro-industrial trade policy was not typical of any autonomous country in the poor periphery during the 19th century. One reason is that revenue needs dominated. So it was that tariff revenues were the most important source of income for the Mexican government: import duties accounted for about half of federal revenue between 1825 and 1845 (Coatsworth and Williamson 2004a, b). Given that textiles represented between 60 and 70 percent of total imports from 1821 to 1830 (table 8.1), tariffs on foreign textiles obviously generated critical fiscal resources for the new republic. Since the primary goal of the Mexican government was to generate revenue, imported cotton textiles were not taxed at higher rates than other goods. This policy was true more generally for all of Latin America before the 1860s. What is more astonishing, however, is that Mexican cotton producers were able to lobby effectively for the prohibition of import of raw "cotton, cotton yarn up to weight number sixty, and cotton ribbon" (Potash 1983: 14), and these were crucial inputs into cotton textile production. Indeed, raw cotton accounted for two-thirds of the total cost of cotton cloth while the share was even higher for cotton yarn (Clark 1987: 144). Obviously this policy could hardly have helped the domestic textile producer since it lowered the *effective rate* of protection, perhaps even erasing its protective impact entirely. The only legislation that unambiguously offered some net protection was the fact that domestic cotton and woolen textiles were exempted from the 4 percent increase in the sales tax (up from 8–12 percent) that was imposed on foreign textiles (Potash 1983: 15).

The (Very) Gradual Move to a More Pro-industrial Policy

Mexican tariff policies became more obviously protectionist in 1824. The 12 percent duty on foreign goods was replaced with the higher *derecho de internación*, a duty of "18 3/4% of the value of imported articles . . . levied when they left the port of entry for any interior destination" (Potash 1983: 20). Moreover state governments were allowed to impose an additional 3 percent tax

on foreign goods sold within their respective jurisdictions. Imported merchandise thus paid a series of duties, state and federal, which totaled 51 3/8 percent of their appraised value. Domestic textiles, in contrast, were subject only to the state *alcabala* of 8 percent. (Potash 1983: 21)

In 1827 a single ad valorem tax of 40 percent was placed on all imports, an effective strategy in terms of short-term revenue collection as well as offering high protection for domestic manufactures. The level of protection rose still further in 1829, when Mexico prohibited the import of coarse cotton and wool textiles—a measure unambiguously designed to protect domestic industries. Of course, there was a big gap between legislated prohibition and smuggled reality. Indeed by the 1840s there was a widespread contraband trade, and smuggled European cottons were displacing Mexican textiles (Salvucci 1987: 154).

The year 1830 marked a shift in the tactics but not in philosophy: the republican government moved to more efficient methods for encouraging better industrial performance, that is, from tariffs to direct subsidy. This was done by dropping the prohibitions on cotton textile imports, imposing modest tariffs in their place, and using a portion of the revenue to subsidize the textile industry. This industrial strategy was illustrated most clearly with the creation of the Banco de Avío, a state development bank that granted loans for the purchase of industrial machinery, particularly in textiles. Some scholars think that the Banco de Avío accomplished its objective (Potash 1983: 125), but one wonders. After all, the bank was officially dissolved in 1842 because of a lack of capital, political interference, and defaults on outstanding loans. Furthermore less than a fifth of total investment in the textile industry during this period came from the Banco de Avío (Potash 1983: 153).

In short, protectionist policy in the early Mexican republic was modest, ineffective and volatile. It was also less protectionist than in the English speaking periphery. For example, northern manufacturing interests in the United States had lobbied to raise tariffs to about 52 percent on dutiable imports in 1830, before an angry export-oriented south demanded a compromise at a lower, but still high, range of 30 to 40 percent on dutiable imports (Irwin 2003: 13–14). Things were much the same in Australia, New Zealand, and Canada (Williamson 2006b), as well as in the United States in the 1840s, Catalonia between the 1830s and the 1860s, and late Meiji Japan.[22]

Things were even worse in Mexico when it came to the *effective* rate of protection. The prohibition on raw cotton imports—a sop for domestic cotton growing interests[23]—remained unchanged through all these years, and it posed a serious constraint on the development of the textile industry. Domestic cotton prices rose up through the 1840s—partly because of the prohibitions and partly because of crop failures, labor shortages, and the unsuitable climate for growing the cotton needed for mechanical spinning. To make matters worse, the increase in raw cotton prices induced the government to grant licenses for the import of raw cotton, which in turn led to a monopoly for raw cotton suppliers. The predictable result was an "inadequate, irregular, and costly supply of raw cotton became a major obstacle preventing the cotton textile industry from . . . competing successfully with imports" (Antuñano 1979: 287).

Clearly, the many short-lived governments that Mexico had during its early republican years were too busy solving urgent fiscal, political, and military problems to worry about the implementation of long-term development projects and policies.

A Mixed Tariff Policy after 1850

Things got little better after mid-century. There was a substantial reduction in the tariffs on cotton manufactures in 1856.[24] The ad valorem tariff on *manta* declined from 76.9 percent in 1855 to 23.1 percent in 1856. However, these new, liberal policies did not have the strong negative impact on the industry that the literature has generally assumed, since the prohibition on raw cotton imports was replaced by a relatively modest ad valorem duty of around 9.5 percent. Thus the effective rate of protection for the industry did not decline at all. Despite the free trade rhetoric, "liberal" policies after 1856 were probably no less protectionist than they were before.[25] However, they were not *more* pro-industrial.

Policy autonomy may have been a necessary condition for effective pro-industrial and pro-growth policy, but it was not a sufficient condition. Republican governments in Mexico were driven by the short-run needs of survival, thus making them easy prey for various interest groups. While Mexican governments were able to give domestic industry some effective protection from foreign competition—something colonial regions elsewhere in the periphery could not, it was not enough to matter.

8.9   Mexico in a Comparative Mirror

By the 1870s the Mexican textile industry was doing better than was the rest of the poor periphery. This chapter has argued that three factors account for this Mexican *exceptionalism*: first, the terms of trade and Dutch disease effects were weak—compared with the rest

of the periphery; second, based on a better relative agricultural productivity performance over time, Mexico maintained better wage competitiveness vis-à-vis the core—compared with the rest of the periphery;
and third, Mexico had the autonomy to devise policies to foster
industry—something the rest of the periphery did not have the autonomy
to do. It appears that the first two were much more important than the
third.

9 Rising Third World Inequality during the Trade Boom: Did It Matter?

9.1 Why Do We Care about Inequality?

What was the effect of the pre-1913 world trade boom on the poor periphery? W. Arthur Lewis (1978a) pioneered the exploration of this question by looking at factor market responses in primary-product exporting economies. He composed a long shopping list of effects including these three: the response of international capital flows, the response of international labor migration and land settlement, and the impact of the terms of trade boom on de-industrialization everywhere around the periphery as primary-product export sectors expanded and import-competing manufacturing contracted. Lewis's shopping list also included a fourth, the impact of these external price shocks on income distribution and thus political power.

Why do we care about globalization-induced distribution effects on the poor periphery? In judging the impact of globalization on any economy, we can focus on the income gains for the average resident (the so-called gains from trade), the distribution impact of those gains (who gains and who loses), and long-run growth impact. So far we have focused on per capita income and the average resident. Social fairness, however, argues that we should explore the extent to which these gains are shared across all groups, regions, and social classes. In addition, if the distribution of income is thought to have an impact on long-run growth performance and thus on the great divergence, we have even more reason to see who gained from globalization in the poor periphery during the first global century before 1913.

The next section will establish what might be called the pre-industrial, and in most cases, pre-global, norm. What was third world income distribution like prior to the industrial revolution, prior to modern economic growth, and prior to the colonization of Asia, Africa, and Latin America? The historical evidence on "ancient" inequality turns out to be more abundant than the reader might have thought. Section 9.3 is the core of the chapter: first, it reviews the theory that predicts the globalization-inequality connection in the poor periphery; second, it explores the facts in the resource-scarce part of the poor periphery; and third, it does the same for the resource-abundant part of the poor periphery. Resource-abundant may sound like a strange phrase to use for the Punjab, Siam, Egypt, or Mexico in 1800, since they were all very poor two centuries ago. But that poverty was dictated by primitive pre-industrial technologies, a scarcity of human capital, and the absence of world commodity demand, not natural resource scarcity. Within that poor environment, most had relatively abundant land, the right climate, or mineral resources, while others had abundant labor. The difference mattered. Section 9.4 reports the magnitude of the colonial "drain" from Spanish Nueva España, British India, and the Dutch East Indies to see how much was taken off the top by the foreign elite and transferred back to Europe. The chapter concludes with a brief assessment of the third world 19th-century connection between inequality and long-run growth.

9.2   The Pre-industrial and Pre-global Inequality Norm

Let us start at the beginning. What was inequality like in pre-industrial societies in what we now call the third world before the first global century? Can it all be characterized as an opulent ruling class at the top extracting every bit of the surplus, and a mass of subservient poor at subsistence?

Income distribution data based on household surveys and population censuses are, of course, unavailable for any pre-industrial society. The earliest income and expenditure surveys date from the late 18th century for England and the mid-19th century for other industrial countries. Yet recent work has suggested that good estimates of pre-industrial inequality can be obtained from what are called *social tables,* where various social classes are ranked from the richest to the poorest with their estimated number of income recipients and their average incomes (Milanovic, Lindert, and Williamson 2008). Social tables are particularly useful in evaluating pre-industrial societies where classes were clearly delineated and the differences in mean incomes between them were substantial.

If class alone determined one's income, and if income differences between classes were large while income differences within classes were small, then most inequality would be explained by average income differences between classes. One of the most famous social tables was constructed by Gregory King for England and Wales in 1688 (Barnett 1936; Lindert and Williamson 1982). King's class list was fairly detailed, but he did not report inequalities within these social groups, so we cannot identify within-class inequality for 1688 England. Yet, when income variance within class is also available for any country offering social table estimates, the differences between measured inequality are typically very small whether within-class variance is included or excluded. In short, the lion's share of inequality in pre-industrial societies is accounted for by between-class average income differences.

The number of social classes into which distributions are divided, and from which we can calculate some summary income inequality statistic like the Gini coefficient, varies considerably. We have only three classes for Nueva España between 1784 and 1799 (comprising the territories of today's Mexico, parts of Central America, and parts of western United States) and 1880 China. In most cases the number of social classes is in the double digits, but sometimes it is much more: thus the data from the 1872 Brazilian occupational census include 813 occupations, but the largest number of observations is provided in the famous 1427 Florentine census that resulted in data for almost 10,000 Tuscan households. As we will see in a moment, these large differences in the number of classes included in the social tables have little systematic effect on the measured Gini.

The Gini estimates are plotted in figure 9.1 against income or GDI per capita. Figure 9.1 also displays what is called the *inequality possibility frontier* (solid line), a curve based on the maximum inequality the elite could have extracted at that income per capita. The maximum is constructed under the assumption that everybody but the elite in such repressive societies would have gotten just the World Bank's estimated subsistence minimum of $PPP 300.[1] The ratio of the actual Gini to the maximum feasible inequality is called the *extraction ratio*. In most cases the calculated Ginis lie pretty close to the inequality possibility frontier (IPF). The countries farthest below the IPF curve—with the lowest extraction ratios—are the most advanced pre-industrial economies in northwestern Europe: Holland between 1561 and 1808, France 1788, and England between 1688 and 1801.

The benchmark observations for England and Wales, and Holland or Netherlands—the only countries for which we have at least three pre-industrial observations—are connected to highlight the evolution of their inequality relative to the IPF. Between 1290 and 1801, and particularly between 1688 and 1759, the increase of the Gini in England and Wales was quite a bit less than the increase in the IPF. Thus the English

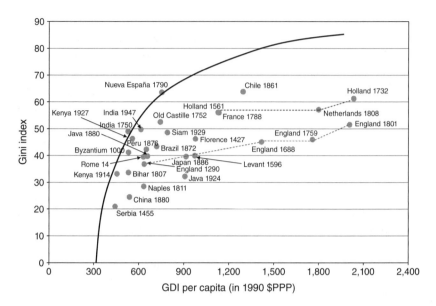

Figure 9.1
Ancient inequalities: Estimated Gini coefficients, and the inequality possibility frontier. The solid IPF line is constructed on the assumption that s = $PPP 300. Source: Milanovic, Lindert, and Williamson (2008: fig. 2).

extraction ratio dropped from about 70 percent in 1290 to about 61 percent in 1801. Or consider the Netherlands between 1732 and 1808 where the extraction ratio decreased from around 72 to 68 percent.

The inequality possibility frontier allows us to better situate these ancient pre-industrial inequality estimates in the modern context. The last panel of table 9.1 provides estimates of inequality extraction ratios for twenty-five contemporary societies. Brazil and South Africa have often been cited as examples of extremely unequal societies, both driven by long experience with racial discrimination, tribal power and regional dualism. Indeed both countries display Ginis comparable to the most unequal pre-industrial societies. But Brazil and South Africa are several times richer than the richest ancient society in our sample, so for these two the maximum feasible inequality is much higher than anything we can see in our ancient sample. Thus the elites in both countries have extracted only a little more than 60 percent of their maximum feasible inequality, and their inequality extraction ratios are about the same as what we find among the *less* exploitative and repressive ancient societies like England between 1801 and 1803 and Japan in 1886.

Table 9.1

Pre-industrial inequality measures

Country/region, year	Gini	Mean income/ s = subsistence (s = $300)	Maximum feasible Gini (IPF)	Inequality extraction ratio (%)
Roman empire 14	39.4	2.1	52.6	75.0
Byzantium 1000	41.1	1.8	43.7	94.1
England and Wales 1290	36.7	2.1	53.0	69.2
Tuscany 1427	46.1	3.3	69.3	66.6
South Serbia 1455	20.9	1.5	32.2	64.8
Holland 1561	56.0	3.8	73.4	76.3
Levant 1596	39.8	3.2	69.1	57.6
England and Wales 1688	45.0	4.7	78.8	57.1
Holland 1732	61.1	6.8	85.2	71.7
Moghul India 1750	48.9	1.8	43.4	112.8
Old Castille 1752	52.5	2.5	59.7	88.0
England and Wales 1759	45.9	5.9	82.9	55.4
France 1788	55.9	3.8	73.5	76.1
Nueva España 1790	63.5	2.5	60.2	105.5
England and Wales 1801	51.5	6.7	85.0	60.6
Bihar (India) 1807	33.5	1.8	43.7	76.7
Netherlands 1808	57.0	6.0	83.3	68.5
Naples 1811	28.4	2.2	52.9	53.7
Chile 1861	63.7	4.3	76.8	83.0
Brazil 1872	43.3	2.4	58.3	74.2
Peru 1876	42.2	2.2	54.0	78.1
Java 1880	39.7	2.2	54.6	72.8
China 1880	24.5	1.8	44.4	55.2
Japan 1886	39.5	3.1	67.2	58.8
Kenya 1914	33.2	1.5	34.2	96.8
Java 1924	32.1	3.0	66.9	48.0
Kenya 1927	46.2	1.9	46.2	100.0
Siam 1929	48.5	2.6	62.1	78.1
British India 1947	49.7	2.1	51.3	96.8
Average	*44.3*	*3.1*	*60.6*	*74.9*

Table 9.1

(continued)

Country/region, year	Gini	Mean income/ s = subsistence (s = $300)	Maximum feasible Gini (IPF)	Inequality extraction ratio (%)
Modern counterparts				
Italy 2000	35.9	62.5	98.3	36.5
Turkey 2003	43.6	22.0	95.4	45.7
United Kingdom 1999	37.4	66.1	98.4	38.0
Serbia 2003	32.2	11.2	91.0	35.4
Netherlands 1999	28.1	72.0	98.5	28.5
India 2004	32.6	6.4	84.2	38.7
Spain 2000	33.0	50.9	97.9	33.7
France 2000	31.2	69.4	98.4	31.7
Mexico 2000	53.8	24.1	95.7	56.2
Chile 2003	54.6	33.7	96.6	56.4
Brazil 2002	58.8	13.9	92.7	63.4
Peru 2002	52.0	12.3	91.8	56.7
Kenya 1998	44.4	4.5	77.6	57.2
Indonesia 2002	34.3	10.7	90.5	37.9
China 2001	41.6	11.5	91.2	45.6
Japan 2002	26.0	70.2	98.5	26.4
Thailand 2002	50.9	21.3	95.2	53.5
Average	*40.6*	*33.1*	*93.6*	*43.6*
Other contemporary countries				
South Africa 2000	57.3	14.7	93.1	61.6
United States 2000	39.9	77.7	98.6	40.5
Sweden 2000	27.3	52.2	98.0	27.9
Germany 2000	30.3	62.0	98.3	30.8
Nigeria 2003	42.1	3.0	66.7	63.1
Congo, D.R., 2004	41.0	1.5	33.3	123.1
Tanzania 2000	34.6	1.8	44.4	77.9
Malaysia 2001	47.9	26.0	96.1	49.9

Source: Milanovic, Lindert, and Williamson (2008: table 2).
Note: Ancient societies ranked by year.

The median Gini in today's world is about 41, a "representative" country having thus extracted just a bit less than 44 percent of feasible inequality, vastly less than did ancient pre-industrial societies (75 percent). Only in the extremely poor countries today, with income per capita less than $PPP 600, do actual and maximum feasible Ginis lie close together as in 2004 Congo Democratic Republic and 2000 Tanzania. But these repressive African countries are exceptions: compared with the maximum inequality possible, today's inequality is *much* smaller than that of ancient societies.

As a country becomes richer, and its surplus above subsistence rises, its feasible inequality expands. Consequently, if recorded inequality is stable, the extraction ratio must fall. This can be seen in figure 9.2 where we plot the inequality extraction ratio against GDI per capita for both ancient societies and their modern counterparts. Thus the social consequences of increased inequality may not entail as much relative impoverishment, or as much perceived injustice, as might appear if we looked only at the

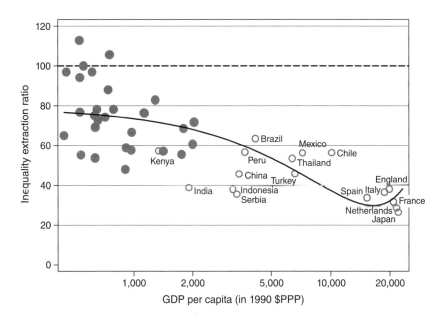

Figure 9.2
Inequality extraction ratio for the ancient society sample and their counterpart modern societies. Modern societies are drawn with hollow circles. Horizontal axis in logs. Inequality extraction ratio shown in percentages.
Source: Milanovic, Lindert, and Williamson (2008: fig. 4).

recorded Gini. This logic is particularly compelling for poor and middle-income countries where increases in income push the maximum feasible inequality up relatively sharply along the steepest part of the IPF curve. The farther a society rises above the subsistence minimum, the less will economic development lift its inequality possibilites, and thus the extraction ratio will be driven more and more by the rise in the actual Gini itself.

Using this information from our ancient pre-industrial societies, can we explain differences in their observed inequality? The Kuznets hypothesis posits that inequality tends to follow an inverted U as average real income increases. Although Kuznets formulated his hypothesis explicitly with a view toward industrializing and industrialized economies, one might wonder whether the Kuznets curve can be found among our pre-industrial economies as well. In addition to average income and its square, table 9.2 includes the urbanization rate, population density and colonial status (a dummy variable). The regression also includes a number of controls for country-specific eccentricities in the data: the number of social groups available for calculating the Gini, whether the social table is based on tax data, and whether the social table for a colony includes the income of resident colonists. The Kuznets hypothesis predicts a positive coefficient on average income and negative coefficient on its square. We also expect higher inequality for the more urbanized countries (reflecting a common finding that inequality in urban areas tends to be higher than in rural areas: Ravallion et al. 2007), and for those that are ruled by foreign elites since powerful colonizers are presumed to be able to achieve higher extraction rates than weaker local elites, and since countries with weak local elites but large surpluses will attract powerful imperialists to extract it (Acemoglu, Johnson, and Robinson 2001).

The empirical results confirm all expectations. Both income terms are of the right sign and significant, supporting a pre-industrial Kuznets curve. The sign on the *urbanization rate* is, as predicted, positive, but since it competes with population density, its statistical significance is somewhat lower. Still each percentage point increase in the urbanization rate (e.g., from 10 to 11 percent) is associated with an increase in the Gini by 0.35 points. Colonies were clearly much more unequal: holding everything else constant, colonies had a Gini about 13 points higher than non-colonies. *Foreigner* is a dummy variable and controls for two observations—south Serbia 1455 and the Levant 1596—that were colonies for which the ancient inequality surveys did not include the incomes and numbers of colonizers at the top. This is therefore simply another control for data eccentricity, and its negative sign shows that being a colony, and not having colonizers

Table 9.2

Regression results for the Gini coefficient

	1	2	3
GDP per capita	360.5***	366.7***	360.2***
	(0.001)	(0.001)	(0.002)
GDP per capita squared	−25.0***	−25.5***	−25.0***
	(0.002)	(0.002)	(0.003)
Urbanization rate	0.349*	0.354*	0.353*
	(0.08)	(0.08)	(0.093)
Population density	−0.105***	−0.100***	−0.107*
	(0.001)	(0.003)	(0.053)
Number of groups	−0.009	−0.009	−0.010
	(0.16)	(0.19)	(0.18)
Colony (0–1)	12.63***	12.93***	12.41***
	(0.001)	(0.001)	(0.002)
Foreigner (0–1)	−9.59	−9.97	−9.26
	(0.25)	(0.25)	(0.29)
Asia (0–1)		−1.28	
		(0.69)	
Tax survey (0–1)	−4.86	−4.85	−4.85
	(0.57)	(0.24)	(0.28)
Constant	−1246***	−1266***	−1245***
	(0.001)	(0.001)	(0.002)
Number observations	28	28	26
Adjusted R squared	0.75	0.73	0.73

Source: Milanovic, Lindert, and Williamson (2008: table 3).
Notes: GDP per capita is in natural logs. Coefficients significant at 10, 5, and 1 percent level denoted, respectively, by three, two and one asterisks, p-values between brackets.

included in the survey, reduces recorded inequality considerably (9 to 10 points).

The number of social groups used in the inequality calculations, or tax census origin of social tables, do not affect the Gini in any significant way. This finding is comforting because it shows that our estimates of inequality are being driven by fundamentals, not by the way the social tables were constructed.

Population density is negatively associated with inequality and significant. Column 1 of table 9.2 reports that an increase in population density by about 10 persons per square kilometer (equivalent to an increase in population density from that of early 19th-century Naples to England and

Wales) is associated with a single Gini point decrease. It might have been expected that the introduction of a dummy variable for more densely populated Asia would have caused the effect of density to dissipate. This is not the case, as shown in column 2. The negative impact of population density on inequality may seem at first sight to be counterintuitive. After all, conventional theory would predict that more population pressure on the land should raise yields and rents, lower labor's marginal product and the wage, thus producing *more* inequality, not less. However, densely populated agrarian societies also had higher food prices than thinly settled societies, so that nominal subsistence had to be much higher to purchase the more expensive foodstuffs, lowering measured inequality. It seems likely that this was the force at work in ancient pre-industrial societies at the start of the 19th century when a world market for grains had not yet developed and local conditions dictated the relative price of food (Latham and Neal 1983; Clingingsmith and Williamson 2008; Dobado Gonzáles and Guerrero 2008).

The stylized picture that emerges is this: inequality follows contours that are consistent with the Kuznets curve hypothesis, a pre-industrial secular rise to a peak, followed by a fall during modern economic growth. It follows that most of the pre-industrial third world had probably reached very high levels of inequality by the early 19th century before the global trade boom. However, the extraction ratio tends to fall as income increases, even during pre-industrial times. This, of course, would invite a European imperialist to plunder where the potential surplus was big, but where the local elite had relaxed their extraction rate. We will return to this issue below.

What about the historical persistence of inequality? For example, has Asia always been less unequal? The answer is no: it does not appear that ancient Asia was significantly less unequal when we control for other factors. Indeed population density is sufficient to identify why ancient Asia had lower levels of inequality than the rest of the pre-industrial world.

What about Latin America? Has it always been more unequal, as implied by the recent work of Stanley Engerman and Kenneth Sokoloff (1997; Engerman, Haber, and Sokoloff 2000). Engerman and Sokoloff offer a hypothesis to account for Latin American growth underachievement during the two centuries following its independence. Their thesis begins with the plausible assertion that high levels of income inequality, and thus of political power, favor rich landlords and rent-seekers, and thus the development of institutions that are compatible with rent-seeking but incompatible with economic growth. Their thesis argues further that high levels of Latin American inequality have their roots in the natural resource endowments present when Iberia colonized the region five centuries ago. Exploitation of the native population and African slaves, as well as their disenfranchisement, reinforced the development of institutions incompatible with growth. Engerman and Sokoloff had no difficulty collecting evidence which confirmed high inequality, disenfranchisement, and lack of suffrage in Latin America compared with the United States. Oddly enough, however, they did not confront their thesis with inequality evidence for the industrial leaders in northwest Europe.

Table 9.3 presents inequality information for pre-industrial western Europe (i.e., prior to 1810) and for pre-industrial and republican Latin America (i.e., prior to 1875). For the former, we have observations from 1788 France, 1561 and 1732 Holland, and 1688, 1759, and 1801 England and Wales. For the latter we have Mexico 1844, Chile 1861, Brazil 1872, and Peru 1876. Engerman and Sokoloff coined their hypothesis in terms of actual inequality. According to that criterion, their thesis must be rejected. That is, the (population weighted) average Latin American Gini

Table 9.3
Inequality in pre-industrial Latin America and western Europe

Country	Year	Source of income data	Population[a]	Actual Gini
Brazil	1872	Occupational census	10,167	43.3
Chile	1861	Occupational census	1,702	54.0
Mexico	1844	Social tables	7,089	51.3
Peru	1856	Social tables	2,469	35.5
Latin America			21,427	
Unweighted average				46.0
Weighted average				45.9
England	1688	Social tables	5,700	45.0
England	1759	Social tables	6,463	45.9
England	1801	Social tables	9,053	51.5
France	1788	Social tables	27,970	55.9
Holland	1561	Census dwelling rents	983	56.0
Holland	1732	Census dwelling rents	2,023	61.1
Western Europe			52,192	
Unweighted average				52.6
Weighted average				52.9

Source: Williamson (2010: table 7).
a. Population in thousands.

(45.9) was considerably *lower* than that of western Europe (52.9), not higher. It is not true that pre-industrial Latin America was unambiguously more unequal than pre-industrial northwest Europe. Thus, if inequality encouraged rent-seeking and discouraged growth in Latin America, it did it even more so in northwest Europe where the industrial revolution first started! However, Latin America was poorer than western Europe, and poorer societies have a smaller surplus for the elite to extract. Thus maximum *feasible inequality* was lower in Latin America (Milanovic et al. 2008). As it turns out, *extraction rates* were considerably higher in Latin America than in western Europe. Thus, while measured inequality does not support the Engerman–Sokoloff thesis, the extraction rate does. We will return to this issue below as well.

9.3   Globalization-Induced Departures from the Pre-global Norm in the Poor Periphery

The Theory

What happened to income distribution in the poor periphery when these pre-industrial societies were exposed to global forces across the 19th century? This question will be answered by focusing on the returns to labor relative to land, or what will be called the wage-rental ratio.[2] The economist reading this should be warned about the rhetoric since the wage-rental ratio label used here certainly does *not* refer to the returns to capital relative to labor's wage. Indeed a well-integrated world capital market ensured that risk-adjusted financial capital costs were pretty much equated the world around (Obstfeld and Taylor 2004). Thus, while trade shocks should have influenced the returns to internationally immobile land and labor, they should not have influenced returns to internationally mobile capital. Furthermore, the distribution of income in the 19th century periphery was determined just as the classical economists modeled it, namely by the relative shares of land (including mineral) rents and wages in national income. To assess the distribution impact of core industrialization and world commodity market integration on the periphery, we should therefore quite naturally focus on labor and land and thus on the wage-rental ratio.[3]

Ever since Eli Heckscher and Bertil Ohlin wrote about the problem almost a century ago (Flam and Flanders 1991), world trade booms have been associated with relative factor price changes. Consider a simple characterization of Lewis's new international economic order where the periphery exports resource-intensive commodities at price p_A in exchange for imports of manufactures from the industrial core at price p_M. If a world trade boom raises p_A/p_M, the rent-to-wage ratio, r/w, should rise in the poor resource-abundant country (since the export boom raises the relative demand for land and mineral resources). Since land and other natural resources were held by the favored few, the pre–World War I world trade boom implied lesser inequality in resource-scarce economies like those in western Europe and East Asia, where land rents (and land values) fell, wages rose, and w/r rose even further. Where industrialization had not yet taken hold in poor resource abundant economies, the pre–World War I world trade boom induced a rise in land (and, more generally, resource) rents, a fall in wages, and an even greater fall in w/r, implying greater inequality in eastern Europe (e.g., Ukraine), the Middle East (e.g., Egypt), sub-Saharan Africa, the Southern Cone, the Punjab, and Southeast Asia, especially where the ownership of land dictated the ownership of wealth.[4] Even in poor countries containing smallholdings, it appears that globalization served to increase land concentration in many regions, like Southeast Asia, thus adding even more to the inequality trends. That is, smallholders moving into cash crops accumulated debt (aided by an integrated world capital market) to finance the increased use of purchased inputs, more extensive irrigation systems, and better transportation, all of which was essential to supply booming world markets. It also exposed them to greater price volatility (chapter 10), and default during slumps converted many of these smallholders into tenants or into "proletarianized" wage labor on large estates. Thus cash tenancy on Burmese rice-producing land rose from 25 to 58 percent between the 1900s and 1930s, and similar trends took place in Indochina, Assam, and Tonkin (Steinberg 1987). The move to large sugar plantations in the Philippines had the same impact on land concentration there as well (Corpuz 1997).

Our central concern, however, is the connection between the terms of trade and the wage–rent ratio. The w/r evidence will be presented below, but first we need to elaborate a bit on the economics. The relevant theory can be found in the work of Max Corden and Fred Gruen (1970), Michael Mussa (1979), and Douglas Irwin (1999), as well as what is known as the magnification effect first elaborated by Ronald Jones (1971). The models are simple, but they isolate what should be important. An increase in the price of the labor-intensive manufactured good (P_M) shifts its isoprice curve outward, and as wages rise, labor is pulled off the land to satisfy new employment demands in manufacturing. As agricultural labor migrates to manufacturing, landlords are left with less labor to cultivate and harvest, lowering land yields and rents. The rent–wage (r/w) ratio falls even more since wages have risen. Furthermore there is a magnification effect, since the rise in w exceeds the rise in P_M. In contrast, if the price of primary products (here called agriculture for short, and thus P_A for its price) rises, the isoprice curve for primary products shifts outward, land (and other resource) rents rise, and the rent–wage ratio rises still more. In this example where favorable price shocks are experienced by the country specializing in commodities, there is a magnification effect since the rise in rents exceeds the rise in P_A. By symmetry, when P_A/P_M falls, the wage–rent ratio rises, again by a magnification effect.

How big is the magnification effect? In an economy with specific-factors,

$$r^* > p_A^* > w^* > p_M^* > i^*,$$

where, once again, the asterisk (*) refers to rates of change. The inequality states that changes in the returns to the sector-specific factors (land and capital) are more pronounced (and of opposite sign) than the return to the mobile factor (labor), a formal result that makes good intuitive sense: after all, while a mobile factor can emigrate from a sector absorbing a bad price shock, an immobile sector-specific factor cannot (like arable land or mineral resources). Furthermore the rent–wage ratio responds as

$$(r^* - w^*) = \Delta (p_A^* - p_M^*),$$

where $\Delta > 1$ denotes the magnification effect. This magnification effect ought to vary from country to country, depending on the size of its primary-product producing sector and the character of technologies in all sectors. Thus globalization shocks can have different effects on wage–rent ratios depending on their size and the structure of the economy in question, but the average value of Δ was about 1.6 in a 19-country sample covering 1870 to 1940 (Williamson 2002: table 5).

The simple Heckscher–Ohlin–Samuelson (HOS) model just exploited limited the story to land and labor, and to manufacturing imports and primary product exports. What about skills, and what about nontradables? Here we are on shakier empirical grounds, but once again, theory helps. Sebastian Galiani, Daniel Heymann, and Nicholás Magud (2009) have recently shown that when the HOS model is expanded to include skill-intensive urban activities (e.g., nontradables), the rise in inequality generated by the rent–wage ratio boom is reinforced by a rise in the wage gap between skilled and unskilled labor. As it turns out, there is some evidence that the Latin American *belle époque* supports this prediction (Arroyo Abad 2008; Arroyo Abad and Santos-Paulino 2009).

So much for theory. What about the facts? As we have seen, export prices boomed in the primary-product specializing countries throughout most of the 19th century. Price trends reversed thereafter. Thus the relative rewards to land and labor—and thus overall income distribution—should have moved in very different directions on either side of World War I. Exactly how they were affected depended, of course, on whether a country's abundant factor was land or labor.

Changing Distribution in the Labor-Abundant Poor Periphery

Consider the canonical land scarce and labor abundant case, Japan. When American gunboats forced Japan to emerge from isolation after 1858, prices of its labor-intensive exports soared, rising toward world market levels, while prices of its land- and capital-intensive imports collapsed, falling toward world market levels. The terms of trade rose 3.5 to 4.9 times over the fifteen years following 1858 (Huber 1971; Yasuba 1996). The higher estimate is used in figure 3.10. However measured, these were massive and permanent relative price shocks. Just how permanent can be seen in figure 3.10: not only did Japan's terms of trade increase almost five times after the country opened up to trade, but it increased still further up to the 1890s. The Heckscher–Ohlin model predicts what the income distribution response should have been in post-1858 Japan: the abundant factor—labor—should have flourished, the scarce factor—land—should have languished, and income inequality should have fallen. Did they?

The available evidence for Japan in mid-century is limited: data documenting trends in land rents or land values are not available until 1885, long after Japan's leap to openness had taken place. But we do have some crude evidence, and it seems to confirm the Heckscher and Ohlin hypothesis. Angus Maddison (1995: 196) estimates that Japan's real GDP per capita increased by only 5.3 percent between 1820 and 1870 (total, not per annum). Assume that all of that very modest increase took place between 1850 and 1870, an unlikely event that argues against the thesis. Some time ago J. Richard Huber (1971) estimated that the real wage for unskilled workers in Osaka and Tokyo increased by 67 percent during this period. True, this huge measured increase is much bigger than the real wage growth others have estimated more recently (Williamson 2000; Bassino and Ma 2004). Nevertheless, consider the implication of Huber's estimates: the nominal wage of unskilled labor, the abundant factor, increased by 43 percent relative to average nominal income in Japan. Under plausible assumptions,[5] this example implies that nominal land rents fell by more than 80 percent. The example also implies that Japan's wage–rent ratio rose by more than 7.3 times (from 1.0 to 1.67/0.20). This is exactly what one would have predicted when a pre-industrial economy is hit with a huge price shock that favors the export good and disfavors the import good: the wage-rental ratio *should* have soared in Japan, with obvious distributional (and political) implications.

A rise in the wage–rent ratio of 7.3 times may seem enormous, but remember the magnification effect discussed in the previous section. To just get a feel for the historical plausibility of these estimates, consider our simple model again. Let θ_{rj} be the share of factor income in sector j going to land rents (with the remainder going to labor). Land was *far* more important in agriculture than manufacturing, so $\theta_{ra} > \theta_{rm}$ and $1/(\theta_{ra} - \theta_{rm}) > 1$. Thus the impact of a relative price shock $(P_M{}^* - P_A{}^*)$—remember, land-scarce Japan exported manufactures—has a magnification effect on the rent–wage ratio:

$$(p_M{}^* - p_A{}^*)/(\theta_{ra} - \theta_{rm}) = (w^* - r^*).$$

If the land share was about 0.4 in agriculture[6] and very small in manufacturing, the magnification effect would be close to 2.5. Thus a rise in Japan's terms of trade by 3.5 times could easily have induced a rise in the wage–rent ratio by 7.3 times.

Of course, these are only informed guesses for pre-modern Japan, but table 9.4 reports more concrete estimates for those countries and time periods that can be documented. Wage–rent ratio trends can be constructed for Japan starting with 1885, Korea starting with 1909, and Taiwan starting with 1904. In contrast with the Punjab after 1873 or Japan after 1858, the early 20th century was not a period of technological quiescence in East Asian agriculture. Instead, the region was undergoing land-saving and labor-using innovation (Hayami and Ruttan 1971: chs. 6 and 7), forces that should have served by themselves to raise the wage–rent ratio. It was also a period of early industrialization, at least in Japan and the Shanghai region (Ma 2004), that pulled labor off the farm (Brandt 1985), another force serving to raise the wage–rent ratio. The period after 1910 was also, as we have seen, one of unfavorable farm price shocks (Kimura 1993; Kang and Cha 1996), an additional force serving to raise the wage–rent ratio. In short, we might expect that East Asian wage–rent ratio trends, initiated by globalization forces in the mid-19th century, to have continued into the 20th century. That is exactly what table 9.4 shows: East Asian wage–rent ratios surged up to the 1920s and 1930s. Land-scarce Europe experienced the same surge in wage–rent ratios during the so-called grain invasion after the 1870s, especially where trade policy remained liberal. Furthermore the

Table 9.4
Wage–rent ratio trends in the third world, 1870 to 1939 (1911 = 100)

Period	Land abundant							Land scarce			
	Argentina	Uruguay	Burma	Siam	Egypt	Punjab	Japan	Korea	Taiwan
1870–1874		1112.5		4699.1		196.7			
1875–1879		891.3		3908.7	174.3	198.5			
1880–1884	580.4	728.3		3108.1	276.6	147.2			
1885–1889	337.1	400.2		2331.6	541.9	150.8	79.9		
1890–1894	364.7	377.2	190.9	1350.8	407.5	108.7	68.6		
1895–1899	311.1	303.6	189.9	301.3	160.1	92.0	91.3		
1900–1904	289.8	233.0	186.8	173.0	166.7	99.8	96.1		68.1
1905–1909	135.2	167.8	139.4	57.2	64.4	92.4	110.4	102.8	85.2
1910–1914	84.0	117.9	106.9	109.8	79.8	80.1	107.5	121.9	96.6
1915–1919	53.6	120.8	164.7	202.1	83.5	82.5	104.9	109.4	111.2
1920–1924	53.1	150.3	113.6	157.9	124.3	81.1	166.1	217.4	140.0
1925–1929	51.0	150.2		114.9	120.8	72.6	202.4	209.2	134.8
1930–1934	58.4	174.3		113.1	116.2	50.4	229.5	194.0	130.7
1935–1939	59.5	213.5		121.6	91.0	33.2	149.9	215.4	123.6

Source: Williamson (2002: table 3).

magnitudes were pretty similar. Over the fifteen years after 1910 to 1914, the average increase in the wage–rent ratio for Japan, Korea and Taiwan combined was about 67 percent (table 9.4). Over the fifteen years after 1890 to 1904, the average increase in the wage–rent ratio for Britain, Ireland, Denmark, and Sweden combined was about 50 percent (O'Rourke, Taylor and Williamson 1996). It might also be relevant to add that politically powerful landed interests were able to secure some protection from these globalization forces in continental Europe by imposing tariffs on grain imports (Rogowski 1989; O'Rourke 1997; Williamson 1997), so that the wage–rent ratio did not rise as fast as it would have under free trade. Japan achieved much the same result with import restrictions on rice (Brandt 1993).

Changing Distribution in the Resource-Abundant Poor Periphery

In contrast with land-scarce East Asia, the Punjab was relatively land abundant, a characterization that is confirmed by the fact that agricultural exports from the Punjab to Europe boomed after the early 1870s, while irrigation investment, immigration, and new settlement made it behave like a frontier region.[7] Globalization should have had the opposite effect on the wage–rent ratio in land abundant Punjab compared with land-scarce East Asia: it should have fallen, and fall it did. Between 1875–1879 and 1910–1914, the wage–rent ratio in the Punjab fell by 60 percent. The Punjab's wage–rent ratio experience was not so different from that of the Southern Cone and other land abundant parts of the poor periphery. Between 1880–1884 and 1910–1914 the wage–rent ratio fell by 85 percent in the combined pair of Argentina and Uruguay (table 9.4). Egypt, riding a cotton boom, conformed to these relative factor price trends: the Egyptian wage–rent ratio fell by 54 percent from the late 1870s to World War I, and by 85 percent from the late 1880s onward (table 9.4).

The recorded decline (rise) in wage–rent (rent–wage) ratios in the land-abundant Southern Cone, the Punjab, and Egypt prior to World War I is simply enormous. But they were even more powerful in land-abundant, labor-scarce, and rice-exporting Southeast Asia: pre-1914 globalization price shocks lowered the wage–rent ratio in both Burma and Siam, and the decline was huge. The wage–rent ratio fell by 44 percent in Burma over the twenty years between 1890–1894 and 1910–1914. In Siam, it fell by 92 percent between 1890–1894 and 1910–1914, and by an even bigger 98 percent between 1870–1874 and 1910–1914. These trends had obvious inequality implications in resource-abundant regions as landed interests gained dramatically relative to labor. As noted above, globalization also served to increase the concentration of land holdings in much of Southeast Asia due to rising smallholder indebtedness as they shifted in to commercial export crops and exposed themselves to greater price volatility associated with many of those crops, resulting in subsequent default for the poorly insured. Smallholders evolved in to tenant or wage labor on large estates, inducing more land and wealth concentration, and even more income inequality as a consequence.

During the pro-global decades before World War I, the wage–rent ratio rose steeply in land and resource scarce countries in the poor periphery—mainly East Asia, while it fell steeply in land- and resource-abundant countries in the poor periphery—in Southeast Asia, the Middle East, and Latin America. We infer that globalization induced a pronounced inequality rise in much of the poor periphery, where countries specialized in export commodities. The opposite was true of East Asia, which increasingly exported manufactures.

9.4   Colonial Drains and the Pre-industrial Norm

The inequality estimates of the colonies listed in table 9.1 do not include any transfer of income from the colony to the European country doing the colonizing, while the inequality estimates of the countries doing the colonizing include that income. How big were these transfers, or what the literature has long called *colonial drains,* and what did they do to actual inequality? If the colonists were resident in the colony, our inequality measures would have picked up their impact on inequality. Indeed table 9.2 estimates that being a colony raised the Gini by 12 to 13 percentage points (that is, raised their inequality by 28 percent = 12.5/44.3). But what about the income transfers, or drains, from poor pre-industrial colony to rich European colonial country? We offer three examples in table 9.5: Nueva España (New Spain) between 1785 and 1800, the Dutch East Indies between 1868 and 1930, and British India from 1801 to 1930.

Nueva España, or what we now call Mexico, was the jewel in the Spanish American crown. Thus, not only did it transfer a share of its annual income to Spain between 1785–1789 (1 percent) and 1796–1800 (2.6 percent), but it also subsidized the rest of the Spanish empire. Adding the two up yields a colonial drain from Nueva España ranging between 4.8 percent in the late 1780s and 7.8 percent in the late 1790s.The drain was even bigger for the Dutch East Indies, or what we now call Indonesia. Between the late 1860s and World War I, the drain from the East Indies averaged 7.5 percent of their income, a figure surprisingly close to that of Nueva España a

Table 9.5
Three examples of colonial drain, 1785 to 1930

Region/period	Share in NNP or GDP (%)	Source
New Spain 1785–1789	1.0	Grafe and Irigoin (2006: table 1, 251)
New Spain 1785–1789 (plus inter)	4.8	Ibid.Includes transfers to rest of empire.
New Spain 1796–1800	2.6	Grafe and Irigoin (2006: table 1, 251)
New Spain 1796-1800 (plus inter)	7.8	Ibid. Includes transfers to rest of empire.
Indonesia 1868–1872	7.4	Maddison (2001: 87)
Indonesia 1911–1915	7.6	Maddison (2001: 87)
Indonesia 1926–1930	10.3	Maddison (2001: 87)
India 1801	6.1	Patnaik (2005: table 6)
India 1811	6.0	Patnaik (2005: table 6)
India 1821	5.3	Patnaik (2005: table 6)
India 1868–1872	1.0	Maddison (2001: 87)
India 1911–1915	1.3	Maddison (2001: 87)
India 1926–1930	0.9	Maddison (2001: 87)

century earlier. But it even rose higher since it reached more than 10 percent in the late 1920s. By these standards, the British imperialists look like pikers. Between 1801 and 1821 the drain to Britain from India averaged 5.8 percent, but the figure fell sharply thereafter, averaging "only" 1.1 percent of Indian income between the 1860s and 1930.

In short, these three imperialists extracted much of the surplus in their colonies. Colonies had far more inequality than did non-colonies and, in addition, lost a significant share of their income in the form of transfers or drains to the colonists' home base.

9.5   Did It Matter?

While income in the poor pre-industrial periphery was already highly unequal when the 19th-century global boom started, by the time that global century was over the poor periphery had become even more unequal everywhere but in East Asia. Did it matter? Theory and fact are both divided.

The arguments for the inequality-breeds growth thesis are many. Here are two. The classical economists thought accumulation was what mattered for growth, and since only the rich had the surplus to invest, anything that increased their share of total income would raise the saving rate. But the classical economists were writing their theory in an economic environment where world capital markets were a thing of the future. Thus countries had to rely on their own savings to achieve accumulation and growth. After the 1870s and after the 1970s, the world was a very different place where financial capital was footloose and looking for the highest returns (Obstfeld and Taylor 2004). Thus countries could rely on foreign investment to finance their local accumulation needs, and domestic saving was not an important constraint. In short, high inequality in the poor periphery was not a necessary or a sufficient condition for accumulation.

Here's the second argument. In contrast with the 19th century, today's economic growth is carried much more by human capital accumulation—education, on the job training, investment in health, and migration—and much less by physical capital. In this new environment, inequality implies big premiums on skills, schooling, and other forms of human capital. Where the premium is big, there is incentive to exploit it by investing in schooling, training, and migration. Thus it can be argued that inequality can cause human capital accumulation and growth.

But the inequality of the 19th-century poor periphery was not caused by earnings inequality or even by high profit rates, but rather by high rents on relatively fixed land and mineral resources. Under these conditions inequality was likely to have caused rent-seeking by the elite, rather than the development of institutions that favored property rights and growth. Thus the globalization-induced inequality in the commodity export parts of the poor periphery probably retarded, rather than stimulated, growth.

10 Export Price Volatility: Another Drag on Third World Growth?

10.1 Commodity Price and Terms of Trade Volatility: The Problem

In the modern world economy, primary products, or export commodities as they are called, have far greater price volatility than do manufactures or services. In addition third world economies that specialize in such products have high export concentration and thus do not spread their risk, yielding even greater volatility in their terms of trade. Table 10.1 summarizes the modern evidence with the latter: from the 1960s to the 1990s, East Asia had terms of trade volatility 1.7 times that of the industrialized economies; the figures were much bigger for the rest of the third world—3.1, 2.6, and 3.8 for, respectively, Latin America, the Middle East and North Africa, South Asia and sub-Saharan Africa. Recent analysis has shown that price volatility of this sort has been very bad for growth over the long run in these poor countries, at least for the past four decades or so. Has it always been that way? Were commodity prices facing periphery countries, and thus their terms of trade, just as volatile in the century or two before 1913 as they are today? And if they were, did the rich periphery countries in North America and Oceana (the second world) find ways to "insure" against the price volatility that the poor periphery countries in Asia, Latin America, and Africa, because of their backwardness, could not? If the answer again is in the affirmative, did commodity price volatility therefore contribute to the great divergence?

This chapter will show that export price and terms of trade volatility for commodities was just as great before 1913 as after 1970, and that it was even greater before 1870 when so much of the great divergence appeared. Furthermore chapter 11 will show that this price volatility diminished growth in the third world, while it did not do so in the second world: indeed it will show that a good share of the great divergence between 1870 and 1939 can be explained by commodity export price

Table 10.1

Comparative terms of trade volatility by region, 1960s to 1990s

Decade	Industrialized economies	East Asia and the Pacific	Latin America and Caribbean	Middle East and north Africa	South Asia	Sub-Saharan Africa
1960s	1.8	5.2	7.2	4.8	12.8	7.2
1970s	5.2	8.2	13	11.5	18	18.2
1980s	3.5	6.1	11	9	10.2	12.2
1990s	2.1	1.9	8.1	7.8	7.8	10.8
Average	3.2 (100)	5.4 (169)	9.8 (306)	8.3 (259)	12.2 (381)	12.1 (378)

Notes: These figures are taken from Loayza et al. (2007: fig. 3, 346). Terms of trade volatility is calculated as the standard deviation of the logarithmic change in terms of trade over each of the four decades 1960 to 2000.

volatility; and it will infer that an even bigger share might be explained for the pre-1870 period. But first: was commodity price and terms of trade volatility big before 1913?

What follows in the next section is a survey of the modern economics literature on the volatility-growth connection. The survey will focus on terms of trade volatility, since it seems to have been the biggest source of macroeconomic volatility *and* it was external or exogenous to the third world economies, at least in the 19th century. Section 10.3 will survey the price volatility evidence for the three centuries from 1700 to the present.

10.2 Commodity Price Volatility: The Modern Economics Literature

Modern observers regularly point to commodity price volatility as a key source of macroeconomic instability in commodity-specialized countries. The same is true of their terms of trade, of course, since commodity export prices are in the numerator while more stable manufacture and service import prices are in the denominator. Furthermore, while the import market basket includes a wide variety of goods and services—thus offering offsets to volatility of any individual item—the export basket is typically concentrated in a few goods.[1] For example, recall chapter 4 (table 4.2) where it was reported that in 1913 the top two export commodities accounted for about 63 percent of total exports for the average Latin American republic, and for some, like Brazil (coffee and rubber, 78 percent),

Chile (nitrates and copper, 78 percent), and Cuba (sugar and tobacco, 92 percent), the share was much higher. Thus high export concentration ensured that commodity price volatility of any given product got translated in to terms of trade volatility. And what we observed for commodity exporters in the 19th century, we observe today in modern Africa (Deaton and Miller 1996; Deaton 1999; Bates et al. 2007).

Until very recently, however, observers paid far less attention to the long-run growth implications of such instability.[2] Like what the economic historian Karl Gunnar Persson calls *les economists* in 17th- and 18th-century Europe (Persson 1999: ch. 1), modern economists stress the investment channel in looking for connections between commodity price volatility and growth. Indeed the development literature offers abundant contemporary microeconomic evidence linking income volatility to lower investment in physical and human capital, and even research and development. In addition the less-risky investment that does take place in the presence of price volatility also tends to be low return. Lower investment and lower returns on less investment means lower growth rates.

Households imperfectly protected from risk change their income-generating activities in the face of income volatility, diversifying toward low-risk alternatives with lower average returns, as well as to lower levels of investment. Macro analysis may fail to see these micro effects in households and small farms, but they have always been present and leave their mark on economywide performance (Roumasset 1976, 1979; Rosenweig and Wolpin 1993; Dercon 2004; Fafchamps 2004). Furthermore severe cuts in health and education follow negative income shocks to poor household in the third world—cuts that disproportionately affect children and hence long-term human capital accumulation. While these forces may have been less critical in the 19th century when land and physical capital were more important sources of growth than human capital, they certainly have been very relevant in the contemporary third world (Jensen 2000; Jacoby and Skoufias 1997; Frankenburg et al. 1999; Thomas et al. 2004).

Poor households find it difficult to smooth their expenditures in the face of shocks because they are rationed in (or even excluded from) credit and insurance markets. Family, friends, and informal community groups cannot offer much help since they share the same shocks, so poor households lower their investments and take fewer risks with what remains. Poor, small family firms (excluded from credit and insurance markets, or unable to find them in a financially backward environment) also find it difficult to smooth net returns on their assets, so they also lower investment and take fewer risks with what remains. That is, households and small firms have always found it difficult to smooth expenditures in the face of an unstable economic environment, and even more so the less developed are financial markets. Thus, whatever can be said about the damaging effects of price volatility on growth for today's third world, can be said with even greater strength in the 19th century when financial institutions and markets were much less developed than they are today, and institutions like the World Bank, the IMF, and NGOs were only in the distant future.

Perhaps most important, revenue sources geared to taxes on import and export trade will, by and large, be volatile. The first-order effect of export price volatility is, of course, directly on export tax revenues, but few third world countries used such taxes before 1913. The bigger second-order indirect effect is on import customs revenues as import demand exhibits the same volatility due to the impact of export earnings on domestic income. In short, poor governments whose revenue sources were mainly taxes on external trade (Coatsworth and Williamson 2004a, b; Williamson 2006b; Bates et al. 2007) had serious difficulty smoothing public investment on infrastructure and education in the face of terms of trade shocks. For example, 19th-century Latin America relied very heavily on customs duties as a source of revenue: the average share of customs duties in total revenues across eleven Latin American republics was 57.8 percent between 1820 and 1890 (Bates et al. 2007: 14–15). Customs revenues were even more important for federal governments (65.6 percent). Latin America and other non-colonies had another problem: their governments could not easily turn to world capital markets to smooth their investment expenditures since those "emerging markets" had to pay large premiums to lenders in Europe and North America even under the best economic conditions (Obstfeld and Taylor 2004; Mauro et al. 2006). But economic conditions were often even worse. While greater volatility increases the need for international borrowing to help smooth public investment expenditures, it has been shown quite persuasively that volatility actually made it harder for commodity exporters to borrow between 1970 and 2001 (Catão and Kapur 2004). It seems likely that the same was true between 1870 and 1913, and even more so before 1870 when a global capital market was only just emerging (Obsfelt and Taylor 2004; Mauro et al. 2006). Lower public investment ensued, and growth rates suffered.

Thus modern economic theory informs us that higher volatility in commodity prices, and hence the terms of trade, should reduce investment and growth in the presence of risk aversion, just as Persson's *les economists* argued regarding investment and productivity in 17th- and 18th-century

European agriculture (Persson 1999). Modern evidence seems to be consistent with the theory. Using data from 92 developing and developed economies between 1962 and 1985, Garey and Valerie Ramey (1995) found government spending and macroeconomic volatility to be inversely related, and that countries with higher volatility had lower mean growth. This result has since been confirmed for a more recent cross section of 91 countries (Fatás and Mihov 2006). Studies like these have repeatedly found that macroeconomic volatility diminishes long-run growth (e.g., Acemoglu et al. 2003; Hnatkovska and Loayza 2005; Loayza et al. 2007), and we now know more about why it is especially acute in poor countries. In an impressive analysis of more than 60 countries between 1970 and 2003, Steven Poelhekke and Frederick van der Ploeg (2007) find strong support for the core–periphery asymmetry hypothesis regarding volatility, and with a large set of controls. Furthermore, while capricious policy and political violence can and did add to volatility in poor countries, extremely volatile commodity prices "are the main reason why natural resources export revenues are so volatile" (Poelhekke and van der Ploeg 2007: 3) and thus why those economies are themselves so volatile. We will return to the Poelhekke and van der Ploeg post-1970 findings in chapter 11.

Philippe Aghion and his collaborators (2005, 2006) offer some other reasons why poor countries face higher volatility and why that higher volatility costs them so much more in diminished growth rates: macroeconomic volatility driven either by nominal exchange rate or commodity price movements will depress growth in poor economies with weak financial institutions and rigid nominal wages.[3] Both of these conditions characterized all poor economies in the past even more than it characterizes them today. While the literature cited on global financial capital markets documents that financial institutions only emerged in poor periphery countries in the late 19th century, the same can be said of domestic capital markets in developing countries today (Rousseau and Sylla 2005, 2006; Bordo and Rousseau 2006). Furthermore low-level equilibrium "subsistence" wages were common throughout the poor third world (Lewis 1954: chs. 6–8).

Finally, we will see in chapter 11 that recent work has confirmed that price volatility was also bad for growth in poor countries (but not in rich) between 1870 and 1939 (Blattman et al. 2007).

10.3 Commodity Price and Terms of Trade Volatility from 1700 to 1939

So how volatile were commodity prices in the 19th century compared with the 21st century?

When the world went global after about 1820, two forces were at work. First, as the poor periphery increasingly specialized in primary-product exports, they must have suffered greater price variability as a consequence, since commodities undergo more volatile price behavior than do manufactures. That is, by following comparative advantage, the poor periphery increasingly collected fewer and fewer eggs in their export basket—sometimes leaving only one or two eggs there—so that price movements of the fewer eggs had less chance to offset each other. Second, as local markets for commodities became increasingly integrated with global markets, price volatility of all commodities might well have fallen, since shocks to demand and supply in local markets must have been muted by conditions in larger world markets. Which dominated, the first or the second? In addition, as the rich periphery in North America and Oceana industrialized, primary products diminished as a share of total exports, while more price-stable manufactures increased their share (for the Australian example, see Bhattacharyya and Williamson 2009). To the extent that the poor periphery missed the industrial revolution, or to the extent that it was delayed, their exports remained dominated by primary products. Thus terms of trade volatility should have become more and more an attribute of the poor periphery alone.

Finally, since much of the modern third world has moved away from primary-product exports since 1950, the same commodity price volatility translates in to less terms of trade volatility. For all developing countries, the share of their exports that are manufactures rose from only about 17 percent of total exports in 1970 to about 64 percent by 1998, and this figure has become even higher a decade later. Most of the third world is now labor abundant and natural resource scarce, so they specialize in labor-intensive manufactures. Thus the classic image of third world specialization in primary products has been obsolescing, and fast (see Martin 2003; Lindert and Williamson 2003: 249). Even sub-Saharan Africa is shifting out of mineral and agricultural exports and into manufactures, although it only became apparent in the early 1990s. The share of manufactures in total exports in this region was only 12 or 13 percent in 1991, while it was almost 50 percent in 1998 (Martin 2003: fig. 6). The moral of the story is this: there is reason to think that today's manufactures-exporting third world faces less terms of trade volatility than the primary-product exporting third world did more than a century ago.

Terms of Trade Volatility from 1865 to 1939

Let us begin with the period which was Nobel laureate W. Arthur Lewis's (1978a) window on the third world—from the late 1860s to the eve of

World War II—when he was writing three decades ago. Just how volatile was the terms of trade for the poor periphery between 1865 and 1939?

Table 10.2 reports a measure of volatility for 24 countries in the poor periphery, and the three major colonial powers in the European core, France, Germany, and the United Kingdom. The volatility measure is based on the Hodrick–Prescott (HP) filter, a measure that is commonly used in the volatility literature on the modern third world commodity exporters (i.e., Mendoza 1997; Blattman et al. 2007). Basically the HP filter serves to calculate how prices deviate from the trend. The measure is calculated by decade and by country in the original source (the database underlying Blattman et al. 2007), and then table 10.2 takes unweighted averages for longer periods and regional groupings.

The basic finding in table 10.2 is that between the 1860s and World War I terms of trade volatility was about 2.7 times bigger for the poor periphery than it was for the European colonizing core (8.1 vs. 3). It is of some interest to note that the ratio of terms of trade volatility between industrialized economies and the third world in the 1990s was 2.9.[4] Apparently there has been a lot of historical persistence in the price volatility data since the late 19th century. Hence what is true today was also true of the half century before World War I: external price volatility was a special attribute of the poor commodity exporters. Both for the recent period and the pre-1914 period, the world was pro-global with integrated commodity markets, and these were also periods of relative macro stability. Neither of those conditions held for the two world wars and the interwar decades of antitrade policy, postwar readjustment, and the great depression. Thus it is not surprising that price instability rose everywhere, but it *is* surprising that it rose *more* in the industrial core so that the "volatility gap" diminished from the 1910s to the 1930s. Still the gap persisted: the poor periphery underwent 40 percent more terms of trade volatility than the industrial core (10.2 vs. 7.3) between 1913 and 1939.

Next, consider which regions in the poor periphery had to face the greatest price volatility in the late 19th century. At the top of the list was Latin America (just as it was in the late 20th century: table 10.1), with a volatility measure a bit above three times that of the core. Foreign markets were, it appears, a lot more stable for the southern cone—exporting wheat, hides, and meat—than for the rest—exporting minerals, sugar, and intermediates for manufacturing. If Argentina and Uruguay are removed from the Latin American group, the regional average rises from 8.9 to 10.1 (not shown in the table). Among these, Brazil, Colombia, and Cuba suffered by far the greatest terms of trade volatility. If volatility is bad for growth, it follows that these three countries must have suffered a huge growth

Table 10.2
Terms of trade volatility, 1865 to 1939

	1860s–1900s	Relatives	1910s–1930s	Relatives	1860s–1930s	Relatives
Latin America	8.916	302	11.773	161	10.345	202
Argentina	5.314		12.216		8.765	
Brazil	14.492		17.380		15.936	
Chile	7.216		10.321		8.769	
Colombia	15.155		12.038		13.597	
Cuba	9.607		13.290		11.449	
Mexico	7.461		8.856		8.159	
Peru	6.663		8.651		7.657	
Uruguay	5.419		11.434		8.427	
South and Southeast Asia	7.780	264	11.036	151	9.408	183
Burma	6.945		13.463		10.204	
Ceylon	15.154		13.044		14.100	
India	5.352		9.233		7.293	
Indonesia	9.558		6.904		8.231	
Philippines	7.823		10.004		8.914	
Thailand	8.036		13.569		10.803	
East Asia	7.518	255	5.879	80	6.699	131
Japan	7.929		5.510		6.720	
China	7.106		6.248		6.677	

Table 10.2
(continued)

Middle East	8.039	273	15.090	206	11.565	225
Egypt	11.863		18.591		15.227	
Greece	6.512		15.182		10.847	
Serbia	7.983		12.057		10.020	
Turkey	5.796		14.528		10.162	
European periphery	8.195	278	7.008	96	7.602	148
Italy	14.021		4.349		9.185	
Portugal	4.285		8.250		6.268	
Russia	9.482		9.318		9.400	
Spain	4.990		6.113		5.552	
Poor periphery	8.090	274	10.157	139	9.124	178
Three core colonizers	2.948	100	7.311	100	5.130	100
France	4.038		6.728		5.383	
Germany	2.089		7.380		4.735	
United Kingdom	2.716		7.825		5.271	

Source: Data underlying Blattman et al. (2007).
Note: Volatility is measured by the Hodrick–Prescott filter with a smoothing parameter = 300. The regional averages are unweighted.

burden, even compared to others in Latin America where volatility was so pronounced.

The most price stable region was East Asia (just as it was in the late 20th century: table 10.1), but its terms of trade volatility was still two and a half times that of the core. The other poor periphery regions recorded price volatility which lay between East Asia and Latin America (just as they did in the late 20th century: table 10.1). Four countries stand out: Italy in the European periphery (14.0), Egypt in the Middle East (11.9), and Ceylon (15.2) and Indonesia (9.6) in South and Southeast Asia. All of these four countries were exporting commodities that had especially high price volatility in world markets, and depending on the results of chapter 11 where the impact of volatility is assessed, they must have suffered lower growth as a consequence.

Terms of Trade Volatility before 1870

Consider now the earlier period before 1870 where the data are harder to come by. Table 10.3 uses this new data base to document terms of trade volatility for the century before 1870, but also up to World War I so as to check comparability with the better 1870 to 1914 data in table 10.2. While there is considerable overlap between the country sample we just analyzed in table 10.2 and this one in table 10.3, there are some modest differences. The new table includes the Levant (composing present-day Iraq, Israel, Lebanon, Palestine, Jordan, and Syria) and Malaya but excludes Burma, Colombia, Greece, and Peru. Also table 10.3 now takes the United Kingdom by itself as representative of the core. That said, terms of trade volatility was much greater in the United Kingdom during the wartime years 1782 to 1820, than it was in the peacetime *pax britannica* century that followed. This result is hardly surprising given what we know about the volatility of the conflict itself and its stop-go impact on trade (Findlay and O'Rourke 2007), and given that the same was true for the decades 1910–1920 and 1940–1950 (not reported in table 10.3). The peacetime years after 1820 were another matter entirely. First, terms of trade volatility in the poor periphery was more than three times what it was in the United Kingdom, either between 1820 and 1870 (9.18/2.91 = 3.2) or between 1870 and 1913 (7.09/2 = 3.5). Recall that the ratio of terms of trade volatility between industrialized economies and the third world in the 1990s was 2.9, somewhat *lower* than it was between 1820 and 1913. Second, terms of trade volatility in the periphery rose over the century, from 6.5 before 1820 to 9.2 between 1820 and 1870, and to 7.1 after 1870, a trend consistent with evolving export concentration as the poor

Table 10.3
Terms of trade volatility, 1782 to 1913

Region	Starting year in the series	Pre-1820	1820–1870	1870–1913
United Kingdom	1782	11.985	2.910	2.006
Europe periphery		4.036	10.720	7.058
Italy	1817	0.922	19.003	11.214
Russia	1782	3.226	10.722	6.104
Spain	1782	7.959	6.472	6.023
Portugal	1842	na	6.681	4.891
Latin America		3.728	6.429	8.140
Argentina	1811	4.409	6.961	8.303
Brazil	1826	na	2.174	10.283
Chile	1810	5.116	6.367	7.865
Cuba	1826	na	9.435	6.822
Mexico	1782	1.658	5.531	5.379
Venezuela	1830	na	8.108	10.185
Middle East		2.902	13.611	7.316
Egypt	1796	2.982	17.861	11.760
Ottoman Turkey	1800	2.821	6.549	3.289
Levant	1839	na	16.423	6.898
South Asia		11.876	9.628	5.364
Ceylon	1782	17.860	7.590	7.532
India	1800	5.891	11.666	3.196
Southeast Asia		7.788	6.977	7.303
Indonesia	1825	na	3.202	6.678
Malaya	1882	na	na	9.199
Philippines	1782	7.992	9.778	6.603
Siam	1800	7.583	7.951	6.732
East Asia		15.554	10.527	4.952
China	1782	15.554	19.752	4.311
Japan	1857	na	1.302	5.592
Average periphery		6.460	9.176	7.089

Source: Williamson (2008: table 3).
Note: Volatility measured using the Hodrick–Prescott filter with smoothing parameter 6.25, which is appropriate for annual observations. The periphery average is unweighted.

periphery exploited comparative advantage. Third, and as we saw for the 1865 to 1913 years, terms of trade volatility varied considerably around the periphery early in the 19th century. Between 1820 and 1870 the highest volatility measures were recorded in the European periphery (especially Italy and Russia), the Middle East (especially Egypt and the Levant), and East Asia (especially China), regions whose long-run economic progress must have suffered accordingly. Latin America and Southeast Asia consistently recorded lower volatility than the rest of the periphery, but it was still more than twice that of the United Kingdom, and it rises in the 1870 to 1913 years when Colombia and Peru are added. South Asia was about average, but it was still more than three times that of the United Kingdom. If we are looking for countries in the periphery where terms of trade volatility would have had an especially powerful deleterious effect on GDP growth performance before 1870, the places to look would be China, Cuba, Egypt, India, Italy, the Levant, the Philippines, and Russia. But with the exception of Brazil and Japan, every periphery country had much higher price volatility than did the European core before 1870. There were no exceptions after 1870: every country in the poor periphery had higher price volatility than did the United Kingdom.

Commodity Price Volatility after 1700

The farther back in time we reach, the fewer the country terms of trade we can document: we lose eight countries when exploring the period 1782 to 1820, and we lose all the rest before 1782. But while we cannot report country terms of trade for most of the 18th century,[5] we *can* report the price volatility of primary product commodities and finished manufactures.

So did commodities exhibit greater volatility than manufactures even in the 18th century? The answer is unambiguous: yes. Table 10.4 reports the price volatility of all items, primary-product commodities (COM), and final manufactured goods (MAN) for the 250 years between 1700 and 1950. The volatility of COM and MAN relative to all items is also reported in parentheses. In every case over the 250 years, the relative volatility indicator is less than 100 for MAN. In some cases where the MAN sample is very small, that ratio is small, like between 1720 and 1775 for Philadelphia (only 3 MAN observations), but apart from that case manufacture price volatility was from 74 percent less (Denmark 1750–1800) to 9 percent less (Britain 1790–1819). The unweighted average between 1775 and 1950 tells us that manufactured goods prices were 25 percent lower than all items, while

Table 10.4

Commodity versus manufactures price volatility, 1700 to 1950

	All items	Commodities (COM)	Manufactures (MAN)
American prices: Bezanson et al.			
1720–1775	0.084	0.085 (101)	0.082 (98)
1770–1790	0.122	0.126 (103)	0.104 (85)
1784–1861	0.067	0.073 (109)	0.048 (72)
1852–1896	0.074	0.079 (107)	0.056 (76)
English prices: Clark			
1700–1819	0.137	0.143 (104)	0.108 (79)
1820–1869	0.131	0.137 (105)	0.105 (80)
British prices: Gayer–Rostow–Schwartz			
1790–1819	0.056	0.057 (102)	0.051 (91)
1820–1850	0.056	0.057 (102)	0.047 (84)
Dutch prices: Posthumus			
1750–1800	0.043	0.044 (102)	0.037 (86)
Danish prices: Friis–Glamann			
1750–1800	0.076	0.082 (108)	0.020 (26)

Source: Jacks et al. (2009: table 3).

commodities were 5 percent higher; alternatively, the price volatility for commodities was 40 percent higher than for manufactures.

Are commodity prices more volatile during world anti-global episodes? If local shocks to supply and demand are stabilized when the local economy trades with the large world economy, commodity prices should have been less volatile when the world was more pro-global. Thus did commodity prices become less volatile when the world went global in the 19th century after the European wars, and did commodity prices become more volatile when the world went autarkic between the World Wars? Table 10.4 answers these questions in the affirmative. The Clark series for England, the Friis-Glamann series for Denmark, and the Posthumus series for the Netherlands all show higher price volatility during war (1776–1819) than during peace. The Bezanson series also shows higher price volatility during war (1776–1819 and 1861–1872) than during peace. But the biggest anti-global world regime was the autarkic stretch of two World Wars, two postwar adjustments, and one great depression between 1914 and 1950. During these four decades, price volatility was twice as great as during the peacetime decades that preceded them.

10.4   Moving toward a Final Reckoning

In chapters 4 through 8 we showed how the terms of trade boom caused de-industrialization in the poor periphery. To the extent that industrialization is a carrier of growth, the latter must have suffered in the de-industrializing third world. Chapter 9 documented how the terms of trade boom and the subsequent export expansion raised inequality in those parts of the poor periphery that exported commodities. We were able to document the size of that increase between 1870 and 1913 in a number of key places. To the extent that the terms of trade and inequality were positively correlated, one can only infer the inequality rise must have been even greater before 1870 when the terms of trade had the greater rise as well. And to the extent that these forces rewarded rent-seeking (and the institutions that favored it) and penalized accumulation and risk-taking (and the institutions that favored them), growth must have suffered. This chapter has added a third drag on growth in the poor periphery: it faced much greater terms of trade volatility than did the core, implying that growth must have suffered in the former compared to the latter.

We now have three reasons for suspecting that 19th-century globalization forces were less favorable to growth in the third world compared with the core, thus contributing to the great divergence.

11 Tying the Knot: The Globalization and Great Divergence Connection

11.1 Waiting for the Jury to Report Out

Chapter 1 showed how the great divergence between Europe and the third world rose to huge heights across the 19th century: that is, the third world fell behind. Chapter 2 showed how the first global century between about 1815 and 1913 was characterized by a world trade boom during which what we now call the third world enjoyed a spectacular improvement in its terms of trade. Thus, for most of the century its primary-product export prices soared and its manufactures import prices plunged. Was this correlation between world globalization, the third world terms of trade, and the great divergence spurious or was it causal? For two hundred years hot debates over the question have raged with no resolution, simply because nobody did the hard empirical work—until now.

Before we press on with the evidence, let us be very clear what this chapter is *not* proposing. It is *not* proposing that there were no gains to trade for the third world. Indeed theory and the historical record both argue unambiguously that rich *and* poor countries gained from trade (although, as chapter 9 showed, some residents gained more than others). Thus the chapter is not proposing that the third world was made poorer by trade: income per capita *levels* were clearly increased by trade. Furthermore this chapter is *not* proposing that there was no per capita GDP growth in the poor periphery during the great trade boom. Some grew faster than others, of course, but the faster growers were typically those with the greater terms of trade booms and those that exploited those booms by moving resources in to their export sectors with speed and efficiency.

So much for what this chapter does *not* propose. What this chapter *does* propose, however, is that the great trade boom across the 19th century raised growth rates by much more in the rich countries than in the poor countries—indeed it lowered it in many places, thus contributing to the great divergence. The chapter argues that globalization and the world trade boom had an asymmetric impact on country growth performance, favoring the rich industrial core over the poor agricultural periphery.

As the last chapter suggested in its conclusion, there were at least three ways that these powerful global forces might have favored growth in the rich industrial core by far more than in the poor agricultural periphery. First, there was the potential impact of de-industrialization. Not only did the third world participate in the trade boom, but as mentioned many times in this book, its commodity export prices soared and its manufactured import prices plunged over the century before World War I. The third world and the first world both responded exactly the way conventional theory has predicted since Adam Smith and David Ricardo—they both exploited their increasingly powerful comparative advantages, the third world specializing increasingly in commodity exports and Europe (plus their English-speaking offshoots) specializing increasingly in manufactures. Another way of saying the same thing is that the third world became less industrial (chapters 4–8) while the European core became more industrial, moving, in the language of formal economics, to the corners (Krugman and Venables 1995) or, in W. Arthur Lewis's (1978a) words, to the "new world economic order."

To the extent that industrialization is a carrier of growth, third world development must have suffered by the de-industrialization, relative to first world development. This view was embedded in the writings of Albert Hirschman (1958) and Gunnar Myrdal (1957) a half century ago, and they were made more formal thirty years later by, for example, Kevin Murphy, Andrei Shleifer, and Robert Vishny (1989). In the past twenty years this view has been greatly richened and dubbed *endogenous growth*. The belief is that positive externalities are sector- and location-specific, favoring urban and industrial clusters. These

externalities between firms [and industries] can be either technological or pecuniary, the former arising when actions of one firm affect another without going through a market and the latter when the interaction is through a market . . . . [In both cases] firms are not able to capture the full benefits . . . of their actions. (Venables 2007: 271)

These effects imply increasing returns (Krugman 1981, 1991a, b): the key is that traditional agriculture obeys constant returns to scale, and diminishing returns to land, while industry obeys increasing returns to scale (Matsuyama 1991, 1992).

According to these endogenous growth (and endogenous comparative advantage) theories, once a country starts specializing in manufactures, its comparative advantage in industry will be reinforced and its overall growth stimulated. Not so for the commodity exporter. Paul Krugman, Anthony Venables, and others, have shown formally how a world trade boom can contribute to economic divergence between trading partners (Krugman 1991a, b; Krugman and Venables 1995; Fujita, Krugman, and Venables 1999; Gylfason et al. 1999; Sachs and Warner 2001; Venables 2007: 275–79), and we argue here, to the great divergence across the 19th century. Or so says the theory, but in the words of Venables, while "these views are suggestive, . . . empirical work has not yet been undertaken to confirm them" (Venables 2007: 279).

Second, there was the potential impact of rising inequality given its source. Chapter 9 documented how the terms of trade boom and the subsequent export expansion raised inequality in those parts of the poor periphery that exported commodities. We were able to document the size of that increase between 1870 and 1913 in a number of key locations, and it was driven by the spectacular rise in rents on natural resources and thus to the incomes of those who owned them. To the extent that the terms of trade and inequality were positively correlated, one is encouraged to infer that the inequality (and natural resource rent) rise must have been even greater before 1870 when the terms of trade underwent a greater rise as well. And to the extent that these forces rewarded rent seeking (and the institutions that favored it), penalized accumulation and risk-taking (and the institutions that favored them), or even caused social unrest and conflict over who owned the rising natural resource rents—what Aaron Tornell and Philip Lane (1999) called the *voracity effect*, growth had a second reason to have been raised by less than in the industrial core. Certainly the argument that natural resource specialization tends to create an institutional weakness that inhibits growth can found frequently in the recent literature (Gelb 1998; Ross 1999; Auty 2001; Torvik 2002; Isham et al. 2005).[1]

This second reason has a name, the *resource curse*. Jeffrey Sachs and Andrew Warner (1995, 2001), for example, have observed that resource-rich countries tend to grow more slowly than resource-poor countries. A popular explanation, due to Raúl Prebisch (1950), Hans Singer (1950), and others, is, as we have noted, that the pattern of comparative advantage forces resource-rich countries to specialize in sectors with little potential for learning and productivity improvement.[2] An alternative story is that resource sectors are inherently more vulnerable to expropriation, and thus capital flight (Tornell and Lane 1999), colonial intervention (Acemoglu et al. 2002), conflict (Collier 2000; Bates 2001; Bates et al. 2001; Bannon and Collier 2003), and poor growth. Anne Krueger (1974), for example, famously argued that resource-owning elites may suppress growth through rent-seeking in poor and resource-abundant countries. In addition to Sachs and Warner, empirical support for the resource curse view has been confirmed many times on modern data (Gylfason et al. 1999; Neumayer 2004; Mehlum et al. 2006; Lederman and Maloney 2007), most recently by Robert Lucas (2009). Historical support for the thesis has also been reported by Yael Hadass and the author (2003) who found that between 1870 and World War I, positive terms of trade movements reduced growth in poor commodity exporters. Our sample, however, covered few of the commodity exporters that remained poor up to WWII, and we did not control for the impact of a third factor, which follows.

The previous chapter added a third potential drag on growth in the third world primary-product exporter: it faced much greater export price and thus terms of trade volatility than did the industrial core. Theory tells us that price volatility is bad for growth in these poor countries by encouraging low-risk and low-returns investment projects as well as less investment. This kind of reasoning implies that growth must have suffered in the third world compared with the first world.

While supported by economic theory, all of this is pure speculation, at least as it applies to the great divergence across the 19th century. The rest of this chapter will try to persuade the reader that the historical evidence unambiguously supports the speculation. Two hundred years of history will be broken up in to three parts. The next section will explore the episode that informed Prebisch and Singer's work and helped support the third world antitrade policies up to the 1970s. The trade-divergence effects were indeed significant during this Singer–Prebisch period between 1870 and 1939, as the conventional literature has hypothesized. However, we will see that the source was not so much terms of trade trends, but its volatility. Section 11.3 explores the period before 1870 where it appears that the trade-divergence effects were most powerful, and when secular terms of trade forces *were* doing much of the work. Section 11.4 turns to the modern era since 1970, during which time the trade-divergence effects have moderated throughout the third world and disappeared completely from a lot of it. Where it still exists, mostly in Africa, price volatility is mostly still at work. Where it does not, those countries now export labor-intensive manufactures (Martin 2003, 2007).

11.2   Trade-Divergence Effects during the Singer–Prebisch Episode 1870–1939

The recent work of Chris Blattman, Jason Hwang, and myself (2007) stretches over three twenty-year periods—the rapid expansion of global markets from 1870 to 1889, their maturation from 1890 to 1909, and the tumultuous interwar years from 1920 to 1939. These periods were chosen because they represent episodes of global integration and disintegration, inducing large terms of trade changes and economywide responses. The two World War decades were excluded because of the absence of data and the gross distortions to trade and prices attributable to war demands, blockades, and skyrocketing transport costs.[3] With the help of Michael Clemens (Clemens and Williamson 2004), we collected new terms of data for 35 countries, data that have been used elsewhere in this book. Table 11.1 lists our sample, with summaries of incomes, exports, and terms of trade. The first step was to obtain the largest sample possible for periphery countries where the terms of trade might be considered exogenous, and then to examine more and more conservative assumptions about which of the countries in the periphery was truly a price-taker. Six industrial leaders are included in a parsimonious definition of the core: Austria-Hungary, France, Germany, Italy, the United Kingdom, and the United States. By 1870 these countries were already wealthy, industrialized, major exporters of both primary commodities and manufactures, and price-makers in world markets. The periphery was mostly poor, commodity-dependent, and highly concentrated in one or two export products. Our sample includes eight from the European periphery (Denmark, Greece, Norway, Portugal, Serbia, Spain, Sweden, and Russia), eight from Latin America (Argentina, Brazil, Colombia, Chile, Cuba, Mexico, Peru, and Uruguay), ten from Asia and the Middle East (Burma, Ceylon, China, Egypt, India, Indonesia, Japan, the Philippines, Siam, and Turkey), and three European offshoots (Australia, Canada, and New Zealand). The sample represents more than 85 percent of world population and more than 95 percent of world GDP in 1914.

The published paper supplies the details regarding the database (Blattman et al. 2007). The export share is calculated as the ratio of exports to national income. The share of exports in primary products follows a definition similar to that in Sachs and Warner (1997) and is the ratio of all exports except manufactured products and specie to total exports. Population growth rates are straightforward. The schooling level is calculated by dividing primary school enrollment by the population under age of 14.

Table 11.1
The 1870 to 1939 sample

| | GDP per capita | | | Exports | | | Terms of trade | | |
	1870	1939	Average growth	Value ('000s)	Primary products (%) 1870	1939	Average growth	Average volatility	Exogeneity
Core									
Austria	974	4,123	2.03	1,918	28	36	-0.18	9.70	*
France	1,858	4,748	1.77	7,000	44	41	-0.18	5.67	*
Germany	1,913	5,549	2.17	5,017	38	18	0.85	4.76	*
Italy	1,467	3,444	1.18	1,096	88	45	-0.39	13.19	*
United States	2,457	6,568	1.46	4,488	86	48	0.88	5.84	*
United Kingdom	3,263	5,979	0.91	11,811	11	24	0.43	4.83	*
European periphery									
Denmark	1,927	5,766	1.74	355	96	85	0.20	7.24	
Greece	1,295	2,687	0.94	84	94	94	-0.29	7.38	
Norway	1,303	4,108	1.62	217	97	58	0.58	8.81	
Portugal	1,085	1,739	0.73	183	96	61	1.20	8.02	
Russia	1,023	2,237	1.27	2,456	98	82	0.04	7.36	†
Sweden	1,664	5,029	1.95	411	91	56	0.57	4.09	
Serbia	822	1,412	0.83	59	96	86	0.54	9.26	
Spain	1,376	2,127	0.73	796	71	84	-0.16	6.72	
European offshoots									
Australia	3,801	5,631	0.84	861	97	95	-0.25	9.47	†
Canada	1,620	4,518	1.66	588	95	74	-0.20	7.84	‡
New Zealand	3,115	6,492	0.80	116	100	99	-0.17	6.82	

Table 11.1
(continued)

Latin America								
Argentina	1,311	4,143	2.15	302	100	97	-0.01	7.20	‡
Brazil	740	1,307	0.82	1,055	100	100	-0.82	17.52	†
Chile	927	3,178	2.21	292	99	100	-0.49	7.74	†
Colombia	1,183	1,905	0.65	69	97	98	-0.37	19.05	
Cuba	1,568	978	-1.08	967	80	97	-1.15	10.62	
Mexico	710	1,428	1.07	225	100	98	-1.00	7.82	
Peru	389	1,884	2.15	296	99	100	-0.83	7.06	
Uruguay	1,311	4,148	2.15	101	100	100	0.19	7.66	
Asia and Middle East								
Burma	602	681	-0.20	154	93	98	0.12	8.08	
Ceylon	769	1,01_	0.47	206	98	99	-0.03	14.93	
China	523	76_	0.54	1,116	99	82	-0.99	6.75	†
Egypt	271	787	1.77	442	93	95	-1.00	11.51	
India	558	64_	0.20	2,108	93	72	-0.40	6.76	†
Indonesia	657	1,12_	0.52	309	98	98	-0.55	9.70	
Japan	741	2,709	1.60	164	71	23	-0.73	6.79	‡
Philippines	912	1,476	0.58	291	99	94	-1.38	8.30	†
Thailand	717	833	0.27	61	99	99	-0.05	9.17	
Turkey	508	1,430	1.61	1,022	100	94	-0.11	7.63	

Source: Blattman et al. (2007: table 2).

Notes: * Initially industrialized countries; low initial commodity dependence; high degree of market power. † Produce more than a third of the global share of exports in any commodity. ‡ Produce between a third and a fourth of the global share of exports in any commodity.

Commodity Price and Terms of Trade Behavior

The most important feature of commodity prices during this Prebisch–Singer episode is not their long-term drift but rather their volatility. Figure 3.2 shows that the Prebisch–Singer period only includes two decades of the great 19th-century third world terms of trade boom, since it peaked between the 1870s and 1890s. The remainder of the period from the 1890s to the 1930s covered the terms of trade collapse that attracted the attention of Prebisch, Singer, and their followers. From their vantage point shortly after World War II, Prebisch and Singer were certainly correct in reporting a secular decline in the periphery's terms of trade, a decline that pretty much erased the boom from 1870 to the peak.

While there was no secular boom over the full seven decades between 1870 and 1939, commodity price volatility was another matter. Chapter 10 reported that some primary products were very volatile (e.g., coffee and tobacco), while others were relatively stable (e.g., wheat and iron). Furthermore the price volatility between commodities often differed by a factor of two or three, and in some cases by a factor of six or seven. What's more, while some commodity prices rose (e.g., tobacco and wool), others suffered sharp reversals (e.g., rubber, which was supplanted by cheaper synthetics in the interwar period). Since most countries specialized in a handful of commodities, these differences in price behavior translated into diverse country experiences—a true commodity lottery (Díaz-Alejandro 1984).

In short, the terms of trade during this period of 1870 to 1939 exhibited considerable year-to-year fluctuations and cycles, but little long-term trend, suggesting that, in contrast with the pre-1870 period, terms of trade volatility mattered far more than did secular trend.

Empirical Strategy

This chapter has two interests. First, it attempts to explain the diversity in economic performance among primary-product exporters. After all, there is a tremendous divergence in incomes and growth rates within the commodity-dependent sample (table 11.1), variation that is at least as interesting and meaningful as that between industrial Europe and the periphery. Second, it attempts to explain differences in growth performance between core and periphery—the great divergence. The relationship between the terms of trade and income growth may be fundamentally different in industrial countries than it is in the commodity-dependent countries. If industrialization is a carrier of growth, and positive terms of trade movements reinforce global patterns of trade, then secular improvements in the terms of trade may be beneficial for growth in the core but less so, or even damaging, in the periphery. Indeed we *expect* to find asymmetry.

The basic empirical specification used is a regression of the average annual growth rate, *GR*, on measures of the growth and volatility in the terms of trade, *TOTG* and *TOTV*:

$$GR_{it} = \beta_0 + \beta_1 TOTG_{it} + \beta_2 TOTV_{it} + \mathbf{Z_{it}\Phi} + \mu_i + v_t + \varepsilon_{it} \qquad (11.1)$$

for country *i* and time period *t*, a vector of controls *Z*, country and time period dummies *μ* and *υ*, and residuals *ε*. Since the persistence of commodity shocks is fairly high (Deaton and Laroque 1992), a decade is taken as the unit of observation. Thus the dependent variable is the average annual growth of GDP per capita over each decade. Terms of trade growth is measured as the percent change in the terms of trade trend over the decade. There are several options for decomposing terms of trade movements into trend and volatility. Enrique Mendoza (1997) employed the terms of trade growth rate and the standard deviation of the growth rate, while Parantap Basu and Darryl McLeod (1992) and others have used the Hodrick–Prescott (HP) filter, the option employed here. As it turns out, the HP data filter and the Mendoza method generate very similar results, and the findings reported here are robust to both. All our specifications include country and decade fixed effects in order to control for unobserved fundamentals that were also determining growth performance, fundamentals that are not the focus of this book.

Were Periphery Terms of Trade and Comparative Advantage Exogenous?
There are two main sources of concern about what might be called our identification assumption: (1) endogeneity of the terms of trade shock in cases where countries are not international price-takers and (2) the presence of an invisible third force (e.g., the quality of institutions and governance) that result in both poor growth and the choice of a commodity export with high price volatility and poor price trends.

The first concern is that some countries in our sample were large enough producers of a particular commodity to affect the world price. While it may certainly have been true, there are two reasons why this is unlikely to be a problem for the analysis. First, violations of this assumption (e.g., Chile with its nitrates or even copper) will cause our results to *understate* the predicted positive impact of a terms of trade boom on growth. For instance, if a reduction in the supply of Chilean copper caused the world market price to rise just as copper output (and hence GDP) in Chile fell, there would be a negative correlation between the terms of trade trend and output growth, biasing the coefficient on trend growth downward. Second, the results are very robust to the exclusion of periphery countries that may be suspected of being price-makers rather than price-takers. Table 11.1 identifies major exporters who produced between a quarter and a third of world exports of any commodity and those that exported more than a third. According to the more than one-third criteria, Australia, Brazil, Chile, China, India, the Philippines, and Russia should be omitted.[4] Excluding in addition all countries that supplied more than a quarter of world exports of any commodity, would imply that Japan, Canada, and Argentina should be added to the omit list. The one-third export share seems like a reasonable lower bound on world market share before a country begins to have a significant impact on world price, but the terms of trade results are highly to robust to even more severe assumptions about exogeneity of the terms of trade.

The second concern is that an omitted force, such as the quality of institutions, is driving both the choice of primary commodity and the pattern and rate of development. It might be suspected, for instance, that countries with particularly poor governance or "extractive" institutions might systematically choose more volatile commodities, and so volatility would be negatively correlated with growth because it acts as a proxy for poor institutions rather than for its own sake. This suspicion is unwarranted. To the extent that initial institutional quality influenced the choice of commodity, it should be captured by country fixed effects. In virtually every periphery country in our sample, the choice of commodities was made long before 1870 and persisted until the end of our period. Any impact of institutional quality on commodity choice is therefore largely time invariant and will be swept out with fixed effects. In addition the historical and empirical evidence strongly support the commodity lottery view—the choice of which commodity to produce and export was not a choice at all, but rather was an outcome determined by geography, factor endowments, and international demand, not institutional quality. The new world provides concrete examples. Where minerals were produced—whether nitrates in Chile or silver in Mexico—the commodity choice was essentially a function of what was under the ground and distance from port. The range of agricultural products available for export was likewise a function of the local endowments and transport costs. The mountainous Andean countries could never compete in wheat production with the Canadian prairie or the Argentine pampas, and hence Canada remained specialized in wheat (and lumber) while Argentina remained specialized in wheat and beef. In Colombia the cost of road and rail construction over three mountain ranges alone meant that overland transport was almost prohibitively expensive,[5] and was justified only for high value-to-weight export products, such as gold, tobacco, and coffee.[6]

Third, where institutions and commodity choice are related, such as in the plantation-style production of sugar or cotton, both poor institutions and high-price volatility seem to have sprung from the same source—local factor endowments. Stanley Engerman and Kenneth Sokoloff (1997) have argued convincingly that the commodity choice, the organization of production, and later institutions in the new world were all functions of factor endowments, including climate and the availability of forced labor. It was not the case that initially poor institutions by themselves resulted in the production and export of volatile commodities. True, we might expect countries with better institutions to handle commodity price shocks better because of a greater ability to borrow and smooth investment and government finances, or because of a reduced likelihood of civil conflict (Bhattacharrya and Williamson 2009). But within the periphery we see virtually no systematic relationship between institutional quality and subsequent volatility.

Empirical Findings

Table 11.2 illustrates two important aspects of historical growth before World War II that have never before received attention. First, not only does high commodity price volatility help explain poor economic performance in the periphery compared with the core, but it also helps explain poor relative performance *within* the periphery. Second, there were asymmetric growth effects between core and periphery. After controlling for volatility, secular increases in the terms of trade have *no* impact on growth in the periphery while they have *positive and significant* impact on growth in the core. Development economists since Prebisch and Singer have thought that declining terms of trade inhibits development. Our evidence suggests their concern was misplaced, since it appears the much-lamented correlation between slow income growth and terms of trade deterioration was probably spurious, at least after 1870. The correlation in the periphery between the secular terms of trade boom *before* 1870, de-industrialization, and poor income growth may, however, have more to support it, as we will see below. After controlling for trend changes in the terms of trade, terms of trade volatility has a *negative and significant* impact on growth in the periphery but *no* impact on growth in the core. Price volatility mattered in contributing to the great divergence, a fact that has been ignored previously in the historical literature.

Table 11.2
GDP growth and the terms of trade, 1870 to 1939

Dependent variable: Decadal average GDP per capita growth

	(1) Core	(2) Periphery	(3) Core	(4) Periphery
TOT trend growth	0.411 [0.181]**	−0.041 [0.135]	0.735 [0.319]**	−0.378 [0.153]**
TOT volatility	0.015 [0.036]	−0.105 [0.042]**	0.017 [0.036]	−0.100 [0.038]***
(TOT growth) × (Exports/GDP)			−3.366 [2.093]	2.382 [0.897]***
Exports/GDP			−1.237 [4.424]	7.531 [3.811]*
Constant	1.154 [0.764]	3.119 [0.443]***	1.280 [0.824]	1.898 [0.700]***
Observations	79	125	79	125
R-squared	0.45	0.34	0.48	0.42
Decade dummies	Y	Y	Y	Y
Country dummies	Y	Y	Y	Y
Mean values (standard deviation)				
GDP growth	1.38 [1.28]	0.99 [1.79]	1.38 [1.28]	0.99 [1.79]
TOT growth	0.36 [1.09]	−0.49 [1.53]	0.36 [1.09]	−0.49 [1.53]
TOT volatility	7.67 [5.56]	9.46 [5.52]	7.67 [5.56]	9.46 [5.52]
(TOT growth) × (Exports/GDP)			0.03 [0.13]	−0.09 [0.35]
Exports/GDP			0.10 [0.06]	0.14 [0.12]
Marginal Impact				
TOT trend growth	0.41	−0.04	0.41	−0.04
TOT volatility	0.02	−0.11	0.02	−0.10
Impact of a 1 standard deviation increase				
TOT trend growth	0.45	−0.06	0.45	−0.06
TOT volatility	0.08	−0.58	0.09	−0.55

Source: Underlying Blattman et al. (2007).
Notes: Robust standard errors in brackets * significant at 10%, ** significant at 5%,
*** significant at 1%.

These results are displayed for the full period, 1870 to 1939, omitting the war decade, and all 35 countries are treated as price-takers. We will examine more conservative definitions of who were price takers in a moment. Note also the top half of table 11.2 reports the point estimates and standard errors for the terms of trade (henceforth TOT) effects that were just summarized above. The bottom half reports the quantitative and economic importance of these TOT effects, including sample means and standard deviations of the independent variables, and the impact of a one-standard-deviation increase in TOT growth and volatility.

As for the bottom half of table 11.2, the marginal effect of an increase in TOT volatility is to decrease income growth in the periphery by about 0.1 percentage points. Furthermore a periphery country with a one standard deviation greater level of volatility than the mean will grow almost 0.6 percentage points per annum more slowly than the sample average. Given that the average annual rate of GDP per capita growth in the periphery was about 1 percent per year, the volatility effects are quite powerful—the marginal effect is 10 percent of average growth, and the standard deviation change close to an astonishing 60 percent (–0.58/0.99).

TOT trend growth was also interacted with export share in columns 3 and 4 of table 11.2 to see whether the terms of trade impact was contingent on the level of export dependence. It seems reasonable that more export-oriented countries would respond more forcefully to external shocks, and so they did. The terms of trade trend growth effects in the periphery are now both significantly negative, strengthening the asymmetric effects between core and periphery. For the periphery, the interaction term is positive and significant, suggesting that an increase in the terms of trade trend growth is associated with a smaller fall in income growth in the most export-oriented countries, perhaps even a rise in the biggest. The effects of volatility remain unchanged with the addition of the interaction.

Blattman et al. (2007) report the results when TOT movements are not decomposed into trend and volatility, as as we do here in table 11.2. The decomposition is critical. The failure to find robust coefficients on TOT growth has led many observers to discount its importance. However, we now see that the failure to find statistically significant results is largely a consequence of measurement error, a problem that is in large part overcome through the decomposition into trend and volatility.

To forestall concern that commodity price fluctuations are not exogenous to all 35 countries in the sample, Blattman et al. (2007) examined the sensitivity of these results to various assumptions about which countries were truly price-takers. All in all, nearly half of the sample can be dropped and the point estimates for TOT volatility in table 11.2 are virtually unchanged. Finally, the robustness of these results are also confirmed with respect to all of the following: inclusion of the war decade, alternative period lengths, alternative methods of decomposing terms of trade series into trend and volatility, the dropping of countries and decades with lower quality income data, alternative functional forms, and the inclusion of institutional quality proxies.

What were the channels of terms of trade impact? Capital accumulation must certainly have been one, and it does turn out that gross capital flows from the United Kingdom to periphery countries were decreasing in TOT volatility. This result is consistent with what we find today. Namely, while greater volatility may increase the need for international borrowing to help smooth domestic activity, a recent IMF study has shown that more volatility actually made it harder to borrow between 1970 and 2001 (Catão and Kapur 2004). Furthermore between 1870 and 1939 smaller countries were more vulnerable to exogenous commodity price fluctuations, and the effect of volatility on investment seems to grow the smaller the country. In general, trend growth in the terms of trade does not appear to be robustly related to increases in levels of UK investment. In the absence of data on capital stocks, we can only speculate as to whether the terms of trade impact on domestic capital accumulation was big or small. It seems likely, however, that domestic savings were even more powerfully influenced by terms of trade shocks than were foreign capital flows, a proposition that remains to be investigated.

Bottom Line for the 1870 to 1939 Decades

This analysis suggests that commodity choice, dependence, and the associated price trends and their volatility were powerful determinants of growth in the periphery up to World War II. In focusing on the forces that led to industrialization and diversification in western Europe and the United States, scholars may have forgotten that the rest of the world—rich and poor—took a different path. Some of the primary-product producing nations did quite well by this strategy—witness Australia, Canada, Egypt, or Norway. Some, like Burma, Ceylon, Colombia, or Cuba, did quite poorly. Others were somewhere in the middle. The commodity-specialized countries were not uniformly slow growing and poor. Neither were the prices of their commodities uniformly volatile and decreasing. In reconstructing nearly a century of terms of trade experience from 1870 to 1939 and assessing its impact on economic performance, we see that some commodities proved more volatile in price than others, and that those countries with more volatile terms of trade grew more slowly: countries with just one standard deviation higher volatility grew more than half a percentage point per annum slower. The economic effects of these estimates are big: producing and exporting a commodity with half the average level of volatility was associated with an annual increase in the rate of growth of a third to a half of a percentage point. What is especially notable about these results is the asymmetry between core and periphery. Where terms of trade volatility was present in the periphery, it created a significant drag on output growth. This was not true of the core: where larger, diversified industrial nations experienced the same high price volatility, they did not experience the same drag on growth. The gap in growth rates in per capita income between core and periphery in our sample is about 0.4 percentage points. If the periphery had experienced the same volatility as the core, ceteris paribus, this would have added 0.2 percentage points to average GDP per capita growth rates in the periphery. This alone accounts for half of the output per capita growth gap. Furthermore, when the terms of trade in the periphery underwent a secular decline after the 1890s, the core growth rate was raised, adding more to the great divergence growth gap.

11.3   Trade-Divergence Effects during the Statistical Dark Age before 1870

If the negative effects of resource curse and de-industrialization have the effects theory suggests, why don't we see even more evidence of it during the Singer–Prebisch episode after 1870? Secular change in the terms of trade—up or down—did not have a really big impact on long-run growth among the poor commodity exporters between 1870 and 1939. Why? Two likely explanations stand out. First, if domestic industry had already been badly damaged by foreign imports during the terms of trade boom up to 1870, there might not have been much left to de-industrialize. Thus the negative impact of de-industrialization on growth would already have had its day. Second, there was no terms of trade boom during the seven decades after 1870, but rather a boom followed by an equal-sized bust. Perhaps the impact of a secular change in the terms of trade never got a chance to be assessed fully during the Prebisch–Singer years. Since dramatic de-industrialization and a huge terms of trade boom were both present before 1870, and if the volatility conditions were equally or even more powerful, there is reason to believe that trade lowered growth in the poor periphery a lot more during the half century or so before 1870 than after.

The problem, however, is that we do not have the data to make the same econometric assessment for pre-1870 that we just reported for post-1870. Suppose, however, that we assume that underlying relationships connecting trade to growth were roughly the same in both periods. If we can show that domestic industries in the poor periphery were big in 1815 (while they were small in 1870), that the terms of trade boom was big in 1815 to 1870 (while it was small 1870–1939), and that terms of trade volatility prior to 1870 was greater than or equal to after 1870, then we might reasonably conclude that trade must have played an even greater role in contributing to the great divergence before 1870 than after (when it probably accounted for half of it).

Was the industrial sector in the poor periphery big in 1815 and small in 1870? We need only recall chapter 5 and especially tables 5.1 through 5.3 to establish that point. For example, third world per capita levels of industrialization were almost comparable to that of the European core in 1750. By 1830, the third world industrialization index had fallen by almost 25 percent. By 1860, third world industry was only 60 percent of its 1750 level (while the European core was almost three times its 1750 level). In contrast, between 1860 and 1913, the third world per capita industry index rose. Table 5.3 offers another window on third world de-industrialization before 1870 by reporting the share of the home textile market supplied by local industry: between 1833 and 1877, it fell from 95 to about 38 percent in British India; between the 1820s and the 1870s, it fell from 97 to about 25 percent in the Ottoman empire; between 1822 and 1870, it fell from 82 to 38 percent in Dutch Indonesia; and between the 1800s and 1879, it fell from 75 to 60 percent in Mexico.

Was the third world terms of trade boom bigger before 1870 than after? Absolutely, and the differences were huge. Figure 3.2 showed that the average terms of trade everywhere in the periphery but East Asia soared from about 1800 to the early 1870s, moved along a volatile plateau up to the mid-1890s, and then underwent its big Prebisch–Singer slide down to World War II. Between 1800 and 1860 the third world terms of trade increased at the spectacular annual rate of more than 1.4 percent per year (table 3.1).

Was third world terms of trade volatility before 1870 greater than or equal to that after 1870? Absolutely. Table 10.3 showed that third world terms of trade volatility was almost 30 percent higher before 1870 than after (9.18 vs. 7.09), while it was already very high in the post-1870 Prebisch–Singer years. Between 1820 and 1870 terms of trade volatility was more than three times that of the United Kingdom (table 10.3: 9.18/2.91 = 3.15), a ratio that is even bigger than it has been in recent years (table 10.1: 9.56/3.2 = 2.99).

It follows that the world trade boom contributed even more to the great divergence before 1870 than after. Since we estimate that about half of the growth gap between core and periphery can be explained by trade effects between 1870 and 1939, it seems reasonable to guess the figure to have been perhaps three-quarters before 1870.

11.4 Trade-Divergence Effects during the Modern Era since 1970

[G]iven the high volatility of primary commodity prices . . . we expect resources-rich countries with poorly developed financial systems to have poor growth performance. (Poelhekke and van der Ploeg 2007: 6)

This statement by Steven Poelhekke and Frederick van der Ploeg is certainly true as far as it goes. But two important third world characteristics—critical aspects of Lewis's new economic order—have slowly disappeared since 1960 or 1970. First, an increasingly large number of poor countries have evolved from commodity exports to unskilled–labor-intensive manufactured exports. Recall that the share of third world exports that are manufactures rose from only about 17 percent of their total exports in 1970 to about 64 percent by 1998, and this figure has become even higher a decade later. As chapter 10 pointed out, most of the third world is now labor abundant and natural resource scarce, so it specializes in labor-intensive manufactures (Martin 2003, 2007). Thus the classic image of third world specialization in primary products has been obsolescing, and fast. Even sub-Saharan Africa has been shifting in to manufactures since the early 1990s, the share of manufactures in its total exports rising to about half by 1998 (Martin 2003: fig. 6). In short, there is reason to think that today's third world faces far less terms of trade volatility than did the commodity-exporting third world more than a century ago.

Second, the Prebisch–Singer announcement of a secular deterioration in commodity-exporters terms of trade was, at it turned out, premature. Since the Korean War, the terms of trade facing commodity exporters has not shown any trend. As John Spraos (1980) noted some time ago, when the 20th-century series is extended beyond 1950 the downward trend in the periphery's terms of trade disappears. This finding of no modern terms of trade trend has been replicated many times in the literature since Spraos wrote (see Grilli and Yang 1988, Bleaney and Greenaway 1993, and

Cuddington et al. 2007 for surveys). Thus modern terms of trade forces are not serving to reinforce primary-product specialization in the third world as it did in the 19th century.

11.5 It All Depended on the World Environment

Up to 1870, terms of trade volatility and secular boom served to lower growth rates in the third world relative to the European core, enough to explain perhaps three-quarters of the growth rate gap between core and periphery and the great divergence. Between 1870 and 1939, these forces weakened mainly because the terms of trade secular boom ceased: yet perhaps half of the growth rate gap was still explained by trade forces. Since 1950, these trade forces have weakened even more as third world exports have shifted from commodities to labor-intensive manufactures.

The third world has gained from trade since 1800: per capita income levels are higher than they would have been in isolation. But their growth rates suffered, especially compared to the industrial core. Could countries in the periphery have lessened the bad growth impact of export prices through judicious use of policy? These questions await us in chapter 13 but only after chapter 12 deals with the third world industrial revival in the late 19th and early 20th centuries.

12 Better Late Than Never: Industrialization Spreads to the Poor Periphery

12.1 When Did the Industrial Revolution Start to Penetrate the Poor Periphery?

There are some parts of Africa and Asia where modern factories are rare even today, where the majority still till the soil with primitive techniques, and where only the minority live in cities. But in some parts of the poor periphery modern industrialization started more than a century ago. Latin America had two emerging industrial leaders in the late 19th century—Brazil and Mexico; Asia had four—Bengal, Bombay, Japan, and Shanghai; and the European periphery had at least three—Catalonia, the north Italian triangle, and Russia. Why the late 19th century and why these places?

No doubt the answer is as complex as any question dealing more generally with the causes of modern economic growth, and no doubt any answer should include fundamentals like culture, geography, institutions, and good government. There is, of course, one simple explanation that would appeal to the growth theorist: As the great divergence took place, labor became increasingly expensive in the industrial core relative to the poor periphery. Thus the poor periphery became increasingly competitive in labor-intensive manufacturing. But what about the relative price of manufacturing output? What about trade and exchange rate policy? What about the timing and location of early industrialization in the poor periphery? Here, global forces have a chance to shine.

This chapter dwells on Brazil and Mexico to help identify the global-industrialization connection, but the penultimate section argues that the Latin American findings generalize to other parts of the poor periphery.

12.2   Measuring an Industrial Liftoff in Latin America

It has long been appreciated that industrialization started long before the 1930s in Latin America, indeed even before World War I. Ezequiel Gallo (1970) made the case for Argentina almost forty years ago when dependency theory and export-led growth were the dominant development paradigms. Warren Dean (1969) made the case for Brazil about the same time, and Henry Kirsch (1977) did so for Chile. Two decades later Stephen Haber (1989, 1990) made the case for Mexico. What is missing from this pioneering literature, however, is an explicit assessment of the timing and pace of industrialization in Latin America compared with the rest of the poor periphery, as well as a comprehensive assessment of its causes.

Since textile production dominated late 19th-century manufacturing, we start there. Imports satisfied a significant part of Latin American home textile demand in the 1870s. Chapter 8 reported that Mexico, an industrial leader in Latin America, imported 40 million square meters of cloth in 1879, compared with 60 million square meters produced domestically. Thus domestic producers were able to claim 60 percent of the local market, a fairly big number for a country that had been flooded with cheap, factory-made European textiles for almost a century. This certainly was not true for all of Latin America: indeed the local market share claimed by Colombian producers was only 10 percent in the 1870s (Gómez Galvarriato and Williamson 2009: table 2). Furthermore Mexico stacks up well against other parts of the poor periphery (table 5.3). India's domestic textile producers claimed only 35 to 42 percent of their local market in 1887, the latter much lower than Mexico's 60 percent in 1879, a decade earlier. Deindustrialization forces in the first three-quarters of the 19th century had been even more powerful in the Ottoman empire where the local textile industry's market share of domestic demand was only 11 to 38 percent in the early 1870s. In Dutch Indonesia, the local textile industry's market share of domestic demand was 38 percent in 1870, about the same as India and the Ottoman empire. Thus, despite the importance of foreign imports in the home market, the Mexican textile industry was doing fairly well by the 1870s, at least compared with the rest of the poor periphery. Mexico was poised for an industrial liftoff from a higher platform than most of the poor periphery.

More to the point, however, is that some parts of Latin America underwent significant industrialization between the 1870s and World War I. By 1907 Brazil's domestic textile industry had carved out an impressive share of its local market, about 65 percent, while Mexico's share had risen to almost 78 percent in 1906 to 1908 (Gómez Galvarriato and Williamson 2009: table 2). Of course, not all of Latin America was industrializing: for example, Argentina's textile industry claimed only 15 to 18 percent of the home textile market in 1913.[1] Textiles are light industry, the sort of labor-intensive manufacturing that every early industrializer exploits first, before moving farther up the skill and technology ladder. Thus it is no surprise that the local market shares for heavy (capital- and skill-intensive) industrial product groups were much smaller even among the industrial leaders. Yet even these higher tech sectors expanded at the end of the period: the domestic producers' share of the Mexican iron and steel market rose from 6 to 28 percent between 1903 and 1911, while that for coke rose from 17 to 47 percent (Gómez Galvarriato and Williamson 2009: table 2).

These facts offer strong support for the view that the Latin American industrial leaders did indeed experience an industrialization liftoff[2] before 1913, and certainly *long* before the 1930s and the initiation of its anti-global and anti-market ISI policies. The harder questions, however, are exactly *when* the liftoff took place, *where* it took place, and *why*.

Stephen Haber dates the beginning of the Mexican industrial liftoff in the late 1880s. In the decade that followed,

the industry more than doubled in size. By 1911, the industry had grown an additional 50 percent. Estimates of total factor productivity (TFP) growth . . . indicate increases of between 1.5 percent . . . and 3.3 percent . . . per year. Labor productivity grew even faster . . . between 3.0 and 4.7 percent per year (Haber 2002: 7–8).

Such growth rates meant that Mexican textile producers had displaced most imported cloth by 1914 (Haber 2002: 11). Furthermore by about 1910 the Mexican textile industry had a machine index per worker 77 percent that of Britain, suggesting that Mexican technology had been partially catching up on the world's light industry leaders over the previous four decades (Clark 1987: 148 and 152). Indeed Aurora Gómez Galvarriato (2007) has shown that one leading Mexican firm had achieved the labor productivity levels of similar sized textile firms in the United States and the United Kingdom at the beginning of the 20th century.

Table 12.1 and figure 12.1 report evidence on exports to Latin America from the United States and the United Kingdom that better identify Latin American industrial leaders and the timing of their industrialization experience in the decades before World War I. These manufacturing intermediates were the main suppliers of energy and capital goods to Latin American industry, so we can assume that manufacturing machinery, iron and steel, and coal imports (all in constant US dollars) are good proxies for relative

Table 12.1
Growth rates per annum in intermediates and capital goods imports from the United
States and United Kingdom, 1871 to 1911 (in US$)

Period	Argentina	Brazil	Chile	Mexico	Unweighted average
1871–1881	3.9	3.8	0.6	14.9	5.8
1881–1891	11.9	7.2	8.3	7.0	8.6
1891–1901	1.9	−2.9	0.4	9.9	2.3
1901–1911	9.6	7.8	7.1	−2.6	5.5
1871–1891	7.8	5.5	4.4	10.9	7.1
1871–1901	5.8	2.6	3.0	10.5	5.5
1871–1911	6.7	3.9	4.0	7.1	5.4
1871–1891	7.8	5.5	4.4	10.9	7.1
1891–1911	5.7	2.3	3.7	3.5	3.8

Source: The import data are reported US and the UK exports of iron and steel, coal,
and manufacturing machinery in 1890 to 1914 in US dollars. Gómez Galvarriato
and Williamson (2008: table 3).

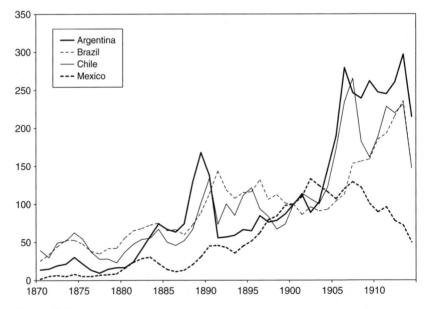

Figure 12.1
Index of coal, iron, and steel and of machinery imports in constant US dollars
(1900 = 100).
Source: Gómez Galvarriato and Williamson (2009: fig. 3).

industrial growth. The data in table 12.1 and figure 12.1 allow us to compare industrial progress between 1870 and 1914 within the four big Latin American countries—Argentina, Brazil, Chile, and Mexico, each of which exhibited impressive growth over the four decades. True, three of them underwent very high volatility: Argentina, Brazil, and Chile all recorded big booms in the late 1880s to early 1890s and again in the run up to World War I, as well as a big bust in the 1890s (see also chapter 10). Mexico did not undergo this volatility before 1900, but it did undergo a secular slow down from 1902 onward, up to and during the revolution (1910–1920). But the combination of imported machinery, iron, and coal as a share of Mexican gross domestic product (in 1990 US dollars) increased seven times up to 1902!

Now consider the growth rates of those intermediate and capital goods imports in table 12.1. Between 1871 and 1901 this industrial proxy grew almost twice as fast in Mexico than the average for the four (10.5 vs. 5.5 percent per annum), and it grew faster even when the run up to the revolution is included (1871–1911, 7.1 vs. 5.4 percent per annum). In addition the table shows that the liftoff started during the first two decades, not just after 1890 as Haber suggests. Note also that the Mexican industrial index grew more than twice as fast as did its GDP over those four decades up to 1911[3] (7.1 vs. 3.4 percent per annum), implying the dramatic structural change we have come to expect from early industrial revolutions. Over the four decades following 1871, the industrial proxy grew 1.6 times as fast as its GDP in Brazil (3.9 vs. 2.4 percent per annum), but it grew only a fifth faster than GDP in Chile (4 vs. 3.3 percent per annum), and it barely grew faster at all in Argentina (6.7 vs. 6 percent per annum).

To summarize, industrialization of the Latin American economic leaders—Brazil and Mexico—was very impressive between 1870 and 1913, especially compared with the rest of the poor periphery, the industrial liftoff started well before 1890; Mexico recorded the most rapid industrialization before 1901; and after 1900, Argentina, Chile, and Brazil all recorded rapid industrial growth well in excess of their GDP growth. What makes this performance all the more striking is that it was preceded by seven decades of de-industrialization. It looks like the 1870s recorded a big turnabout for Brazil and Mexico, from de-industrialization to re-industrialization.

12.3   Some Potential Explanations for the Latin American Industrial Liftoff

What explains the timing and the pace of the Latin American industrial liftoff? Consider five leading candidates.

First, we now know that Latin America was far more protectionist than anywhere else in the late 19th century (Coatsworth and Williamson 2004a, b). Indeed Latin America had the highest tariffs in the world from the late 1880s onward,[4] and before the late 1880s only the United States had higher average tariff rates. Still the typical average tariff rate in Latin America did not rise between 1870 and 1914, and it is changes in protection that matter.

If average levels of protection did not rise over the four decades, what about the protection of manufacturing, and what about the effective rate of protection there? Here the evidence is much more supportive of an active role for pro-industrial policy. The leader of the policy pack, Mexico, adopted far more coherent and consistent pro-industrial tariff policies under the Porfiriato regime. Policy makers in late 19th-century Latin America were certainly aware of infant industry arguments (Bulmer-Thomas 1994: 140), but tariffs were not used specifically or consciously to foster industry in Mexico, or elsewhere in Latin America, until early in the 1890s, a decade or two after the industrial liftoff began. Mexico increased its average tariff rates sharply in 1890 and graduated from having the lowest levels of protection among major Latin American countries to having levels similar to the rest. But this policy transformation did not just entail a change in average tariff levels. It also entailed a profound change in the tariff structure, a change that served to raise the *effective* rate of protection for manufacturing.[5] Edward Beatty (2000) and Graciela Márquez (2002) have shown that the 1880s and 1890s saw the introduction of a modern pro-industrial policy in Mexico, including a rational structure of protection. Haber agrees with Márquez and Beatty:[6]

In 1891 Mexico was using tariffs to protect the cotton textile industry which perhaps would have otherwise been uncompetitive. This meant high tariffs on competing goods and low tariffs on inputs. The tariff on imported cloth tended to be twice that of the tariff on imported raw cotton. The result was an effective rate of protection that varied from 39 to 78 percent. (Haber 2002: 16)

This explanation helps account for the fast Mexican industrial liftoff compared with the rest of the periphery, especially given that most of Asia, Africa, and the Middle East did not have the autonomy to pursue pro-industrial commercial policies. We also know that the pro-industrial Mexican policy led the rest of the autonomous Latin American republics by a decade or two: the policy was followed with a lag by Brazil and Chile a little later in the 1890s, and by Colombia in the early 1900s (Márquez 2002; Coatsworth and Williamson 2004a; b). Argentina failed to follow suit, a policy that helped put the brakes on industrialization there.[7]

A more rational tariff policy clearly increased its support for local industry in Mexico, Brazil, and Chile from the 1890s onward. However, the
industrial liftoff started earlier, in the 1870s. Thus we need to search for
additional explanations for Latin American re-industrialization, especially
for the leaders, Brazil and Mexico.

Consider four other influences that might have contributed to the
industrial liftoff in Latin America, perhaps even more so than tariff policy.
The first is world prices and the terms of trade. There was a big secular
change in world relative prices facing the Mexican economy after the
1870s, a change that no longer penalized local manufacturing. Chapter
8 argued that a good part of the exceptionally modest Mexican de-
industrialization experience in the half century before 1870 was due to
an exceptionally modest terms of trade shock compared to the rest of
Latin America, Asia, the Middle East, and even the European periphery.
It appears likely that the same was true of the half century after 1870, but
in the opposite direction: Latin America's terms of trade fell earlier and
faster than anywhere else in the periphery, especially Mexico. Since it
imported manufactures, the relative price of industrial goods rose in
home markets, favoring industry. Second, there was also an acceleration
in total factor productivity growth in one key export activity in Latin
America, mining. This served to contribute to the fall in the net barter
terms of trade, but given a price elastic demand facing silver, copper,
and other metals, it also served to raise the income terms of trade,[8] fostering the import of relatively cheap capital goods and manufacturing intermediates (including coal), thus favoring an industrial liftoff. These
productivity events were unusual for the poor periphery at that time,
including much of Latin America. It gave Mexico an edge. Third, there is
the depreciation of local currencies to consider. The biggest real exchange
rate depreciation between 1870 and 1913 took place in Brazil and Mexico,
forces that must also have contributed to their impressive industrialization
performance.

Finally, economic success in the industrial core raised the cost of
labor there relative to the poor periphery, eventually offering the later
an industrial escape from resource specialization. Thus Latin American
industry could have become more competitive to the extent that it faced
weaker upward pressure on the nominal wage due to slower overall economic growth, but in addition weaker upward pressure on food prices
could have strengthened their competitiveness. The latter can be explained
by elastic food import supplies and domestic market integration by the
railroads.

12.4 No More Dutch Disease in Latin America?

Most of Latin America faced a big secular change in world relative price trends over the four decades before 1913, a change that, as we have noted above, no longer penalized local manufacturing. The region's terms of trade reached a secular peak in the mid-late 1870s, leveled off up to the early-mid 1890s, after which it fell far more dramatically up to the early 1900s than almost anywhere else in the poor periphery. Between 1870–1874 and 1909–1913, its terms of trade actually fell by 10 percent, this after rising by 174 percent over the seven decades between 1800–1804 and 1870–1874 (figure 3.6; table 3.1)! Only the European periphery underwent a similar collapse in its terms of trade, where the secular peak was even earlier, the 1850s, and the fall even steeper (figure 3.5). In contrast, the rest of the periphery underwent no net fall over the four decades: the Middle East and Southeast Asia underwent a continuous terms of trade improvement from the mid-1870s onward, while South Asia and East Asia underwent no change either way. Which parts of Latin America underwent the biggest changes in terms of trade trend? Consider first the two industrial leaders. Mexico underwent a big fall in its terms of trade after the early mid-1890s: the Mexican terms of trade was cut in half between 1890 and 1902,[9] twice as big as the rest of Latin America. Furthermore the primary product price boom in the decade or so before 1913 was very modest in Mexico, and it didn't come close to recovering the secular peak in the late 1870s and early 1880s. Indeed the Mexican terms of trade fell by more than 37 percent between 1870–1874 and 1910–1913, while it rose by 11 percent in the rest of Latin America. Mexico was exceptional compared with the Latin American average. While Brazil underwent great terms of trade volatility, it hardly underwent any secular change at all in its terms of trade over the four decades (a total rise of only 1.3 percent between 1870–1874 and 1910–1913). This secular stability certainly represented a marked change in world economic conditions after seventy years of rising terms of trade and thus falling relative prices of manufactures. In contrast with these immense price changes facing the two industrial leaders, Argentina and Chile continued its terms of trade boom up to World War I; between 1870–1874 and 1910–1913, Chile's terms of trade rose by a huge 81 percent, while the figure for Argentina was still a big 21 percent.

In summary, a fall (or no rise) in the net barter terms of trade implied a rise (or no fall) in the relative price of imported manufactures, an event that favored (or no longer penalized) domestic industry. If a rising terms of trade caused de-industrialization and Dutch disease in the six or seven decades before the 1870s, it follows that a falling or stable terms of trade after 1870 should have contributed greatly to the impressive Mexican and Brazilian industrialization experience up to 1913.

12.5   The *Income* Terms of Trade, and Export-Led Growth in Latin America

So far we have assumed that the Latin American republics had no influence over their export or import prices, and thus that their terms of trade was determined exogenously in world markets, an issue that the previous chapter already explored. While commodity exports were only a small share of world exports of any specific commodity for Argentina (maize, wheat), Columbia (coffee, gold), Cuba (sugar, tobacco), Peru (copper), Uruguay (wool, meat), and Venezuela (coffee, cacao), the shares were much bigger for Chile (nitrates, copper), Mexico (silver), and Brazil (coffee, rubber); see tables 4.2 and 11.1. Indeed Edward Beatty (2000) has argued persuasively that Mexican mineral supplies to the world market, especially silver, helped precipitate the big decline in its net barter terms of trade: by flooding the market with silver, Mexico lowered the world price and worsened its terms of trade. Beatty also argues that it was rapid productivity advance in Mexican mining that produced that result, but since the demand for minerals was price elastic, total export values and foreign exchange earnings boomed, creating export-led growth. It also reduced the relative price of imported capital goods, energy sources, and other intermediates in to manufacturing, thus fostering industrial growth.

While a very big decline in its net barter terms of trade (after a long secular boom) was consistent with a very big increase in its income terms of trade (table 12.2), Mexico appears to be the Latin American exception. That is, Beatty's supply side argument cannot apply to mineral-producing Chile, since its net barter terms of trade did not fall but rather rose mightily. Beatty's hypothesis also gets only weak support for Brazil where the net barter terms of trade was stable after the long and spectacular pre-1870 boom while the income terms of trade underwent only a modest increase (table 12.2).

12.6   Industrial Competitiveness: Keeping the Lid on Latin American Wages?

The share of the labor force in manufacturing never exceeded 25 percent anywhere in Latin America in 1895.[10] This implies that real wages

Table 12.2
Income terms of trade growth in Latin America, 1870 to 1913 (1900 = 100)

	(1) NBTT 1870–1874	(2) 1870X volume	(3) (1)(2)/100 = INCTT 1870	(4) NBTT 1909–1913	(5) 1913X volume	(6) (4)(5)/100 = INCTT 1913	(7) INCTT growth (%)
NBTT increase							
Argentina	103.3	19.2	19.8	138.8	170.1	236.1	5.9
Chile	83.1	38.6	32.1	148.4	163.3	242.3	4.8
Colombia	103.1	114.0	117.5	118.3	267.0	315.9	2.3
Uruguay	85.3			106.2			
NBTT decrease							
Mexico	142.5	18.3	26.1	89.4	178.9	159.9	4.3
Cuba	135.3			105.9			
Peru	134.9	114.8	154.9	97.8	232.4	227.3	0.9
NBTT no change							
Brazil	115.1	47.2	54.3	115.9	104.4	121.0	1.9
Venezuela	107.9			105.9			
Latin America	118.1			106.9			

Sources: A 1870 population weighted average is used for Latin America. The export volume data are taken from Maddison (1989: 140) and (1995: 236). The INCTT = (NBTT)(X), or $X p_X / p_M$, where p_X is export price and p_M import price. The table uses the first equation. Gómez Galvarriato and Williamson (2008: table 6).

(w/pc, where pc refers to the cost of living) were determined by labor productivity elsewhere in the economy—mining, agriculture, construction, and services—not in manufacturing. Slow-growing labor productivity in the rest of the economy would have given Latin American manufacturing the advantage of modest upward pressure on per unit wage costs, making it more competitive with North America and western Europe, where the upward pressure was much stronger. It was, of course, the own-wage that mattered to employers in manufacturing, that is, the nominal wage divided by the price of manufactures (w/p_M). If the price of foodstuffs (p_F) was the central determinant of the cost of living in Latin America, and if p_F/p_M was falling, we would have another reason to expect Latin American manufacturing to have undergone increasing wage competitiveness compared with foreign firms. Is there any reason to think that p_F/p_M should have fallen? Yes, and for two reasons: first, to the extent that the post-1870s grain invasion from Argentina, North America, and Ukraine flooded Latin American food deficit regions, where most Latin American manufacturing was located;[11] and second, to the extent that newly built railroads brought the cheaper foreign grain to those same urban interior markets (Dobado and Marrero 2005b). The issue is how much?

Mexico recorded the biggest p_F/p_M decline between 1874–1878 and 1913, 34 percent, and Brazil the second, 21 percent (Gómez Galvarriato and Williamson 2009: fig. 10). Thus the grain-invasion-cum-railroads prediction is confirmed, and furthermore the two fastest industrializing countries recorded the biggest fall in p_F/p_M.

But did cheaper grains necessarily mean lower nominal wages and thus greater wage competitiveness for local manufacturing? Did the own-wage facing manufacturing (w/p_M) fall, at least for the four countries that offer the necessary time series data—Brazil, Chile, Mexico, and Uruguay? It appears that Brazil and Uruguay had the industrial advantage on this score, since the upward pressure on the own-wage in manufacturing was much greater in Chile and Mexico (Gómez Galvarriato and Williamson 2009: fig. 11). Indeed over the period 1870 to 1913 the own-wage in Brazil grew no faster than it did in the United States, the former remaining competitive with the latter on that score at least. By the same criteria, wage competitiveness deteriorated in Mexico (but not nearly as much as Chile). Of course, there were other forces determining competitiveness, but if we are looking for explanations for precocious industrialization in Brazil and Mexico, *better* wage competitiveness was not one of them.

12.7   Did Real Currency Depreciation Increase Manufacturing Profitability in Latin America?

Depreciation of the domestic currency favors local manufacturing in primary-product exporting countries since it makes imported manufactures more expensive in the local market. Currency appreciation does the opposite. When trading partners have different rates of inflation, the nominal exchange rate must be adjusted to take account of the differential inflation rates, yielding a real exchange rate. The real exchange rate (RER) is yet another force that could have helped account for the timing and pace of industrialization in Latin America before 1913, especially given that Latin America did not rush to join the gold standard club while most European colonies did.[12]

Figure 12.2 plots the RER for the four big Latin American republics—Argentina, Brazil, Chile, and Mexico. The figure makes it quite clear that manufacturing in Chile must have been greatly disadvantaged by real exchange rate trends since it underwent significant real currency appreciation. Argentina underwent no secular change in its real exchange rate

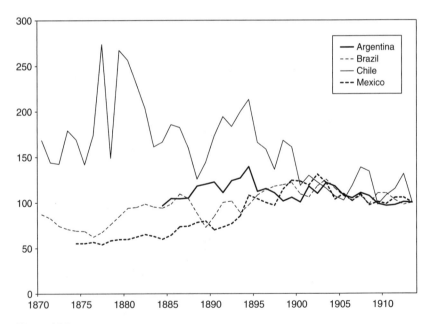

Figure 12.2
Real exchange rate trends in Latin America, 1870 to 1913 (1913 = 100).
Source: Gómez Galvarriato and Williamson (2009: 687–89).

between 1884 and 1913, so it could not have been a source of any stimulus to import-competing manufacturing there. However, the real exchange rate did undergo secular depreciation in Brazil and Mexico, and the magnitudes appear to have been big: Mexico underwent a real currency depreciation of 137 percent between the mid-1870s and 1902, when capital goods imports surged. Mexican real currency depreciation for the whole period was an enormous 81 percent. While not quite as big, Brazil also underwent a significant real currency depreciation of 34 percent between 1870–1874 and 1913.

In short, some part of the industrial liftoff in Brazil and Mexico can indeed be explained by a real exchange rate depreciation up to 1913.

12.8   What about the Rest of the Poor Periphery?

To the extent that pro-industrial tariff and exchange rate policy mattered, it seems clear that the best place to look for early industrialization evidence elsewhere in the poor periphery would be where there was policy autonomy over tariffs and currency regimes. Unfortunately, there are few places to look in Asia and Africa since most of it was controlled by the colonists who favored keeping the new economic order in place: that is, they certainly didn't want to foster manufacturing competition in their colonies. To the extent that world market forces mattered, it seems clear that the best place to look for early industrialization evidence elsewhere in the poor periphery would be where world market forces were driving up the relative price of manufactures in local markets. So where do we see the terms of trade for primary-product exporters dropping early and big, or where in East Asia—whose natural comparative advantage was not in primary products but in labor-intensive manufacturing—do we see the terms of trade soaring? These, after all, would be places where the relative price of manufactures was on the rise, thus favoring early industrialization. Unless these forces were too weak to offset other "fundamental" hindrances to modern economic growth, we should see—at least compared with the rest of the poor periphery—early industrialization there.

Table 12.3 inverts the changing terms of trade (p_X/p_M) evidence in the poor periphery between 1870–1874 and 1910–1913—except for East Asia—so as to measure changes in the relative price of imports (p_M/p_X) that we take to be a crude proxy for changes in the relative price of manufactures in home markets. Big negative numbers identify those regions where de-industrialization and Dutch disease forces were still powerful: Argentina, Chile, Indonesia, Egypt, and the Levant are all well above the

Table 12.3
Percentage change in the relative price of imports in home markets, 1870–1874 up to 1910–1913

Latin America	
Argentina	−23.3
Brazil	−4.9
Chile	−44.6
Mexico	55.1
Venezuela	−3.2
East Asia	
China	10.7
Japan	50.7
South Asia	
Ceylon	50.6
India	−9.3
Southeast Asia	
Indonesia	−57.2
Philippines	19.2
Siam	9.6
Middle East	
Egypt	−25.3
Ottoman	−1.1
Levant	−23.7
European periphery	
Italy	1.7
Portugal	32.5
Russia	10.6
Spain	13.9
All periphery	−9.2

Source: Taken from the database underlying Williamson (2008).
Notes: 1870 population weights used to construct "all periphery." Except for East Asia, the figures are simply the percent change in the inverse of the net barter terms of trade, or p_M/p_X. For East Asia, it is p_X/p_M.

1870 population weighted average for the periphery as a whole (a 9.2 percent fall in the relative price of manufactures proxy). Big positive numbers identify those regions where world market forces were giving a powerful stimulus to early industrialization: Mexico in Latin America; China and Japan in East Asia; Portugal, Russia, and Spain in the European periphery; and three Asian surprises, Ceylon, Siam, and the Philippines. The rest show no powerful world market forces one way or the other.

Since the determinants of industrialization are complex, it is hardly surprising that the correlation between changing world market conditions and industrialization in the poor periphery was imperfect. Yet four parts of the world where industrialization of the late comers was most dramatic were also those parts where the pro-industrial world market forces were most dramatic—Mexico, China (Shanghai), Japan, and the European periphery.

12.9   Decomposing the Sources of the Industrial Liftoff in the Poor Periphery

This chapter does not offer any explicit empirical decomposition of the sources of the industrial liftoff (or its absence) in the poor periphery between 1870 and World War I. At this point the historical evidence is not yet sufficient for that demanding task: rather we have been content to lay out the competing explanations, to offer some plausible support for them, and to set out an agenda. Still, when future research offers an explicit empirical decomposition of the late 19th-century industrial liftoff in some precocious locations around the poor periphery, this chapter will have shown how those decompositions are likely to have differed across countries, and where these forces are likely to have mattered most.

My guess is that *changing* fundamentals will end up playing a much more modest role in contributing to the industrial liftoff than the current neo-institutional literature supposes: those fundamentals may help explain *where* industrialization started in the poor periphery, but changing fundamentals are unlikely to explain *when* and by *how much*. I stress the word *changing* since it had to have been *changing* fundamentals raising productivity in manufacturing, or *changing* external terms of trade, or *changing* domestic wage competitiveness, or *changing* tariffs, or *changing* real exchange rates improving profitability in manufacturing. It would have been those *changes* that accounted for the liftoff, not *levels* of any of these contending forces.

The reader must have noted that this chapter has paid little attention to rising total factor productivity in manufacturing around the poor periphery. There are two explanations for its omission. First, only rarely has manufacturing productivity growth been estimated anywhere in the poor periphery over the four decades after 1870. Second, the United States, Britain, and other competitors to local manufacturing in the poor periphery were themselves undergoing rapid productivity advance, so we'd have to find evidence of total factor productivity *catching up* in the periphery leaders like Catalonia, the northern Italian triangle, Russia, Japan, Shanghai, Bombay, Bengal, Brazil, and Mexico. Such evidence will be hard to find. Maybe rapid manufacturing productivity catch up played a role, but based on Latin American experience, it probably did not explain most of the industrial liftoff in the leading parts of the poor periphery. If not productivity catch-up, what was it?

Changing external terms of trade must have played a big role, as the immense pre-1870 boom in the external terms of trade switched to a post-1870 bust; that is, a pre-1870 fall in the relative price of imported manufactures reversed trend to become a post-1870 rise. What had been a sickly Dutch disease before 1870 became a healthy Dutch revival after 1870, at least in some parts of the poor periphery. These forces were strong and it is time that the literature paid more attention to them.

Changing tariff and real exchange rate policy also must have played a big role, but only in those parts of the poor periphery where there was policy autonomy. Average tariff rates in Latin America rose hardly at all over these four decades, but the effective rate of protection for manufacturing rose a lot as the tariff structure was rationalized. Since Mexico led the way, it had the first-strike advantage of effective pro-industrial policy, and this long before the early-ISI protectionist policies of the 1930s. In addition the real exchange rate depreciated for both Brazil and Mexico, offering more benefits to import-competing industry in those Latin American industrial leaders. Since South Asia, Southeast Asia, Africa, the Middle East, and the other parts of the poor periphery did not undergo the same real currency depreciation (tied as they were to gold and/or the mother country's currency), these two leaders enjoyed a first strike pro-industrial advantage—this long before the well-known real currency depreciations of the 1930s.

It is time for us to confront trade policy in detail, and that's the agenda for the next chapter.

13 Policy Response: What Did They Do? What Should They Have Done?

13.1 Thinking about Policy Responses in the Poor Periphery

This chapter is *not* about the impact of anti-trade policies on economic performance in the poor periphery over the century before the 1930s. Research has already confirmed that tariff walls did not alone improve growth rates in the poor periphery (Vamvakidis 2002; Clemens and Williamson 2004).[1] Indeed it seems likely that the openness–growth causation probably went the other way round in the poor but autonomous (e.g., not colonial) periphery. For example, countries achieving rapid GDP per capita growth also underwent faster growth in import duties and other parts of the tax base, thus reducing the revenue need for high tariff *rates*, even to finance a growing government expenditure share. Countries suffering slow growth would have kept tariff *rates* high to ensure adequate revenues for government expenditure needs, and they would have *raised* those tariff rates if their intent was to increase their expenditure shares on the military, infrastructure, and other public goods.

Instead, this chapter first establishes that tariffs were much higher in the autonomous periphery than in the European industrial core, and that the tariffs there rose steeply across the late 19th century. Furthermore the rise in tariff rates even took place in Asia, where European colonies were so common. These facts alone may come as a surprise to the reader, so we dwell on then at length. Second, we then ask why tariffs were so high (and rising) in the periphery. Was this anti-trade policy backlash motivated by industrialization targets, by compensation of the losers from trade, by government revenue needs, or by other goals?

13.2   What Did the Poor Periphery Do about Tariffs?

Figure 13.1 reports the ad valorem tariff rates[2] for six regions of the world between the 1860s and the 1930s: the United States and the average of three members of the European industrial core (France, Germany, United Kingdom), three English-speaking European offshoots (Australia, Canada, New Zealand), ten from the industrially lagging European periphery (Austria-Hungary, Denmark, Greece, Italy, Norway, Portugal, Russia, Serbia, Spain, Sweden), ten from Asia and the Middle East (Burma, Ceylon, China, Egypt, India, Indonesia, Japan, the Philippines, Siam, Turkey), and eight from Latin America (Argentina, Brazil, Chile, Colombia, Cuba, Mexico, Peru, Uruguay).

The figure documents the well-known interwar protectionist surge in the 1920s and 1930s. What is much less well-known, however, is the persistent protectionist drift worldwide between 1865 and about 1900, a thirty-five year drift sufficiently pronounced that tariffs were at least as

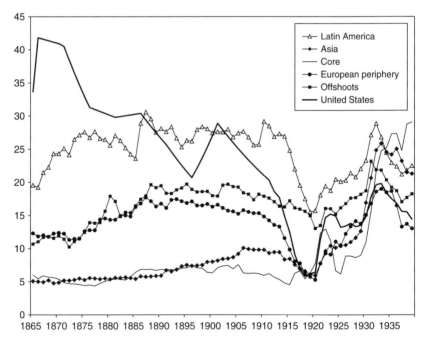

Figure 13.1
Unweighted average of regional tariffs before World War II.
Source: Coatsworth and Williamson (2004: fig. 2).

high in 1900 as they were in 1938 everywhere in the periphery except Asia. There was a very pronounced secular rise in tariffs across Latin America, the English-speaking European offshoots (the United States being the only exception) and the European periphery. This steep rise up to the 1890s in the periphery's tariff rates (and their persistence at those high levels up to World War I) *far* exceeds that of the European core. This is an especially notable fact given that almost nothing has been written on this anti-trade trend in the periphery, while so much has been written about the far more modest backlash on the European continent (e.g., Gerschenkron 1943; Kindleberger 1951; Bairoch 1989).

In addition there was enormous variance in levels of protection between these regional averages. The richer European offshoots had levels of protection almost three times that of the European core around the turn of the century.[3] The European periphery had tariffs in 1925 about two and a half times higher than those in the European industrial core. The independent Latin American republics had tariffs in 1885 almost five times those in the dependent parts of Asia (Burma, Ceylon, China, Egypt, India, Indonesia, and the Philippines). However, the independent parts of Asia (Siam, Ottoman Turkey, and Japan) had tariff rates about the same as the dependent parts of Asia. Colonial status, lack of autonomy, and "unequal treaties" all played an obvious role in Asia, but local conditions seem to have mattered too.

The industrial core had the lowest tariffs.[4] Most members of the poor periphery in Asia were colonies or quasi-colonies of the industrial core (Burma, Ceylon, Egypt, India, Indonesia, the Philippines), or were forced to sign free trade agreements with the core in mid-century when the latter trained naval guns on their potential trading partners (China, Japan), or the former viewed nearby gunboats as a sufficient threat to go open on their own (Siam). Thus Asian tariff rates were pretty much like those of the core early on, but they started drifting upward after the 1880s, when the unequal treaties had expired and long before the post–World War II independence movement.

As was suggested above, colonial status did not necessarily imply lack of local influence on tariff policy. There are five colonies in our Asian sample—Burma, Ceylon, India, Indonesia, and the Philippines, although foreign influence was strong enough to make Egypt behave like a colony. While colonial tariff policy did indeed mimic that of their masters, local conditions mattered as well (Clemens and Williamson 2002): for example, while India's ad valorem tariff rates were on average about the same as free-trading Britain, those of Burma and Ceylon were 4 or 5 percentage points higher, and those of Egypt were 10 points higher. Clearly, local conditions mattered even in colonies of the same colonist. But who the colonist was also mattered: tariff rates in the Philippines were unrelated to those in Spain before 1898, but very closely related to those in the United States afterward.

There is plenty of evidence of rising world protection before World War I, but much of that anti-trade reaction took place in the periphery; as was indicated above, the much-studied European continental backlash plotted in figure 13.1 looks pretty modest compared with what happened in the periphery. Except for the United States (which had the highest tariffs in the world for some time), tariffs rose everywhere in the English-speaking offshoots up to 1900: Canada by about 3 percentage points; Australia by more than 7 percentage points; and New Zealand by almost 12 percentage points. The anti-trade surge in Latin America was led by Columbia (up almost 7 percentage points) and Uruguay (up more than 10 percentage points). The European periphery leaped to high levels of protection after the 1870s, with Russia leading the way. And while Asia had the lowest tariffs in 1865, by 1914 they had been raised to levels that approached that of the protectionist English-speaking European offshoots. Thus these tariff data offer three surprises. First, while economic historians have long understood that the European continent raised tariffs partly in response to the "grain invasion" of the 1870s, this move to higher tariffs on the continent was repeated in the European periphery (up 4.2 percentage points to 16.8 percent) and in the Latin American republics (up 6.9 percentage points to 34 percent). Second, while the traditional literature teaches us that the Latin American reluctance to go open in the late 20th century was the product of the great depression and the import substitution industrial (ISI) strategies that arose in its wake (Díaz-Alejandro 1984; Corbo 1992), Latin America already had the highest tariffs in the world by the late 19th century (Coatsworth and Williamson 2004a, b). Third, it is not true that Asia waited for post–World War II independence to switch to protectionist policies: there was an upward surge in tariff rates in Asia after the 1880s and early 1890s, illustrated best by Burma, India, the Philippines, Siam, and Turkey. Presumably the upward surge in Asian tariffs after the 1880s was due to a weakening colonial grip and to the expiration of those "unequal treaties" signed decades earlier, both of which would have given the region the increasing autonomy to set higher tariffs accommodating local political economy forces that must have been pushing in that direction for some time.

Table 13.1
Structure of protection: World in 1913

Region	Average tariff (%) on	
	Manufactures	Wheat
Rich industrial core	6	13
Continental Europe	11	25
United Kingdom	0	0
Autonomous poor periphery	41	16
Argentina	22	0
Brazil	60	0
Columbia	50	20
Mexico	45	42
Japan	28	18
Semi-dependent poor periphery	5	4
China	5	0
Iran	4	0
Siam	3	3
Turkey	8	11

Source and notes: Bairoch (1993: table 3.2, 37). Figures are rounded. For manufactures, continental Europe from Bairoch (1993: table 3.3, 40) includes Austria, Belgium, Denmark, France, Germany, Netherlands, and Switzerland.

Finally, we should note that so far we have been talking about average tariff rates. Since the major import-competing industry in the core countries was grain production, perhaps we should be looking at protection against grain imports there. Since the major import-competing industry in the poor periphery was manufactures, perhaps we should be looking at protection against manufactured imports there. In short, we should pay attention to what is called the *structure of protection*. Table 13.1 uses Paul Bairoch's (1993) summary to show what the structure of protection looked like the world around in 1913. First, the highest tariffs in the world (excepting the United States) were on manufactures in the autonomous poor periphery. Second, the lowest tariffs in the world were on all imported products in the semi-dependent poor periphery and on manufactures in the European core. Third, the structure of protection favored import-competing industries the world around: industrial Europe placed higher tariffs on wheat than manufactures, more than twice as high; and the poor periphery placed higher tariffs on manufactures than on wheat, two and a half times higher in the autonomous poor periphery.

13.3 Explaining Tariff Responses in the Poor Periphery

Was It to Protect Infant Industry?

Two centuries of history have persuaded public authorities that industrialization is a carrier of development. Furthermore third world authorities were persuaded for much of the mid-late 20th century that protection was the only way to foster that process. Indeed they often cited 19th-century experience to help support these claims. In what follows, this motivation will be called the infant industry argument for short, with the understanding that it includes development and industrial policy.

Could policy makers in the autonomous parts of the poor periphery have seen any evidence that protection fostered growth? They did not, of course, have the models, methods, and evidence that we have today, but they certainly would have had the intuition. The late 20th-century evidence strongly supports the position that protection *hinders* growth.[5] But what about the pre-modern era? Did protection in the periphery foster[6] growth in the century before World War II when tariffs were so high? Certainly not in Latin America where high tariffs were correlated with *slow* growth before 1914 (Coatsworth and Williamson 2004a), just as it has been in the late 20th-century developing world. But the poor periphery could have been looking instead at the new industrial leader, the United States, with its high tariff wall, just as they looked at isolationist Soviet Russia for their mid- to late 20th-century confirmation of anti-trade ISI strategies.

Policy makers in those parts of the periphery that had tariff autonomy were certainly aware of the infant-industry argument offered for the German *Zollverein* by Frederich List and for the United States by Alexander Hamilton. This was certainly true of late 19th-century Latin America (Bulmer-Thomas 1994: 140) and the European periphery (Bairoch 1989). However, it is important to stress "late" in the previous sentence since the use of protection specifically and consciously to foster industry does not occur in the poor periphery until Mexico led the way in the early 1890s, Brazil and Chile following a little later in the 1890s, Colombia in the early 1900s (Márquez 2002; Coatsworth and Williamson 2004a, b), and Tsarist Russia about the same time (Bairoch 1989). In short, protection for industrial development became a significant motivation for tariffs in the periphery only near the turn of the previous century; it was not a significant motive for protection in the 19th century.

Thus we must look elsewhere for explanations for the exceptionally high tariffs in the autonomous periphery in the century before 1914.

Was It Stolper–Samuelson?

Until the race toward autarky in the 1930s, the free traders were members of the industrial core, their colonies, or those who had been intimidated by gunboats to open up. The rest had erected high tariff walls. But simply to show high and rising tariffs in the periphery is not enough. Did globalization backlash account for it?

The most elegant backlash explanation has its roots in the economics of Eli Heckscher (1919: translated in Flam and Flanders 1991) that showed how foreign trade effected the distribution of income, opening the way for Wolfgang Stolper and Paul Samuelson (1941) to elaborate the corollary (in English and mathematics), namely that the scarce factor should favor protection and the abundant factor should favor free trade. About twenty years ago, Stolper–Samuelson thinking was used with great skill by Ronald Rogowski (1989) who applied it to country trade policy the world around from 1840 to the present. But there were two limitations to the way Rogowski used the Stolper–Samuelson corollary. First, the corollary only tells us who cares about what, not who has the vote. Since the landed elite dominated voting in land scarce Europe,[7] the import-competing sectors got the protection from foreign grains that the landed elite wanted. Their political influence waned over time, however, since the power of the scarce factor at the polls shrinks as its relative size shrinks, and shrink it did as industrialization took place. However, what happens when the scarce factor does not have the vote at all, which was true of labor throughout most of the world before the 1930s?[8] Did labor get the protection of import-competing manufacturing that it should have wanted in labor scarce Latin America, in the labor scarce English-speaking new world, and in labor scarce southeast Asia? Second, Rogowski used the corollary to speak to *levels* of protection but not to *changes* in protection. Can the *rise* in protection be attributed to compensation of the global-induced injured scarce factor?

So, when the import-competing sector was injured by an adverse price shock—an improvement in the country's terms of trade induced by world market events or by declining seaborne transport costs that reduced import prices and raised export prices, was there a "compensation effect" that drove up tariffs? The answer will depend in part on whether the factors in the slumping sector could escape by migrating to the booming sector. Of course, the scarce factor can never completely escape injury by emigrating from the import competing sector, since these effects leave their mark economy wide, but the mark is much smaller. Thus Stolper–Samuelson economics has a far better chance of explaining 19th-century tariff policy when, after all, most trade was in primary products where immobile specific factors—land and minerals—played such a big role. The more trade was dominated by immobile, sector-specific factors, the more would those factors complain loudly when hit by unfavorable price shocks.[9]

Capitalists in the autonomous periphery should have been looking to form protectionist coalitions as soon as the first global century began to threaten them with freer trade. They did not have far to look in Latin America, either because they managed to dominate oligarchic regimes that excluded other interests or because they readily found coalition partners willing to help, or both (Rogowski 1989; Coatsworth and Williamson 2004a).

Why no scarce labor in the Latin American tale? Growth, peace, and political stability during the *belle époque* after the 1860s certainly did not produce democratic inclusion. Most of Latin America limited the franchise to a small minority of rich adult men until well into the 20th century, and suffrage for the working man would come even later in the Asian and Middle Eastern periphery. Thus the pre-modern periphery tended to produce oligarchic or despotic governments in which free-trading urban merchants who were linked to external trade and world finance played a dominant role. Free-trading landowners and mineral interests formed the second dominant part of the ruling oligarchy in countries that specialized in the export of agricultural products. The third dominant part of the ruling oligarchy was pro-protectionist manufacturing capitalists. The same was true of Russia, the Ottoman empire, Siam, and other autonomous parts of the periphery.

De-industrialization and Scarce Factor Compensation

Tariffs in the poor periphery could not have been used to foster industrialization and growth until the 1890s, but they could have been used to compensate for the massive de-industrialization damage caused by the 19th-century terms of trade boom favoring primary products.

Three ingredients were essential to the survival of any import-competing industry in the periphery: low costs of inputs—like labor, power, and raw materials; high productivity in the use of those inputs; and high market prices of output. Policy makers in the periphery could not do much about the first two,[10] but they could do a great deal about the third by pushing up tariff barriers, excluding foreign imports and thus raising the domestic price of manufactures relative to other commodities produced for home or foreign markets. When industrial productivity advance in the core was fast, world prices of manufactures declined relative to other products, and foreign firms became increasingly competitive in local periphery markets. Thus policy makers who favored industry, and/or the scarce factors used by industry, had reason to raise tariffs in response to any sharp decline in the relative price of manufactures in world markets. In short, if the periphery had experienced de-industrialization and feared more of the same, and if it wanted to compensate scarce factors damaged by foreign competition, it would have raised tariffs in response to falling relative prices of manufactures in world markets.

Evaporating Geographic Barriers and Scarce Factor Compensation

High transport costs on imported goods can be just as protective as high tariffs. When new transport technologies induced the dramatic fall in freight costs documented in chapter 2, the winds of competition thus created must have given powerful incentives to import competing industries (and scarce factors) to lobby for more protection. The 19th-century transport revolution gave plenty of incentive for manufacturing interests in the periphery and agricultural interests in the core to lobby for protection as the natural barriers afforded by transport costs melted away. This connection was confirmed long ago by the "invasion of grains" into the European industrial core. But what about the "invasion of manufactures" into the poor periphery?

The transport revolution took many forms, but, as we have seen, two mattered most: a decline in sea freight rates, and the penetration of railroads into interior markets. Freight rates fell everywhere, but especially on routes carrying high bulk intermediates and foodstuffs to Europe. Meanwhile railroads penetrated interior markets everywhere in the poor periphery, and this must have been especially relevant for tariff policy where markets were mainly located in the interior. If railroads exposed previously isolated manufacturing firms to increased foreign competition, those interests should have lobbied for more protection. These railroad forces were especially important in Latin America, eastern Europe, Ottoman Turkey, and even India.

Tariffs for Revenue

Were revenues a strong motive for high tariffs? Tariff revenue can be expressed as $R = tpM$, where R is revenue, t is the average ad valorem tariff rate, p is the average import price, and M is import volume.[11] For the governments in the periphery that had in mind some target revenue share in GDP ($R/Y = r$) and could not rely on foreign capital inflows to balance the current account (so $pM = X$), then $r = tpM/Y = tX/Y$. Clearly, if foreign exchange earnings from exports were booming (caused either by a terms of trade boom, denoted here by a fall in the relative price of imports, p, or by a supply-side expansion that increased export quantities, X, or both), then the target revenue share could have been achieved at lower tariff rates, t. That is, the bigger the export boom, the higher the export share, the bigger the import share, and the lower the necessary tariff rate. Of course, countries in the periphery that were successful in getting external finance would have had less reason to use high tariffs to augment revenues in the short run and medium term. Since world capital markets became increasingly well integrated up to 1913 (Obstfeld and Taylor 2003, 2004), high tariffs that were necessary in 1860 would have been far less necessary in 1913 if revenue smoothing was a key motivation. Furthermore countries that developed internal tax sources would have had less need for high tariffs, an event that started in the late 19th century industrial core, accelerating during the interwar rise of the welfare state (Lindert 1994, 2003). However, such developments lagged way behind in the periphery.

So, did autonomous governments in Latin America, the European periphery and Asia act as if they were meeting revenue targets? Ceteris paribus, did they lower tariff rates during secular booms in primary product markets when their export shares were high and rising, and did they raise them during primary product slumps?

A Minor Actor: Strategic Trade Policy

A well-developed theoretical literature on strategic trade policy predicts that nations have an incentive to inflate their own terms of trade by raising tariffs, unless, of course, trading partners agree to mutual concessions (e.g., Dixit 1987; Bagwell and Staiger 2002). According to this kind of thinking, a country's own tariffs will depend at least in part on the country's external tariff environment. For the two decades before World War I, every region in the periphery (except Latin America) faced much lower tariff rates in their main export markets than they themselves erected against competitors in their own markets (Blattman, Clemens, and Williamson 2002). The explanation, of course, is that their main export markets were located in the European core, where tariffs were much lower, although this was not true of Latin America for whom the protectionist United States was such an important market.

While the strategic trade policy thesis holds promise in helping account for higher tariffs in Latin America trading with the heavily protected

United States, and in that part of the European periphery trading with more protectionist France and Germany, it holds less promise for that part of the European periphery whose exports were sent to free-trading France, United Kingdom, and the Netherlands. Indeed between 1900 and World War I a decline in partner tariffs took place everywhere in the periphery *except* in the European periphery, suggesting a leader–follower reaction that varied across the periphery depending on who the dominant trading partner was—for example, an ultra-protectionist United States lowering tariffs, a moderately protectionist France and Germany raising tariffs, or a free trade Britain standing pat (Blattman, Clemens, and Williamson 2002).

13.4   The Political Economy of Tariffs: Looking at the Evidence

The potential explanations for tariff policies discussed above can be allocated to three main motives: scarce factor compensation, revenue needs, and infant industry arguments. The pages above argued that the latter is a modern motivation (at least in the poor periphery), and thus it will be ignored in what follows. While the remaining two motives need not have been competing, we would still like to know which played the biggest role, and in which periods and places. Elsewhere, an econometric attack was launched on the question (Blattman, Clemens, and Williamson 2002; Clemens and Williamson 2002; Coatsworth and Williamson 2004a): first, by treating the tariff experience as comparative economic history, and second, by exploring the cross-sectional tariff variance across countries. Here we will just summarize those results.

   We start with the time series and comparative economic history for the decades between 1870 and 1939. First, an improvement in a country's terms of trade generated a strong anti-trade reaction. For the poor periphery, this took the form of a de-industrialization reaction, since an improvement in the relative price of their primary-product export implied a fall in the relative price of imported manufactures, inviting a tariff-raising lobbying reaction by urban-industrial interests at home. For the European core, this took the form of a grain invasion reaction, as a fall in the relative price of imported foodstuffs invited a tariff-raising lobbying reaction by landed interests at home. In addition a decrease in sea freight costs was associated with an offsetting rise in tariff barriers, and an increase in the length of the domestic rail network was associated with a symmetric rise in tariffs. As geographic barriers evaporated, import-competing industries were compensated by higher tariffs. Second, revenue motivation is confirmed since export booms were associated with lower tariff rates, and slumps with higher tariff rates. As far as controls are concerned, here are the three that mattered most: Tariff rates fell with increases in GDP per capita, a result consistent with modern surveys of attitudes toward free trade (Mayda and Rodrik 2001; O'Rourke and Sinnott 2001). Internal market size also mattered, and in the predicted way: large countries had lower tariff rates. Suffrage—proxied by schooling and urbanization—served to give the vote to urban labor who sought to protect their industrial jobs.

Fair enough, but why were tariffs on the rise nearly everywhere in the decades before 1900, especially in the autonomous periphery? Growing GDP per capita and local market size were serving to *lower* tariffs everywhere, but these were overwhelmed by countervailing tariff-raising forces (Blattman, Clemens, and Williamson 2002). The push for higher tariffs came mostly from two sources: first, domestic political economy forces carried by a shift of voting power to urban interests; and second, a protectionist reaction serving to compensate import-competing industries as openness was thrust upon them by advances in transportation technology and world market forces lowering the relative price of manufactures in local markets. Falling transportation costs certainly did contribute to rising tariff barriers in the European core, the English-speaking European offshoots, and Asia. But transport revolutions along the sea lanes had little impact on tariffs in Latin America and the European periphery, simply because the fall in overseas freight rates was more modest there. The big impact came from railway penetration of their interiors. Finally, tariffs were pushed up by de-industrialization in the periphery, joining and even preceding the reaction to grain invasion in the core. Overall, it appears to have been rising levels of railway penetration, suffrage, and improving terms of trade (at least up to the 1890s) that drove tariffs upward in the periphery. The revenue motive was a force but not a dominant one after 1870. However, the revenue motive *was* a dominant force before 1870 (Coatsworth and Williamson 2004a, b).

Anti-trade forces that had pushed up tariffs before the 1890s ebbed afterward, finally overwhelmed by surging pro-trade forces. The terms of trade now had a pro-trade influence in the poor periphery since a stable or falling terms of trade there eliminated much of the compensation argument for tariffs. That is, as the long-run deterioration in the relative price of primary products started after the 1870s or 1890s, the relative rise in the price of imported foreign manufactures eased the competitive pressure on local industry. Furthermore much of the railroad system in the poor periphery was completed, and the transport revolution on the sea lanes was losing steam. Thus upward pressure on tariffs eased since there were fewer injured parties to compensate.

The cross-country results are consistent with the comparative time series. So, why were tariffs so low across Asia and the Middle East? Certainly lack of autonomy and the fact that the colonists were free-traders played a central role. Yet these two regions still obeyed the same political economy forces that prevailed in autonomous Latin America and the European periphery. Also bigger colonies with bigger internal markets were ones in which local industry could find niches and thus had less need for protective tariffs. Smaller domestic markets in many Latin American and English-speaking European offshots made it harder for manufacturing firms to survive in a niche without walls to protect them. The revenue motive also helps account for some of the difference between the autonomous and nonautonomous parts of the poor periphery: the colonies had revenue sources that the poor republics did not.

A summing up might be useful at this stage. Revenue needs were an important determinant of tariff rates in the periphery before the 1870s, and especially for young republics with limited tax bases and limited access to foreign capital. As world capital markets improved in the late 19th century, and as periphery governments broadened their tax bases, revenue needs gradually lost their influence on tariff setting. De-industrialization and fears of more of it were a major determinant of tariff policy in the periphery before World War I, especially before the 1890s when the relative price of imported manufactures underwent almost a century of dramatic secular decline (chapter 3). After the 1860s, grain-invasion fears in the European core joined de-industrialization fears in the periphery (which chapters 4–8 reported having been pronounced at least since the 1820s). Finally, geography mattered, so that where and when the natural protection of distance and topography was conquered by transport technology, tariffs rose to compensate the injured import-competing industries.

Addendum: Policy Packages and the Real Exchange Rate

Few policies are decided in isolation. Indeed there were other ways that governments could have improved the competitive position of import-competing industries, if such protection was their goal, and they explored many of these alternatives in the 1930s and in the ISI years that followed. Yet they clearly understood these alternatives even before World War I. One powerful alternative involved allowing real exchange depreciation. If governments chose to go on the gold standard or to peg to a core currency, they got more stable real exchange rates in return (and an attractive advertisement for foreign capital: Meissner 2005). However, since protection via real exchange rate depreciation was forgone, tariff rates would have to go up to reclaim that protection lost. We know industrial countries exploited this trade-off during the 1930s (Eichengreen and Irwin 2009), but did the periphery also exploit this trade-off before World War I? It turns out that some did. So where, when, and how much did the exchange rate depreciation foster industrialization in the poor periphery? As chapter 12 stressed, depreciation of the domestic currency favored local manufacturing in the poor periphery since it made imported manufactures more expensive in the local market. Currency appreciation did the opposite. The real exchange rate makes adjustments for different rates of inflation between the periphery country and the rest of the world. Obviously the real exchange rate can change either by changing nominal exchange rates or by changing domestic price levels, but if the country opts for fixed nominal exchange rates (gold standard, pegs on a major currency) changes in its price level are limited. In short, by electing to stay off the gold standard, real exchange rate depreciation could have fostered industrialization. Two countries did so in Latin America: Mexico (on a silver standard until 1905) underwent a real currency depreciation of 137 percent between the mid-1870s and 1902, and the real currency depreciation for the whole period was an enormous 81 percent. While not quite as big, Brazil (fiat currency until 1906) also underwent a significant real currency depreciation of 34 percent between 1870–1874 and 1913 (Gómez Galvarriato and Williamson 2009). The rest of the periphery did not follow suit since most stuck to the gold standard or other fixed exchange rate currency arrangements. Some exceptions were China, Spain, and Venezuela, which never went on the gold standard, and Japan and Russia, which waited until the 1890s or even later (Meissner 2005: table 1, 391).

13.5 What Should They Have Done?

If the goal was to favor industrial development or simply to compensate losers from the de-industrialization damage generated by trade, theory tells us that tariffs were a poor way to do it. For compensation purposes, the first best way would have been to use tax-transfer mechanisms that would not have had the distortions associated with tariffs. So much for theory! Unfortunately, no country, and certainly no poor periphery country, had the fiscal sophistication or the political will to implement any such tax-transfer scheme. For industrial development purposes, we know that the first-best policy was not tariffs but rather subsidies for industrial inputs like education, capital goods, R&D, and learning by doing. These tools were rarely used in the poor periphery before the 1930s, although there were exceptions like Mexico and Japan. Presumably these tools were not used because there was no political will to do so by the oligarchies in power.

But if the goal was industrialization and growth, and if the major policy tool available to achieve it in the poor periphery was tariffs, then they should have offered high effective rates of protection to industries that were skill-intensive and generated positive externalities to other industries. They did not do so. This is hardly surprising since Nathan Nunn and Daniel Trefler have shown that developing countries did not do so even between 1972 and 2000 (Nunn and Trefler 2007: see also Grossman and Helpman 1994). Nunn and Trefler show that third world tariffs are used to satisfy rent-seeking behavior, just as we have shown that they were used to compensate the global (import-competing) losers in the poor periphery before 1939. And since labor-intensive sectors were much bigger in the poor periphery than were sophisticated skill-intensive sectors generating positive externalities, they had much bigger lobbies and thus got the protection.

14   Morals of the Story

The long 19th century up to World War I produced two big economic events. First, the west European leaders (and their English-speaking offshoots) underwent an industrial revolution, but the poor periphery did not. The living standard and income per capita gap between the industrial leaders and the poor periphery widen dramatically to levels much like they are today. Second, the world went global. Trade barriers fell steeply and commodity trade boomed. The poor periphery enjoyed almost a century of soaring terms of trade, as the demand for the intermediates to feed Europe's (and their English-speaking offshoots) factories and for the luxury foodstuffs consumed by their economically successful citizens boomed. The poor periphery exploited that boom well by specializing increasingly in the export of primary products, while western Europe specialized in the export of manufactures. Given those two events, *Trade and Poverty* posed the following question in the first chapter: Was the positive correlation between the world going global and the sharply rising economic gap between poor and rich countries causal? Did the former contribute to the latter?

The answer clearly is yes. We got that answer first by exploring what are called the channels of impact. *Trade and Poverty* stressed three: de-industrialization, rising inequality, and primary product price volatility.

First, consider de-industrialization. If trade benefited the rich core by more than it did the poor periphery—thus contributing to the great divergence—then it must have done so by the fact that world trade reinforced industrialization in the core while suppressing it in the periphery. Early in *Trade and Poverty*, we saw that most economists think that industry is a carrier of growth, at least in its early stages. Thus economists commonly embed that view in their theories of endogenous growth. Fair enough: then did the trade boom cause de-industrialization in the poor periphery? It did indeed, although some regions were able to fend off the destructive effects of de-industrialization better than others. Did this harm average incomes in the poor periphery? No, it did not. Rather, the poor periphery improved its growth performance as a consequence. The terms of trade gift from the industrial core raised their incomes, and they also exploited the gains from trade by increasingly specializing in primary product exports. But the trade-induced rise in their growth rates was far lower since they did not get the endogenous growth kick from industrialization that the rich core did.

Second, the global trade boom raised inequality dramatically in most of the poor periphery. A rich oligarchy owned the land, the mines and other natural resources that were the basis of their primary product export boom. Better prices for those exports raised the return to the natural resources—land rents and income from the mines soared—augmenting incomes at the top. Rising inequality increased the political power of the oligarchy, and their interest was to reinforce institutions and government policies that rewarded their rent-seeking, while suppressing those that might have fostered growth. These pro–rent-seeking forces were absent in land scarce countries specializing in manufactures. While the landlords lost there, the urban working class and their capitalist employers gained. As their political power increased, institutions and policies shifted from rent-seeking toward pro-growth. The land scarce countries included, of course, relatively rich, capital-abundant western Europe. But the land scarce countries also included relatively poor, capital scarce East Asia, whose industry was also stimulated by the trade boom. Political power shifted the same way.

Third, primary-product specialization in the poor periphery exposed them to greater price and income volatility, and volatility was bad for growth. Primary-product prices have always been more volatile than that of manufactures and services, and thus the terms of trade in the poor periphery was much more volatile than in the rich core, even as early as the 18th century. To add to the volatility, trade encouraged specialization and in the poor periphery this meant concentrating exports in just one or two commodities. As they gave up diversification for specialization, export concentration meant even more price and thus income volatility.

Having established these three channels of impact, *Trade and Poverty* then explored the evidence in support of the asymmetric trade impact thesis: Did a terms of trade boom raise growth in the rich core but not in the poor periphery? Did terms of trade volatility do less damage in the rich core than in the poor periphery? The test was performed on a world sample of thirty-five countries comprising more than 95 percent of world GDP in

1914. The sample included nine from the rich core (western Europe and its English-speaking offshoots), and twenty-six from the poor periphery in Asia, the Middle East, Latin America, and the lagging parts of Europe. The test was to see whether, between 1870 and 1939, trends and volatility in the terms of trade had very different effects on growth rates in the core than in the periphery. It did: a terms of trade boom augmented growth in the rich core but had no effect in the poor periphery; terms of trade volatility hurt growth in the poor periphery but not in the rich core. The data are not available to perform the same test for the half century before 1870, but it is likely that the test would be even more supportive there. After all, the terms of trade boom was bigger, the de-industrialization forces were more powerful, and terms of trade volatility was even greater.

We conclude that history supports the theory, both on the three channels of impact and on the overall impact. The world trade boom up to World War I helped contribute to the great divergence, and that contribution was very big. But it wasn't just trade that did it: it was a huge rise in the terms of trade in the poor periphery that did it.

Trade and Poverty concluded with two more issues. First, if the secular terms of trade boom up to the 1870s or 1890s (a fall in the relative price of manufactures) caused de-industrialization in the poor periphery, then wouldn't a terms of trade bust after the 1870s or 1890s (a rise in the relative price of manufactures) favor industrialization in the poor periphery? There seems to be some evidence supporting this view: after about 1870, most early industrializers in the poor periphery faced a significant fall in their terms of trade. Second, did those poor periphery countries which had the autonomy to do so raise tariff barriers to fend off the invasion of manufactures and the forces of de-industrialization? We know this is not the best way to foster industrialization, but did they do it? Yes, where they had the autonomy to do so tariffs in the poor periphery were far higher (and rising) than they were in the rich European core. But no, the motivation was not some pro-industrial policy. Rather, the motivation was compensation of the losers. A pro-industrial policy motivation had to wait until the 1930s and the start of anti-trade and anti-market ISI strategies.

Are there lessons from this history? Yes. Terms of trade booms in the poor periphery can still put the brakes on growth for countries looking to develop. That much has not changed over the past century or two. But countries that have the power and the political will to do so can and have significantly weakened, or even eliminated, that correlation. By adopting pro-growth policies, most of the third world has shifted from specializing in primary-product exports to labor-intensive exports, thus breaking the power of primary-product prices on their economies. By adopting the relevant institutions and policies, many countries have found ways to smooth the impact of price volatility. And as the third world gives the vote to the working poor and small urban capitalists, institutions and policies have developed to offset the economic power of rent-seeking interests. Where this process is slow, as in Africa, the old 19th-century economic order prevails. Where this process is fast, as in East Asia, the European periphery, and much of Latin America, the old 19th-century economic order is long gone.

Notes

Chapter 2

1. The next few paragraphs draw heavily on Findlay and O'Rourke (2007: 395–96), who relied on O'Rourke and Williamson (1999: chs. 3 and 6), who relied heavily on Bairoch (1989).

2. Niall Ferguson claims that "no organization in history has done more to promote the free movement of goods, capital and labour than the British Empire in the nineteenth and early twentieth centuries" (Ferguson 2003: xxi).

3. This section draws on Williamson (2006a: ch. 2).

4. Recent work has been able to uncover little or no evidence of commodity price convergence between Europe and Asia in the three centuries after 1500. The big globalization turning point was the 1820s (O'Rourke and Williamson 2002a, 2002b), after which commodity price convergence was dramatic.

5. The "tyranny of distance" was the apt phrase that Geoffrey Blainey (1982) used to describe its importance to Australian development. Export shares in GDP were only 3.4 percent for Asia in 1913, but 25 percent for Latin America and 20 percent for Africa and Egypt combined (Blattman et al. 2007: table 1).

6. See also Gallup, Gaviria, and Lora (2003: 47–50). Of course, there were other factors at work too, like institutions, demography, slavery and luck in world commodity markets. But many of these were themselves influenced by geography and endowments, as Stanley Engerman and Kenneth Sokoloff (1997; with Haber 2000) have argued.

7. The industrial output figures start with 1750 while the GDP figures start with 1700. Since the 18th century was a transition to modern economic growth, growth rates trended up a bit even then. Thus, if we had industrial output for 1700 to 1830, the growth rate would be lower than the 0.96 figure report in table 2.2 for the developed countries. Also, and in contrast with the GDP sample, the industrial

output sample includes some late industrializers—Austria-Hungary, Russia, Spain—that drag the acceleration down.

8. Revisions of Maddison (1995) found in Estevadeordal et al. (2003: fig. I).

Chapter 3

1. Unless otherwise noted, the terms of trade phrase used in the text always refers to the *net barter* terms of trade, that is, the ratio of the average price of exports to that of imports.

2. Until the 1780s, long time series on the terms of trade in the poor periphery appears to be available only for Mexico and Spain. See Williamson (2008: app.).

3. Carlos Díaz-Alejandro (1984) made this point some time ago, and called it the "commodity lottery."

4. The other member of the East Asian sample is Japan, but it does not enter the sample until 1857. Thus all the differences between the series with and without East Asia can be attributed to China before the late 1850s. In the second half of the century, the population weight for China is so huge that China still dominates the East Asian terms of trade trends.

5. It should be noted that one other country, Cuba, showed "exceptional" terms of trade experience. The Cuban terms of trade is not plotted in figure 3.6, but it *fell* by 49 percent between 1826 and 1860, and by 50 percent up to 1885 through 1890. The source of the decline lay, of course, with sugar prices.

6. I am not suggesting here that the price of opium was exogenous to the Chinese market. Indeed rising Chinese demand helped account for part of the price boom, and monopoly behavior by the East India Company probably accounted for the rest.

7. The text should not be interpreted as suggesting that the price of silk or tea were exogenous to China. Indeed China was a major supplier of both to world markets.

8. Mexico is an exception. See Dobado, Gómez, and Williamson (2008) and Williamson (2007).

9. The Levant is not shown in table 3.1, since the series starts only with 1839, but it underwent a milder terms of trade boom.

10. One explanation for the weak terms of trade boom is that India remained a gross (but not a net) exporter of cotton goods even when British factory textiles flooded India's domestic economy. Since cotton textiles influenced India's export prices, and since the latter were falling dramatically up to 1850, the net barter terms of trade did not enjoy quite the same boom in India that it did in the rest of the poor periphery.

Chapter 4

1. These are taken from Blattman et al. (2007), but see also Hanson (1986).

2. The term was first used in the late 1970s to describe the decline of manufacturing in the Netherlands after the discovery of North Sea natural gas deposits in the 1960s.

3. Richard Auty (1993) first used this expression to describe the paradox that countries rich in natural resources are often relatively poor and record slow growth. Since then, the empirical literature has exploded on the topic. See, for example, Sachs and Warner (1995) and Gylfason (2000).

4. Formal models linking resource booms to rent-seeking can be found in Murphy et al. (1991, 1993), Tornell and Lane (1999), Baland and Francois (2000), and Torvick (2002), among others.

5. There is a considerable difference between Hanson's 20 poor periphery countries in table 4.3 and our 24 in table 4.2. Hanson excludes some we include: Colombia, Cuba, Mexico, Venezuela, Burma, Turkey, Greece, Portugal, Serbia, Spain, and Russia. Hanson includes some we omit: Algeria, British Guiana, British West Indies, Costa Rica, French West Indies, Mauritius, Reunion, San Salvador, and Senegal. Hanson also allocates Argentina to the core. See the note to table 4.3.

6. A more complete statement of the model can be found in Clingingsmith and Williamson (2008).

7. Wrigley (2006: 477) paraphrases Adam Smith (1776/1904: I, 381) this way: "An efficient agriculture meant cheap food, which in turn led to low wage costs" and thus a competitive industry.

8. The own wage is defined as the nominal wage divided by the price of the output produced by that industry.

9. For example, agriculture employed 68 percent of the Indian labor force even as late as 1901 (Roy 2002: 113).

Chapter 5

1. $[M_{IC}/M_W]/[GDP_{IC}/GDP_W] = [M_{IC}/GDP_{IC}]/[M_W/GDP_W] = 1.22$, where IC = India plus China and W = world.

2. $[M_{DC}/GDP_{DC}]/[M_W/GDP_W] = 1.23$, where DC = developed core.

3. The penetration of the Ottoman domestic market started somewhat earlier with an Indian "invasion" over the three centuries before 1800 (İnalcık 1993: 269–96).

4. For a survey, see Issawi (1961), and his citations there. See also Batou (1990: 459–60; 1991: 181–217).

5. Batou's (1991: table 1) estimates of machine cotton spindles per capita give an Egyptian 1834 figure of 80, which ranked Egypt in a tie for fifth with Spain, both of which were below Great Britain, Switzerland, United States, and France but above all others.

6. Pamuk (2006: table 1) estimates Egyptian GDP per capita growth between 1820 and 1870 at 0.4 percent per annum. No doubt that modest figure was even lower between 1805 and 1849, the Mohamed Ali anti-global and anti-market years, since the 1820 to 1870 span includes the cotton-export boom of the 1850s and 1860s.

7. Malaya between 1882 and 1913 is also plotted in figure 3.9, but it starts much too late to be included in this analysis.

8. It is somewhat of an irony that the term Dutch disease can be applied best to the Dutch East Indies.

9. The data underlying figure 3.10 are taken from Yasuba (1996: table 2, geometrically interpolating between his benchmark observations for 1857, 1865, 1875), and linked to the annual series in Yamazawa (1975: 539).

10. As we will see, Karl Marx, the theorist, was not paying attention to the evidence when he said, in "China the spinners and weavers have suffered greatly under this foreign competition [that is, the importation of English cottons]" (Marx 1853, cited in Feuerwerker 1992: 123).

11. See also Feuerwerker (1970; 1980: 28–40).

Chapter 6

1. Terms of trade increases up to the 1860s were also much bigger for the European periphery. In addition after the 1840s their increase was much bigger for Japan and the Mideast (Williamson 2006a, b, 2008). Like India, the terms of trade boom was also modest for Mexico between 1750 and 1870, and Dutch disease forces were weaker as a consequence. But why was Mexico better able to minimize de-industrialization effects (Dobado, Gómez Galvarriato, and Williamson 2008) than India? An answer is offered in chapter 8.

2. Domestic consumption of cotton cloth was 60 million rupees in Bengal, and 16 million rupees were exported by both Asian and European merchants (Chaudhury 1999: 143, 175, 188, 198, 211). See also Roy (2009).

3. Some have argued that deteriorating weather conditions helped precipitate the collapse of the Mughal empire (Grove and Chappell 2000: 15), but the alleged connection is not central to the issues raised here.

4. India is assumed to have been a price taker for textiles and other manufactures. Given this assumption, domestic demand did not matter in determining the performance of Indian industry. Only price and competitiveness on the supply side

mattered. Thus we ignore as irrelevant any argument that appeals to a rise in the demand for cloth as per capita income rose (Harnetty 1991: 455, 506; Morris 1983: 669).

5. Robert Allen (2005: table 5.3, 121) estimates that rice and peas combined accounted for 49 percent of the budget for common workers in India around 1595. More generally, food accounted for 91 percent.

6. English merchants and English ships were the main suppliers to the Atlantic trade, a lot of it the so-called re-export trade. While the share of Indian textiles in the West African trade was about 38 percent in the 1730s, it had fallen to 22 percent in the 1780s and 3 percent in the 1840s (Inikori 2002: 512–13 and 516). By the end of the 17th century, Indian calicos were a major force in European markets (Landes 1998: 154). For example, the share of Indian textiles in total English trade with southern Europe was more than 20 percent in the 1720s, but this share fell to about 6 percent in the 1780s and less than 4 percent in the 1840s (Inikori 2002: 517). India was losing its world market share in textiles during the 18th century, long before the industrial revolution.

7. To make matters worse, India, which had captured a good share of the English market in the 17th century, had—as an English defensive response—already been legislated out of that market by Parliamentary decree between 1701 and 1722 (Inikori 2002: 431–32), thus protecting local textile producers. But Parliament kept the Atlantic economy as a competitive free trade zone. Of course, the large Indian Ocean market was also a free trade zone, and India had dominated this for centuries (Chaudhuri 1978; Landes 1998: 154). It should be stressed that India also had a technological edge over England in the early 18th century (Prakash 2004: 268–69). Before the machines of Hargraves, Arkwright, and Crompton, Indian spinners were the only ones capable of producing yarn strong enough for the warp, and thus could produce pure cotton cloth. European spinners could not do this, and thus could only produce a mixed cotton-linen cloth.

8. A recent survey of the Bengal economy by Roy (2009) finds no evidence of growth *or* decline over the 50 years before British colonization.

9. Agriculture employed 68 percent of the Indian labor force even as late as 1901 (Roy 2002: 113).

10. Since grain is taken to have been nontradable internationally, any secular tendency for domestic demand to outpace domestic supply would have raised grain prices. An exogenous acceleration of population growth would have lowered labor productivity on the land, reduced food supply relative to demand, and thus raised the price of food. However, population grew at only 0.26 percent per annum between 1700 and 1820, and this was only a trivial increase over what preceded it (Moosvi 2000: 322). Thus other forces are needed to explain any observed rise in the relative price of grains.

11. Maddison (2001: 184 and 214) estimates that in 1820 the GDP of the India (including present-day Bangladesh and Pakistan) was about three times that of the United Kingdom, but the industrial share must have been a lot smaller in India. The text assumes that these offsetting forces were roughly comparable.

12. The same seems to apply to the 19th-century Indonesian "drain" to Holland, which averaged about 6 percent of GDP in 1835 to 1860 (van Zanden 2002: fig. 1). However, the Dutch colonists used coffee rather than textiles to facilitate the transfer.

13. Peter Harnetty would appear to agree, although he was speaking of the Central Provinces in the 1860s, not the century starting roughly with 1750. Harnetty says (1991: 460): "The combination of high food prices and cheap cloth imports had a depressing effect on the local industry."

14. This Indian 1800 figure of 15 to 18 percent compares favorably with that of other periphery regions almost a century later: Mexico in 1895 at 11.7 percent, and the United States 1880 at 18.8 percent. Gómez Galvarriato and Williamson (2008: table 5).

15. The literature insists on some qualifications to this big de-industrialization fact. First, many workers who gave up industry over the century were working only part-time. Second, the import of machine-made goods only helps explain the demise of textiles. Third, the literature also argues that cheaper imported yarn would have reduced the production costs facing handloom weavers, thus making them more competitive. Since cheaper European factory-produced yarn would have lowered the production costs not just for Indian handloom weavers but for weavers the world around, it is not clear how this made Indian weavers more competitive with imported cloth.

16. Among the most well-known examples is the powerful image quoted by Karl Marx in *Das Kapital*: "The misery hardly finds a parallel in the history of commerce. The bones of the cotton-weavers are bleaching the plains of India" (1977 [1867], vol. 1: 558). Marx attributed this quote to the governor-general of India in 1834 to 1835, who was Lord William Bentinck. However, Morris D. Morris has pointed out that the quoted words do not appear in Bentinck's report of that year or in his papers (Morris 1969: 165, n.152). The true source of this first report of de-industrialization remains a mystery.

17. Hamilton spent nearly $20 million (2005 US$) on the survey, and his information appears to be of high quality (Martin 1838).

18. The percentage of industrial workers who were spinners fell from 82 to 15 between 1809–1813 and 1901.

19. This is a reasonable assumption up to the mid-19th century. Grains became tradable commodities throughout Asia in the late 19th century, but for the 18th

and early 19th century, it is more accurate to treat them as nontradables. See chapter 4.

20. If this formal "cost competitiveness" and "own wage" language seems awkward when applied to household spinners and weavers, think instead of the grain that could be bought with nominal earnings in those households.

21. The grain price series includes prices for rice, wheat, bajra, and jower from locations spanning the subcontinent. Restricting the included series to rice and wheat for Bengal and north India, which comprise the longest and most regionally consistent prices, shows the same patterns as the overall series. The main difference is that the rise in grain prices of 1780 to 1850 is smoother in the restricted series. A full description of how the wage and price data were constructed can be found elsewhere (Clingingsmith and Williamson 2008: data app.).

22. A full description of the wage data can also be found in Clingingsmith and Williamson (2008: data app.).

23. Note that Broadberry and Gupta's north India grain wage series contains no data points between 1690 and 1874, so it is impossible to discern trends within the 18th century from it.

24. In any case, since agriculture was so huge, it must have dominated nationwide labor scarcity conditions, and not just those in manufacturing.

25. After 1860, global trade in grains changed conditions considerably. Thus the assumption that grains were nontradable is increasingly untenable as the late 19th century concludes. Cheaper imported grains (and railroad development within India) could have played a role in lowering the own wage in manufacturing after the 1860s or 1870s, and thus could have contributed to re-industrialization in India.

Chapter 7

1. Alternatively, if the country is "large" and has an influence on world prices, then it will suffer a terms of trade deterioration, in that it has to share part of the labor productivity gains in the agricultural export sector with its trading partners. The "large" country conditions probably began to apply to Egypt and its cotton exports after the 1860s, but Egypt is not included in this chapter's Ottoman empire definition. The empire definition here excludes Egypt because it had different endowments, different commodity specialization, significant policy autonomy, and Mohamed Ali.

2. This must have placed local industry at a significant disadvantage relative to foreign products. Yet the literature offers no explicit assessment of its impact, nor of the political economy that produced it.

3. Export duties are a tax on trade and thus offer partial relief to import-competing industries. It appears that the literature had failed to appreciate this fact, since it offers no explicit assessment of its impact.

4. The figure is for *average* tariff rates, but the rates were even higher on imported manufactures.

5. Quataert cites the Indian de-industrialization literature in pointing out terminological problems: "Some India scholars suggest that the term [de-industrialization] be abandoned altogether because its meaning is not clear. They argue that there are too many holes in the data to support the level of generalization that use of the term implies" (Quataert 1994: 898). Obviously, I disagree. Labels are useful for narratives, but theory and measurement are the keys to understanding the de-industrialization experience, regardless of descriptive labels.

6. Pamuk (1987: 121), and see his appendix V for the details of the reconstruction.

7. That is, p_T and p_C are assumed to be exogenous to the Ottoman economy.

8. The literature often fails to appreciate that *changes* in policy, transport costs and world prices matter, not levels. After all, de-industrialization implies a change, namely a decline in the relative or even absolute importance of manufacturing.

9. The share of transportation costs in the price of a good moved to and from the Ottoman interior varied substantially according to the good (low-value, high-bulk primary products vs. high-value, low-bulk textiles, but also wheat vs. other primary goods) and the distance from port. Hence the estimates underlying table 7.2 are rough. Quataert (1977: 143–54) offers an excellent discussion of this issue and some international comparisons with wheat transport on the Anatolian railway after 1890. The cereal growing areas in Anatolia could not send any wheat to Istanbul or Izmir before the railroad, but they did send some to the southern port of Mersin on the Mediterranean via camel caravans. Quataert indicates that per ton-kilometer costs in transporting Anatolian wheat to all three ports by railroad were initially significantly higher than on the routes between Chicago and New York. However, he estimates that ton-kilometer charges for wheat and barley accounted for 22 percent of the final price in Istanbul at the end of the period. Other export commodities produced in the interior, like fruits, nuts, and tobacco, benefited to a smaller extent from the arrival of the railroads (Kurmus 1974). Table 7.2 summarizes this evidence by assuming that between the 1860s and 1913 the railroads alone lowered textile prices in the interior by about 7 percent and raised primary product prices in the interior by about 21 percent, all relative to coastal prices.

Chapter 8

1. The "continental European periphery" is here taken as the unweighted average of Czechoslovakia, Denmark, Finland, Italy, Norway, Spain, Sweden, and Russia.

2. Coatsworth (2003, 2005). The *Insurgencia* started in 1810, and, after years of violence and economic dislocation, the Mexican Republic emerged in 1821.

3. Maddison (2003) estimates a 0.32 percent annual rate of population growth, and Coatsworth (2003) estimates 0.73 percent. Clearly, further research is needed to resolve this immense demographic difference.

4. Calculated around 1800 from cities with 10,000 inhabitants or more reported in Humboldt (1822).

5. There is one dissenting voice which rejects the majority "lost decades" view (Prados 2009).

6. Between 1796 and 1828 cochineal export values averaged more than 15 percent of total exports (Baskes 2005: 192–93). Cochineal was used to dye textiles.

7. The average excludes the years 1805 to 1806 and 1809, when international hostilities sharply reduced Atlantic trade.

8. Miño (1983: 244). The economywide manufacturing estimate comes from Humboldt (1822: 451).

9. Based on capital invested, this *indianilla* factory was bigger than the largest *obraje* in Nueva España, Tacuba in 1752 (Miño 1998: 48 and 191).

10. Miño (1998: 266–67). Table 8.1 estimates that textile imports were 55.5 percent of total imports between 1802 and 1828, while another estimate places the figure even higher at 85 percent between 1806 and 1818 (Thomson 2002: 105).

11. Florescano (1969: 68–82). A later version of the Florescano thesis can be found in Brian Hamnett (1980).

12. According to Hamnett (1980: 23), the value of domestically produced textiles fell by one half between the 1800s and the 1820s.

13. The Latin American examples can be easily multiplied, but here's what W. Arthur Lewis had to say about Columbia: "the result of successful exporting was an influx of cheap cottons and metalwares which set back the domestic production . . . of manufactures" in Columbia (Lewis 1978b: 218–19). See also McGreevey (1971: 164–73).

14. However, Mexican mills were smaller than were those in the core competitors. While the average Mexican mill in 1843—in terms of spindles per mill—was not much smaller than the average United States mill in 1831, by 1879 it was only 20 percent of the average 1880 American mill.

15. The words corn, Indian corn, and maize are used interchangeably.

16. The Lewis assumption has been criticized extensively since his famous labor surplus article appeared in 1954. Yet development economists and economic

historians still find it a useful way to assess economywide behavior in low-income societies. Figure 8.5 suggests that the assumption is confirmed by Mexican experience over the half century 1780 to 1830, but not before or after. We will deal with the post-1830 deviation in what follows below.

17. The price of textiles and the British export price index were highly correlated for the years 1800 to 1828.

18. Of course, the Dutch disease literature reminds us that the terms of trade between tradables and nontradables can be at least as important as the external terms of trade, but that issue will be explored below.

19. The true increase in Mexico's terms of trade may have been somewhat "larger because of the tradition of using export prices of a major exporter as a proxy for Latin American import prices—meaning that the statistics tend to understate the improvement in Latin America's [net barter terms of trade] by neglecting declining transport costs, which lower import prices" (Prados 2004: 80). Perhaps, but any downward bias would be shared by other regions in the periphery, so it should not affect any comparisons.

20. As was noted earlier, Mexico could have had relatively low agricultural productivity, and certainly compared with England. But the text refers to *trends* in agricultural productivity, not levels.

21. These real wage movements suggest that inequality rose to independence and then fell, trends that have recently been confirmed (Williamson 2009).

22. On the antebellum United States, see Bils (1984) and Harley (1992); on Catolonia, see Rosés (1998) and Thomson (2005); and on Japan, see Clark (1987).

23. Raw cotton was grown extensively in Mexico, but it was not competitive in world markets. Thus, behind tariffs and prohibitions, domestic cotton prices were higher than world prices.

24. Cosio Villegas (1931: 13, 43, 92); Gómez Galvarriato (1999: 208).

25. To add to the ambiguity, the elimination of domestic geographic barriers to trade—especially with the introduction of the railroads—also exposed domestic producers to greater foreign competition.

Chapter 9

1. This is less than Maddison's (1998: 12) assumed subsistence minimum of $PPP 400, which, in principle, covers more than physiological needs. Note that a purely physiological minimum "sufficient to sustain life with moderate activity and zero consumption of other goods" (Bairoch 1993: 106) was estimated by Bairoch to be $PPP 80 at 1960 prices, or $PPP 355 at 1990 prices. Our minimum is also consistent with the World Bank absolute poverty line, which is 1.08 per day per capita in 1993

$PPP (Chen and Ravallion 2007: 6). This works out to be about $PPP 365 per annum in 1990 international prices. Since more than a billion people are calculated to have incomes less than the World Bank global poverty line, it seems reasonable to assume that the physiological minimum income must be less. One may also recall that Colin Clark's (1957: 18–23) pioneering study of incomes, distinguished between international units (the early PPP dollar) and oriental units, the lower dollar equivalents that he thought held for subtropical or tropical regions where calorie, housing, and clothing needs are considerably less than those in temperate climates. Since our sample includes a fair number of tropical countries, this gives us another reason to use a conservatively low estimate of the physiological minimum.

2. Where agriculture is "big" in pre-industrial economies, the changing wage–rent ratio can be a very effective proxy for trends in inequality, and the evidence for it can be found in Williamson (1997, 1998, 2000, 2002a), Lindert and Williamson (2003), and Milanovic et al. (2008). A "big" agriculture is one in which the share of agricultural land in total economywide tangible wealth is more than a third and/or in which the agricultural employment share is more than a half. Around the turn of the last century, the agriculture employment share in the poor periphery was the following: Egypt 69.6, India 67.3, Indonesia 73.1, Japan 70, Taiwan 70.3, and Turkey 81.6 (Mitchell 1998b: 91–101); Mexico 71.9 (Mitchell 1993: 101); Portugal 66.9, and Spain 70.2 (Mitchell 1998a: 155–57).

3. In contrast, the modern distribution literature focuses on wages by skill and the earnings distribution. Skills and financial capital were not critical factors of production in the pre-modern periphery, and thus were only marginally relevant to income distributions.

4. Goldsmith (1985: table 40, 123) reports the share of agricultural land in tangible national wealth around World War I. The figures for three in the periphery were (in percent): Japan 29.7, Mexico 23, and Italy 33.3. Around 1850 the shares were much bigger, but Goldsmith offers only one observation, Italy 41.8. Presumably the shares were even bigger in much of the (undocumented) primary-product oriented periphery. If livestock, farm structures, and commodity inventories were added to agricultural land, the shares would be bigger still.

5. The arithmetic is simple enough. Let national income (Y) equal the sum of wages (w_L, the wage per worker times the total labor force) and land rents (r_D, rent per hectare times total hectares), so that $Y = w_L + r_D$. Then per worker income growth is (where an asterisk refers to the percentage growth over the fifteen or twenty years after 1858) $Y^* - L^* = w^*\theta_w + L^*(\theta_w - 1) + r^*\theta_r$. Assume further that the share of income accruing to labor (θ_w) was 60 percent and to land (θ_r) 40 percent. The land share in the 1880s has been estimated to have been about 37 percent (see note 103), close to the 40 percent assumed here. Assume also that land hectarage was fixed, and that labor force growth was 7.6 percent between 1850 and 1870 (the measured rate of population growth in Maddison 1995: 106). If some of the GDP per capita growth

between 1820 and 1870 actually took place before 1850, then land rents fell by even more than what is estimated in the text. If the wage actually rose by less than Huber estimates, then land rents per hectare also rose by less, but the big wage–rent ratio rise would have been much the same.

6. The figure for 1883 to 1892, the earliest estimate available for agriculture in Japan, was 36.7 percent (Hayami 1975: table 2–11, 36; land rent as a share in the sum of land rent plus wages, the latter including imputed wages).

7. Chaudhuri (1983), Tomlinson (1993), and Whitcomb (1983). It is relative endowments that count for specialization and trade. Presumably both labor and land had low productivity in the Punjab compared with western Europe. The *effective* stocks of labor and land were both very low, accounting for low per capita income.

Chapter 10

1. Since third world commodity exports are first world commodity imports, why doesn't commodity price volatility cause terms of trade volatility for both the first and the third worlds? The answer, of course, is that while the price volatile goods dominate third world exports, they do not dominate first world imports. Thus export commodities with volatile prices translate in to volatile terms of trade for the third world, but they do not for the first world, or even the second world that also exports primary products, like Australia, Canada, and the United States.

2. For important early exceptions, see Easterly et al. (1993), Deaton and Miller (1996), Mendoza (1997), Deaton (1999), Kose and Reizman (2001), and Bleaney and Greenway (2001). The more recent (booming) literature is reviewed below in the text.

3. See also Aizenman and Marion (1999), Flug et al. (1999), Elbers et al. (2007), and Koren and Tenreyro (2007).

4. Loayza et al. (2007: data underlying fig. 3, 346) where volatility is calculated as the standard deviation of the logarithmic change.

5. The missing evidence are the trade weights to attach to the prices.

Chapter 11

1. For a historian's survey of the recent commodity export literature, see Barbier (2005).

2. In Prebisch's words, "industrialization is the only means by which the Latin American countries may fully obtain the advantages of technical progress." Cited in Cuddington et al. (2007: 103).

3. We stop at 1909, not 1913, because the trend and volatility data for are only comparable if they are based on a full decade.

4. We do not have data on world export shares of gold and silver, but several countries (e.g., Mexico) are major producers. These countries need not be dropped, however, because the prices of these precious metals were generally fixed, so no feedback effects were possible. The silver price was pegged in world markets by the bi-metallic core Franco countries during most of our period. As for gold, it too was pegged by the gold standard except for wars and the 1930s.

5. In Colombia, 35 to 60 cents per ton-mile, as compared to 2 to 4 cents in the United States over the same period (Safford and Palacios 2002: 34).

6. The tobacco case is particularly instructive. In the 1870s plantations in Java began producing cheap, high quality tobacco, permanently lowering the world price and shutting Colombia out of the market. Colombia scrounged for new products for several years, cycling through indigo and cinchona bark (for quinine) before eventually finding a profitable niche in the rising world demand for high-quality coffee, which their mountains became famously known for producing cheaply. Such a trend was not uncommon in the periphery; when export products and mixes did change, the pattern was typically one of substitution, not diversification, with any new export product replacing the old. Peru, for instance, focused on cotton and sugar export only after guano and silver stocks depleted. Brazil failed to find a real replacement for natural rubber until almost a generation after the invention of a synthetic substitute that destroyed the market.

Chapter 12

1. It should be pointed out that these figures are inconsistent with Fernando Rocchi's (2006) recent book that stresses industrialization in Argentina, perhaps because Rocchi does not report sector or market shares.

2. The term "liftoff" should not be confused with Walt Rostow's term "takeoff in to self-sustained growth" coined nearly a half century ago (Rostow 1964). I use the term only to describe an acceleration, and, to my knowledge, it was first used by Haber (2002).

3. All of the GDP estimates cited here are from Maddison (2008).

4. The tariff rates would, of course, be even higher if we looked only at manufacturers.

5. The effective rate of protection includes not just the impact of the tariff on imported final goods (e.g., cotton textiles), but also on inputs (e.g., raw cotton). Before Mexican tariffs were rationalized, high tariffs on raw cotton tended to offset any benefits from high tariffs on cotton textiles.

6. By 1960 Mexico had much lower tariffs on capital goods and industrial raw materials than did Argentina or Brazil (Taylor 1998; Haber 2006: table 13.8, 574).

7. Rocchi (2006: 208a) also notes that Argentina did not join this pro-industrial policy trend.

8. The income terms of trade is defined as $p_X X/p_M$ or export revenue $(p_X X)$ over import price (p_M), or the quantity of imports that export earnings will buy. To the extent that foreign exchange earnings were used to buy imported capital goods and intermediates, manufacturing was favored.

9. The real exchange rate also depreciated by about 50 percent just between 1885 and 1892 (Catão 1998: 74), and it never recovered. We return to this below.

10. Data on the percentage of the labor force in manufacturing come from Kirsch (1977: 41), Seminario (1965: 48), and Dorfman (1970: 310).

11. On the European grain invasion, see O'Rourke (1997).

12. Except for Argentina, Chile, Columbia, and Uruguay, the rest of Latin America did not adopt fixed metallic (gold or silver, or both) exchange rates until after 1900 or never did. Even India, Japan, and Russia waited until the 1890s, and Bulgaria, China, and Spain never did. See Meissner (2005: table 1).

Chapter 13

1. Note that this statement refers to the poor periphery. Bairoch (1989), O'Rourke (2000), and O'Rourke and Lehmann (2008) have shown, however, that high tariffs were associated with rapid growth in the rich industrial countries before 1913.

2. Ad valorem tariffs are applied as a percentage of import value. While most countries favored specific duties (pesos per bag, dollars per barrel, pence per pound), these are converted to ad valorem (percentage) rate equivalents in figure 13.1 and table 13.1.

3. When the United States is shifted to the rich European offshoot club, the ratio of European offshoot tariffs to that of the core is more than three to one.

4. Prior to World War I, tariffs were much higher in the rich European offshoots than anywhere else. But they would have been even higher had one of the most protectionist, the United States, been allocated to the offshoot region rather than the core. The United States has always presented a problem to historians and economists alike. The canonical frontier economy with scarce labor and abundant resources, by 1900 it was also the world's industrial leader (Wright 1990) and a central market for the exports from the rest of the world, especially Latin America. So, while the United States was certainly a rich European offshoot, it is allocated to the industrial core.

5. The literature is huge and often ambiguous on the growth gains from openness. See, for example, Dollar (1992), Sachs and Warner (1995), Frankel and Romer (1999), Rodriguez and Rodrik (2001), and Irwin and Terviö (2002). To paraphrase words in a survey by Lindert and Williamson (2003: 252), all statistical studies showing that third world protection since 1950 has helped augment their economic growth, or that liberalization has harmed it, forms an empty set.

6. Caution suggests using the phrase "was associated with" rather than the causal word "fostered." I press on without caution, but subject to this understanding.

7. In 1831 only 8.6 percent of the adult males in the United Kingdom had the right to vote, and the figure was still only 17.8 percent in 1866. These were, of course, the wealthy at the top of the distribution. Countries on the continent had even lower suffrage rates.

8. As late as 1940 the share of the adult male population voting in Latin America was never higher than 19.7 percent (Uruguay), while the lowest figures were for Ecuador, Bolivia, Brazil, and Chile (3.3, 4.1, 5.7, and 6.5 percent, respectively). Engerman, Haber, and Sokoloff (2000: table 2, 226). Of course, de jure and de facto political power are two different things. Labor could, and sometimes did, express their economic preferences de facto by taking to the streets. But it was very costly for them to do so.

9. Stolper–Samuelson economics has a much poorer chance of explaining modern tariff policy when, instead, trade is dominated by manufactures and most factors— labor, skills, and capital—are mobile. Today mobile factors can escape most of the trade-induced injury by fleeing the sector hit by bad price shocks. This statement even applies to the modern third world where manufactures have been a rapidly rising share of output and exports in the modern era. Among all developing countries, manufactures rose from about 15 percent of commodity exports in 1965 to about 82 percent by 1998 (Martin 2003: fig. 3). Alternatively, the residual—agriculture and mining exports fell from about 85 to 18 percent. Much of the third world is now labor abundant and natural resource scarce, so it exports labor-intensive manufactures. Thus the growth of trade now helps it industrialize. No longer does the third world just specialize in primary products.

10. Except, of course, that they could keep the price of imported raw material intermediates low by giving such imports tariff concessions, thereby raising the *effective* rate of protection on value added.

11. Totally differentiating with respect to t, and assuming that the typical 19th-century country in the periphery was a price taker for manufacturing imports, yields $dR/dt = pM + (tp)dM/dt$. The revenue-maximizing tariff rate, t^*, is found by setting $dR/dt = 0$, in which case $t^* = -1/(1 + \eta)$, where η is the price elasticity of demand for imports. Douglas Irwin (1998a: 14) estimates the price elasticity to have been about –2.6 for the United States between 1869 and 1913. Since the import mix for

countries around the periphery was similar to that of the United States, taking the price elasticity for the former to have been around -3 can't be too far off the mark. Under those assumptions the revenue-maximizing tariff in the autonomous periphery would have been very high indeed, about 50 percent. This argument can, of course, be extended to export duties in those cases where the periphery country controlled a significant share of world markets, and thus faced a (price-inelastic) downward-sloping demand curve, like Brazilian coffee or Chilean nitrates. On the latter, see Lüders and Wagner (2009).

References

Acemoglu, D. 2009. *Introduction to Modern Economic Growth*. Princeton: Princeton University Press.

Acemoglu, D., S. Johnson, and J. Robinson. 2001. The colonial origins of comparative development. *American Economic Review* 91 (5): 1369–1401.

Acemoglu, D., S. Johnson, and J. Robinson. 2002. Reversal of fortune: Geography and institutions in the making of the modern world income distribution. *Quarterly Journal of Economics* 117 (November): 231–94.

Acemoglu, D., S. Johnson, and J. Robinson. 2005. The rise of Europe: Atlantic trade, institutional change and economic growth. *American Economic Review* 95 (June): 546–79.

Acemoglu, D., S. Johnson, J. Robinson, and Y. Thaicharoen. 2003. Institutional causes, macroeconomic symptoms: Volatility, crises, and growth. *Journal of Monetary Economics* 50 (1): 49–122.

Aghion, P., G.-M. Angeletos, A. Banerjee, and K. Manova. 2005. Volatility and growth: Credit constraints and productivity-enhancing investments. NBER working paper 11349. National Bureau of Economic Research, Cambridge, MA.

Aghion, P., P. Bacchetta, R. Rancière, and K. Rogoff. 2006. Exchange rate volatility and productivity growth: the role of financial development. CEPR discussion paper 5629. Centre for Economic Policy Research, London.

Aizenman, J., and N. Martion. 1999. Volatility and investment: Interpreting evidence from developing countries. *Economica* 66: 157–79.

Alam, M. 1986. *The Crisis of Empire in Mughal North India: Awadh and the Punjab, 1707–48*. Delhi: Oxford University Press.

Allen, R. C. 2001. The great divergence in European wages and prices from the Middle Ages to the First World War. *Explorations in Economic History* 38 (October): 411–47.

Allen, R. C. 2005. Real wages in Europe and Asia: A first look at the long-term patterns. In R. C. Allen, T. Bengtsson, and M. Dribe, eds, *Living Standards in the Past: New Perspectives on Well-being in Asia and Europe*. Oxford: Oxford University Press, 111–30.

Allen, R. C. 2007a. The Industrial Revolution in miniature: The Spinning Jenny in Britain, France, and India. Working paper 375. Department of Economics, Oxford University.

Allen, R. C. 2007b. India in the great divergence. In T. J. Hatton, K. H. O'Rourke, and A. M. Taylor, eds., *The New Comparative Economic History: Essays in Honor of Jeffrey G. Williamson*. Cambridge: MIT Press, 9–32.

Allen, R. C., J.-P. Bassino, D. Ma, C. Moll-Murata, and J. L. van Zanden. 2009. Wages, Prices and Living Standards in China, 1738–1925: In Comparison with Europe, Japan, and India. Working paper 2009-3. Center for Economic Institutions, Institute for Economic Research, Hitotsubashi University.

Andaya, B. W. 1989. The cloth trade in Jambi and Palembang society during the seventeenth and eighteenth centuries. *Indonesia* 48 (April): 27–46.

Antuñano, E. 1979. *Documentos para la historia de la industrialización en México, 1833–1846*. 2 vols. Mexico City: Secretaría de Hacienda y Crédito Público.

Arroyo Abad, L. 2008. Inequality in republican Latin America: Assessing the effects of factor endowments and trade. GPIH working paper 12. University of California, Davis.

Arroyo Abad, L., and A. Santos-Paulino. 2009. Trading inequality? Comparing the two Latin American globalization waves. Presented at the conference on Latin American Inequality in the Long Run, Madrid (May 8–9).

Auty, R. M. 1993. *Sustaining Development in Mineral Economies: The Resource Curse Thesis*. London: Routledge.

Auty, R. M. 2001. The political economy of resource-driven growth. *European Economic Review* 45: 839–46.

Bagchi, A. 1976a. Deindustrialization in India in the nineteenth century: Some theoretical implications. *Journal of Development Studies* 12 (January): 135–64.

Bagchi, A. 1976b. Deindustrialization in Gangetic Bihar 1809–1901. In D. Banerjee, B. Chattopadhyay, B. Chaudhuri, B. De, A. Ray, A. Sen, M. Sen, and P. Sinha, eds., *Essays in Honour of Prof. S. C. Sarkar*. New Delhi: People's Publishing House, 499–522.

Bagwell, K., and R. W. Staiger. 2002. *The Economics of the World Trading System*. Cambridge: MIT Press.

Baier, S. L., and J. H. Bergstrand. 2001. The growth of world trade: Tariffs, transport costs, and income similarity. *Journal of International Economics* 53 (1): 1–27.

Bairoch, P. 1982. International industrialization levels from 1750 to 1980. *Journal of European Economic History* 11 (Fall): 269–333.

Bairoch, P. 1989. European Trade Policy, 1815–1914. In P. Mathias and S. Pollard, eds., *The Cambridge Economic History of Europe*, vol. 3. Cambridge: Cambridge University Press, 1–159.

Bairoch, P. 1991. How and not why? Economic inequalities between 1800 and 1913: Some background figures. In J. Batou, ed., *Between Development and Underdevelopment: The Precocious Attempts at Industrialization of the Periphery 1800–1870.* Genève: Librairie Droz, 1–42.

Bairoch, P. 1993. *Economics and World History: Myths and Paradoxes.* New York: Harvester Wheatsheaf.

Baland, J.-M., and P. Francois. 2000. Rent-seeking and resource booms. *Journal of Development Economics* 61 (April): 527–42.

Bannon, I., and P. Collier, eds. 2003. *Natural resources and violent conflict: Options and actions.* Washington, DC: World Bank.

Baptista, A. 1997. *Bases cuantitativas de la economía venezolana 1830–1995.* Caracas: Fundación Polar.

Barbier, E. B. 2005. Natural resource-based economic development in history. *World Economy* 6 (3): 103–52.

Barnett, G. E. 1936. *Two Tracts by Gregory King.* Baltimore: Johns Hopkins University Press.

Baskes, J. 2005. Colonial institutions and cross-cultural trade: Repartimiento credit and indigenous production of cochineal in eighteenth-century Oaxaca, Mexico. *Journal of Economic History* 65 (March): 186–210.

Bassino, J.-P., and D. Ma. 2004. Japanese wages and living standards in 1720–1913: An international comparison. Presented to the conference Towards a Global History of Prices and Wages, Utrecht (August 19–21).

Basu, P., and D. McLeod. 1992. Terms of trade fluctuations and economic growth in developing economies. *Journal of Development Economics* 37: 89–110.

Bates, R. H. 1997. *Open Economy Politics: The Political Economy of the World Coffee Trade.* Princeton: Princeton University Press.

Bates, R. H. 2001. *Prosperity and Violence: The Political Economy of Development.* New York: Norton.

Bates, R. H. 2008. *When Things Fell Apart: State Failure in Late-Century Africa*. New York: Cambridge University Press.

Bates, R. H., J. H. Coatsworth, and J. G. Williamson. 2007. Lost Decades: Postindependence Performance in Latin America and Africa. *Journal of Economic History* 67 (December): 917–943.

Bates, R. H., A. Grief, and S. Singh. 2001. Organizing violence. Weatherhead Center for International Affairs, Harvard University, Cambridge.

Batou, J. 1990. *One Hundred Years of Resistance to Underdevelopment: Latin American and Middle Eastern Industrialization and the European Challenge 1770–1870*. Genève: Librairie Droz.

Batou, J., ed. 1991. *Between Development and Underdevelopment: The Precocious Attempts at Industrialization of the Periphery 1800–1870*. Genève: Librairie Droz.

Bayly, C. 1983. *Rulers, Townsmen, and Bazaars: North Indian Society in the Age of British Expansion, 1770–1870*. Cambridge: Cambridge University Press.

Beatty, E. 2000. The impact of foreign trade on the Mexican economy: Terms of trade and the rise of industry 1880–1923. *Journal of Latin American Studies* 32: 399–433.

Bengston, T., C. Campbell, J. Lee, et al. 2004. *Life under Pressure: Mortality and Living Standards in Europe and Asia, 1700–1900*. Cambridge: MIT Press.

Bernhofen, D. M., and J. C. Brown. 2004. A direct test of the theory of comparative advantage: The case of Japan. *Journal of Political Economy* 112 (1): 48–67.

Bernhofen, D. M., and J. C. Brown. 2005. An empirical assessment of the comparative advantage gains from trade: Evidence from Japan. *American Economic Review* 95 (March): 208–24.

Bértola, L. 2000. *Ensayos de Historia Económica: Uruguay y la región en la economia mundial 1870–1990*. Montevideo: Ediciones Trilce.

Bértola, L., and J. G. Williamson. 2006. Globalization in Latin America before 1940. In V. Bulmer-Thomas, J. Coatsworth, and R. Cortes Conde, eds., *Cambridge Economic History of Latin America*. Cambridge: Cambridge University Press, 11–56.

Bhattacharyya, S., and J. G. Williamson. 2009. Commodity price shocks and the Australian economy since federation. NBER working paper 14694. National Bureau of Economic Research, Cambridge, MA.

Bils, M. 1984. Tariff protection and production in the early U.S. cotton textile industry. *Journal of Economic History* 44 (December): 1033–45.

Blattman, C., M. A. Clemens, and J. G. Williamson. 2002. Who protected and why? Tariffs the world around 1870–1938. Presented to the Conference on the Political Economy of Globalization, Trinity College, Dublin (August 29–31).

Blainey, G. 1966. *The Tyranny of Distance: How Distance Shaped Australia's History.* Melbourne: Macmillan (rev. 1982 ed.).

Blattman, C., J. Hwang, and J. G. Williamson. 2007. The impact of the terms of trade on economic development in the periphery, 1870–1939: Volatility and secular change. *Journal of Development Economics* 82 (January): 156–79.

Bleaney, M., and D. Greenway. 1993. Long-run trends in the relative price of primary commodities and in the terms of trade of developing countries. *Oxford Economic Papers* 45: 349–63.

Bleaney, M., and D. Greenway. 2001. The impact of terms of trade and real exchange rate volatility on investment and growth in sub-Saharan Africa. *Journal of Development Economics* 65 (August): 491–500.

Booth, A. 1998. *The Indonesian Economy in the Nineteenth and Twentieth Century.* New York: St. Martin's Press.

Bordo, M., and P. Rousseau. 2006. Legal-political factors and the historical evolution of the finance-growth link. *European Review of Economic History* 10 (December): 421–44.

Bowen, H. V., M. Lincoln, and N. Rigby, eds. 2003. *The World of the East Indian Company.* Rochester, NY: Brewer.

Bowring, Sir John. 1840. *Report on Egypt 1823–1838 under the Reign of Mohamed Ali.* London: HMSO (reprinted Trade Exploration Ltd. 1998).

Brading, C. W. 1969. Un analisis comparativo del costo de la vida en diversas capitales de hispanoamerica. *Boletin Historico de la Fundacion John Boulton* 20 (March): 229–63.

Brandt, L. 1985. Chinese agriculture and the international economy 1870–1913: A reassessment. *Explorations in Economic History* 22 (April): 168–80.

Brandt, L. 1993. Interwar Japanese agriculture: Revisionist views on the impact of the colonial rice policy and the labor-surplus hypothesis. *Explorations in Economic History* 30 (January): 127–45.

Braun, J., M. Braun, I. Briones, J. Diaz, R. Lüders, and G. Wagner. 2000. *Economia Chilena 1810–1995: Estadisticas Historicas.* Santiago: Pontifica Universidad Catolica de Chile.

Broadberry, S., and B. Gupta. 2005. The early modern great divergence: Wages, prices and economic development in Europe and Asia, 1500–1800. Unpublished manuscript. University of Warwick.

Bulmer-Thomas, V. 1994. *The Economic History of Latin America since Independence.* Cambridge: Cambridge University Press.

Caggiano, G., and G. Huff. 2007a. Globalization and labour market integration in late nineteenth- and early twentieth-century Asia. *Research in Economic History* 25: 255–318.

Caggiano, G., and G. Huff. 2007b. Globalization, immigration and Lewisian elastic labor in pre–World War II Southeast Asia. *Journal of Economic History* 67 (March): 33–68.

Caron, F. 1983. France. In P. K. O'Brien, ed., *Railways and the Economic Development of Western Europe, 1830–1914,* New York: St. Martin's Press, 28–48.

Catão, L. 1998. Mexico and export-led growth: The Porfirian period revisited. *Cambridge Journal of Economics* 22 (January): 59–78.

Catão, L. 2006. Export growth, the exchange rate, and machinery investment in early development: The cases of Brazil and Mexico. Washington, DC: IMF (February).

Catão, L., and S. Kapur. 2004. Missing link: Volatility and the debt intolerance paradox. Unpublished manuscript. International Monetary Fund, Washington, DC.

Chaudhuri, K. N. 1978. *The Trading World of Asia and the English East India Company, 1660–1760.* Cambridge: Cambridge University Press.

Chaudhuri, K. N. 1983. Foreign trade and balance of payments (1757–1947). In D. Kumar and M. Desai, eds., *The Cambridge Economic History of India,* vol. 2. Cambridge: Cambridge University Press, 804–77.

Chaudhury, S. 1999. *From Prosperity to Decline: Eighteenth Century Bengal.* New Delhi: Manohar Publishers.

Chen, S., and M. Ravallion. 2007. *Absolute Poverty Measures for the Developing World, 1981–2005.* Washington, DC: World Bank Research Development Group.

Chowdhury, B. 1964. *Growth of Commercial Agriculture in Bengal.* Calcutta: R.K. Maitra.

Chowning, M. 1997. Reassessing the prospects for profit in nineteenth-century Mexican agriculture from a regional perspective: Michoac'an, 1810–1860. In S. Haber, ed., *How Latin America Fell Behind?* Stanford: Stanford University Press, 179–215.

Clarence-Smith, W. G. 2005. Cotton textiles on the Indian Ocean periphery, c1500–c1850. Presented at the Global Economic History Network, Conference 8, Pune, India (18–20 December).

Clark, C. 1950. *Conditions of Economic Progress,* 2nd ed. London: Macmillan.

Clark, C. 1957. *Conditions of Economic Progress*, 3rd ed. London: Macmillan.

Clark, G. 1987. Why isn't the whole world developed? Lessons from the cotton mills. *Journal of Economic History* 47 (March): 141–73.

Clark, G. 2004. The condition of the working-class in England, 1200–2000: Magna Carta to Tony Blair. Unpublished manuscript. Department of Economics, University of California, Davis.

Clark, G. 2007. *A Farewell to Alms: A Brief Economic History of the World*. Princeton: Princeton University Press.

Clark, G., K. H. O'Rourke, and A. M. Taylor. 2008. Made in America? The new world, the old, and the Industrial Revolution. *American Economic Review* 98 (May): 523–28.

Clemens, M. A., and J. G. Williamson. 2002. Closed jaguar, open dragon: Comparing tariffs in Latin America and Asia before World War II. NBER working paper 9401. National Bureau of Economic Research, Cambridge, MA.

Clemens, M., and J. G. Williamson. 2004. Why did the tariff-growth correlation reverse after 1950? *Journal of Economic Growth* 9 (March): 5–46.

Clingingsmith, D., and J. G. Williamson. 2008. Deindustrialization in 18th and 19th century India: Mughal decline, climate shocks and British industrial ascent. *Explorations in Economic History* 45 (July): 209–34.

Coatsworth, J. H. 1979. Indispensable railroads in a backward economy: The case of Mexico. *Journal of Economic History* 39 (4): 939–60.

Coatsworth, J. H. 1981. *Growth against Development: The Economic Impact of Railroads in Porfirian Mexico*. Dekalb: Northern Illinois University Press.

Coatsworth, J. H. 2003. Mexico. In J. Mokyr, ed., *The Oxford Encyclopaedia of Economic History*, vol. 3. New York: Oxford University Press, 501–7.

Coatsworth, J H. 2005. Structures, endowments, and institutions in the economic history of Latin America. *Latin American Research Review* 40 (3): 126–44.

Coatsworth, J. H., and J. G. Williamson. 2004a. Always protectionist? Latin American tariffs from independence to Great Depression. *Journal of Latin American Studies* 36 (part 2): 205–32.

Coatsworth, J. H., and J. G. Williamson. 2004b. The roots of Latin American protectionism: Looking before the Great Depression. In A. Estevadeordal, D. Rodrik, A. Taylor, and A. Velasco, eds., *Integrating the Americas: FTAA and Beyond*. Cambridge: Harvard University Press, 37–73.

Collier, P. 2000. *Economic Causes of Civil Conflict and Their Implications for Policy*. Washington, DC: World Bank.

Comin, D., W. Easterly, and E. Gong. 2008. Was the wealth of nations determined in 1000 B.C.? Unpublished paper (September).

Corbo, V. 1992. Development strategies and policies in Latin America: A historical perspective. Occasional paper 22. International Center for Economic Growth, San Francisco.

Corden, W. M., and F. H. Gruen. 1970. A tariff that worsens the terms of trade. In I. A. McDougall and R. H. Snape, eds., *Studies in International Economics*. Amsterdam: North Holland, 55–58.

Corpuz, O. D. 1997. *An Economic History of the Philippines*. Quezon City: University of the Philippines Press.

Cosío Villegas, D. 1931. *La Cuestión Arancelaria en México: Historia de la Política Aduanal III*. Mexico City: Ediciones del Centro Mexicano de Estudios Económicos.

Cuddington, J. T., R. Ludema, and S. A. Jayasuriya. 2007. Prebisch–Singer redux. In D. Lederman and W. E. Maloney, eds., *Natural Resources: Neither Curse nor Destiny*, Stanford: Stanford University Press, 103–82.

Darwin, C. [1859] 1972. *The Origin of the Species*. London: Dent and Sons.

Datta, R. 1999. Markets, bullion and Bengal's commercial economy: An eighteenth century perspective. In O. Prakash and D. Lombard, eds., *Commerce and Culture in the Bay of Bengal, 1500–1800*. Delhi: Manohar, 329–59.

Dean, W. 1969. *The Industrialization of São Paulo 1880–1945*. Austin: University of Texas Press.

Deane, P., and W. A. Cole. 1967. *British Economic Growth, 1688–1959: Trends and Structure*, 2nd ed. Cambridge: Cambridge University Press.

Deaton, A. 1999. Commodity prices and growth in Africa. *Journal of Economic Perspectives* 13 (3): 23–40.

Deaton, A., and G. Laroque. 1992. On the behaviour of commodity prices. *Review of Economic Studies* 59 (January): 1–23.

Deaton, A., and R. I. Miller. 1996. International commodity prices, macroeconomic performance and politics in sub-Saharan Africa. *Journal of African Economies* 5 (suppl.): 99–191.

Dercon, S. 2004. *Insurance against Poverty*. Oxford: Oxford University Press.

de Vries, J. 1994. The Industrial Revolution and the industrious revolution. *Journal of Economic History* 54 (June): 249–70.

de Vries, J. 1984. *European Urbanization, 1500–1800*. Cambridge: Harvard University Press.

Diamond, J. M. 1997. *Guns, Germs, and Steel: The Fates of Human Societies*. New York: Norton.

Díaz-Alejandro, C. 1984. Latin America in the 1930s. In ed. R. Thorp, ed., *Latin America in the 1930s: The Role of the Periphery in World Crisis*. Basingstroke, England: Macmillan, 17–49.

Dixit, A. 1987. Strategic aspects of trade policy. In T. F. Bewley, ed., *Advances in Economic Theory: Fifth World Congress*. New York: Cambridge University Press, 329–62.

Dobado Gonzáles, R., A. Gómez Galvarriato, and J. G. Williamson. 2008. Mexican exceptionalism: Globalization and de-industrialization 1750–1877. *Journal of Economic History* 68 (September): 1–53.

Dobado Gonzáles, R., and G. A. Marreno. 2001. Minería, crecimiento económico y costes de la Independencia en México. *Revista de Historia Económica* 19 (3): 573–611.

Dobado Gonzáles, R., and G. A. Marreno. (2005a), The "mining-led growth" in Bourbon Mexico, the role of the state and the economic cost of independence. Global Economic History Network Conference (Istanbul).

Dobado Gonzáles, R., and G. A. Marreno. 2005b. Corn market integration in Porfirian Mexico. *Journal of Economic History* 65 (March): 103–28.

Dobado Gonzáles, R., and D. Guerro. 2008. What 18th century grain prices show. Unpublished manuscript. Instituto Complutense de Estudios Internacianales, Universidad Complutense de Madrid.

Dollar, D. 1992. Outward-oriented developing economies really do grow more rapidly: Evidence from 95 LDCs, 1976–1985. *Economic Development and Cultural Change* 40 (April): 523–44.

Dorfman, A. 1970. *Historia de la Industria Argentina*. Buenos Aires: Solar.

Drelichman, M. 2005. The curse of Moctezuma: American silver and the Dutch disease. *Explorations in Economic History* 42 (July): 349–80.

Dyson, T., ed. 1989. *India's Historical Demography: Studies in Famine, Disease and Society*. London: Curzon Press.

Easterly, W., M. Kremer, L. Pritchett, and L. H. Summers. 1993. Good policy or good luck? Country growth performance and temporary shocks. *Journal of Monetary Economics* 32 (December): 459–83.

Easterly, W., and R. Levine. 2003. Tropics, germs, and crops: How endowments influence economic development. *Journal of Monetary Economics* 50 (January): 3–40.

Eichengreen, B., and D. A. Irwin. 2009. The protectionist temptation: Lessons from the Great Depression for today. VOX, Center for Policy Research, London (March 17).

Elbers, C., J. W. Gunning, and B. Kinsey. 2007. Growth and risk: Methodology and micro evidence. *World Bank Economic Review* 21 (1): 1–20.

Engerman, S., S. Haber, and K. Sokoloff. 2000. Institutions, factor endowments, and paths of development in the new world. *Journal of Economic Perspectives* 14 (Summer): 217–32.

Engerman, S. L., and K. L. Sokoloff. 1997. Factor endowments, inequality, and differential paths of growth among new world economies. In S. Haber, ed., *How Latin America Fell Behind*. Stanford: Stanford University Press, 260–304.

Esteban, J. C. 2001. The British balance of payments, 1772–1820: India transfers and war finance. *Economic History Review* 54 (February): 58–86.

Estevadeordal, A., B. Frantz, and A. M. Taylor. 2003. The rise and fall of world trade, 1870–1939. *Quarterly Journal of Economics* 118 (May): 359–407.

Fafchamps, M. 2004. *Rural Poverty, Risk and Development*. Chattenham: Edward Elgar.

Fatás, A., and I. Mivhov. 2006. Policy volatility, institutions and economic growth. Unpublished manuscript. INSEAD, Singapore and Fontainebleau, France.

Farrington, A. 2002. *Trading Places: The East Indian Company and Asia, 1600–1834*. London: British Library.

Federico, G., and K. G. Persson. 2007. Market integration and convergence in the world wheat market 1800–2000. In T. J. Hatton, K. H. O'Rourke, and A. M. Taylor, eds., *The New Comparative Economic History: Essays in Honor of Jeffrey G. Williamson*. Cambridge: MIT Press, 87–113.

Ferguson, N. 2003. *Empire: How Britain Made the Modern World*. New York: Penguin.

Feuerwerker, A. 1970. Handicraft and manufactured cotton textiles in China, 1871–1910. *Journal of Economic History* 30 (June): 338–78.

Feuerwerker, A. 1980. Economic trends in the late Ch'ing empire, 1870–1911. In J. K. Fairbank and K-C. Liu, eds., *The Cambridge Economic History of China:* Vol. 2: *Late Ch'ing, 1800–1900, Part 2*. Cambridge: Cambridge University Press, 1–69.

Feuerwerker, A. 1992. *Studies in the Economic History of Late Imperial China*. Ann Arbor: University of Michigan Press.

Findlay, R., and K. H. O'Rourke. 2007. *Power and Plenty: Trade, War, and the World Economy in the Second Millennium*. Princeton: Princeton University Press.

Flam, H., and M. J. Flanders. 1991. *Heckscher–Ohlin Trade Theory*. Cambridge: MIT Press.

Florescano, E. 1969/1986. *Precios Agrícolas del Maíz y Crisis Agrícolas en México 1708–1810*. Mexico City: Era (first published 1969, republished 1986).

Flug, K., A. Splilimbergo, and A. Wachtenheim. 1999. Investment in education: Do economic volatility and credit constraints matter? *Journal of Development Economics* 55 (2): 465–81.

Flynn, D. O., and A. Giraldez, eds. 1997. *Metals and Monies in an Emerging Global Economy*. Brookfield, Vt.: Variorum.

Fogel, R. W. 1964. *Railroads and American Economic Growth: Essays in Econometric History*. Baltimore: Johns Hopkins Press.

Frankel, J., and D. Romer. 1999. Does Trade Cause Growth? *American Economic Review* 89 (June): 379–99.

Frankenberg, E., K. Beegle, B. Sikoki, and D. Thomas. 1999. Health, family planning and well-being in Indonesia during an economic crisis: Early results from the Indonesian family life survey. RAND Labor and Population Program working paper 99–06. Rand Corporation, Santa Monica, CA.

Fremdling, R. 1983. Germany. In P. K. O'Brien, ed., *Railways and the Economic Development of Western Europe, 1830–1914*. New York: St. Martin's Press, 121–47.

Fujita, M., P. Krugman, and A. J. Venables. 1999. *The Spatial Economy: Cities, Regions, and International Trade*. Cambridge: MIT Press.

Furber, H. 1948. *John Company at Work: A Study of European Expansion in India in the Late Nineteenth Century*. Cambridge: Harvard University Press.

Galiani, S., D. Heymann, and M. Magud. 2009. On the distributive effects of terms of trade shocks: the role of non-tradable goods. Unpublished manuscript (January). SSRN, http://SSRN.com.

Gallo, F. 1970. Agrarian expansion and industrial development in Argentina, 1880–1930. In R. Carr, ed., *Latin American Affairs*. Oxford: Oxford University Press, 45–61.

Gallup, J. L., A. Gaviria, and E. Lora. 2003. *Is Geography Destiny? Lessons from Latin America*. Stanford: Stanford University Press.

Gallup, J. L., J. D. Sachs, and A. D. Mellinger. 1999. Geography and economic development. In B. Plsekovic and J. Stiglitz, eds., *Annual World Bank Conference on Development Economics, 1998/1999*. Washington, DC: World Bank, 127–78.

Galor, O., and A. Mountford. 2006. Trade and the great divergence: The family connection. *American Economic Review* 96 (May): 299–303.

Gelb, A. 1988. *Oil Windfalls: Blessing or Curse?* New York: Oxford University Press.

Gerschenkron, A. 1943. *Bread and Democracy in Germany*. Berkeley: University of California Press.

Gerschenkron, A. 1962. *Economic Backwardness in Historical Perspective*. Cambridge: Harvard University Press.

Glazier, I., V. Bandera, and R. Brenner. 1975. Terms of trade between Italy and the United Kingdom 1815–1913. *Journal of European Economic History* 4 (Spring): 5–48.

Glick, R., and A. M. Taylor. 2010. Collateral Damage: Trade Disruption and the Economic Impact of War. *Review of Economics and Statistics* 92 (February): 102–27.

Goldsmith, R. W. 1985. *Comparative National Balance Sheets: A Study of Twenty Countries 1688–1978*. Chicago: University of Chicago Press.

Gómez Galvarriato, A. 1999. Industrial development under institutional frailty: The development of the Mexican textile industry in the nineteenth century. *Revista de Historia Económica* 17 (special issue): 191–223.

Gómez Galvarriato, A. 2002. Manufacturing in Latin America from colonial times to 1850. Draft, prepared for V. Bulmer-Thomas, J. H. Coatsworth, and R. Cortes Conde, eds., *Cambridge Economic History of Latin America*, vol. 1. Cambridge: Cambridge University Press (2006).

Gómez Galvarriato, A. 2007. The political economy of protectionism: The Mexican textile industry, 1900–1950. In S. Edwards, G. Esquivel, and G. Márquez, eds., *The Decline of Latin American Economies: Growth, Institutions, and Crisis*. Chicago: University of Chicago Press, 363–406.

Gómez Galvarriato, A., and J. G. Williamson. 2009. Was it prices, productivity or policy? The timing and pace of Latin American industrialization after 1870. *Journal of Latin American Studies* 41 (December): 663–94.

Gómez Mendoza, A. 1982. *Ferrocarriles y Cambio Económico en Espa a (1855–1913) un Enfoque de Nueva Historia Económica*. Madrid: Alianza.

Grilli, E. R., and M. C. Yang. 1988. Primary commodity prices, manufactured goods prices, and the terms of trade of developing countries: What the long run shows. *World Bank Economic Review* 2: 1–48.

Grossman, G. M., and E. Helpman. 1994. Protection for sale. *American Economic Review* 84 (4): 833–50.

Grove, R. H. 1997. *Ecology, Climate and Empire: Colonialism and Global Environmental History, 1400–1940*. Cambridge: White Horse Press.

Grove, R. H., and J. Chappell. 2000. El Niño chronology and the history of global crises during the little ice age. In R. H. Grove and J. Chappell, eds., *El Niño—History and Crisis: Studies from the Asia-Pacific Region*. Cambridge: White Horse Press, 5–34.

Grove, R. H., V. Damodaran, and S. Sangwan, eds. 1998. *Nature and the Orient: The Environmental History of South and Southeast Asia*. Delhi: Oxford University Press.

Gylfason, T. 2000. Natural resources, education and economic development. CEPR discussion paper 2594. Centre for Economic Policy Research, London.

Gylfason, T., T. T. Herbertsson, and G. Zoega. 1999. A mixed blessing: Natural resources and economic growth. *Macroeconomic Dynamics* 72 (2): 603–33.

Haber, S. 1989. *Industry and Underdevelopment: The Industrialization of Mexico*. Stanford: Stanford University Press.

Haber, S. 1990. La economía mexicana, 1830–1940: Obstáculos a la industrialización (II). *Revista de Historia Económica* 8 (2): 335–62.

Haber, S. 2002. It wasn't all Prebisch's fault: The political economy of twentieth century industrialization in Latin America. Unpublished manuscript. Stanford University.

Haber, S. 2006. The political economy of industrialization. In V. Bulmer-Thomas, J. Coatsworth, and R. Cortés-Conde, eds., *The Cambridge Economic History of Latin America*, vol. 2. Cambridge: Cambridge University Press, 537–84.

Habib, I., ed. 1977. *The Cambridge Economic History of India*. Cambridge: Cambridge University Press.

Habib, I. 1985. Studying a colonial economy without perceiving colonialism. *Modern Asian Studies* 19 (special issue): 355–81.

Habib, I. 2003. The eighteenth century in Indian economic history. In P. J. Marshall, ed., *The Eighteenth Century in Indian History: Evolution or Revolution*. Oxford: Oxford University Press, 100–19.

Hadass, Y, and J. G. Williamson. 2003. Terms-of-trade shocks and economic performance, 1870–1940: Prebisch and Singer revisited. *Economic Development and Cultural Change* 51 (April): 629–56.

Hamilton, E. J. 1934. *American Treasure and the Price Revolution in Spain*. Cambridge: Harvard University Press.

Hamnett, B. R. 1980. The economic and social dimensions of the revolution of independence in Mexico, 1800–1824. *Ibero-Amerikanisches Archiv* 6 (1): 1–27.

Hanson, J. R. 1977. Diversification and concentration of LDC exports: Victorian trends. *Explorations in Economic History* 14 (January): 44–68.

Hanson, J. R. 1986. Export shares in the European periphery and the third world before World War I: Questionable data, facile analogies. *Explorations in Economic History* 23 (January): 85–99.

Harlaftis, G., and V. Kardasis. 2000. International shipping in the eastern Mediterranean and the Black Sea: Istanbul as a maritime center. In Ş. Pamuk and J. G. Williamson, *Globalization Challenge and Economic Response in the Mediterranean before 1950*. London: Routledge, 233–65.

Harley, C. K. 1988. Ocean freight rates and productivity, 1740–1913: The primacy of mechanical invention reaffirmed. *Journal of Economic History* 48 (December): 851–76.

Harley, C. K. 1992. International competitiveness of the antebellum American cotton textile industry. *Journal of Economic History* 52 (September): 559–84.

Harnetty, P. 1991. "Deindustrialization" revisited: The handloom weavers of the central provinces of India c.1800–1947. *Modern Asian Studies* 25 (July): 455–510.

Harrison, L. E. 1985. *Underdevelopment Is a State of Mind: The Latin American Case*. Cambridge: Harvard University.

Hawke, G. R. 1970. *Railways and Economic Growth in England and Wales, 1840–1870*. Oxford: Clarendon.

Hayami, Y. 1975. *A Century of Agricultural Growth in Japan*. Tokyo: University of Tokyo Press.

Hayami, Y., and V. Ruttan. 1971. *Agricultural Development: An International Perspective*. Baltimore: Johns Hopkins Press.

Helpman, E. 2004. *The Mystery of Economic Growth*. Cambridge: Harvard University Press.

Herranz-Loncán, A. 2003. Railroad impact in backward economies: Spain, 1850–1913. Unpublished manuscript. Universitat de Barcelona.

Hirschman, A. O. 1958. *The Strategy of Economic Development*. New Haven: Yale University Press.

Hnatkovska, V., and N. Loayza. 2005. Volatility and Growth. In J. Aizenmann and B. Pinto, eds., *Managing Economic Volatility and Crises*. Cambridge: Cambridge University Press, 65–100.

Huber, J. R. 1971. Effect on prices of Japan's entry into world commerce after 1858. *Journal of Political Economy* 79 (3): 614–28.

von Humboldt, A. [1822] 1984. *Political Essay on the Kingdom of New Spain*, trans. J. Black. London: Longman, Hurst, Rees, Orne and Brown.

Hurd, J. 1975. Railways and the expansion of markets in India, 1861–1921. *Explorations in Economic History* 12 (3): 263–88.

İnalcık, H. 1993. *The Middle East and the Balkans under the Ottoman Empire*, vol. 9. Bloomington: Indiana University Turkish Studies.

Inikori, J. 2002. *Africans and the Industrial Revolution in England*. Cambridge: Cambridge University Press.

Irwin, D. A. 1999. Ohlin versus Stolper Samuelson? Presented to the Centennial Celebration of Bertil Ohlin, Stockholm, October 1999.

Irwin, D. A. 2003. New estimates of the average tariff of the United States, 1790–1820. NBER working paper 9616. National Bureau of Economic Research, Cambridge, MA.

Irwin, D. A., and M. Terviö. 2002. Does trade raise income? Evidence from the twentieth century. *Journal of International Economics* 58 (1): 1–18.

Isham, J., M. Woolcock, L. Pritchett, and G. Busby. 2005. The varieties of resource experience: Natural resource export structures and the political economy of economic growth. *World Bank Economic Review* 19 (2): 141–74.

Issawi, C. 1961. Egypt since 1800: A study in lop-sided development. *Journal of Economic History* 21 (March): 1–25.

Issawi, C. 1966. *The Economic History of the Middle East, 1800–1914*. Chicago: Chicago University Press.

Issawi, C. 1982. *An Economic History of the Middle East and North Africa*. New York: Columbia University Press.

Issawi, C. 1988. *The Fertile Crescent 1800–1914: A Documentary Economic History*. New York: Oxford University Press.

Jacks, D. S. 2006. What drove 19th century commodity market integration? *Explorations in Economic History* 43 (July): 383–412.

Jacks, D. S., C. M. Meissner, and D. Novy. 2008. Trade costs, 1870–2000. *American Economic Review* 98 (May): 529–34.

Jacks, D. S., C. M. Meissner, and D. Novy. 2009. Trade booms, trade busts, and trade costs. NBER working paper 15267. National Bureau of Economic Research, Cambridge, MA.

Jacks, D. S., and K. Pendakur. 2007. Global trade and the maritime transport revolution. Presented at the New Comparative Economic History Conference in Honor of Peter Lindert, University of California, Davis (June 1–3).

Jacks, D. S., K. H. O'Rourke, and J. G. Williamson. 2009. Commodity price volatility and world market integration since 1720. NBER working paper 14748. National Bureau of Economic Research, Cambridge, MA.

Jacoby, H. G., and E. Skoufias. 1997. Risk, financial markets, and human capital in a developing country. *Review of Economic Studies* 64 (July): 311–35.

Jensen, R. 2000. Agricultural volatility and investments in children. *American Economic Review* 90 (May): 399–404.

Jones, R. W. 1971. A three-factor model in theory, trade, and history. In J. N. Bhagwati, R. W. Jones, R. A. Mundell, and J. Vanek, eds., *Trade, Balance of Payments, and Growth*. Amsterdam: North-Holland, 3–20.

Kang, K. H., and M. S. Cha. 1996. Imperial policy or world price shocks? Explaining interwar Korean living standards. Presented to the Conference on East and Southeast Asian Economic Change in the Long Run, Honolulu, Hawaii (April).

Kapuscinski, C. 2000. Agricultural productivity in India: The role of climate information in forecasting yields of foodgrains. In R. H. Grove and J. Chappell, eds., *El Niño—History and Crisis: Studies from the Asia–Pacific Region*. Cambridge: White Horse Press, 196–223.

Keller, W., and C. H. Shiue. 2008. Tariffs, trains, and trade: The role of institutions versus technology in the expansion of markets. NBER working paper 13913. National Bureau of Economic Research, Cambridge, MA.

Kindleberger, C. P. 1951. Group behavior and international trade. *Journal of Political Economy* 59 (February): 30–46.

Kirsch, H. W. 1977. *Industrial Development in a Traditional Society: The Conflict of Entrepreneurship and Modernization in Chile*. Gainesville: University Presses of Florida.

Klein, H. S. 1998. *The American Finances of the Spanish Empire*. Albuquerque: New Mexico University Press.

Koren, M., and S. Tenreyro. 2007. Volatility and development. *Quarterly Journal of Economics* 122 (1): 243–87.

Korthals, W. L. 1994. *Changing Economy in Indonesia*. Vol. 15: *Prices (Non-rice) 1814–1940*. The Hague: Royal Tropical Institute.

Kose, M. A., and R. Reizman. 2001. Trade shocks and macroeconomic fluctuations in Africa. *Journal of Development Economics* 65 (1): 55–80.

Krueger, A. 1974. The political economy of the rent-seeking society. *American Economic Review* 64 (June): 291–303.

Krugman, P. 1981. Trade, accumulation, and uneven development. *Journal of Development Economics* 8: 149–61.

Krugman, P. 1991a. Increasing returns and economic geography. *Journal of Political Economy* 99: 483–99.

Krugman, P. 1991b. *Geography and Trade*. Cambridge: MIT Press.

Krugman, P., and A. Venables. 1995. Globalization and the inequality of nations. *Quarterly Journal of Economics* 110 (November): 857–80.

Kurmus, O. 1974. *The Role of British Capital in the Economic Development of Western Anatolia 1850–1913*. PhD thesis, University of London.

Kurmus, O. 1983. The 1838 Treaty of Commerce re-examined. In J.-L. B. Grammont and P. Dumont, eds., *Economie et societies dans l'empire Ottoman*. Paris: Centre National de la Recherche Scientifique, 411–17.

Laffut, M. 1983. Belgium. In P. K. O'Brien, ed., *Railways and the Economic Development of Western Europe, 1830–1914*. New York: St. Martin's Press, 203–26.

Lains, P. 1995. *A Economia portuguesa no seculo XIX*. Lisbon: Imprensa Nacional Casa da Moeda.

Landes, D. S. 1998. *The Wealth and Poverty of Nations*. New York: Norton.

Lardinois, R. 1989. Deserted villages and depopulation in rural Tamil Nadu c.1780–c.1830. In T. Dyson, ed., *India's Historical Demography: Studies in Famine, Disease and Society*. London: Curzon Press, 16–48.

Latham, A. J. H. 1986. The international trade in rice and wheat since 1868: A study in market integration. In W. Fischer, R. M. McInnis, and J. Schneider, eds., *The Emergence of a World Economy 1500–1914*. Wiesbaden: Franz Steiner, 645–65.

Latham, A. J. H., and L. Neal. 1983. The international market in rice and wheat 1868–1914. *Economic History Review* 36 (May):260–75.

Lederman, D., and W. E. Maloney, eds. 2007. *Natural Resources: Neither Curse nor Destiny*. Stanford: Stanford University Press.

Legarda, B. J. 1999. *After the Galleons: Foreign Trade, Economic Change and Entrepreneurship in the Nineteenth-Century Philippines*. Madison: University of Wisconsin Press.

Lewis, W. A. 1954. Economic development with unlimited supplies of labour. *Manchester School of Economic and Social Studies* 28 (2): 139–91.

Lewis, W. A. 1970. The export stimulus. In W. A. Lewis, ed., *Tropical Development, 1880–1913*. Evanston, IL: Northwestern University Press.

Lewis, W. A. 1978a. *The Evolution of the International Economic Order*. Princeton: Princeton University Press.

Lewis, W. A. 1978b. *Growth and Fluctuations, 1870–1913*. Boston: Allen and Unwin.

Lewis, W. A. 1980. The slowing down of the engine of growth. *American Economic Review* 70 (September): 555–64.

Lindert, P. H. 1994. The rise in social spending, 1880–1930. *Explorations in Economic History* 31 (January): 1–36.

Lindert, P. H. 2003. *Growing Public: Social Spending and Economic Growth since the Eighteenth Century*. Cambridge: Cambridge University Press.

Lindert, P. H., and J. G. Williamson. 1982. Revising England's social tables, 1688–1812. *Explorations in Economic History* 19 (4): 385–408.

Lindert, P. H., and J. G. Williamson. 2003. Does globalization make the world more unequal? In M. Bordo, A. M. Taylor, and J. G. Williamson, eds., *Globalization in Historical Perspective*. Chicago: University of Chicago Press, 227–71.

Loayza, N. V., R. Rancière, L. Servén, and J. Ventura. 2007. Macroeconomic volatility and welfare in developing countries: An introduction. *World Bank Economic Review* 21 (3): 343–57.

Lockwood, W. W. 1954. *The Economic Development of Japan: Growth ad Structural Change 1868–1938*. Princeton: Princeton University Press.

López-Córdova, J. E., and C. M. Meissner. 2003. Exchange-rate regimes and international trade: Evidence from the classical gold standard era. *American Economic Review* 93 (March): 344–53.

Lucas, R. E. 2009. Trade and the diffusion of the Industrial Revolution. *American Economic Journal Macroeconomics* 1 (January): 1–25.

Lüders, R., and G. Wagner. 2009. Export tariff, welfare and public finance: Nitrates from 1880 to 1930. Presented to the 15th World Economic History Congress, Utrecht (August 3–7).

Ma, D. 2004. Why Japan, not China, was the first to develop in East Asia: Lessons from sericulture, 1850–1937. *Economic Development and Cultural Change* 52 (2): 369–94.

MacAlpin, M. B. 1979. Dearth, famine and risk: The changing impact of crop failures in western India, 1870–1920. *Journal of Economic History* 39 (1): 143–57.

Maddison, A. 1995. *Monitoring the World Economy 1820–1992*. Paris: OECD.

Maddison, A. 1998. *Chinese Economic Performance in the Long Run*. Paris: OECD Development Centre.

Maddison, A. 2001. *The World Economy: A Millennial Perspective*. Paris: OECD.

Maddison, A. 2003. *The World Economy: Historical Statistics*. Paris: OECD.

Maddison, A. 2007. World Population, GDP and Per capita GDP, 1–2003AD (August 2007 update). www.ggdc.net/Maddison.

Maddison, A. 2008. World Population, GDP and Per capita GDP, 1–2006AD (October 2008 update). www.ggdc.net/Maddison.

Magee, S. P., W. A. Brock, and L. Young. 1989. *Black Hole Tariffs and Endogenous Policy Theory*. Cambridge: Cambridge University Press.

Márquez Colín, G. 2002. Monopoly and trade in colonial Latin America. Paper given at the 13th International Economic History Conference, Buenos Aires (July).

Marshall, P. J. 1987. *Bengal: The British bridgehead: eastern India, 1740–1828.* Cambridge: Cambridge University Press.

Marshall, P. J., ed. 2003. *The Eighteenth Century in Indian History: Evolution or Revolution?* New Delhi: Oxford University Press.

Martin, R. 1838. *The History, Antiquities, Topography, and Statistics of Eastern India.* London: H.W. Allen.

Martin, W. 2003. Developing countries' changing participation in world trade. *World Bank Research Observer* 18: 187–203.

Martin, W. 2007. Outgrowing resource dependence: Theory and developments. In D. Lederman and W. L. Maloney, eds. *Natural Resources: Neither Curse nor Destiny.* Stanford: Stanford University Press, 323–55.

Marx, K. [1867] 1977. *Capital,* vol. 1, transl. by B. Fowkes. New York: Vintage Books.

Matsuyama, K. 1991. Increasing returns, industrialization, and indeterminacy of equilibrium. *Quarterly Journal of Economics* 106 (May): 617–50.

Matsuyama, K. 1992. Agricultural productivity, comparative advantage, and economic growth. *Journal of Economic Theory* 58 (2): 317–34.

Mauro, P., N. Sussman, and Y. Yafeh. 2006. *Emerging Markets, Sovereign Debt, and International Financial Integration: 1870–1913 and Today.* Oxford: Oxford University Press.

McGreevey, W. P. 1971. *An Economic History of Colombia 1845–1930.* Cambridge: Cambridge University Press.

Mehlum, H., K. Moene, and R. Torvik. 2006. Institutions and the resource curse. *Economic Journal* 116: 1–20.

Meissner, C. 2005. A new world order: Explaining the emergence of the classical gold standard. *Journal of International Economics* 66 (July): 385–406.

Mendels, F. F. 1972. Proto-industrialization: the first phase of the industrialization process. *Journal of Economic History* 32 (March): 241–61.

Mendoza, E. 1997. Terms of trade uncertainty and economic growth. *Journal of Development Economics* 54 (December): 323–56.

Milanovic, B., P. H. Lindert, and J. G. Williamson. 2008. Ancient inequality. Revised NBER working paper 13550. National Bureau of Economic Research, Cambridge, MA.

Miño Grijalva, M. 1983. Espacio económico e industria textil: los trabajadores de Nueva España, 1780–1810. *Historia Mexicana* 23 (April–June): 231–61.

Miño Grijalva, M. 1993. *La Protoindustria colonial Hispanoamericana*. Mexico City: El Colegio de México.

Miño Grijalva, M. 1998. *Obrajes y tejedores de Nueva España*. Mexico City: El Colegio de México.

Mitchell, B. R. 1978. *European Historical Statistics 1750–1970*. New York: Columbia University Press.

Mitchell, B. R. 1993. *International Historical Statistics: The Americas 1750–1988*, 2nd ed. New York: Stockton Press.

Mitchell, B. R. 1998a. *International Historical Statistics: Europe 1750–1993*, 4th ed. London: Macmillan.

Mitchell, B. R. 1998b. *International Historical Statistics: Africa, Asia and Oceania 1750–1993*, 3rd ed. London: Macmillan.

Mitchell, B. R. 2003. *International Historical Statistics: Europe 1750–2000*, 5th ed. Hampshire, UK: Palgrave Macmillan.

Mitchell, B. R., and P. Deane. 1962. *Abstract of British Historical Statistics*. Cambridge: Cambridge University Press.

Mitchener, K. J., and M. Weidenmier. 2008. Trade and empire. NBER working paper 13765. National Bureau of Economic Research, Cambridge, MA.

Miyamoto, M., Y. Sakudo, and Y. Yasuba. 1965. Economic development in preindustrial Japan, 1859–1894. *Journal of Economic History* 25 (December): 541–564.

Mokyr, J. 1993. *The British Industrial Revolution: An Economic Perspective*. Boulder: Westview Press.

Moosvi, S. 2000. The Indian economic experience 1600–1900: A quantitative study. In K. N. Panikkar, T. J. Byres, and U. Patnail, eds., *The Making of History: Essays Presented to Irfan Habib*. New Delhi: Tulika, 328–58.

Moosvi, S. 2002. Studying a colonial economy—Without perceiving colonialism. In I. Habib, ed., *Essays in Indian History*. London: Anthem Press, 336–66.

Morris, M. D. 1969. Trends and tendencies in Indian economic history. Indian Economy in the Nineteenth Century: A Symposium, Indian Economic and Social History Association (Delhi).

Morris, M. D. 1983. The growth of large-scale industry to 1947. In D. Kumar and M. Desai, eds., *The Cambridge Economic History of India*, vol. 2. Cambridge: Cambridge University Press, 553–676.

Mukerjee, R. 1939. *The Economic History of India: 1600–1800*. London: Longmans, Green and Company.

Mulhall, M. G. 1892. *The Dictionary of Statistics*. London: Routledge.

Murphy, K., A. Shleifer, and R. Vishny. 1989. Industrialization and the big push. *Journal of Political Economy* 97: 1003–26.

Murphy, K., A. Shleifer, and R. Vishny. 1991. The allocation of talent: Implications for growth. *Quarterly Journal of Economics* 106 (May): 503–30.

Murphy, K., A. Shleifer, and R. Vishny. 1993. Why is rent seeking so costly for growth? *American Economic Review* 83 (Papers and Proceedings): 409–14.

Mussa, M. L. 1979. The two sector model in terms of its dual: A geometric exposition. *Journal of International Economics* 9 (4): 513–26.

Myrdal, G. 1957. *Economic Theory and Under-developed Regions*. London: Duckworth.

Nehru, J. 1947. *The Discovery of India*. London: Meridian Books.

Neumayer, E. 2004. Does the "resource curse" hold for growth in genuine income as well? *World Development* 32 (10): 1627–40.

Newland, C. 1998. Exports and terms of trade in Argentina, 1811–1870. *Bulletin of Latin American Research* 17 (3):409–16.

North, D. C. 1958. Ocean freight rates and economic development 1750–1913. *Journal of Economic History* 18 (December): 538–55.

North, D. C. 1990. *Institutions, Institutional Change and Economic Growth*. Cambridge: Cambridge University Press.

North, D. C. 2005. *Understanding the Process of Economic Change*. Princeton: Princeton University Press.

North, D. C., and R. P. Thomas. 1973. *The Rise of the Western World*. Cambridge: Cambridge University Press.

North, D. C., and B. Weingast. 1989. Constitutions and commitment: The evolution of institutions governing public choice in 17th century England. *Journal of Economic History* 48 (December): 803–32.

Nunn, N., and D. Trefler. 2007. The political economy of tariffs and long-term growth. Unpublished manuscript. Harvard University.

O'Brien, P. K., ed. 1999. *Oxford Atlas of World History*. New York: Oxford University Press.

O'Brien, P. K. 2004. Colonies in a globalizing economy 1815–1948. LSE working paper 08/04. Global Economic History Network, London School of Economics.

Obstfeld, M., and A. M. Taylor. 2003. Globalization and capital markets. In M. Bordo, A. M. Taylor, and J. G. Williamson, eds., *Globalization in Historical Perspective*. Chicago: University of Chicago Press, 121–83.

Obstfeld, M., and A. M. Taylor. 2004. *Global Capital Markets: Integration, Crisis, and Growth.* Cambridge: Cambridge University Press.

Ocampo, J. A. 1994. Una breve historia cafetera de Colombia, 1830-1938. In S. Kalmanovitz et al., eds., *Minagricultura 80 años. Transformaciones en la Estructura Agraria.* Bogotá-Caracas-Quito: Tercer Mundo Editores, 177–223.

Ohkawa, K., and H. Rosovsky. 1973. *Japanese Economic Growth: Trend Acceleration in the Twentieth Century.* Stanford: Stanford University Press.

Olson, M. 1963. *The Economics of Wartime Shortage.* Durham, NC: Duke University Press.

O'Rourke, K. H. 1997. The European grain invasion, 1870–1913. *Journal of Economic History* 57 (December): 775–801.

O'Rourke, K. H. 2000. Tariffs and growth in the late 19th century. *Economic Journal* 110 (April): 456–83.

O'Rourke, K. H. 2006. The worldwide economic impact of the French Revolutionary and Napoleonic Wars, 1793–1815. *Journal of Global History* 1: 123–49.

O'Rourke, K. H., and S. H. Lehmann. 2008. The structure of protection and economic growth, 1870–1913. NBER working paper 14493. National Bureau of Economic Research, Cambridge, MA.

O'Rourke, K. H., and R. Sinnott. 2001. The determinants of individual trade policy preferences: International survey evidence. In S. M. Collins and D. Rodrik, eds. *Brookings Trade Forum 2001.* Washington, DC: Brookings Institute Press, 157–206.

O'Rourke, K. H., A. M. Taylor, and J. G. Williamson. 1996. Factor price convergence in the late nineteenth century. *International Economic Review* 37 (3): 499–530.

O'Rourke, K. H., and J. G. Williamson. 1999. *Globalization and History.* Cambridge: Cambridge University Press.

O'Rourke, K. H., and J. G. Williamson. 2002a. After Columbus: Explaining Europe's overseas trade boom, 1500–1800. *Journal of Economic History* 62 (June): 417–56.

O'Rourke, K. H., and J. G. Williamson. 2002b. When did globalization begin? *European Review of Economic History* 6 (pt. 1): 23–50.

O'Rourke, K. H., and J. G. Williamson. 2005. From Malthus to Ohlin: Trade, growth and distribution since 1500. *Journal of Economic Growth* 10 (January): 5–34.

O'Rourke, K. H., and J. G. Williamson. 2009. Did Vasco da Gama matter to European markets? *Economic History Review* 62 (August): 655–84.

Overman, H. G., S. Redding, and A. J. Venables. 2001. The economic geography of trade, production and income: A survey of empirics. In E. Kwan-Choi and J. Harrigan, eds., *Handbook of International Trade.* London: Basil Blackwell, 353–87.

Owen, E. R. J. 1969. *Cotton and the Egyptian Economy 1820–1914*. Oxford: Oxford University Press.

Owen, E. R. J. [1983] 1993. *Middle East in the World Economy 1800–1914* London: I.B Tauris.

Pamuk, Ş. 1986. The decline and resistance of Ottoman cotton textiles 1820–1913. *Explorations in Economic History* 23 (April): 205–25.

Pamuk, Ş. 1987. *The Ottoman Empire and European Capitalism, 1820–1913: Trade, Investment and Production*. Cambridge: Cambridge University Press.

Pamuk, Ş. 2006. Estimating economic growth in the Middle East since 1820. *Journal of Economic History* 66 (September): 809–28.

Pamuk, Ş., and J. G. Williamson. 2009. Ottoman de-industrialization 1800–1913: Assessing the shock, its impact and the response. NBER working paper 14763. National Bureau of Economic Research, Cambridge, MA.

Parthasarathi, P. 1998. Rethinking wages and competitiveness in the eighteenth century: Britain and South India. *Past and Present* 158 (February): 79–109.

Patrick, H., ed. 1976. *Japanese Industrialization and Its Social Consequences*. Berkeley: University of California Press.

Persson, K. G. 1999. *Grain Markets in Europe, 1500–1900*. Cambridge: Cambridge University Press.

Petmezas, S. D. 1990. Patterns of protoindustrialization in the Ottoman empire: The case of eastern Thessaly, ca. 1750–1860. *Journal of European Economic History* 19 (Winter): 575–603.

Pires, T. 1944. *The "Suma Oriental" of Tomé Pires*. London: Hakluyt Society.

Poelhekke, S., and F. van der Ploeg. 2007. Volatility, financial development and the natural resource curse. CEPR discussion paper 6513. Centre for Economic Policy Research, London.

Polanyi, K. 1944. *The Great Transformation*. New York: Rinehart.

Pollard, S. 1982. *Peaceful Conquest: The Industrialization of Europe 1760–1970*. Oxford: Oxford University Press.

Pomeranz, K. 2000. *The Great Divergence: China, Europe, and the Making of the Modern World*. Princeton: Princeton University Press.

Ponzio, C. A. 2005. Globalisation and economic growth in the third world: Some evidence from eighteenth century Mexico. *Journal of Latin American Studies* 37 (August): 437–67.

Ponzio, C. A. 2005. Looking at the dark side of things: Political instability and economic growth in post-independence Mexico. Unpublished manuscript. Harvard University.

Potash, R. A. 1983. *Mexican Government and Industrial Development in the Early Republic: The Banco de Avío*. Amherst: University of Massachusetts Press.

Prados de la Escosura, L. 2003. Assessing the economic effects of Latin American independence. Working paper 03–12. Economic History and Institutions, Universidad Carlos III de Madrid, Madrid.

Prados de la Escosura, L. 2004. Draft of "The economic consequences of independence in Latin America." In V. Bulmer-Thomas, J. H. Coatsworth, and R. Cortés Conde, eds., *The Cambridge Economic History of Latin America*, vol. 1. Cambridge: Cambridge University Press.

Prados de la Escosura, L. 2009. Lost decades? Economic performance in postindependence Latin America. *Journal of Latin American Studies* 41(2): 279–307.

Prakash, O. 2004. *Bullion for Goods: European and Indian Merchants in the Indian Ocean Trade, 1500–1800*. New Delhi: Manohar.

Prakash, O. 2005. The great divergence: Evidence from eighteenth century India. Presented at the GEHN Conference on Imperialism, Istanbul (September 11–12).

Prebisch, R. 1950. *The Economic Development of Latin America and Its Principal Problems*. Lake Success, NY: United Nations, Department of Economic Affairs. Reprinted in *Economic Bulletin for Latin America* 7 (1962): 1–22.

Puryear, V. J. [1935] 1969. *International Economics and Diplomacy in the Near East*. Stanford: Archon Books.

Quataert, D. 1977. Limited revolution: The impact of the Anatolian railway on Turkish transporation and the provisioning of Istanbul, 1890–1908. *Business History Review* LI (Summer): 139–60.

Quataert, D. 1992. *Manufacturing and Technology Transfer in the Ottoman Empire, 1800–1914*. Istanbul: Isis Press.

Quataert, D. 1993. *Ottoman Manufacturing in the Age of the Industrial Revolution*. Cambridge: Cambridge University Press.

Quataert, D. 1994. The age of reforms, 1812–1914. In H. Inalcyk and D. Quataert, eds., *An Economic and Social History of the Ottoman Empire, 1300–1914*. Cambridge: Cambridge University Press, 759–946.

Ramey, G., and V. A. Ramey. 1995. Cross-country evidence on the link between volatility and growth. *American Economic Review* 85 (5): 1138–51.

Raychaudhuri, T. 1983. The mid-eighteenth-century background. In D. Kumar and M. Desai, eds., *The Cambridge Economic History of India*, vol. 2. Cambridge: Cambridge University Press, 3–35.

Redding, S., and A. J. Venables. 2004. Economic geography and international inequality. *Journal of International Economics* 62 (1): 53–82.

Reid, A. 1988. *Southeast Asia in the Age of Commerce, 1450–1680.* Vol. 1: *The Lands below the Winds.* New Haven: Yale University Press.

Resnick, S. A. 1970. The decline of rural industry under export expansion: A comparison among Burma, Philippines, and Thailand, 1870–1938. *Journal of Economic History* 30 (March): 51–73.

Ricardo, D. 1817. *On the Principles of Political Economy and Taxation.* London: J. Murray.

Rocchi, F. 2006. *Chimneys in the Desert. Industrialization in Argentina during the Export Boom Years, 1870–1930.* Stanford: Stanford University Press.

Rodríguez, F., and D. Rodrik. 2001. Trade policy and economic growth: A skeptic's guide to the cross-national evidence. In B. Bernanke and K. S. Rogoff, eds., *Macroeconomics Annual 2000.* Cambridge: MIT Press for NBER, 261–325.

Rogowski, R. 1989. *Commerce and Coalitions: How Trade Effects Domestic Political Arrangements.* Princeton: Princeton University Press.

Romer, P. M. 1986. Increasing returns and long-run growth. *Journal of Political Economy* 94 (October): 1002–37.

Romer, P. M. 1990. Endogenous technological change. *Journal of Political Economy* 98 (October: pt. 2): S71–S102.

Rosenweig, M. R., and K. I. Wolpin. 1993. Credit market constraints, consumption smoothing, and the accumulation of durable production assets in low income countries: Investments in bullocks in India. *Journal of Political Economy* 101 (2): 223–44.

Rose, M. B. 2000. *Firms, Networks and Business Values. The British and American Cotton Industries since 1750.* New York: Cambridge University Press.

Rosés, J. R. 1998. The early phase of Catalan industrialisation, 1830–1861. Unpublished PhD thesis. European University Institute.

Ross, M. L. 1999. The political economy of resource curse. *World Politics* 51 (January): 297–322.

Rostow, W. W. 1964. *The Stages of Economic Growth: A Noncommunist Manifesto.* London: Cambridge University Press.

Roumasset, J. A. 1976. *Rice and Risk: Decision-Making among Low-Income Farmers.* Amsterdam: North-Holland.

Roumasset, J. A., J.-M. Boussard, and I. Singh, eds. 1979. *Risk, Uncertainty and Agricultural Development.* New York: Agricultural Development Council.

Rousseau, P., and R. Sylla. 2005. Emerging financial markets and early U.S. growth. *Explorations in Economic History* 42 (January): 1–26.

Rousseau, P., and R. Sylla. 2006. Financial revolutions and economic growth: Introducing this EEH symposium. *Explorations in Economic History* 43 (January): 1–12.

Roy, T. 2000. *The Economic History of India 1857–1947*. Delhi: Oxford University Press.

Roy, T. 2002. Economic history and modern India: Redefining the link. *Journal of Economic Perspectives* 16 (Summer): 109–30.

Roy, T. 2009. Economic conditions in early modern Bengal: A contribution to the divergence debate. CEPR discussion paper 7522. Centre for Economic Policy Research, London.

Sachs, J. D. 2001. Tropical underdevelopment. NBER working paper 8119. National Bureau of Economic Research, Cambridge, MA.

Sachs, J. D., and A. M. Warner. 1995. Natural resource abundance and economic growth. NBER working paper 5398. National Bureau of Economic Research, Cambridge, MA.

Sachs, J. D., and A. Warner. 1997. Economic reform and the process of economic integration. *Brookings Papers on Economic Activity* 1: 1–53.

Sachs, J. D., and A. M. Warner. 2001. The curse of natural resources. *European Economic Review* 45: 827–38.

Safford, F., and M. Palacios. 2002. *Colombia: Fragmented Land, Divided Society*. Oxford: Oxford University Press.

Salvucci, R. J. 1987. *Textiles and Capitalism in Mexico: An Economic History of the Obrajes, 1539–1840*. Princeton: Princeton University Press.

Salvucci, R. J. 1992. *Textiles y capitalismo en México: una historia económica de los obrajes, 1539–1840*. Mexico City: Alianza.

Sánchez Santiró, E. 2006. Recuperación y expansión de la agroindustria azucarera mexiquense en un contexto de crisis (1821–1854). *Investigaciones de Historia Económica* (Fall): 41–72.

Sánchez Santiró, E. 2007. El desempeño de la economía mexicana tras la independencia, 1821–1870: Nuevas evidencias e interpretaciones. Presented at the Seminario de Historia Económica, Fundación Ramón Areces *Obstáculos al Crecimiento Económico en Iberoamérica y España 1790–1850*, May 18–19, Madrid.

Schell, W., Jr. 2001. Silver symbiosis: Re-orienting Mexican economic history. *Hispanic American Historical Review* 81 (February): 90–133.

Schmitz, C. J. 1979. *World Non-ferrous Metal Production and Prices, 1700–1976*. London: Frank Cass.

Schonhardt-Bailey, C. 2006. *From Corn Laws to Free Trade: Interests, Ideas, and Institutions in Historical Perspective*. Cambridge: MIT Press.

Seminario de Historia Moderna de México. 1965. *Estadísticas Económicas del Porfiriato,Fuerza de Trabajo y Actividad Económica por Sectores*. México: El Colegio de México.

Shah Mohammed, S., and J. G. Williamson. 2004. Freight rates and productivity gains in British tramp shipping 1869–1950. *Explorations in Economic History* 41 (April): 172–203.

Shinohara, M. 1972. *Mining and Manufacturing* (vol. 10 of K. Ohkawa, M. Shinohara, and M. Umemura, eds., *Estimates of Long-Term Economic Statistics of Japan since 1868*). Tokyo: Toyo Keizai Shinposha.

Simmons, C. 1985. "Deindustrialization," industrialization, and the Indian economy, c. 1850–1947. *Modern Asian Studies* 19 (special issue): 593–622.

Singer, H. W. 1950. The distribution of gains between investing and borrowing countries. *American Economic Review* 40: 473–85.

Slaughter, M. J. 1995. The antebellum transportation revolution and factor-price convergence. NBER working paper 5303. National Bureau of Economic Research, Cambridge, MA.

Smith, A. [1776] 1904/1976. *An Inquiry into the Nature and Causes of the Wealth of Nations*, 5th ed., 2 vols. (ed. E. Cannan) Dunwoody, GA: Norman S. Berg.

Smith, T. C. 1955. *Political Change and Industrial development in Japan: Government Enterprise, 1868–1880*. Stanford: Stanford University Press.

Sonmez, A. 1970. *Ottoman Terms of Trade, 1878–1913*. Ankara: METU Studies in Development

Spraos, J. 1980. The statistical debate on the net barter terms of trade between primary commodities and manufactures. *Economic Journal* 90: 107–28.

Steinberg, D. J. 1987. *In Search of Southeast Asia*. Honolulu: University of Hawaii Press.

Stemmer, J. E. O. 1989. Freight rates in the trade between Europe and South America. *Journal of Latin American Studies* 21 (pt. 1): 22–59.

Stolper, W., and P. Samuelson. 1941. Protection and real wages. *Review of Economic Studies* 9: 58–73.

Studer, R. 2008. India and the great divergence: Assessing the efficiency of grain markets in eighteenth and nineteenth century India. *Journal of Economic History* 68 (June): 393–437.

Sugiyama, S. 1987. The impact of the opening of the ports on domestic Japanese industry: The case of silk and cotton. *Economic Studies Quarterly* 38 (4): 338–53.

Sugiyama, S. 1988. *Japan's Industrialization in the World Economy, 1859–1899.* London: Athlone Press.

Summerhill, W. 2001. Economic consequences of Argentine railroads, 1857–1913. Unpublished manuscript. University of California, Los Angeles.

Summerhill, W. 2005. Big social savings in a small laggard economy: Railroad-led growth in Brazil. *Journal of Economic History* 65 (1): 72–102.

Taylor, A. M. 1998. On the costs of inward-looking development: Price distortions, growth, and divergence in Latin America. *Journal of Economic History* 58 (March): 1–28.

Thomas, D., K. Beegle, E. Frankenberg, B. Sikoki, J. Strauss, and G. Teruel. 2004. Education in a Crisis. *Journal of Development Economics* 74 (June): 53–85.

Thomson, G. P. C. 1991. Continuity and change in Mexican manufacturing, 1800–1870. In J. Batou, ed., *Between Development and Underdevelopment.* Geneva: Librairie Droz, 255–302.

Thomson, G. P. C. 2002. *Puebla de los Angeles: industria y sociedad de una ciudad mexicana, 1700–1850.* Mexico City: Benemérita Universidad de Puebla.

Thomson, J. K. J. 2005. Explaining the "take-off" of the Catalan cotton industry. *Economic History Review* LVIII (November): 701–35.

Thorner, D. 1962. Deindustrialization in India 1881–1931. In D. Thorner and A. Thorner, eds., *Land and Labour in India.* Bombay: Asia Publishing House, 70–81.

Tomlinson, B. R. 1993. *The New Cambridge History of India.* Vol. 3: *The Economy of Modern India, 1860–1970.* Cambridge: Cambridge University Press.

Tornell, A., and P. Lane. 1999. The voracity effect. *American Economic Review* 88 (5): 22–46.

Torvik, R. 2002. Natural resources, rent seeking, and welfare. *Journal of Development Economics* 67 (2): 455–70.

Tulloch, G. 1967. The welfare costs of tariffs, monopolies and theft. *Western Economic Journal* 5 (December): 224–32.

Vamplew, W. 1971. Railways and the transformation of the Scottish economy. *Economic History Review* 24 (1): 37–54.

van der Eng, P. 2007. De-industrialization and colonial rule: The cotton textile industry in Indonesia, 1820–1941. Unpublished manuscript. Australian National University, Canberra.

van Zanden, J. L. 2002. Colonial state formation and patterns of economic development in Java, 1800–1913. Unpublished manuscript. Utrecht University.

Venables, A. 2007. Trade, location, and development: An overview of theory. In D. Lederman and W. F. Maloney, eds., *Natural Resources: Neither Curse nor Destiny*. Stanford: Stanford University Press, 259–87.

Ward, H. G. 1991. *México en 1827*. Puebla: Secretaría de Cultura.

Weisdorf, J. L. 2006. From domestic manufacturing to Industrial Revolution: Long-run growth and agricultural development. *Oxford Economic Papers* 58 (April): 264–87.

Whitcombe, E. 1983. Irrigation and railways. In D. Dumar, ed., *The Cambridge Economic History of India*: Vol. 2: *c. 1757–c.1970*. Cambridge: Cambridge University Press, 677–761.

Williamson, J. G. 1990. The impact of the Corn Laws just prior to repeal. *Explorations in Economic History* 27 (April): 123–56.

Williamson, J. G. 1997. Globalization and inequality, past and present. *World Bank Research Observer* 12 (2): 117–35.

Williamson, J. G. 1998. Globalization, labor markets and policy backlash in the past. *Journal of Economic Perspectives* 12 (Fall): 51–72.

Williamson, J. G. 2000. Globalization, factor prices and living standards in Asia before 1940. In A. J. H. Latham, ed., *Asia Pacific Dynamism 1500–2000*. London: Routledge, 13–45.

Williamson, J. G. 2002a. Two centuries of globalization: Backlash and bribes for the losers. WIDER annual lecture. Copenhagen (September 5).

Williamson, J. G. 2002b. Land, labor and globalization in the third world 1870–1940. *Journal of Economic History* 62 (1): 55–85.

Williamson, J. G. 2006a. *Globalization and the Poor Periphery before 1950*. Cambridge: MIT Press.

Williamson, J. G. 2006b. Explaining world tariffs 1870–1938: Stolper–Samuelson, strategic tariffs and state revenues. In R. Findlay, R. Henriksson, H. Lindgren, and M. Lundahl, eds., *Eli Heckscher, 1879–1952: A Celebratory Symposium*. Cambridge: MIT Press, 199–228.

Williamson, J. G. 2006c. Globalization, de-industrialization and underdevelopment in the third world before the modern era. [Revista de Historia Económica] *Journal of Iberian and Latin American Economic History* 24 (Primavera): 9–36.

Williamson, J. G. 2007. Lost decades: Dealing with independence and globalization in 19th Century Latin America. Inaugural lecture. Third International Congress in Economic History, Cuernavaca, Mexico (October 29–31).

Williamson, J. G. 2008. Globalization and the great divergence: Terms of trade booms and volatility in the poor periphery 1782–1913. *European Review of Economic History* 12 (December): 355–91.

Williamson, J. G. 2009. History without evidence: Latin American inequality since 1491. NBER working paper 14766. National Bureau of Economic Research, Cambridge, MA.

Williamson, J. G. 2010. Latin American growth-inequality trade-offs: The impact of insurgence and independence. NBER working paper 15680. National Bureau of Economic Research, Cambridge, MA.

Williamson, J. G., and P. H. Lindert. 1980. *American Inequality: A Macroeconomic History*. New York: Academic Press.

Williamson, J. G., and T. Yousef. 2008. Globalization, policy and competitiveness: De-industrialization in Egypt, 1790–1913. (ongoing).

Wright, G. 1990. The origins of American industrial success, 1879–1940. *American Economic Review* 80 (September): 651–68.

Wrigley, E. A. 2006. The transition to an advanced organic economy: half a millennium of English agriculture. *Economic History Review* 59 (3):435–80.

Yasuba, Y. 1978. Freight rates and productivity in ocean transportation for Japan, 1875–1943. *Explorations in Economic History* 15: 11–39.

Yasuba, Y. 1996. Did Japan ever suffer from a shortage of natural resources before World War II? *Journal of Economic History* 56 (September): 543–60.

Yamazawa, I., and Y. Yamamoto. 1979. *Foreign Trade and Balance of Payments* (vol. 14 of *Estimates of Long-Term Economic Statistics of Japan since 1868*). Tokyo: Toyo Keizai Shinposha.

Index

Acemoglu, Daron, 2
Africa
in 1960 economic order, 2
sub-Saharan
absence of data for, 28
terms of trade volatility in, 167,
168
Aghion, Philippe, 171
Agricultural productivity
decline in, 130
in India
decline in, 78–79, 81–82, 84, 85, 86,
91–92, 95, 96, 98, 99, 135
epoch of high level in, 83–84, 91
in Mexico
and manufacturing competitiveness,
130
as relatively stable, 133–34, 143
and textile sector wages, 55
Ali, Mohamed (Egyptian leader), 66–67,
68, 109, 112
Anglo-Turkish Commercial
Convention, 102–103
Anti-trade backlash, 9, 215, 217, 218.
See also Protectionism; Tariffs
Argentina
commodity exports from, 207
export concentration in, 52
export shares in GDP for, 47
GDP/exports/terms of trade in
(1870–1939), 187

imports of intermediate and capital
goods to, 202
industrialization in, 203
pro-industrial policies absent in, 204
railway mileage in (1850–1910), 16
real exchange rate for, 210
tariffs in, 219
terms of trade for, 206, 211, 212
income terms of trade, 208
terms of trade data for, 29, 37
terms of trade volatility for, 174, 177
textile industry of, 201
wage–rent ratios in, 161
Asia
export shares in GDP for, 47
inequality in, 154
in 1960 economic order, 2
per capita levels of industrialization
in, 64
tariffs in, 216, 218, 227
for dependent and independent
parts, 217
and transport revolution, 18–19
Assam, cash tenancy in, 157
Asymmetric trade impact, 48, 171,
185–87, 191, 232–33
Australia
GDP/exports/terms of trade for
(1870–1939), 186
and industrialization, 172
as primary-product producer, 194

Australia (cont.)
railway mileage in (1850–1910), 16
tariffs in, 141, 218
Austria-Hungary, 185
free trade in (19th century), 13
GDP/exports/terms of trade for
(1870–1939), 186
railway mileage in (1850–1910), 16

Bairoch, Paul, 61, 63, 77, 88, 219
Banco de Avío (Mexico), 128, 139,
141
Beatty, Edward, 204, 207
Belgium, free trade in (19th century),
13
Bengal, industrialization in, 199
as periphery leader, 214
Bombay, industrialization in, 199
as periphery leader, 214
Booth, Anne, 70
Bowring, Sir John, 67
Brazil
commodity exports from, 207
export concentration in, 52, 168
export shares in GDP for, 47
GDP/exports/terms of trade for
(1870–1939), 187
imports of intermediate and capital
goods to, 202
industrialization in, 199, 203
per capita levels of, 64
as periphery leader, 214
inequality measures for, 148, 149,
150, 155
extraction ratio, 151
pro-industrial policies in, 204–205
real currency depreciation for, 228
real exchange rate for, 210, 211
tariffs in, 219, 220
terms of trade for, 206, 207, 212
income terms of trade, 208
terms of trade boom for, 37
terms of trade data sources for, 30

terms of trade volatility in, 173, 174,
177
textile mills in, 128, 200
and wage competitiveness, 209
Britain. *See* United Kingdom
British transportation cost index, 16
Burma
cash tenancy in, 157
de-industrialization in, 70–71
export concentration in, 52
export shares in GDP for, 47
and free trade, 14
GDP/exports/terms of trade for
(1870–1939), 187
as primary-product producer, 194
tariffs in, 217–18
terms of trade volatility for, 174
wage–rent ratios in, 161, 162
Byzantium, inequality measures for,
148, 149

Canada
GDP/exports/terms of trade for
(1870–1939), 186
as primary-product producer, 194
railway mileage in (1850–1910), 16
tariffs in, 141, 218
Capital accumulation, and terms of
trade impact, 194
Catalonia, industrialization in, 199
as periphery leader, 214
tariffs in, 141
Ceylon
export concentration in, 52
export shares in GDP for, 47
and free trade, 14
GDP/exports/terms of trade for
(1870–1939), 187
industrialization in, 213
as primary-product producer, 194
tariffs in, 217–218
terms of trade for, 212
terms of trade boom for, 37, 119

terms of trade data sources for, 30
terms of trade volatility for, 174, 176, 177
Chappell, John, 83
Chile
    commodity exports from, 207
    export concentration in, 52, 168–69
    export shares in GDP for, 47
    GDP/exports/terms of trade for (1870–1939), 187
    imports of intermediate and capital goods to, 202
    industrialization in, 203
    inequality measures for, 148, 149, 150, 155
    extraction ratio, 151
    pro-industrial policies in, 204–205
    real exchange rate for, 210
    tariffs in, 220
    terms of trade for, 206, 207, 211, 212
    income terms of trade for, 208
    terms of trade boom for, 37
    terms of trade data sources for, 30
    as terms of trade example, 189–90
    terms of trade volatility for, 174, 177
    and wage competitiveness, 209
China, 1
    de-industrialization in, 61–63, 72–73, 74
    Dutch disease effects in, 72–73
    exceptionalism of, 33–34, 72–73
    and exchange rates, 228
    export concentration in, 52
    export shares in GDP for, 47
    free trade forced on, 13–14
    GDP/exports/terms of trade for (1870–1939), 187
    industrialization in, 213
    per capita levels of, 64
    inequality measures for, 148, 149, 150
    extraction ratio, 151

manufacturing output share of, 77, 88
railway mileage in (1850–1910), 16
tariffs in, 219
terms of trade for, 72, 212
terms of trade boom absent from, 26, 37
terms of trade data for, 30
terms of trade volatility for, 174, 177
    and GDP growth, 178
trade liberalization in, 71, 72
Clarence-Smith, William, 69
Clark, Colin, 87
Clark, Gregory, 138
Clemens, Michael, 185
Climate, and Indian de-industrialization, 82–84
Clingingsmith, David, 83
Cobden–Chevalier Treaty, 13
Colombia
    commodity exports from, 207
    export concentration in, 52
    export shares in GDP for, 47
    export substitution in, 190–91, 247n.6
    GDP/exports/terms of trade for (1870–1939), 187
    as primary-product producer, 194
    pro-industrial policies in, 204–205
    tariffs in, 218, 219, 220
    terms of trade (income) for, 208
    terms of trade volatility for, 173, 174
Colonial drain, 84, 146, 163–64
Colonialism
    vs. early industrialization, 211
    and Indian de-industrialization, 85–86
    and inequality, 152
    and tariffs, 217, 227
Commodity price volatility, 232
    and economic growth, 171, 191, 194–95
    and institutional quality, 190–91
    as globalization downside, 51–53

Commodity price volatility (cont.)
and great divergence, 167
modern economics literature on,
168–71
in 1700–1939 period, 171–79
during Prebisch–Singer period
(1870–1939), 188
Comparative advantage, 45, 53, *See also*
Gains from trade
and de-industrialization, 77–78, 101
endogenous, 183
for Europe vs. third world, 182
export concentration from, 172
and Latin American primary products,
137–38
and question of exogeneity of terms
of trade, 189–90
and resource curse, 183
and terms of trade volatility in poor
periphery, 178
Congo, Democratic Republic of,
inequality measures for, 150
Congress of Vienna, and Rhine
navigation, 14
Corden, Max, 157
Core nations. *See* Rich industrial core
Corn Laws, abolition of, 12
Cottage industries
in Britain, 88, 105
factory-based productivity brings
demise of, 127
in India, 88
and Ottoman empire, 105
putting-out system of, 61, 124
Cotton spinning. *See also* Textiles
in India (decline of), 87–88
in Mexico, 126, 129
in Ottoman empire, 105, 106
Cuba
commodity exports from, 207
exceptionalism of, 236n.5
export concentration in, 52, 168–69
export shares in GDP for, 47

GDP/exports/terms of trade for
(1870–1939), 187
as primary-product producer, 194
terms of trade (income) for, 208
terms of trade boom absent from, 26,
37
terms of trade data for, 30
terms of trade volatility in, 173, 174,
177
and GDP growth, 178
Currency depreciation, and Latin
American industrialization, 205,
214
and manufacturing profitability,
210–11
Currency unions, in first global
century, 11, 14, 23

Darwin, Charles, 83
Dean, Warren, 200
De-industrialization, 8–9, 60, 231–32
absolute, 56, 57, 60, 90, 94, 104, 114
causes of, 77–78
contentious aspects of, 104
and great divergence, 182
relative, 56–57, 60, 90, 95, 114
and terms of trade, 225
De-industrialization in poor periphery,
59–60, 74, 211
in China, 72–73
comparative qualitative assessment of,
65–66
comparative quantitative assessment
of, 61–65
differences between parts of, 59, 60
and economic growth, 180
during Singer–Prebisch episode, 195
in Egypt, 66–68
as globalization result, 27, 49–50, 60
in India, 62, 75–78, 98–99
causal hypotheses on, 78–86
measurement of, 86–89
and neo-Ricardian model, 89–91

relative prices and own wage in manufactures in, 91–97
in Indonesia, 65, 68–71, 74
and local share of domestic textile market, 64–65, 106–107, 196
in Mexico, 74, 129, 205
and neo-Ricardian model, 130–31
and pro-industrial policies, 139–42, 143
and question of failure to compete more effectively, 137–39
and terms of trade, 131–33
in transition before *Porfiriato*, 120–23
and wage competitiveness, 133–37, 143
in young Republic, 123–30
for Ottoman empire, 105–10
and barriers to trade, 102–104
causes of, 105–106, 114–17, 242n.9
and eastern Mediterranean debate, 104–105
and external terms of trade, 110–12
neo-Ricardian model of, 112–14, 116
vs. other nations in periphery, 118
and textile industry 200
neo-Ricardian model of, 53–57
for India, 89–91
for Mexico, 130–31
for Ottoman empire, 112–14, 116
and tariffs, 222–23, 225, 227, 233
and terms of trade boom, 57, 119, 145, 180, 222, 225
textiles as gauge of, 60–61
and trade boom, 7, 231–32
Denmark
commodity vs. manufacturing price volatility for, 179
free trade in (19th century), 13
GDP/exports/terms of trade for (1870–1939), 186
post-Napoleonic trade policy of, 12
Depreciation of local currencies. *See* Currency depreciation

Depressions, 23
Great Depression of 1930s, 28
Developed countries, GDP and industrial output performance in, 22. *See also* Rich industrial core
Discovery of India (Nehru), 85
Distribution of income. *See* Income distribution
Divergence between rich core nations and poor periphery, 1, 43–44, 198. *See also* Poor periphery; Rich industrial core; Third world
and asymmetric trade impact, 48, 171, 185–87, 191, 232–33
and channels of impact, 182, 231–32
emergence of, 2–4, 27
and globalization, 48, 181–84
in pre-1870 period, 195–97
during Singer-Prebish period (18701939), 184, 185–195, 232–33
origin of, 1–2
and terms of trade boom, 185–87, 232–33
and trade boom, 4–7
Domestic capital accumulation, terms of trade impact on, 194
Drought, and Indian de-industrialization, 83
Dutch disease, 49–50
in China, 72–73
in Egypt, 66–68
in European poor periphery, 36
in India, 86
in Indonesia, 68–71
in Japan, 71–72
and Latin America, 39, 206–207
and Mexico, 120, 132, 133, 139, 142
in poor periphery, 74, 211, 214
and de-industrialization, 33, 119
as globalization result, 27
Dutch East Indies. *See* Indonesia
Dutt, R. C., 85

East Asia. *See also* Gang of four
exceptionalism of, 33–34
and free trade, 13
GDP per capita growth of, 6
growth performance in (1700–1820), 3
land scarcity in, 232
old order disappeared in, 234
and terms of trade, 206
and industrialization, 211
terms of trade boom in, 28, 36, 37,
42–43
terms of trade volatility in, 167, 168,
174, 176, 177
wage–rent ratios in, 160
East Asia less China, GDP per capita
growth of, 5
Eastern Europe, railroads in, 223
Eastern Mediterranean
de-industrialization debate, 104–105
Economic growth
and commodity price volatility, 171,
191, 194–95
and institutional quality, 190–91
and de-industrialization, 180, 195
determinants of (1870–1939), 194
in first global century, 11
and inequality, 164–65, 180
in Latin America (and income
inequality), 154–55
and protectionism, 220
and rent-seeking, 183, 184
and terms of trade boom, 181, 198,
233
and terms of trade volatility, 119, 180,
184, 198
Economic order, world (1960), 102
Economic order of Lewis. *See* New
international economic order
Egypt
de-industrialization and Dutch disease
in, 66–68, 74
vs. rest of poor periphery, 118
export concentration in, 52

export shares in GDP for, 47
GDP/exports/terms of trade for
(1870–1939), 187
and lowered transportation costs,
108
as primary-product producer, 194
as resource-abundant, 146
and tariffs, 217–18
terms of trade for, 111–12, 133, 211,
212
terms of trade boom for, 37, 39–40,
66, 118, 119
terms of trade data sources for, 30
terms of trade volatility for, 175, 176,
177
and GDP growth, 178
wage–rent ratios in, 161, 162
El Niño, 82–83
Endogenous growth, 182–83
Engerman-Sokoloff hypothesis, 154–56,
191
"Engine of growth"
positive effects of globalization as,
27
trade as, 46, 48
English-speaking offshoots, GDP per
capita growth of, 5
Erie Canal, 14–15
European core, per capita levels of
industrialization in, 64. *See also* Rich
industrial core
European periphery
export shares in GDP for, 47
GDP per capita growth of, 5, 6
growth performance in (1700–1820), 3
industrialization in, 213
old order disappeared in, 234
tariffs in, 216, 217, 218, 220
terms of trade boom in, 28, 35, 36
terms of trade volatility for, 175,
177
*Evolution of the International Economic
Order* (Lewis), 33

Exchange rate depreciation, in Brazil
    and Mexico, 205
Export boom, 53–54
    and inequality, 232
    lower tariff rates from, 224, 225–26
Export concentration
    as globalization downside, 51–53,
    232
    in third world economies, 167,
    168–69, 172
Export shares, in GDP, 47, 48
Externalities, positive, 182
    from tariff protection, 229
Extraction ratio, 147. *See also*
    Inequality
    for ancient and modern societies,
    149–50, 151
    for Latin America vs. western Europe,
    156

Factor endowments
    and choice of primary commodity,
    190–91, 247n.6
    and Engerman–Sokoloff hypothesis,
    155, 191
Factory building
    in Mexico, 128
    in Middle East, 66–67, 109
Feuerwerker, Albert, 73
Financial drain, as Indian
    de-industrialization offset, 84–85
Florescano, Enrique, 126
Fogel, Robert, 19
France, 185
    GDP/exports/terms of trade for
    (1870–1939), 186
    inequality measures for, 148, 149,
    150, 155
    extraction ratio, 151
    railway mileage in (1850–1910),
    16
    terms of trade volatility for, 175
Freight rate index, real, 17

Gains from trade, 48, 181
    distribution of, 145 (*see also* Income
    distribution)
    in poor periphery, 45–48, 181, 198
Galiani, Sebastian, 158
Gallo, Ezequiel, 200
Gang of four, 1, 21
GDP
    short-run increase in, 101
    and terms of trade (1870–1939), 192
GDP per capita
    from 1870 to 1939 by country,
    186–87
    growth of in core (1800–1913), 26
    growth of in poor periphery, 181
    world growth performance of
    (1820–1913), 5
    world growth performance of
    (1913–1940), 6
Germany, 185
    and free trade (1870s), 13
    GDP/exports/terms of trade for
    (1870–1939), 186
    inequality measures for, 150
    internal trade barriers destroyed in, 15
    railway mileage in (1850–1910), 16
    terms of trade volatility for, 175
Gerschrenkron, Alexander, 54, 79, 115
Gini coefficient, 147, 148
Global century, first, 11–12, 25–28
    growth miracle in, 21–22
    question of most prominent force in,
    22–24
    trade liberalization in, 12–14, 23
    and world transport revolution, 14–21
Global economy, before 19th century,
    12
Globalization, 231. *See also* Trade
    boom, world; Terms of trade boom
    asymmetric growth from, 48, 49, 232
    and de-industrialization in third
    world, 27, 49–50, 60
    in India, 75–76

Globalization (cont.)
and divergence between rich core and
poor periphery, 48, 181–84
in pre-1870 period, 195–97
during Singer–Prebish period
(1870–1939), 184, 185–95, 232–33
downsides of, 48
commodity price volatility and
export concentration, 51–53 (see
also Commodity price volatility)
de-industrialization, 49–50, 60, 75–76
(see also De-industrialization in poor
periphery)
Dutch disease, 49–50 (see also Dutch
disease)
rent-seeking and resource curse,
50–51 (see also Rent-seeking;
Resource curse)
first century of (early 19th century to
World War I), 4, 6
impact(s) of, 145
and income distribution, 156–59
in labor-abundant part of poor
periphery, 159–62
in resource-abundant part of poor
periphery, 162–63
and Indian de-industrialization,
75–76, 85–86
positive vs. negative effects of for
periphery, 27
and price volatility, 179
Gold standard
in first global century, 11, 14, 23, 25
and real exchange rates, 227, 228
Gómez-Galvarriato, Aurora, 138–39,
201
Grain, economic role of, 54–55. See also
Agricultural productivity
Grain invasion
in European core, 160, 218, 223, 225,
226, 227
in Latin America, 209
Grain wages, 79–80, 89, 94

Great depression of 1930s, 28
Great divergence. See Divergence
between rich core nations and poor
periphery
Great Divergence, The: China, Europe,
and the Making of he Modern World
(Pomeranz), 3
Greece
export concentration in, 52
export shares in GDP for, 47
GDP/exports/terms of trade for
(1870–1939), 186
terms of trade volatility for, 175
Grove, Richard, 83
Growth miracles
in rich core nations (1820–1913),
21–22
in 20th century, 21
Gruen, Fred, 157

Haber, Stephen, 200, 201, 204
Hamilton, Alexander 139, 220
Hamilton, Francis Buchanan, 87
Hanson, John, 51–53
Heckscher, Eli, 156, 221
Heckscher–Ohlin model, 159
Heckscher–Ohlin–Samuelson model,
158
Heymann, Daniel, 158
Hirschman, Albert, 182
Hodrick–Prescott (HP) filter, 173,
189
Hong Kong, 1
Huber, J. Richard, 159
Human capital
and economic growth, 165
and negative income shocks, 169
Humboldt, Alexander von, 134

Import substitution industrial (ISI)
strategies, 218, 220, 233
Income distribution
and economic growth, 164–65

and globalization, 145, 156–59
  in labor-abundant part of poor
    periphery, 159–62
  in resource-abundant part of poor
    periphery, 162–63
  under pre-industrial and pre-global
    inequality, 146–56 (see also
    Inequality)
Income terms of trade, in Latin
  America, 207, 208
India, 1. See also South Asia
  colonial drain from, 164
  de-industrialization in, 61–63, 74,
    75–78, 98–99
  causal hypotheses on, 78–86
  measurement of, 86–89
  and neo-Ricardian model, 89–91
  relative prices and own wage in
    manufactures in, 91–97
  textile import penetration in, 65,
    106
  export concentration in, 52
  export shares in GDP for, 47
  exports to Indonesia from, 69
  and free trade, 14
  GDP/exports/terms of trade for
    (1870–1939), 187
  inequality measures for, 148, 149, 150
  extraction ratio, 151
  local share of domestic textile market
    for, 64, 65, 106–107, 129, 196,
    200
  manufacturing output share of, 88
  own wage in textiles in, 137
  per capita levels of industrialization
    in, 64
  railroads in, 19, 223
  railway mileage in (1850–1910), 16
  tariffs in, 217–18
  terms of trade for, 75, 76, 86, 118,
    212
  and terms of trade boom, 37, 40–41,
    236n.10

terms of trade data sources for, 30
terms of trade volatility for, 174, 177
and GDP growth, 178
Indochina, cash tenancy in, 157
Indonesia
  colonial drain from, 163–64
  de-industrialization and Dutch disease
    in, 65, 68–71, 74
  export concentration in, 52
  export shares in GDP for, 47
  foreign import share of domestic
    market in, 77
  and free trade, 14
  GDP/exports/terms of trade for
    (1870–1939), 187
  inequality measures for, 148, 149, 150
  extraction ratio, 151
  local share of domestic textile market
    for, 65, 106–107, 196, 200
  tariffs in, 217–18
  terms of trade for, 42, 133, 211,
    212
  terms of trade boom for, 37, 119
  terms of trade data sources for, 30
  terms of trade volatility for, 174,
    177
Industrialization
  early, 9, 62, 201, 213, 232
  in Japan, 160
  in poor periphery, 199, 211
  in Shanghai region, 160
  and exchange rate depreciation, 228
  in Japan, 43, 71–72
  in Mexico, 120
  and openness, 27
  in poor periphery, 199, 211–14
  in Latin America, 200–205, 207, 209,
    210–11
  in poor periphery vs. rich core, 232
Industrial Revolution, 231
  GDP growth rates raised in, 4
  and Ottoman spinners vs. weavers,
    108

Industrial Revolution (cont.)
and periphery vs. core, 27
and relative textile prices, 131
slow spread of through Europe, 36
Inequality, 231, 232
and colonial drain, 163–64
and economic growth, 164–65, 180,
183
and globalization, 156–59
in labor-abundant part of poor
periphery, 159–62
in resource-abundant part of poor
periphery, 162–63
and Kuznets curve hypothesis, 152,
154
pre-industrial and pre-global, 146–56
vs. current societies, 151
as result of globalization for
periphery, 27
and terms of trade boom, 180
Inequality extraction ratio. See
Extraction ratio
Inequality possibility frontier, 147, 148
Infant industry view, 220, 225
and Latin American policy makers,
204
and Mexican textile industry, 139
Intersectoral terms of trade, in India
(textiles and agriculture), 86, 93–94,
98
Investment, and price volatility, 169
Iran, tariffs in, 219
Irwin, Douglas, 157
Issawi, Charles, 102, 104, 105, 109,
111
Italy, 185
export shares in GDP for, 47
GDP/exports/terms of trade for
(1870–1939), 186
inequality measures for, 150
inequality measures for (Naples 1811),
148, 149
extraction ratio, 151

north Italian triangle (industrialization
in), 199, 214
railway mileage in (1850–1910), 16
terms of trade for, 212
terms of trade boom for, 36, 119
terms of trade data for, 30
terms of trade volatility for, 174, 176,
177
and GDP growth, 178

Japan
exceptionalism of, 34
and exchange rates, 228
export concentration in, 52
export shares in GDP for, 47
GDP/exports/terms of trade for
(1870–1939), 187
industrialization in, 71–72, 160, 199,
213
and Dutch disease, 72, 74
as periphery leader, 214
inequality measures for, 148, 149,
150
extraction ratio, 151
railway mileage in (1850–1910), 16
and subsidy policies, 229
tariffs in, 141, 219
terms of trade in, 212
terms of trade boom in, 42–43, 71,
159
terms of trade data for, 30
terms of trade volatility for, 174,
177
trade policy liberalization of, 13
wage–rent ratio in, 159–62
Johnson, Simon, 2
Jones, Ronald, 54, 157

Kenya, inequality measures for, 148,
149, 150
extraction ratio, 151
King, Gregory, 146–47
Kirsch, Henry, 200

Korea, 14
  trade liberalization in, 71
  wage–rent ratio trends in, 160, 161
Kosambi, D. D., 85
Krueger, Anne, 184
Krugman, Paul, 183
Kurmus, Orhan, 104–105
Kuznets hypothesis, 152, 154

Labor costs, and Latin American
  industrialization, 205. See also
  Wages
Labor market, and Mexican textile
  industry, 138
Land holdings, concentration of
  (Southeast Asia), 162–63
Lane, Philip, 183
Latin America. See also specific
  countries
  commodity price volatility for, 173
  customs duties as revenue for, 170
  and Dutch disease, 206–207
  export concentration in, 52, 168–69
  export shares in GDP for, 47
  and free trade, 13
  freight-rate decline for, 18
  GDP per capita growth of, 5, 6
  growth performance in (1700–1820), 3
  industrialization levels per capita in
    (1750–1913), 64
  industrial liftoff in, 200–203
  and currency depreciation, 205,
    210–11
  potential explanations for, 203–205
  and wage competitiveness, 207, 209
  inequality in, 154–55
  in 1960 economic order, 2
  old order disappeared in, 234
  protectionism in, 204, 222
  and Mexican industry, 139, 140, 141,
    142
  railroads in, 209, 223
  tariffs in, 216, 217, 218, 220, 224

  terms of trade for, 119, 133
  income terms of trade, 207, 208
  and industrialization, 205, 206–207
  terms of trade boom in, 28, 35, 36,
    37, 38–39, 76, 119
  terms of trade volatility for, 176, 177
  and transport costs, 20
  and Panama Canal, 19
  and railroads, 19–20
  wage gap in, 158
Latin America and Caribbean, terms of
  trade volatility in, 167, 168
Levant, 176
  inequality measures for, 148, 149, 152
  terms of trade for, 211, 212
  terms of trade data for, 30
  terms of trade volatility for, 177
  and GDP growth, 178
Lewis, W. Arthur, 27, 28, 33, 46, 48,
  51, 54, 79, 115, 130, 145, 172–73
  new international economic order of,
    28, 63, 64, 156, 182, 197
List, Frederick, 139, 220

Maddison, Angus, 63, 120, 159
Magnification effect, 157, 158, 160
Magud, Nicholás, 158
Malaya
  terms of trade in, 42
  terms of trade data for, 30
  terms of trade volatility for, 177
Malaysia, inequality measures for, 150
Marketing board, in Egypt, 67–68
Márquez, Graciela, 204
Marx, Karl, 41, 73, 75, 240n.16
Mendoza, Enrique, 189
Mexico (Nueva España), 119–20
  colonial drain from, 163, 164
  commodity exports from, 207
  de-industrialization in, 74, 129, 205
  neo-Ricardian model of, 130–31
  and pro-industrial policies, 139–42,
    143

Mexico (Nueva España) (cont.)
  and question of failure to compete
    more effectively, 137–39
  and terms of trade, 131–33
  in transition before *Porfiriato*,
    120–23
  and wage competitiveness, 133–37,
    143
  in young Republic, 123–30
  exceptionalism of, 119–20, 132, 133,
    139–40, 142–43
  export concentration, 52
  export shares in GDP for, 47
  foreign import share of domestic
    market in, 77
  GDP/exports/terms of trade for
    (1870–1939), 187
  imports of intermediate and capital
    goods to, 202
  industrialization in, 39, 199, 203, 213
  per capita levels of, 64
  as periphery leader, 214
  inequality measures for, 148, 149,
    150, 155
    extraction ratio, 151
  local share of domestic textile market
    for, 65, 106–107, 129, 196, 200
  obraje production in, 123, 125
  pro-industrial tariff policies of, 204,
    214
  railroads in, 19, 20
  railway mileage in (1850–1910), 16
  real currency depreciation in, 228
  real exchange rate for, 210, 211
  as resource-abundant, 146
  and subsidy policies, 229
  tariffs in, 219, 220
  terms of trade for, 127, 131–33, 142,
    206, 212
    income terms of trade, 208
    internal for agriculture, 135
    terms of trade boom for, 37, 132
    and de-industrialization, 238n.1

terms of trade data sources for, 30
  terms of trade volatility for, 174, 177
  textile import penetration in, 65, 106
  and wage competitiveness, 209
Middle East. *See also* Levant
  export shares in GDP for, 47
  GDP per capita growth of, 5, 6
  growth performance in (1700–1820), 3
  tariffs in, 227
  and terms of trade, 206
  terms of trade boom in, 28, 35, 36,
    37, 39–40, 76
  terms of trade volatility for, 175, 177
Middle East and north Africa, terms of
  trade volatility in, 167, 168
Mohamed Ali (Egyptian leader), 66–67,
  68, 109, 112
Monsoons, and Indian
  de-industrialization, 82–83
Most-favored-nation (MFV) clause, in
  19th-century treaties, 13
Mughal collapse hypothesis, on Indian
  de-industrialization, 78–82, 83–84,
  86, 98
Murphy, Kevin, 182
Mussa, Michael, 157
Myrdal, Gunnar, 182

Naoroji, Dadabhai, 85
Nehru, Jawaharlal, 85
Neo-Ricardian model of
  de-industrialization, 53–57
  for India, 89–91
  for Mexico, 130–31
  for Ottoman empire, 112–14, 116
Netherlands (Holland)
  commodity vs. manufacturing price
    volatility for, 179
  free trade in (19th century), 13
  inequality measures for, 148, 149,
    150, 155
    extraction ratio, 151
  post-Napoleonic trade policy of, 12

New England, unskilled textile labor in,
138
New international economic order, 28,
33, 44, 51, 63, 64, 156, 197
New Zealand
GDP/exports/terms of trade for
(1870–1939), 186
tariffs in, 141, 218
Nigeria, inequality measures for, 150
North, Douglas, 2
North index, 16
North Italian triangle, industrialization
in, 199
as periphery leader, 214
Norway
free trade in (19th century), 13
GDP/exports/terms of trade for
(1870–1939), 186
as primary-product producer, 194
Nueva España. *See* Mexico
Nunn, Nathan, 229

O'Brien, Patrick, 63
OECD. *See also* Rich industrial core
manufactures as specialization of, 44
vs. third world, 1–2
Ohlin, Bertil, 156
"Open" economies, 7–8
and colonial Mexico, 122
and industrialization in rich core, 27
Opium, Chinese import of, 34
Origin of the Species, The (Darwin), 83
Ottoman empire, 101
de-industrialization in, 105–10
and barriers to trade, 102–104
causes of, 105–106, 114–17, 242n.9
and eastern Mediterranean debate,
104–105
neo-Ricardian model of, 112–14, 116
vs. rest of poor periphery, 118
and textile industry, 200
foreign import share of domestic
market in, 77

free trade treaties of (1838–1841),
102–103, 116
local share of domestic textile market
for, 64–65, 106–107, 129, 196, 200
protectionism in, 222
terms of trade for, 108, 110–12, 116,
118, 133, 212
terms of trade boom for, 101, 106,
110–11, 112, 118, 119
*Ottoman Empire and European
Capitalism, The* (Pamuk), 105
Ottoman Turkey. *See also* Turkey
de-industrialization in, 74
and eastern Mediterranean debate,
104–105
export concentration in, 52
export shares in GDP for, 47
railroads in, 223
terms of trade boom for, 37, 39–40
terms of trade data sources for, 30
terms of trade volatility for, 177
Owen, Roger, 104
Own-wage, 209
and de-industrialization, 56–57
in Indian manufacturing, 91–97

Pamuk, Şevket, 103, 104, 105, 106, 109
Panama Canal, 18, 19–20
Parthasarathi, Prasannan, 79, 89
Peace, and trade boom, 24
Peel, Robert, 12
Persson, Karl Gunnar, 169, 170–71
Peru
commodity exports from, 207
export concentration in, 52
export shares in GDP for, 47
GDP/exports/terms of trade for
(1870–1939), 187
inequality measures for, 148, 149,
150, 155
extraction ratio, 151
terms of trade (income) for, 208
terms of trade volatility for, 174

Philippines
de-industrialization in, 70–71
export concentration in, 52
export shares in GDP for, 47
GDP/exports/terms of trade for
(1870–1939), 187
industrialization in, 213
tariffs in, 217–18
terms of trade for, 212
terms of trade boom for, 37, 42, 119
terms of trade data sources for, 30
terms of trade volatility for, 174, 177
and GDP growth, 178
Poelhekke, Steven, 197
Policy responses in poor periphery,
215
misguided choices of, 228–29
and real exchange rates, 227–28
tariffs, 215–19
and political economy, 226–27
protecting infant industry, 220, 225
and railroads as facilitating
competition, 223, 227
for revenue, 223–24, 225–26, 226
and scarce factor compensation,
222–23, 225, 227
and Stolper–Samuelson corollary,
221–22
and strategic trade policy, 224–225
Political situations
and breakup of Mughal empire, 80–82
and choice of suboptimal tariffs,
228–29
and inequality, 232
institutional quality as determining
commodity export, 190–91
and Mexican exceptionalism, 120
in Mexico
and limitation on textile industry,
138, 139
and protection for domestic industry,
140, 142
and Ottoman trade, 103

and protectionism
in continental Europe, 162, 221
in Latin America, 222
and resource curse, 51
and tariffs, 226–27
Pomeranz, Kenneth, 3
Poor periphery, 1. See also Divergence
between rich core nations and poor
periphery; Third world
colonial drain from, 146, 163–67,
232
commodity price volatility in, 167,
172, 173, 176, 191, 194–95 (see also
Commodity price volatility)
de-industrialization in, 59–60, 74
(see also De-industrialization in poor
periphery)
comparative qualitative assessment
of, 65–66
comparative quantitative assessment
of, 61–65
differences in between parts of
periphery, 59, 60
and globalization, 27, 49–50, 60
(see also Globalization)
and local share of domestic textile
market, 64–65, 106–107, 196
neo-Ricardian model of, 53–57,
89–91, 112–14, 116
and primary-product specialization,
32–33, 53, 54, 63, 131, 225
and tariffs, 222–23, 225, 227, 233
(see also Tariffs)
and terms of trade boom, 57, 119,
145, 180, 222, 225
textiles as gauge of, 60–61
diversity in economic performance
within, 48, 188, 191
eastern Mediterranean vs. rest of
periphery, 118
and domestic capital markets, 171
export concentration in, 51–53, 167,
168–69, 172, 232

export shares in GDP for (1870 and 1913), 47, 48
as gaining from trade, 45–48
income distribution in, 156–59
and growth, 164–65
in labor-abundant part, 159–62
in resource-abundant part, 162–63
industrialization in, 199, 211–14
in Latin America, 200–205, 207, 209, 210–11
price of manufactures in, 26
and price volatility, 167–68 (*see also* Commodity price volatility; Terms-of-trade volatility)
primary-product specialization in, 26, 44, 64, 194, 231, 232 (*see also* Primary-product exports; Primary-product specialization)
simple household-based technology in, 105, 109 (*see also* Cottage industries)
terms of trade in, 53, 197–98, 211, 212, 214, 224–25, 226 (*see also* Terms of trade)
terms of trade boom in, 26, 28, 30–33, 34–35, 36–37, 44, 145 (*see also* Terms of trade boom)
terms of trade volatility in, 172, 173, 175, 176, 178, 184, 191, 232, 233 (*see also* Terms of trade volatility)
Population density, and inequality, 153–54
Portugal
export concentration in, 52
export shares in GDP for, 47
GDP/exports/terms of trade for (1870–1939), 186
industrialization in, 213
terms of trade for, 212
terms of trade data for, 30
terms of trade volatility for, 175, 177
Prebisch, Rául, 28. *See also* Singer–Prebisch episode

Price volatility, as result of globalization for periphery, 27, 53, 157 (*see also* Commodity price volatility)
Primary-product exports, 1, 145. *See also* Commodity price volatility
by country (1870–1939), 186–87
diversity in economic performance among exporters, 188
and Dutch disease, 49
export share definition for, 185
as growth-diminishing, 7
in Mexico, 132–33, 137
and terms of trade boom, 8, 131, 132–33, 181
and transport revolution, 14, 21
and wage–rent ratio, 158
Primary-product specialization, 26, 44, 64, 194, 231
and de-industrialization, 32–33, 53, 54, 63, 131, 225
and income distribution, 159
lack of quality improvement in (vs. manufactures), 30
as obsolescent, 197, 198
in Ottoman empire, 110
and railroads, 116
poor-periphery variation in, 34–35
and price volatility, 27, 51, 53, 167, 172, 178, 179, 181, 184, 188, 232
shift from, 233 34
Product price volatility, 231 (*see also* Commodity price volatility)
Pro-industrial policies, in Latin America, 204–205
in Mexico, 139–42, 143, 204, 205, 214
Protectionism, 27, 102, 128, 216–17, 218. *See also* Tariffs
in Asia, 218
in continental Europe, 162
against grain imports in core countries (structure of protection), 219

Protectionism (cont.)
infant-industry argument for, 139, 204, 220, 225
in Latin America, 204, 222
and Mexican industry, 139, 140, 141, 142
and railroads as facilitating competition, 223
as reaction to lowered price of manufactures, 226
Proto-industrial cottage industries, 105. See also Cottage industries
Punjab
globalization in, 162
as resource-abundant, 146
wage–rent ratios in, 160, 161
Putting-out cottage industry system, 61, 124, 127. See also Cottage industries

Quataert, Donald, 103, 104, 109, 110

Railroads, 15, 19, 27. See also Transport revolution
for interior markets, 223, 226
and Latin American wage competitiveness, 209
and Ottoman trade, 104, 116, 117
world mileage of (1850–1910), 16
Real exchange rate (RER)
depreciation of, 227–28
and industrialization in Latin America, 210, 214
Real wages, and de-industrialization, 88–89
Refrigeration, trade implications of, 18
Re-industrialization, 59, 99. See also Industrialization
in India, 92, 99
in Latin America, 205
Rent-seeking
and economic growth, 180, 183, 184

as globalization downside, 50–51
and inequality, 165, 232
power of curbed, 234
and third world tariffs, 229
Rent–wage ratio, 157–58
Resource curse, 183–84
as globalization downside, 50–51
and Singer–Prebisch episode, 195
Ricardo, David, 45, 182. See also Neo-Ricardian model of de-industrialization
Rich industrial core, 1. See also Divergence between rich core nations and poor periphery
in examination of trade-divergence effects 185
growth miracle in (1820–1913), 21–22
tariffs in, 216
Robinson, James, 2
Rogowski, Ronald, 221
Roman empire, inequality measures for, 148, 149
Russia
and exchange rates, 228
export concentration in, 52
export shares in GDP for, 47
GDP/exports/terms of trade for (1870–1939), 186
industrialization in, 199, 213
as periphery leader, 214
protectionism in, 222
railway mileage in (1850–1910), 16
tariffs in, 218, 220
terms of trade for, 212
terms of trade boom for, 36, 119
terms of trade data for, 30
terms of trade volatility for, 175, 177
and GDP growth, 178
Rybzynski effect, 61

Sachs, Jeffrey, 183
Salvucci, Richard 123, 125–26

Samuelson, Paul, 221. *See also* Stolper-
Samuelson corollary
Serbia
export concentration in, 52
export shares in GDP for, 47
GDP/exports/terms of trade for
(1870–1939), 186
inequality measures for, 150
extraction ratio, 151
for south Serbia (1455), 148, 149,
152
terms of trade volatility for, 175
Shanghai, industrialization in, 160,
199
as periphery leader, 214
Shimoda and Harris ("unequal")
treaties, 13, 71
Shleifer, Andrei, 182
Siam (Thailand)
de-industrialization in, 70
export concentration in, 52
export shares in GDP for, 47
GDP/exports/terms of trade for
(1870–1939), 187
industrialization in, 213
inequality measures for, 148, 149,
150
extraction ratio, 151
protectionism in, 222
as resource-abundant, 146
tariffs in, 219
trade liberalization of, 14
terms of trade for, 212
terms of trade boom for, 37, 42
terms of trade data sources for, 30
terms of trade volatility for, 174, 177
trade liberalization in, 71
wage–rent ratios in, 161, 162
Singapore, 1
Singer, Hans, 28
Singer-Prebisch episode (1870–1939),
and relation of globalization to great
divergence, 184, 185–95

Small country assumption
for Mexico, 131
for Ottoman empire, 101
Smith, Adam, 6, 54, 79, 115, 182
Social tables, 146–47, 152
South Africa, inequality measures for,
150
South Asia. *See also* India
and free trade, 14
GDP per capita growth of, 6
growth performance in (1700–1820), 3
and terms of trade, 206
terms of trade boom in, 28, 35, 36,
37, 40–41, 41–42, 118
terms of trade volatility in, 167, 168,
177
South Asia less India, GDP per capita
growth of, 5
Southeast Asia
GDP per capita growth of, 5, 6
growth performance in (1700–1820), 3
and terms of trade, 206
terms of trade boom in, 28, 35, 36,
37, 41–42, 76
terms of trade volatility for, 177
South and Southeast Asia, terms of
trade volatility for, 174
South Korea, 1. *See also* Korea
Spain
and exchange rates, 228
export concentration in, 52
export shares in GDP for, 47
GDP/exports/terms of trade for
(1870–1939), 186
industrialization in, 213
inequality measures for, 148, 149,
150
extraction ratio, 151
terms of trade for, 212
terms of trade boom for, 36, 119
terms of trade data for, 30
terms of trade volatility for, 175, 177
Spraos, John, 197

Steamships, 15, 18. *See also* Transport
    revolution
    and Ottoman trade, 104
Stolper, Wolfgang, 221
Stolper–Samuelson corollary, 221–22,
    249–50n.9
Strategic trade policy, 224–25
Structure of protection, 219
Suez Canal, 18, 19, 73
Supply-side forces
    and Indian de-industrialization, 41,
        77, 86, 89, 91, 98, 99
    and drought frequency, 78
    in Mexican de-industrialization,
        126–27, 130
    and Mexican terms of trade, 130, 207
    and Ottoman empire, 112, 113
    and third world de-industrialization,
        54, 74
Sweden
    free trade in (19th century), 13
    GDP/exports/terms of trade for
        (1870–1939), 186
    inequality measures for, 150

Taiwan, 1
    wage–rent ratio trends in, 160, 161
Tanzania, inequality measures for, 150
Tariffs, 215–19
    and de-industrialization, 222–23, 225,
        227, 233
    and industrialization in poor
        periphery, 214
    vs. internal tax sources (core vs.
        periphery), 224
    in Mexico, 139–42, 143
    in Ottoman empire, 103
    and political economy, 226–27
    protecting infant industry, 220, 225
    preferable alternative to, 228–29
    preferable types of, 229
    and railroads as facilitating
        competition, 223, 226

    for revenue, 223–24, 225–26, 226
    and scarce-factor compensation,
        222–23, 225, 227
    and Stolper–Samuelson corollary,
        221–22
    and strategic trade policy, 224–25
Tax-transfer mechanisms, as
    compensation, 228
Technology transfer
    and Ottoman de-industrialization,
        110
    from trade, 46
Telegraph, 11
Terms of trade, 7, 236n.1. *See also*
    Gains from trade
    for China, 72, 212
    and comparative advantage in
        agriculture, 101
    for core vs. periphery, 188–89
    and economic growth, 8, 46
    for Egypt, 111–12, 133, 211, 212
    from 1870 to 1939 by country,
        186–87
    and GDP (1870–1939), 192
    for India, 75, 76, 86, 118, 212
    for Indonesia, 42, 133, 211, 212
    and India, 37, 40–41, 236n.10
    in Japan, 212
    for Latin America, 119, 133
    income terms of trade, 207, 208
    and industrialization, 205, 206–207
    measure of, 29
    for Mexico, 127, 131–33, 142, 206,
        212
    income terms of trade, 208
    internal for agriculture, 135
    and openness, 27
    for Ottoman empire, 106, 108,
        110–12, 116, 118, 133, 212
    for poor periphery, 53, 212, 214, 226
    absence of detrimental trend in,
        197–98
    and de-industrialization, 60, 74, 225

and industrialization, 211
slump in, 9
stability of (18th century), 30, 31
and tariffs, 224–25
variance in, 34–35
and wage–rent ratio, 157
during Prebisch–Singer period
(1870–1939), 188
question of exogeneity of, 189–90,
207
Terms of trade boom, 8–9, 25, 27–28,
231
and de-industrialization in neo-
Ricardian model, 57
and great divergence, 185–87, 232–33
in poor periphery, 26, 28, 30–33, 44,
145
Ceylon, 119
and Chinese or East Asian
exceptionalism, 33–34, 72–73
data gathered for, 28–30
and de-industrialization, 119, 145,
180, 222, 225
East Asia, 28, 36, 37, 42–43
and economic growth, 181, 198, 233
Egypt, 37, 39–40, 66, 118, 119
European periphery, 28, 35, 36
India, 37, 40–41, 236n.10
Indonesia, 37, 119
and inequality, 180 (see also
Inequality)
Italy, 119
Japan, 42–43, 71, 159
Latin America, 28, 35, 36, 37, 38–39,
76, 119
vs. living standards, 119
Mexico, 37, 132, 238n.1
Middle East, 28, 35, 36, 37, 39–40,
76
Ottoman empire, 101, 106, 110–11,
112, 118, 119
Ottoman Turkey, 37, 39–40
Philippines, 37, 42, 119

pre-1870 period, 196
and resource curse, 50–51
Russia, 119
South Asia, 28, 35, 36, 37, 40–41,
41–42, 118
Southeast Asia, 28, 35, 36, 37, 41–42,
76
Spain, 119
United Kingdom, 32
variance in, 34–35, 36–37
Terms of trade slump, 9, 27
Terms of trade volatility, 167, 232,
233
and economic growth, 119, 180, 184,
198
and great divergence, 191–94, 195
in 1700–1939 period, 171–79
Textile boom, as Indian
de-industrialization offset, 84–85
Textiles. See also Cotton spinning
Britain's technological lead in, 135
cotton as input for, 21
as de-industrialization gauge, 60–61
and India
absence of productivity advance in,
94
exports of, 79, 84, 239n.7
in Latin American economy, 200–201
as import, 21
and local share of domestic textile
market, 64, 65, 106–107, 129, 196,
200
in Mexican economy, 123–29, 135,
138, 140
and government policy, 141–42
in neo-Ricardian model of
de-industrialization, 54–57
Thailand. See Siam
Third world. See also Poor periphery
GDP growth rate average in (1820–
1913), 46
GDP and industrial output
performance in, 22

Third world (cont.)
  industrialization in, 196
  vs. OECD, 1
  recent move to manufacturers in, 172,
    197, 198
Thomson, Guy, 139
Tonkin, cash tenancy in, 157
Tornell, Aaron, 183
Total factor productivity, 214
  and Latin American industrialization,
    205
  and Mexican industrial liftoff, 201
Trade. *See also* Terms of trade
  in first global century, 11
  liberalization of (19th century), 12–14,
    23
  and "openness," 7–8, 27
  and transportation-cost decline,
    16–18
Trade boom, world, 15, 25. *See also*
    Globalization; Terms of trade boom
  and great divergence, 4–7
  in pre-1870 period, 197
  and growth miracle (1820–1913), 21,
    22–23
  and growth in rich vs. poor countries,
    181–82
  and poor periphery, 145
  de-industrialization in, 7, 231–32
Transport costs
  decrease in, 16, 17, 27
  and Egyptian cotton, 68
  and Ottoman trade, 103
  in sea freight rates, 60
  and Indian bullock power, 82
  and Ottoman de-industrialization,
    116, 117, 242n.9
  and protectionism, 223
  and tariffs, 226
Transport revolution, 11, 14–21
  and Indian de-industrialization, 75
  and Ottoman industry, 108
  price convergence from, 29

and primary products vs.
    manufacturers, 20–21
  world grain market from, 54–55
Trefler, Daniel, 229
Turkey. *See also* Ottoman Turkey
  GDP/exports/terms of trade for
    (1870–1939), 187
  inequality measures for, 150
  extraction ratio, 151
  tariffs in, 219
  terms of trade volatility for, 175
Tuscany, inequality measures for, 148,
    149

United Kingdom (Britain), 185
  capital flows out of, 194
  commodity vs. manufacturing price
    volatility for, 179
  exports share for (1830s), 63
  free trade adopted by (19th century),
    12
  GDP/exports/terms of trade for
    (1870–1939), 186
  inequality measures for, 150
  inequality measure for (England), 155
  extraction ratio, 151
  inequality measures for (England and
    Wales 1290), 148, 149
  internal trade barriers destroyed in, 15
  own wage for textiles in (England),
    96, 137
  productivity improvement in, 59–60,
    75, 105–106, 127, 135
  railway mileage in (1850–1910), 16
  tariffs in, 219
  terms of trade in, 31, 32
  terms of trade volatility for, 175, 176,
    177
United States, 185, 249n.4
  commodity vs. manufacturing price
    volatility for, 179
  GDP/exports/terms of trade for
    (1870–1939), 186

inequality measures for, 150
internal trade barriers destroyed in, 15
railroads in, 15, 19
railway mileage in (1850–1910), 16
tariffs in, 141, 216, 217, 218, 219, 220, 224, 225
Uruguay
commodity exports from, 207
export concentration, 52
export shares in GDP for, 47
GDP/exports/terms of trade for (1870–1939), 187
tariffs in, 218
terms of trade (income) for, 208
terms of trade volatility for, 174
and wage competitiveness, 209
wage–rent ratios in, 161

van der Eng, Pierre, 70
van der Ploeg, Frederick, 197
van Zanden, Jan Luiten, 70
Venables, Anthony, 183
Venezuela
commodity exports from, 207
and exchange rates, 228
export concentration, 52
terms of trade for, 212
income terms of trade, 208
terms of trade boom for, 37
terms of trade data sources for, 30
terms of trade volatility for, 177
Vishny, Robert, 182
Voracity effect, 183

Wage competitiveness, Mexican, 133–37
Wage–rent(al) ratio, 156
for Britain, Ireland, Denmark, and Sweden, 162
in East Asia, 160
in Europe, 160
in Japan, 159–60
for Japan, Korea, and Taiwan, 162

in Korea, 160
in Punjab, 160
in Taiwan, 160
in third world (1870–1939), 161
Wages
and Latin American industrialization, 205, 207, 209
real wages and de-industrialization, 88–89
War, and price volatility, 179
Ward, Henry George, 127–28
Warner, Andrew, 183
Waterloo, battle of, as turning point, 12
Western Europe. *See also* Rich industrial core
GDP per capita growth of, 5, 6
GDP and industrial performance in, 22
growth performance in (1700–1820), 3
inequality in, 155
in 1960 economic order, 2
Western Europe offshoots, GDP and industrial output performance in, 22
World economic order (1960), 102
World market integration, 23